Scenographic Imagination

SCENOGRAPHIC IMAGINATION
Third Edition

Darwin Reid Payne

Southern Illinois University Press
Carbondale

Library of Congress Cataloging-in-Publication Data

Payne, Darwin Reid.
    Scenographic imagination / Darwin Reid Payne.—3rd ed.
        p.   cm.
    Includes bibliographical references and index.
    1. Theaters—Stage-setting and scenery.   I. Title.
PN2091.S8P354   1993
792'.025—dc20   92-13216
ISBN 0-8093-1850-4 (cloth).—ISBN 0-8093-1851-2 (paper)   CIP

Printed on recycled paper ♻

For John Bury

Contents

Illustrations

Preface

It has been twelve years since *The Scenographic Imagination* was published. The last decade has seen many changes in the theater, and the role of the scenographer, while not changing significantly, has altered enough to make a revision of the earlier text warranted. I would venture to say that the most important change that has taken place is the increasing role of the computer in all phases of life; and it can be demonstrated, I believe, that use of this tool has in many ways made the work of the scenographer more productive. While we are still in the infancy of computer graphics, already it is evident that this one area will continue to grow as computer technology is expanded and refined. An additional area that is still some time in the future is the development of the CD-ROM, which will open vast new possibilities for the research necessary for successful scenographic design. That is the bright side of the picture for the present and for the future. There is a darker side I would also address in the following pages.

The subject to which I refer concerns the general education of the scenographic artists who are in training today. I am not alone when I call attention to the narrowing of vision we continue to detect in today's student of theater design. The impression persists among many instructors that those we teach are not as interested in the areas of education we thought important, are not curious enough about the legacies of the past we found, and still find, indispensable to our work. Nor do we believe that the fault lies in the natural atrophying of our own aging minds.

On the other hand, during the past thirty years there has been an increased emphasis given to perfecting technological production practices. The reason I wrote *Design for the Stage* and subsequently *The Scenic Imagination* was that I felt those important philosophical roots of scenography needed to be evaluated in the light of technical advances. For that main reason I have retained much of the text that dealt with the philosophical education of scenographers and have emphasized even more strongly the need for theater artists to seek a deeper commitment to theater's human roots. It is, of course, tempting to spend one's student years searching out new ways to move scenery faster; to dazzle audiences with the possibilities of hydraulic lifts, poured foam, and rubber casting; to astound with projections and laser light. (Nor could any scenographer long deny the fascinations with the constantly increasing possibilities computer graphics technology gives to scenographers.) Still, I think it is time to examine again the basic reasons there are visual artists in the theater; to ask ourselves: *for what purpose do we work and to what basic philosophy do we turn for guidance*. In my own mind, the answer becomes clearer with age and experience. I would like to share some of those reasons with those who are beginning to form questions of their own.

What is presented in this book is the substance of what I consider important to the scenographic student training today. I continue to believe Arthur Eddington's comment: "We often think that when we have completed our study of *one* we know all about *two*, because *two* is *one* and *one*. We forget that we still have to make a study of *and*." It is still the *and* of the visual arts of the theater I wish to pursue in the present revision—the often disregarded, almost always hidden way in which the motion of the scenographer's mind becomes physical realities on the stage. More than ever I am convinced that this area of the scenographer's education demands attention and study. As I wrote in 1980, I cannot assure the success of my attempt; nevertheless, I renew here my pledge to continue the path charted there.

Although many have contributed to this book, both directly and indirectly, I continue to be in the debt of Mordecai Gorelik and his many hours of helpful counsel and personal instruction as well as the always useful example of his own work; although Mr. Gorelik died in the last year of this revision, his philosophy of what constitutes the art of scenography still informs much of what is presented in the following pages. I would also like to thank the three principal photographers who have so conscientiously sought to bridge the three-dimensional world of the theater with the two-dimensional limitations of the printed page: Bob Jones, Elliott Mendelson, and particularly Myers Walker. A debt of gratitude must also be paid to the following publishers and copyright holders who have so generously allowed me to quote from their works:

"Against Falsehood," a lecture by John Bury. Reprinted by permission of John Bury.

"La Môme Bijou," from *The Secret Paris of the 30's*, by Brassaï, translated from the French by Richard Miller. English translation Copyright © by Random House, Inc., New York, and Thames and Hudson, Ltd., London. Reprinted by permission of Random House, Inc., and Thames and Hudson, Ltd.

"Epic Scene Design," by Mordecai Gorelik from *Theatre Arts*, October 1959. Reprinted by permission of Mordecai Gorelik.

"A Setting for Ibsen's *Ghosts* from a Director's Diary, 1905." First published in *The Drama Review* 9, no. 1, T25 © 1964 by *The Drama Review*. Reprinted by permission. All Rights Reserved.

Portion of a letter reprinted from "To Directors and Actors: Letters, 1948–1959," by Michel de Ghelderode, translated by Bettina Knapp. First published in the *Tulane Drama Review* (Summer 1965). Reprinted by permission of Bettina Knapp.

"The Building or the Theatre," by Sean Kenny, from *Theatre Crafts Magazine* 2, no. 1 (January–February 1968). Reprinted by permission of *Theatre Crafts Magazine* © Rodale Press 1968.

A review by Robert Lewis Shayon of *Death of a Salesman*, from *Saturday Review*, May 28, 1966. Reprinted by permission of Robert Lewis Shayon.

"A Director Views the Stage," by Tyrone Guthrie, from *Design Quarterly*, no. 58 (1963). Reprinted by permission of *Design Quarterly*, copyright Walker Art Center.

"Theory of Design," by Norman Bel Geddes, from *Encyclopaedia Britannica*. Reprinted by permission of *Encyclopaedia Britannica*.

"*How I See the Woman without a Shadow*," by Robert O'Hearn, from Opera News, 17 September 1966. Reprinted by permission of Robert O'Hearn.

"Weigel's Props," by Bertolt Brecht, translated by John Willet. Reprinted by permission of John Willet.

Introduction

Can this cockpit hold
The vasty fields of France? Or may we cram
Within this wooden O the very casques
That did affright the air at Agincourt?
O, pardon! since a crooked figure may
Attest in little place a million;
And let us, ciphers to this great acompt,
On your imaginary forces work.

Thus begins *The Life of Henry the Fifth,* Shakespeare's popular historical drama. In all dramatic literature there is no more abject apology for the imperfections and limitations of the physical theater. Nor, for that matter, is there any more powerful inducement to enter into that admittedly imperfect world than the words *"let us, ciphers to this great acompt, on your imaginary forces work."*

Almost four hundred years have passed since those words were first spoken, and much has changed in the institution of theater. It was, for instance, in Shakespeare's day a common attitude to consider playgoing as much an auditory activity as it was a visual spectacle. The audiences of his time needed little prompting to put their individual *imaginary forces* to work; the Elizabethan audience—commoners and aristocrats—have left much evidence that indicates to later times that they were an audience with firm opinions on a wide range of subjects and actively engaged in their pleasures in which the theater ranked high. Action, of course, has always been central to the theatrical experience; this was cer-

tainly true of the Elizabethan theater. Equally important in the theater of the period was the place of words. The English language of the day, still young in comparison to those of Europe and the lands bordering the Mediterranean, was vitally dramatic; it was changing constantly, and the popularity of a playwright depended as much on his ability to provide a wildly extravagant flow of words as it did to concoct a good story. The best of the English playwrights of the period appealed to the ear as well as to the eye. It is very important to keep in mind that it was *through the ear,* so to speak, that much of the stage was set. The small platform stages of the time were limited, but the stage that the playwright set in the spectator's individual imagination knew few limits. The willingness of the audience to have those imaginary forces worked upon by language that evoked locale, time of day or year, as well as mood, is evidenced on every page of the works that come to us from the Elizabethan age. A significant clue to the current attitude toward playgoing occurs when the players in *Hamlet* come to Elsinore to perform: Hamlet greets them with the phrase, "We'll hear a play tomorrow." It is a telling phrase that gives testimony to the importance of language that raises in the mind images not present on the physical stage. There can be little doubt that imagination was a vital part of the theatrical experience of Shakespeare's day.

Since that time theatrical production has altered radically. Audiences have become progressively less inclined to see with the "mind's eye" (another phrase from *Hamlet*); those *imaginary forces,* to a very large extent, have atrophied. During that four-hundred-year span, imagination has largely been replaced by actual pictorial scenery made possible by the development of a highly complex scenic technology: wood and canvas, plastic and steel, hydraulics and computers, have rendered the use of the individual imagination all but impossible. Although it can be interminably debated—as it constantly is—whether this trend from active imagination to explicit picturization has been a healthy development, it cannot be denied that the theater of today is approached with objectives vastly different from the theater of earlier times. In most of the theater of the past, each member of an audience accepted a responsibility that few of their present-day counterparts seem willing to undertake. In the theater of today, setting the scene has been almost entirely relegated to a professional "imaginer": the scenographer. Just what is a scenographer? Why has this person been given the task of "seeing" for others? Most important of all, what are the *actual* responsibilities of such a person in today's theater?

For many years now—as an artist firmly embedded in my own time—I have attempted to define for myself a convincing philosophical basis for the art I practice: scenography; to formulate some few governing principles that I can intellectually defend to others and, not least of all, to myself. For it is important, I believe, that all artists, even the most intuitive, have some positive concept of why they do what they choose to do and why they believe what they believe about those choices. So far, I have not been completely successful in articulating a coherent philosophy. Many aspects of the search remain unresolved; I would like to think that this inability to be precise in my motives for being an artist in the theater is inherent proof that my

work is still evolving and thus prevents an easy analysis or a simple summation. At other times I have been on the point of resolving the question simply by quitting the profession entirely. Somehow that decision never gets made; something always forestalls that final step. Usually it is because I am offered a production to design of some work that has intrigued me for years but that I never had opportunity to do. At times this presents a dilemma but on balance not an altogether unpleasant one.

It is relatively easy to prove scenography's continuing necessity by its ubiquitous existence; never have there been more scenographers at work; never so many projects to engage them; and never so many student scenographers training to take their place or take a place beside those still working. All things considered, the continuance of scenography in the theater seems assured for some time to come.

Still, the old doubts concerning the absolute necessity of such an art persist. I cannot quite overcome a nagging feeling that the theater could very well do without scenography; that the stage might regain some of its former vitality and power if it became more spare in scenic approach or less interested in innovative production. (At the moment of this writing a ghost of that former approach to theater has just emerged: one of the first professional theaters in London, the Rose, has just been rediscovered and its foundations exposed for the first time in four hundred years. Even what little remains of that structure gives strong evidence of the simplicity of approach—as well as its evident demand on an audience's active imaginative participation in the theater—that the theater of today has lost. At the same time this flexible theater emerges from the past, we also have the opportunity to witness a more recently built theater in Hamburg, West Germany, receiving a year-long structural renovation just for the technological demands of a single production: Andrew Lloyd Webber's musical *The Phantom of the Opera.* The juxtaposition of these two events should give us ample pause to reflect on the nature of the theaters we had and those we now have.)

It is this feeling—the need to assess our priorities in all theatrical arts—that I perceive in much of the present-day writing that deals with the philosophy of scenic production. As we do, however we should consider carefully Buckminster Fuller's thoughtful tenet: *less is more*.

These thoughts are especially disquieting to one who not only has spent the past forty years designing for the theater but has had the added responsibility of instructing and guiding others who wish to carry on that practice. Having discussed these feelings and doubts on numerous occasions with other scenographers as well as with directors, actors, and with other related theater artists—a significant number of whom also serve, as I do, both as practicing artists and as instructor—I feel less alone, less a traitor to my profession. I often find they have similar misgivings as to the "lasting" value of their work or the continuing importance of their instruction. Some few, I regret more to find, are positive only in their refusal to consider the questions at all and who think it idly academic to broach any questions beyond the current year or the present project. (Nor can I be sure in my own mind they are not right to adopt such a position, to ignore entirely my questionings; to adopt the attitude that Dylan Thomas once voiced that "the business of posterity was to look after itself.") Many, like myself, continue to grapple with the perceived dilemma: What, we ask, is the best advice to give those who seek instruction for the present and direction for the future? How can we prepare students of theater for a profession that, if the recent past is any guide, will be considerably changed soon? As I write, the twenty-first century is only a decade away; it is irresistible for me and for many others, I feel, *not* to speculate on what that new age will bring.

I have not yet found—nor really expect to find soon—a satisfactory solution to these inquiries. Nevertheless, it seems important not to forget that such questions can be a positive part (indeed, a necessity) of the ongoing educational process of today. In addition, it has become increasingly clear to me that if there are indeed answers, we will find them not so much by attempting to seek out or redefine the nature and needs of an ever more complex contemporary theater but by trying to understand better the basic nature of all present-day theater artists and to study their continuing and evolving relationships. We should, more important still, constantly attempt to gain some insight into why anyone seeks to work in the theater in the first place; to understand better why this kind of work has such an appeal to the imagination of an ever-increasing number. For I very much believe that while all theater people, the scenographer not least among them, want positive reward for their efforts, they must also have, to use a phrase more often applied to spiritual disciplines, a genuine calling to a kind of work that demands an inordinate dedication but that does not automatically promise or produce wide acclaim or great fortune. Further, underlying the motives of the most ambitious of artists, I would expect to find an intense desire to be connected with, and to be important to, a community of dedicated and like-minded artists.

In this book the approach to designing for the stage is treated as an art, not simply as a craft. One must keep in mind that no art is without its underlying structure of craft that the artist must master. More important still, although our focus may not dwell on the craft as much as other texts do, the importance of mastering all the crafts of scenography are assumed. Too often these two aspects of design become separated; students of scenography becomes so intrigued with the making of working drawings, models, and sketches of interesting possibilities for the stage that they forget their contribution is not an end in itself but part of a larger effort involving the work and aesthetic judgments of many others, not theirs alone. Yet it is possible for the scenographer, despite this seemingly severe restriction on personal expression, to make a contribution to the production at the same level as those of the director and performer. Meeting the stated demands of the script or satisfying the specific requests of the director is certainly part of a scenographer's job; but it is also possible, with the scenographer's special vision that spans all the arts, to make suggestions that may extend and amplify the underlying meanings of the production in ways that neither the playwright, director, nor actor had envisioned. This expanded participation is a distinctive twentieth-century contribution to the theater. Giving the scenographer an important interpretative role is not, however, without attendant dangers; some of these are addressed later in the book. Of course no scenographer can meet this responsibility without being an able craftsman; it is imperative that any scenographer be a master of the mechanical skills of the profession to implement the special visions that arise from interpretation. It is entirely possible to be an expert draftsman, carpenter, electrician, and scene painter and still not be an artist of scenography; too often this is the case. While this book is no more than an introduction to that area that lies beyond the basic craft of scenography, it does attempt to expose some of the elemental yet important questions most students have in their initial confrontation with this second aspect of scenography. Although these questions can never be answered completely, certain directions and possibilities they suggest are indicated and discussed. Of course, it is in the lifelong pursuit of these answers that the craftsman can become an artist.

For a number of years I have taught scenography in university theaters. My first impulse—and the course of action I followed for some time—was to teach it solely as a craft, with only passing affirmation that it could be more than that. The considered reason for pursuing that approach was a belief that since one could not be expected to teach a student to be an accomplished artist during some arbitrarily prescribed period, perhaps the subject need not be considered at all. While there has not been in my teaching a complete reversal of the early approach, it has been modified greatly; the mechanical skills of design still must be taught, but the emphases in the classroom now rest more in showing how these serve the highest aims of the theater and drama. It now seems to make more sense to demonstrate from the outset of the scenographer's education that craft and art are not separate activities with different aims, but that each should assist the other to something greater than either one; ideally, each should grow out of the other.

All too often beginning scenographers do not consider very deeply the theoretical basis of their profession. They are impatient with the scholarly approach to this art. They are eager to begin the "real" business of the scenographer: to draw sketches, construct models, and to make working drawings. For many years, in my own classes there was little question of any conceptual approach other than that which was casually and somewhat arbitrarily imposed. Nor did there

ever seem to be time for any study more exhaustive than the unavoidably shallow research into architectural styles or the accurate copying of period design elements. For instance, when a student selected *The Beggar's Opera* as his project, the eighteenth-century ballad-opera by John Gay, he was more interested in the style and dimensions of a Newgate Prison window and only slightly concerned (if at all) with the action that transpired in the room where it was to be placed. Asked what might be taking place in the London street just outside the prison, and whether that action might have any bearing on the dramatic situation inside the prison or on his particular design, the student might reply, "Just what difference does it make?" The fact that what the scenographer creates does have a very real influence on both the actor and director, and ultimately on the way the play itself is perceived, made me realize that mechanical skill was not enough, that there was a great deal more we should be considering in the classroom but were not. Further, I began to realize that it is not uncommon for a scenographer (and not just the student), with the best intentions, to thwart the larger aims of a production, not to mention the work of the other members of the artistic team with which he or she is working, by striving too hard to make a strongly individual impression on an audience. These issues, it became increasingly evident, should be broached and discussed in the formative stages of the scenographer's education. All scenographers must not only know *how*, important as technique is, they must also be fully aware of *why*.

Finally, it should be understood that a basic core of knowledge assimilated from a number of areas spanning all human activity is essential to the student desiring to make the best use of this book. Progress in the art of scenography depends largely on becoming knowledgeable in many areas of human endeavor, not simply those that take place in the physical theater. Briefly, this basic core of knowledge would consist of the following:

1. A general familiarity with, and an understanding of, theater history and the development of the drama

2. A basic knowledge of art history and an understanding of periods and styles of architecture, painting, sculpture, furnishing, and cos-

tume and well as the historical contexts in which these artifacts existed

3. A familiarity with principles, techniques, and materials in pictorial and three-dimensional design

As well as the following that will not fall within the scope of this book:

4. A basic knowledge of stagecraft and theatrical production techniques and materials, including the mechanics of the stage and an understanding of the fundamental principles of stage lighting

5. Skill in fundamental drafting procedure and in executing mechanical drawings, which should include a working knowledge of computer graphics

This may sound like an unusual amount and variety of information and skills for any student to possess. It is. Most scenographers do not have them when they begin to study theatrical design. Many continue to ignore their necessity, but most finally acquire the necessary education and skills, often independently of formal academic education. Still, acquire them they must, for there is no way for the aspiring scenographer to progress without this solid grounding. Indeed, the successful theater artist will have a firm understanding of all the arts, including literature, music, and the dance, as well as those more nearly confined to theater. The truly successful scenographer should be, in the best sense, an educated person who also happens to be an expert technician in his field; the best in the past have been and the best in the future will be just such fully realized artists. Three of the most influential persons of the last hundred years—Gordon Craig, Adolphe Appia, and Robert Edmond Jones—have been keenly interested and vastly knowledgeable in all the arts, not just those of technical theater.

It is time well spent to give a brief moment to examination of the most basic terms used in this book: *scenography* and *scenographer.* Although these are not unfamiliar terms to many persons working in the theater today, they are not as well known as are similar terms such as *choreography* and *choreographer.*

The term *scenographer* is a relatively new one in the American theater. There are many still, I would venture to guess, to whom the term *scenography* automatically implies an activity more grand, certainly more spectacular, than does the term scenic design. Implicit in the use of scenography as the most basic description of a specific profession lies an increasing awareness that many of the old descriptions applied to visual theater artists are no longer accurate. While the word has to some a faintly pretentious ring to it (some seeing a too-foreign influence in its use), others are beginning to see the real differences that lie between *scenographer* and *scenic designer.* Many shades of opinion, it is safe to say, still exist and will persist in the future concerning these terms. It is not the purpose of the this book to champion the use of one title over the other; nor is it the presumption that his text will put the final stamp of authority on the use of the term *scenographer.* The choice made, however, is an attempt to define more precisely the functions of a certain kind of designer, an artist whose training has become increasingly more specialized and demanding. Even descriptions of design functions in theater have changed during the progress of this century. As Denis Bablet, a theater historian who has written widely on scenography in the twentieth century, points out, "The French word 'decor' is a conventional term that we continue to use because habits are deeply rooted, but it is an obsolete one. . . . The designer's task is no longer to ornament or to embellish, to create a shrine for the production. . . . the setting is today an interpreter of the play, an actor. In many cases, of course, it must still specify or evoke the scenes of the action, but above all it acts out and reveals the action, stresses or explains its meanings. . . . A Mertz or a Neher, a Svoboda, a Sean Kenny or an Acquart conceive, in agreement with the director, an organization of the scenic space that is functional in relation to the play, to the staging, to the actor and to the public. They model a stage floor, they portion out acting areas, create different levels. They trace axes, prescribe lines of circulation, in a word, *they establish a scenic architecture of which each element becomes indispensable, brings out the relationship that unites the characters, accentuates the signification of the actor's slightest gesture. They are creators of space.* It is understandable that many designers prefer to style themselves 'scenographers,' the term so justly employed in Central Europe."

Of these figures listed by Bablet, Josef Svoboda is, perhaps, the most important single person to bring the question of *scenography* versus *scenic design* into sharp focus; his definition, although not complete or final, does point the way to a workable understanding of the difference between the two terms: "I'm looking for a word to describe the profession, not the person, the profession with all the means at its disposal, with all its various activities and responsibilities in terms of the *stage* and creative work done in close cooperation with direction, with special emphasis on the free choice of all available means, not merely the pictorial and painted. For example, scenography can mean a stage filled with vapor and a beam of light cutting a path through it. . . . Theatre is mainly in the performance; lovely sketches and renderings don't mean a thing, however impressive they may be; you can draw anything you like on a piece of paper, but what's important is the actualization. True scenography is what happens when the curtain opens and can't be judged in any other way."

Few scenographers contest what Svoboda says here. What he does not give us, however, is any indication as to how the scenographer learns his profession. (In Svoboda's own organization he does not present scenography as an independent course of study; instead, he assigns theatrical projects to advanced students of architecture. He has, on numerous occasions, stated in public lectures that he believes this to be the most effective and productive method of training students of scenography.) In America, while this philosophy is not a prevailing one, it is still understandable why Svoboda has adopted it. Certainly the ability to teach any art is questionable, and scenography, which incorporates many diverse arts and disciplines, presents very special problems not only to students but to the instructors who train them. While all who would make scenography their primary profession must learn the languages of form, color, line, mass, and texture, they must concurrently come to understand the intricate relationships these elements must have with a number of arts outside those of two-dimensional and three-dimensional design: music, drama, poetry, and dance. It is the degree to which students of scenography become sensitive, aware, and knowledgeable in these other arts of communication that will determine professional competence and success.

A Note on Outside Reading Materials and Allied Sources

Not only is reading essential to the scenographer seeking to build a store of practical information, it is also a necessary and positive step toward the creation of a philosophical framework without which craft will lack direction and art loses purpose. Awareness and comprehension of the literature of a scenographer's own discipline as well as that of related arts are important, since the scope of scenography is nothing less than the whole world outside the theater.

Most creative artists, especially in their student days, do not read enough, not only generally but even in their field of major interest. The average student is usually grossly ignorant of the literature of his chosen profession, ignorant of both its extent and nature. It is likely, however, that the same student would read more if such materials were called attention to or given directions as to where to find them; the fact is that texts and articles on scenography are often difficult to locate or not widely available. (After all, it is not a greatly overcrowded profession, and far fewer are writing about it than are practicing it.) At the same time, much of the available material is not very informative; in content a great deal is inadequate, misleading, or too general to be of any real use to the beginning student. In the formal classroom environment, moreover, the student is confronted with a dilemma: assigned to read a certain book or article by a certain time (information the instructor feels is useful or necessary to the student's understanding and development), more often than not the material is checked out of the library or missing. For these reasons, the outside readings in this book are presented in the following manner:

1. As usual in most textbooks, direct quotations of short length are used to make specific points concerning the material under immediate discussion.

2. At certain points, a complete section from a larger work (such as a chapter from a book or an article from a magazine or journal) is inserted into the main body of the text. These sections will allow the student to read a more comprehensive statement (rather than a limited quotation) in its entirety without having to check out from the

library the complete book or to track down the article. Having read a portion of a book will perhaps encourage a further reading in it later.

3. At the conclusion of the book a complete bibliography is given. Recommendations made there include books directly related not only to theater arts but to other art fields as well as texts dealing with allied areas of study.

The approach outlined above should, along with other readings the individual instructor will doubtless wish to include in his own presentation, give the student of scenography a sound basic groundwork on which to build a thorough understanding of the literature in the fields of scenography and other related arts.

A Note to the Instructor

No book can teach a course; only the individual instructor can do that. How helpful any text is to a student is largely dependent on how and to what extent the instructor uses that text within the structure of a course. For these reasons, the basic assumption of the author is that the greater responsibility of teaching any student the fundamentals of scenography is still where it always has been, with the individual instructor.

For approximately twenty years this book, in various forms, has been the basic outline for an introductory course in theater visual art. Undoubtedly it will be more useful as a source book and point of departure than as a rigid all-inclusive guideline. It will become quickly apparent that the book has been written in a strongly personal tone and is primarily based on the personal experiences of the author. The reason for this approach has less to do, however, with ego gratification on the part of the author than it is a tacit admission that no text could ever be written that would set down once and for all inviolable principles. If nothing else, what is suggested here will give both the student and instructor something to react against, and in so reacting create a valuable climate of discussion from which growing artistic awareness may emerge. While this may appear a negative point, artists realize that is the right and duty of those who come after them to question the accomplishments and approaches of their predecessors, certainly not blindly accept or follow them. So while examples

are given within the book that demonstrate or suggest solutions to specific design problems (indeed, the entire second half of the book is primarily devoted to just such examples), they are not the definitive solutions to those problems. Nor would examination of these examples alone further the student's education to any appreciable degree. For this reason let us call attention to the obvious point that it is always the responsibility of the individual instructor to create and evaluate different problems and projects for his own students rather than to rely on a predetermined set of exercises devised by the author of a text. Materials of this nature, therefore, are missing from this book altogether although a certain number of approaches are suggested implicitly and on rare occasions explicitly. After all, the whole point of any creative course is—or should be—to allow the student to think of new solutions to artistic problems rather than to "play back" information recently encountered or assimilated from previous accomplishments. It is important, moreover, that each instructor interpret this book (or take exception to) in the light of personal experience and individual judgment.

Some years ago I attended a symposium on the nature and direction an educational program for visual theater artists should pursue. Asked to state my own thoughts how such a program should be constructed, I responded with a number of goals I believed both necessary and achievable. These included the minimum skills needed to practice professionally: drafting, scenic drawing, knowledge of stage technology and materials, and understanding of stage forms. What I did not give enough attention to or emphasis upon at that gathering was, it now seems to me, to the philosophical base that gives meaning to those more mechanical aspects of scenography. Over the past decade I have attended other forums on scenographic art during which I have taken the opportunity to stress what I consider are important parts of the scenographer's formal education: the intellectual skills that coexist with those craft elements of training. Among those intellectual skills I would list the following:

1. The ability of the scenographer to develop a kind of *time vision*: an ability to *see* historical pasts and other cultures as a living place with living inhabitants

2. The understanding that *seeing* is not as-

sured by 20/20 or corrected vision: that the surfaces of objects, places, and events can only be
penetrated and understood by an *active vision*
and a *prepared vision*

3. To comprehend how space on the stage
differs conceptually from that experienced outside the theater

4. To realize that the art of scenography pre-
sumes the ability to create on the stage dramatic
imagery that supports the purposes of the total
production

5. To develop technical skills that serve the
scenic concepts of the production rather than to
demonstrate the visual virtuosity of an individual scenographer

The aims outlined above, while conceptual in
nature, are of vital importance to any designer
who wishes to participate in the professional
theater. In a book of this length (or in any book
of any length, for that matter), addressing fully
the implications of such goals is not possible. In
defense of the materials presented here, however, I would invoke these slightly pessimistic
but nonetheless comforting words of Aldous
Huxley: "However elegant and memorable,
brevity can never, in the nature of things, do
justice to all the facts of a complex situation. Life

is short and information endless: nobody has
time for everything. In practice we are generally
forced to choose between an unduly brief exposition and no exposition at all. Abbreviation is a
necessary evil, and the abbreviator's business is
to make the best of a job that, though intrinsically
bad, is still better than nothing."

I leave the last word in this note to instructors
to another writer who was also a teacher: Loren
Eisely. One of our century's great essayists,
Eisely knew well the importance of good teaching. His thought on the matter bears repeating
here:

The uses of a great professor are only partly to give us
knowledge; his real purpose is to take his students beyond knowledge into the transcendental domain of the
unknown, the future and the dream—to expand the
limits of human consciousness. In doing this he is creating the future in the minds of men. It is an awe-inspiring
responsibility, and the men to whom this task is given
should be chosen with all the care of which society is
capable. The teacher is genuinely the creator of humanity, the molder of its most precious possession, the
mind. There should be no greater honor given by society than permission to teach, just as there can be no
greater disaster than to fail at the task.

Scenographic Imagination

1

The Scenographic Artist

The learned divide and mark out their ideas more specifically and in detail. I, who see no farther into things than practice informs me, without any system, present my ideas in a general way and tentatively. . . . leave it to artists, and I don't know whether they will succeed in so complex, minute, and fortuitous a thing, to draw up into bands this infinite diversity of forms, to make our inconsistency stand fast, and set it down in order.
—Michel de Montaigne, *Essays*

The Purpose of the Scenographer

Before any philosophy of practice can be formulated or explored, it must first be accepted that there is a uniqueness to that practice that makes it worthy of study. The essential point to remember about the twentieth-century's conception of scenography as an art is that prior to this century it was, almost always, only an adjunct to a production, not necessarily an integral part of it. In fact, there was little coordination between any of the various departments responsible for the mounting of a production. The scenographer (or *scenic artist*, as was the more common designation), while he may have received some general instructions from the owner of a company producing works for the stage, relied on his graphic skills to produce a design rather than on his ability to analyze dramatic texts; any discussion of the appropriateness of a setting for a particular work usually took place after the designs were done. If, however, the designs were grand enough or sufficiently ornate, there is little evidence that anyone voiced the opinion that the settings did not really fit the tone of the play or opera or that they contributed in any real way to the totality of the production. Prior to Richard Wagner and the Duke of Saxe-Meiningen such considerations were not part of prevailing theatrical thought. If, on the other hand, they did please a theater manager's personal visual tastes, the designer quite probably received more commissions. If the settings were not acceptable for any number of reasons, others were given an opportunity to demonstrate their skills; in that respect, the same competitive situation still exists today. But the great difference between then and now lies in the fact that the scenic artist of the past spent very little time working with others—directors, costumers, playwrights—in preproduction planning. Ostensibly the scenic artist's task was to provide pictorial backgrounds in front of which actors and singers performed; the relationship of the performer to his scenic environment was at best a superficial one.

And yet it would not be entirely accurate to maintain that the scenic artists of the eighteenth and nineteenth centuries were only the helpless servants of domineering actor-managers and autocratic playwrights. Often they were highly respected artists in the theater and, more often than not, established architects or painters in the world outside the theater. Moreover, there is ample reason to believe that many of these artists were guilty of considering the actors, singers, and dancers mere additions to their work. Nor is there much proof that the scenic artists of the past made any attempt to study the text in order to integrate his designs into a cohesive whole. It is doubtful if many playwrights were given heed as to how their texts appeared on the stage. It is certainly doubtful that the scenic artist of the baroque or classical periods gave any thought to the purposes that lay beneath the surface—the subtext—of a dramatist's script or a composer's music. If one inspects the pictorial records of the various forms of theater during the eighteenth and nineteenth centuries, the period of time when scenic design gained ascendency in the theater, it appears as if few scenic artists saw much difference between any form of theatrical production; play, opera, masque, and ballet all received much the same treatment. A scenic artist's only real concern was to what extent these works provided an opportunity to create elaborate stage pictures or spectacular visual effects (fig. 1). But in fairness to the visual artists of these periods, it should be also be remembered that this approach was exactly what was expected of them.

Perhaps we should not be too hard on the accepted conventions of another age without understanding some of the reasons why certain practices came into being. For instance, we are now fairly certain that although providing a background for the performer was part of the early scenographer's function, the most important purpose for which scenery was invented lay in a different direction. Service to the performer was not the prime consideration for designing stage settings. In *Changeable Scenery*, Richard Southern sheds light on the attitude of those who designed for the the stage. He reports that "there is one remarkable fact to be found in a study of scenes and scene-changing which outshines even the intriguing details of the machinery by which the scene-changes were worked. This fact is both surprising and important; it clears up many puzzles in the staging of plays of the past, and its recognition is an essential to any understanding of the development of scenery today. This fact is that the changing of scenes *was intended to be visible; it was part of the show; it came into existence to be watched*" (italics mine).

Southern's observations draw our attention to two important points: (1) that engineering ability was a coequal necessity for the stage designer of the past, and (2) that the ability to create appropriate scenic environments for the performers was at best a secondary consideration.

Fig. 1. Design for an opera by Joseph Galli Bibiena

It certainly explains how artists such as Leonardo da Vinci became involved in theatrical projects. Still, it was not until the Restoration of Charles II in 1660 that scenery became an integral part of the dramatic stage. As Gary Taylor tells us in *Reinventing Shakespeare*, "Until this time, Shakespeare's plays [as well as those for every other playwright, Taylor could have added] had been performed in ornate theatres by actors lavishly costumed, but upon stages that gave no pictorial representation of place or time. The action in every play happened on a flat, dusty promontory between 'the heavens' above (an overhang painted with astronomical symbols) and 'hell' below (an invisible hollow, reachable by trapdoors). Location was signaled, if at all, by three-dimensional functional props like thrones, not by two dimensional inert painted scenery. This definition of space is cosmic and human; 'where we are' is determined by theological architecture and portable accessories. The post-Restoration definition of space was, in contrast, Cartesian and Newtonian: there was no theological frame, only a succession of spatial categories—unindividuated 'stock' scenes, generic woods or gardens, city squares or interiors—neoclassical generalities of locale that framed recurring situations in many plays. . . . changeable scenery fundamentally altered the history of Shakespearian performance, criticism, and editing." It profoundly altered, Taylor could have also added, the entire direction of the theater ever since. While the first settings of that post-Restoration theater were almost entirely devoid of three-dimensional scenery, actors still performed on a flat stage in front of flat pictorial images like those shown in figure 1. By the middle of the nineteenth century, however, anyone visiting the theater would expect to see literal representations of specific locations such as that shown in a contemporary illustration for the balcony scene from *Romeo and Juliet* (fig. 2).

For the most part, scenery is no longer created for its own sake (although audiences still take a childlike pleasure in viewing any production that features visible scene changes). As that mode of thought has altered somewhat, so has the scenographer's purpose and function in the theater. We have progressed to the point where scenography is considered an integral part of a production, not merely a decorative adjunct to

it. Not only has the function of the scenographer changed over the years, the basic skills of the profession have also undergone a radical change. From the middle of the sixteenth century until late in the nineteenth, scenic artists were almost without exception painters and quite often architects as well as engineers (especially during the late Renaissance and baroque periods). Moreover, some of these artists not only were famous but possessed immense influence with the governing powers of the day. During Shakespeare's time, Inigo Jones was arguably a more powerful figure than the playwright, and Ben Jonson, a contemporary of Shakespeare, complained bitterly that Jones was paid more for his scenery that he, Jonson, was given for his text.

Even the most famous of these architect-designers, however, were not called upon to understand the underlying meanings of a dramatic text. Nor were they often required to use skills other than those of a draftsman. Manipulation of actual three-dimensional form on the stage did not occur except in nondramatic spectacles. The designs were almost always transferred to the stage in flat pictorial terms, although there was a distinct attempt to produce an illusion of depth of space and solidity of form. Many of the scenographers creating settings for the baroque period, and even for the romantic theater of the nineteenth century, knew that what they had designed could only be realized on the stage as oversized pictures, never as real structures. Quite possibly many took a certain pleasure in being able to allow their imaginations full play without having to consider the limitations of actual structural practice or cost, weight, and unmanageability of gross building materials. Even today many scenographers begin their careers in areas and disciplines that deal primarily with two-dimensional design, painting for instance, and slowly become, as they comprehend that the theater is not just picture come to life, something else than a painter, something more than an architectural draftsman.

Although by the end of the nineteenth century there was a general dissatisfaction with painted scenery, since it did not fit the trend toward realism that theater was taking (Strindberg was only one during this time to inveigh against the antiquated system of scenic art—

Fig. 2. Nineteenth-century *Romeo and Juliet*

"stage doors are made of canvas and swing back and forth at the lightest touch . . . nothing is more difficult than to get a room that looks something like a room although the painter can easily enough produce waterfalls and flaming volcanoes"); even as early as 1808 a few discerning critical voices were beginning to call attention to the essential stupidity of contemporary scenographic practices. Wilhelm Schlegel, a German theater critic of the time, makes us realize that there were some even that long ago who did not blindly accept the current stage conventions as a proper artistic mode of production.

Our system of stage decoration has several unavoidable defects . . . the breaking of the lines on the sides of a scene from every point of view except one; the disproportion of the player when he appears in the background and against objects diminished in perspective; the unfavorable lighting from below and behind; the contrast between painted lights and shades; the impossibility of narrowing the stage at pleasure, so that the inside of a palace and a hut have the same length and breadth. The errors to be avoided are want of simplicity and of great and reposeful masses; the overloading of the scene with superfluous and distracting objects, either because the painter is desirous of showing off his strength in perspective or because he does not know how otherwise to fill up the space; an architecture full of mannerism, often altogether, nay, even at variance with possibility, colored in a motley manner which resembles no species of stone in the world. (Wilhelm Schlegel, quoted by Lee Simonson, *The Art of Scenic Design*)

Although Schlegel's remarks shrewdly anticipate the revolution in the design of stage settings that would take place at the end of the century, at the time his feelings were not widely shared, certainly not heeded.

Nowhere is the attitude of Schlegel's period better exposed than in an event which took place in the Weimar Theater during the last portion of Goethe's reign there as the managing director.

In 1816 the Weimar Theater arranged a special evening for its regular patrons. The occasion was not to present a new play or opera but only to view a new stock of settings especially commissioned by Goethe and executed by a noted scenic painter named Friedrich Christian Beuther. Goethe had been so impressed with Beuther's work that he wished his patrons to be able to examine them without the distraction of performers. Not a single actor performed that evening, nor were any scenes acted in the new settings; they were simply there to be looked at. The curtain rose, a setting was revealed and applauded, the curtain descended, a new scene was set, and thus the evening progressed. At the end of the "performance," the audience was allowed to come to the stage for a closer look at Beuther's artistry. The evening ended, no doubt, with champagne and praise to the scenic artist for settings that would find use in many future productions.

Although it is doubtful that few audiences today would have an interest in such a "performance," some scenographers, even as late as the ninth decade of this century (David Hockney a prime example), strongly uphold the contention that scenography should be first and foremost decorative and visually exciting. In the 1920s this attitude had its strongest champion in Leon Bakst, Diaghilev's greatest designer for his Ballets Russes. Bakst makes a special plea for this point of view when he states: "In the modern theater there are . . . tendencies which, in one way or another, affect the character of decors. The . . . tendency, which I call 'Protestant,' takes as its point of departure renunciation of beautiful, sumptuous, and dominant decor, claiming that such settings impede full apprehension of the word" (Leon Bakst, "Painting and Stage Design," *Art and the Stage in the Twentieth Century*).

There are few scenographers now who would be completely sympathetic with this point of view (although probably there are more than would admit it). Still, by and large, Bakst does not speak to or for most scenographers in today's theater, who are more self-effacing than he would allow himself to be. For if there has been one major change in the visual theater artist's role from the first uses of scenery until now, it is that the scenographer has become less and less a creator of spectacular scenic pictures and more and more an artist who is deeply involved with the concerns of performers who must live in the special world that the playwright has created with his words.

But why did this change come about? Actually the major reforms in theater production did not come until near the very end of the nineteenth century and were in great part due to the work and theories of men who were born near or soon after the peak of the romantic movement, which began around 1815. These men were to have strong influences in the theater of their day and those influences still inform production practice today. Richard Wagner, Gordon Craig, and Adolphe Appia—to name the most important, although not the only influential, visionaries of the past hundred years—are directly responsible for freeing the stage of an increasingly stultifying realism in scenic design. In their writing and practice originated the concept—the most basic one in the whole philosophy of scenography—that this art is not a peripheral theatrical activity (either physically or conceptually) but one that is essential to dramatic production. Not many years after these pioneers, the American theater gained one of its greatest artists, the undisputed father of American scenography, Robert Edmond Jones. Jones's design for the 1915 production of *The Man Who Married a Dumb Wife* heralded not only a new scenographer for the New York stage but also a whole new era in the American theater. More importantly, it was Jones who introduced to America the new movements in scenographic art that flourished in Europe during the last decades of the nineteenth century and the first decades of the twentieth. His book *The Dramatic Imagination*—written in 1941 and reprinted many times since—has become an important document in American theater art.

Returned from Europe, Jones became a stern critic of his native theater. In the theaters of Europe he witnessed many instances of a new attitude toward the stage, a seriousness of purpose to scenic design he did not find at home. The movement he observed was called "the new stagecraft." In production after production there, he saw how all the elements of design, direction, and acting were merged into a unified whole. Here in America, he felt, the prevailing practices of those working in the theater had become shoddy and purposeless; that theater had become primarily "show business," the main purpose of which was to give an unthinking audience an evening of mindless entertainment. The Broadway stage was expert, he knew, in the construction of superficially exciting "shows" with spectacular scenic displays. But it rarely created productions that genuinely moved an audience or gave its patrons food for thought. While Jones believed entertainment was an important part of the theater, he felt it also had the obligation to provide more than that. In Europe he had seen the theater's true power unleashed; he was determined to see that same power exposed on the stages of America. Nor was he alone in his vision of a revitalized theater that would in its visual beauty and dramatic power appeal to the higher instincts of an audience. Norman Bel Geddes, another of the American theater's most important artists during the first thirty years of this century and a contemporary of Jones, also felt that theater could be more than it had been during the last decades of the nineteenth century and the first two of the twentieth. In the fourteenth edition of the *Encyclopaedia Britannica* he wrote the following:

To the Greeks, the theatre was their most vital creative expression, and they succeeded in achieving results that for "pure theatre" have never been surpassed. They built them to look like theatres and to dignify what transpired within them. . . .

Fig. 3. Design for *The Seagull*

We live in an industrial age. We should have theatres that belong to our time, drama that voices this time. Instead our theatre is a secondary expression. . . . The theatre is in a state of sham. The plays, the actors, the scenery, all try to make audiences forget they are in a theatre. The buildings themselves are made to look like office buildings, taverns, museums, Renaissance palaces, Spanish missions or casinos. . . .

To any student of the subject, the development of the theatre since the Greeks shows gradual deterioration. The single item that has most influence these changes is the proscenium arch. . . . Its two dimensional aspect imposes an effect which is deadening, as compared with the exhilaration of an audience surrounding the actors, such as we get in the circus. There is no more reason or logic in asking an audience to look at a play through a proscenium arch than there would be in asking them to watch a prize fight through

Fig. 4. Design for *The Divine Comedy*, Norman Bel Geddes, 1921. Scene: Paradise, "O! Thou Sweet Light . . . " Norman Bel Geddes Collection, Theatre Arts Library, Harry Ransom Humanities Research Center, The University of Texas at Austin, by permission of Edith Lutyens Bel Geddes, executrix

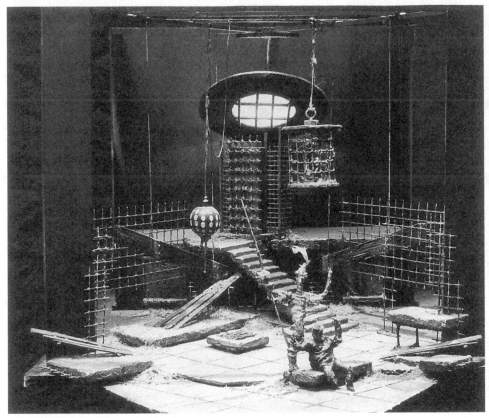

Fig. 5. Design for *Man of La Mancha*

one. . . . In an art gallery, looking at a piece of sculpture, you instinctively walk slowing around the object to view it from different directions, rather than merely standing and looking at it as you would a painting. The exaggerated importance of the picture-frame stage of the past generation is undoubtedly due to lack of imagination of the minds working in the theatre. . . .

The end we seem to be going toward has a more plastic three dimensional stage structure, formal, dignified and neutral, as a basis, its various acting platforms inviting a variety of movement, and provided with adequate space for lighting instead of cramped condition of the present. Such a structure is designed for the playing of a sequence of scenes of diverse mood, locale and character, not imitative in geographical terms, but creative in dramatic terms, with emphasis on the intensity of dramatic action and its projection to an audience.

The style of scenery both Jones and Bel Geddes were reacting against is shown in figure 3. The kind of theater Bel Geddes advocated is shown in figure 4, an unrealized project for *The Divine Comedy* devised to demonstrate his visions for the theater of the future.

While there have been many influences that changed both the look and philosophical thrust of scenography during the last ninety years, the most revolutionary aspects of these influences did not really begin to manifest themselves until after the second world war and the rebuilding of Europe. While it is difficult to enumerate all the directions scenography has taken, a few of these changes could be listed (many of them interrelated) as follows:

1. There is a tendency to prefer radical stage-audience relationships (many of these are open stage or variations of open stage forms, but some like the experimental audience placements of Jerzy Grotowski in Poland, which will be be discussed at a later point in this book) rather than the standard proscenium arch relationship to the audience.

2. First, there is an emphasis toward sculptural building rather than employing flat units

Fig. 6. Design for *The Front Page*

Fig. 7. Technicians using poured foam

painted to represent three-dimensional form, and second, another facet of this same trend, a definite predisposition toward using open skeletal structural forms rather than cutting off the backstage area from the playing area by a single closed-off unit such as a box set (fig. 5).

3. There is a redefinition of the box-setting form by violating the proscenium arch with playing areas that jut into the traditional proscenium-arch auditorium space (fig. 6).

4. Actual three-dimensional textures are used rather than painted simulation of textures, while at the same time, also using twentieth-century materials (lightweight synthetics such as foam plastics, rubber castings, etc.) and technology instead of traditional building materials and stagecraft techniques. Figure 7 shows technicians using poured foam for the snowbanks and vacuum-formed bricks required in the design shown in figure 8.

5. A greater use of consciously selected meta-phorical and symbolic imagery in design concepts (and in many instances using fragmented images or a number of images or forms incongruently juxtaposed) is to be found rather than attempting to copy on the stage details from directly observed natural images or historical structures and locales (fig. 9).

6. There has been a general tendency to simplify scenic environments into forms and materials that directly reflect and relate to the abstract qualities the scenographer and director feel are inherent in the text (fig. 10).

7. With the increased use of multimedia there is now usually more than one focus (if any focus at all) of attention on the stage at one time, the effect and aim of the production being more an accidental and accumulative experience rather than a linear progression of calculated images and rehearsed actions (fig. 11).

8. There has also been a noticeable difference in the manner in which the twentieth-century

Fig. 8. Design for *La Bohème*

Fig. 9. Design for *Don Carlos*

scenographer regards the setting on the physical stage. It could be said that scenographers and directors have during this century rediscovered the theater as a three-dimensional world, not just an animated picture ridgedly framed by a proscenium arch. As the proscenium arch has been violated (or removed altogether), there has been a movement from designs that are primarily viewed as flat background decoration (fig. 12) with a distinctly horizontal bias to designs that employ deeper acting areas and that have scenic elements more vertical in nature (fig. 13).

All these tendencies are evident in the design for *Oedipus* shown in figure 14. Perhaps the greatest single preoccupation of the present-day scenographer—a concern that he directly links his work with that of other theater artists—lies in the manipulation of stage space.

But just what is *stage space*; how does it differ from space outside the theater? These questions are not easy to answer, even by the experienced scenographer who has confronted the problems and implications of spatial relationships on the stage. Much of the text that follows will have meaning to the extent that we come to understand some of those problems and implications. For now, however, let us examine the question of space on the stage in its simplest form and in a rudimentary historical perspective.

Until approximately the turn of this century, the unstated but accepted attitude toward scenery in the theater should be *decorative* rather than *functional*. This attitude could be presented in a diagram such as that shown in figure 15. Here we see that scenery stands on three sides of the performer but does not in any direct way

Fig. 10. Design for *The Crucible*

influence him; the only tangible way in which he relates to this background is by being *seen against it*. The background is something with which the performer does not—in fact, cannot—have an active relationship. Strangely enough, the performer of the seventeenth and eighteenth centuries—and well into the nineteenth—had little conception of how he was seen in relation to his immediate environment; all he could do is perform in spite of it. In some instances, as Wilhelm Schlegel reported earlier, the lines of the perspective painting made actors appear as if they changed sizes as they moved from the back of the stage to the forestage. The actor, although the nearest to the painted background, had little choice but to ignore his surroundings, since interaction with this painted environment was all be impossible.

During the last part of the nineteenth century and during the whole of this one, the director and scenographer, and to some extent the playwright, have literally forced the performer to the real world of form by devising productions that depend upon three-dimensional environments. Performers cannot avoid directly relating to their environment, since the stage is rarely a flat plane surrounded by flat pictures but is often a com-

plex multileveled structure. Even in the opera—which retained the vestiges of the nineteenth-century picture stage well into this century—now routinely fractures playing areas into difficult obstacle courses that must be carefully negotiated while singing difficult music. Figure 16 is a diagram showing an environment that requires performers to be directly related to their surroundings.

The scenographer has, during the last century become more and more responsible for this integration of performer and scenic environment. This has meant, in addition, that the work of the scenographer must be more carefully coordinated with that of other theater artists, most notably, the director of a production. In tandem the director and scenographer have the responsibility for expanding a performer's possibility of movement. This can be accomplished in a number of ways. A performer's movement can be restricted to a set path by having physical obstacles set in his way (fig. 17A) or by causing the performer conform to an accepted convention; while one could physically walk through the "walls" represented by the skeletal structure (fig. 17B), an agreement between actor, director, and scenographer that the path from the outside of

Fig. 11. Design for *Aïda* with projections

the structure to the inside will be similar to that shown. (Just such a convention is adopted in the design of Jo Mielziner for his production of *The Death of a Salesman* discussed later in the text.) A third way to influence the movements of a performer is to provide a carefully delineated path on the stage floor. This can be done with a raised structure like that shown in figure 18 or by simply marking out a pathway on the floor as shown in figure 17B.

All these possibilities have been employed extensively in the stage designs of this century. Fracturing the stage into individual acting areas or creating complex stage forms is no longer considered radical. While the Broadway theater held on to its boxlike stages well into the middle of the century, increasingly scenographers such as Boris Arronson began to violate the arch and bring the setting into the auditorium space. Extending the playing area beyond the curtain line (consequently making the curtain unusable) into the audience's area is now routinely done. Figure 19 is a design that incorporates many of the features just discussed. Many of the examples used in this book show designs approached in the same manner.

Fig. 12. Design for *The Boy Friend*

There are some dangers in creating scenic environments that "reinvent" the stage space. And there is always the temptation for a scenographer to unilaterally create interesting stage shapes that have little to do with the internal needs of the production. It should be emphasized here that the creation of stage shapes must be agreed upon with the director of the production. Peter Brook make a telling point when he says that "the set is the geometry of the eventual play, so that a wrong set makes many scenes impossible to play, and even destroys many possibilities for the actors."

The scenographer's most significant function, then, is that of manipulator of stage space in its relationship to the human actor; the successful scenographer is a master of those relationships. It is in this role that the scenographer has a dangerous assignment, since it is possible—as Brook points out—to limit the actor's movement (and consequently his effectiveness) purposelessly in order to preserve a pictorial effect or a desire for an interestingly shaped stage.

Having examined stage space possibilities in general, let us progress to a discussion of the ways human beings consider space outside the theater. To begin, we might ask a common question posed by many not familiar with the peculiarities of theatrical thought: *What is the difference between the work of the scenographer and that of the interior decorator?* That many—both inside the theater and outside it—see little difference between these two professions makes it imperative that the question is broached early in our study.

First of all, let us determine what we mean by the term *space* in relation to the human being in daily life. And our first step in understanding the various relationships that exist is to separate the term into two major categories: private space and public space. No matter what society we inhabit, our lives are played out in these two kinds of space. In a later part of this text we will consider the implications inherent in public space and how it affects those who use it ("Research into Action: *Romeo and Juliet*" in part 5). For now, however, we will consider the area of private space only.

Private space can be either inside a building structure or outside it, but in both instances there is some attempt to cut off that space—either by

Fig. 13. Design for *Home*

one person or a small group—to make it clearly
personal or somehow unique. The room is probably the most elemental unit of private space; no
matter if the room is owned by the inhabitant(s)
or just being used for a temporary period, it
always, directly or indirectly, shows the effects
of private use and ownership. But in what ways
is the personal quality of a room brought about?
Roughly this happens in three ways:

1. By seeking the help of someone (an interior
decorator most often) who can delineate and coordinate the functions of the room and at the
same time produce a particular "look" and "feel"
that reflect the owner's personal taste and sensi-

bilities (or perhaps what the owner thinks is the
current style in fashion).

2. By the individual who owns the room assuming the responsibility for the planning and
ordering of the room into workable units and an
aesthetically pleasing whole. Many individuals
feel that space they inhabit cannot be arranged or
made pleasing by anyone other than themselves.
Many people approach the planning of their personal spaces with the "I may not know, perhaps,
what is *good*, but I know what I *like*" philosophy.
Rooms consciously planned by their owners often tell what the person occupying them would
like to be accepted as rather than what they actu-

Fig. 14. Design for *Oedipus*

ally may be. In this way personal living spaces serve the same function as costumes or clothes: outward signs of inner promptings.

3. By not consciously considering the planning of the space at all. Once the natural demands of day-to-day living are assured in functional and utilitarian ways, no further thought is given by the person living there to aesthetic considerations. Most dramatic characters live in spaces thus established. They reflect the hypothesis that a person who lives in a particular place for a period of time creates, although unconscious of its happening, a highly distinctive and personal environment.

The resulting space is slow in evolution, however, and overall effect is primarily accumulative in nature, not, as stated before, consciously planned.

Of the three kinds of personal space just described—and one might expect that individual dramatic characters could overlap these categories—this last kind of space is the most difficult for the scenographer to plan and execute, since the key to success lies in fully understanding the characters themselves.

It is little wonder, then, that young scenographers find it difficult to create spaces in which dramatic characters can live out their stories.

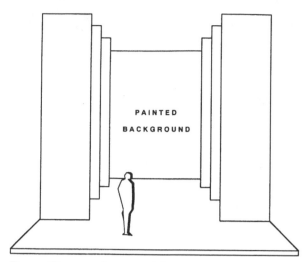

Fig. 15. Diagram of scenery style

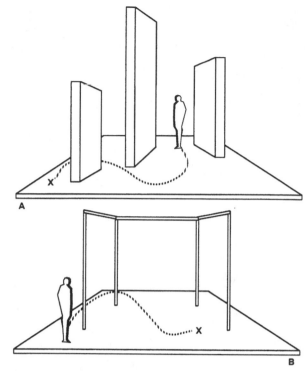

Fig. 17. Actor's possible movements

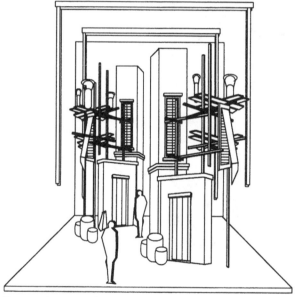

Fig. 16. Diagram of scenery style

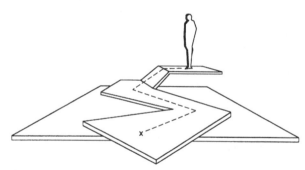

Fig. 18. Actor's possible movements

Moreover, it is characteristic of the fledgling scenographer that he confuses his functions with those of the interior decorator. It is a well-known attitude among professional scenographers that some of their colleagues are little more than interior decorators who happen to work in the theater. In *The Dramatic Imagination*, Robert Edmond Jones devotes much of a long chapter to explaining just what the differences between the two professions are. Ultimately, however, it is not a matter of class distinction or hierarchy that separates the scenographer and the interior decorator; rather, it is a profound difference in pur-

poses and goals. Let us take a moment to examine what those differences are.

Interior decorators have and use in their work certain skills that allow them to analyze a room in ways that scenographers also employ. It is true that interior decorators usually attempt to make rooms they design reflect the personality of their clients; but, at the same time, it is difficult for these designers—usually highly trained in many visual arts and crafts—to keep their own tastes out of the picture. In many instances, an individual decorator is chosen *because* of distinctive approaches to room decoration. Many clients actually expect their chosen decorator to supply

Fig. 19. Design for *A Christmas Carol*

the taste they may feel they lack. And many decorators are happy to supply that taste for a fee.

The essential point to be made here is that interior decorators, while they are greatly interested in making rooms aesthetically pleasing and stylish, are primarily concerned with the predictable functions of those rooms as outlined by a client's stated wishes; they are responsible *only* for the successful resolution of those functions in a agreed-upon style. A decorator may, for instance, be called upon to provide a conversation area for client A larger than that required by client B, since client B does not have as many friends or social gatherings as client A. The task of the interior decorator is to combine all demands—no matter how diverse the individual elements—into a unified and satisfactory whole. Once this has been accomplished, the job is considered finished and the client moves back into the newly decorated space. What is done in that space is no longer the concern of the interior decorator.

We might ask, then, doesn't the scenographer perform many of the same functions as those just detailed? Is not the work of the scenographer also complete when he has provided the characters in the play with a room that satisfies their physical needs, and (like the clients of the interior decorator) is not his job finished when the actors move into the setting? The answer to these questions contains the essential difference between the professions.

Yes, some of the functions mentioned above are similar, some almost identical (both interior decorators and scenographers must be trained in period styles, use of color and form, identification of antiques, etc.); but the scenographer does not consider his task done when the actors take up "tenancy" of the room he has created. What must concern him further *is what they do after they move into the created space.* This is the main distinction and greatest difference between the work of the scenographer and the interior decorator. Let us now examine just what this difference entails.

Although the interior decorator has influenced certain aspects of behavior of the people who inhabit the rooms he designed, he cannot be responsible if, say three weeks after he has completed his work, a murder is committed in that room. But what of the scenographer? Although the scenographer may have created a room that used all the skills and knowledge of the decorator, be identical in almost every way, there is one very important difference between the decorator's room and the scenographer's room: the scenographer must know everything that will transpire in his room for the entire time the room exists. If there is to be a murder in it, the scenographer must be aware that it will happen. In some ways he must plan for the way it will be done.

The relationship of the scenographer to the characters in a play has a greater complexity to it than does that of decorator to her clients because the scenographer must constantly work on many levels at the same time. Not only do the events of the play need understanding and coordination, the characters of the drama, unlike the decorator's clients, never speak directly to the scenographer and very rarely discuss with one another what they feel about the place where they find themselves. In almost every dramatic text, however, it is possible to glean the necessary information concerning their lives and their actions.

This brings us to another important subject, a subject directly related to the matters just discussed: the question of stage space.

What is stage space? In part 2 of this text we will examine in greater detail how scenographers think of space on the stage and how it is used to further the purposes of a text. For the moment, however, let us give one example to demonstrate how it differs from space in the world we experience outside the theater.

It is not uncommon for the playwright sometimes to call upon the scenographer to organize the stage into separate areas that will represent different locales, although actually only a nominal distance from one another. While these locations are supposedly miles apart, they are in reality no more than a few feet, sometimes inches, apart. The same requirement is made in relation to time as well; for example, in Arthur Miller's *Death of a Salesman*, Willy Loman must literally walk in the space of a few feet from his backyard to another city and, at the same time, into the past. This use of space on the stage in such a free unrestricted manner is not a modern innovation, however; Shakespeare, to mention but one playwright from the past, made similar demands on the theater's ability to mold time and space to the needs of the playwright's imagination. The very nature of stage space is fluid and amorphous; it freely bends, sometimes breaks, those natural laws that operate in the world outside the theater. No set of rules, no firm principles can be formulated that will once and forever set the limits as to how stage space may be used. The problems the playwright presents the scenographer must be solved over and over in response to the needs of each new text, each new production. In most cases the problems are reasonably simple. The scenographer must, nevertheless, always be prepared to redefine the total space under his control into workable frameworks that address often illogical demands on distance, space, and time. The questions raised by these demands is a subject that should be addressed early in the education of any scenographer. Considering how such questions are answered is very likely the most significant aspect of theater practice that separates scenography from all other arts.

The Educational Background of the Scenographer

Before beginning the main body of the text, it would be time well spent to examine more closely certain assumptions that underlie the present-day educational climate in which we live and work. These assumptions affect equally the student and the instructor; moreover, it is in the impartial examination of these most basic assumptions that in all the arts student and instructor alike have been negligent, since, like the air we breathe, they are too omnipresent, too all-pervasive to be given much serious attention. Nevertheless, some attempt, although necessarily short as it must be here, should be made to see if these assumptions are valid foundations on which to build for the future.

The most basic assumption made in this book

is that all students training for to be scenographers feel, as an important part of their educational agenda, a strong need to become directly involved in a form of communication that can reveal to others meaningful truths concerning their collective pasts, their current worlds, and their possible futures. Further, all that follows speaks to those students who refuse to limit their fields of inquiry to narrowly defined concepts of those worlds or a theater that reflects only limited views of human possibility. If one accepts Shakespeare's often quoted but nonetheless still current observation that "all the world's a stage and all the men and women merely players," the scenographer must also realize that the stage is a real world where the people who inhabit it are no less real than those who view it. The theater, although a sometimes puzzling and fragmented mirror of that world, is not only a fascinating mechanical toy raised to vast dimensions. On the other hand, the theater is often able to reveal through its mechanical means great subjective truths, truths that would remain essentially unknown or invisible without the theater artist's ability to manipulate physical form and color. We should never forget that the scenographer must become an expert craftsman who links the world of words and ideas, philosophies and histories, myths and tales, to physical things that can be seen and touched in a world of material form and movement. If there is to be a continuing theater, it must rely on steady flow of craftsmen of revelation.

It is important for all students of scenography to understand that although technical expertise is essential in their work, mechanical skill is merely a path to a goal, not the goal itself. The danger always exists in our training that technical prowess and pride in attained skills can lead a student to be more concerned with demonstrating those accomplishments than in employing them for purposes less visible to the public eye. It comes as a surprise to the average theatergoer (and quite probably many a theatrical insider as well) that many mature scenographers very rightly assume that if their own work "shows up" in a production, that if their skill is too readily apparent, they have to some degree failed in their intent. This is not to say that imaginative work should go unperceived or unappreciated by those viewing a production in the

theater, but that perception and appreciation should always be in context—part of a whole, not an isolated accomplishment to be applauded separately.

Judging a scenographic design as something apart from the total production is, of course, certainly nothing new in the theater. In our own time painters such as Picasso, Matisse, Dali, or David Hockney and sculptors such as Henry Moore or Alexander Calder are expected to be instantly recognizable as themselves. They do not attempt to disguise the fact they have contributed their famous names to the production, as well as their work. In all fairness to them, however, artists of this magnitude are expected to display their own distinct personalities. Audiences expect to see recognizable elements of work that has its genesis outside the theater in a different medium.

Scenographic artists, on the other hand, must care less about preserving their own recognizable signatures and hallmarks in the works they create. While certain scenographers may become known both by name and by certain traits in their work, their first obligation is to serve the larger whole, not to shine with individual brilliance. Robert Edmond Jones writes in *The Dramatic Imagination*: "A stage setting has no life of its own. Its emphasis is directed toward the performance. In the absence of the actor it does not exist. Strange as it may seem, this simple and fundamental principle of stage design still seems to be widely misunderstood."

While this statement is more than half a century old, the essential decency of its underlying philosophy still commands the attention and respect of the most modern scenographer. In my own work I have attempted to follow the wisdom of this advice; and I have been most pleased with that work when, in the audiences' applause, I could perceive that it was a performance being rewarded and not individual artists. One can tell that if you listen carefully enough.

Where and when does one begin that certain path that leads to particular interests, interests that eventually become a profession? While some can easily be explained by family influences or early exposure to cultural histories, many of the causes will always remain lost to conscious analysis. The individual artist would do well to be curious concerning those reasons and to do some probing into those initial circumstances that set the path. At least one should attempt some insight into the early activities that triggered a desire to work in the theater. Many theater artists—Ingmar Bergman, to name but one—have written in their memoirs of specific instances that proved to be decisive turning points. Howard Gardner, a writer interested in child development and especially how they become integrated into their individual cultures, makes some important observations that could help us understand the forces that determined an early predisposition to theatrical work. He writes:

We have encountered . . . young children whom we have come to call *patterners*. These youngsters analyze the world very much in terms of the configurations they discern, the patterns and regularities they encounter, and, in particular, the physical attributes of objects—their colors, size, shape, and the like. Such patterners enthusiastically arrange blocks on top of one another, endlessly experiment with forms on the table or in their drawings, constantly match objects with one another, build pairs and trios and the like; but they spend little time reenacting familiar scenes in play and they engage in relatively little social conversation (though they certainly understand what is said).

Sharply contrasted with these youngsters is the population we have touted as *dramatists*. These children are keenly interested in the structure of events that unfold in their vicinity—the actions, adventures, clashes, and conflicts that befall the world of individuals, as well as the fantastic tales describing even more gripping events, which they ask to hear over and over again. While patterners cling to the activities of drawing, modeling with clay, and arrangement of numerical arrays, the dramatists prefer to engage in pretend play, in storytelling, in continuing conversation and social exchange with adults and peers. For them, one of life's chief pleasures inheres in maintaining contact with others and celebrating the pageantry of interpersonal relations. Our patterners, on the other hand, seem almost to spurn the world of social relations, preferring instead to immerse (and perhaps lose) themselves in the world of (usually visual) patterns.

In a very real sense, scenographers must possess leanings toward both the kinds of activities discussed above. Perhaps there is a clue embedded in Gardner's observations that points to the unique nature of scenography itself, since to

practice it one must have a foot in both worlds: one must have the instincts of the patterner as well as those of the dramatist.

Let us now focus on another basic assumption this book makes: not all craftsmen become artists, but every artist must be a craftsman. Further, it would be a dull student indeed who did not know that the term *craftsmanship* is not the same thing in all instances; that craftsmanship in arts is not the same as craftsmanship in, for instance, the building trades. (This is not a class distinction, however, simply a difference in ultimate purpose: a good plumber is not necessarily one who can discourse on the societal implications of indoor plumbing. But a scenographer who thinks his only task is to supply accurate working drawings for flats, platforms, or backdrops or to be able to specify how many instruments are necessary to provide illumination for an acting area is not fulfilling his expected function.)

Norman Potter, in his short but nonetheless excellent book *What Is a Designer: Education and Practice* (a book, by the way, that should be read totally by every serious student of scenography), provides good reasons why the earliest phases of a designer's education are so important. He says: "Design education must, by its nature, dig below the surface, and must at the outset be more concerned to clarify intentions than to get results. If it is sensible to see learning and understanding as rooted in the continuum of life, it may be that a really useful introduction course will only show its value in the full context of subsequent experience, i.e. several years afterwards. Conversely, an education that concentrates on short-term results may give a misleading sense of achievement and fail to provide an adequate foundation for subsequent growth."

Many students are impatient with the discipline required to clarify those essential intentions. They want to seek out the "right way" quickly. These students often ask just which of the two paths—formal art instruction or theater training—is the more important one to pursue in the educational career of the scenographer. Such discussions usually provoke a debate if one (no matter which) is touted over the other. Most students consider it improbable to pursue both courses of study with equal attention or success, since most departments of a college or a university have academic restrictions placed on their programs. A recurring question is this: *If one does arrange an accommodation between these two disciplines, how is it possible to take the liberal arts courses deemed necessary to a full understanding of our main studies?*

To these questions we who teach scenography find no easy answers. Certainly there are no satisfactory quick replies. If such are expected, I usually give this advice: choose neither path, quit now and take up some other less demanding study. While this attitude may seem at first negative, even harsh and evasive, it is very good advice nonetheless. One foot *must* be in formal art training, one in the theater; most important of all, the scenographer's mind must constantly balance numerous often diverse interests simultaneously. There is no quick way. There is no other way.

Students of every art soon realize that their education never ends. Although the scenographer may stop formal instruction, even the most secure find that the process must continue; that as well informed as one is upon the completion of a degree or license, it is, in very real terms, only the beginning, not the close of the artist's education.

An important factor in the continuing education of any artist starting today is to realize that the world has, in many significant ways, become a much smaller place since the beginning of this century. The visual arts of the theater often cross national borders and continental oceans. While there have always been cultural crosscurrents in styles of drama and production approaches, the past ninety years have seen the theater become a more unified world activity rather than a series of isolated cultural phenomena. The cinema, television, videotapes, laser disks, and, not least, an explosion of printed materials have augmented the possibility that previously required physical travel; technology now makes it possible to view important events without leaving home. Additionally, the availability of inexpensive travel options brings numerous theatrical companies to our door step. The net result of this cross-fertilization is the emergence of artists who, although they still come from and serve individual cultures, are not simply representative products of that culture. Paradoxically, as we become more worldly, we at times foster provincial attitudes; as we gain more to choose from we become narrower in point of view. In *The Systems View of the World*, Ervin Laszlo describes just what happens to those whose visions become blurred or atrophied when individuals too narrowly limit their attention:

Given persons can and often do develop interests within their own specialties that set them apart from the rest—or all but a handful among the rest—and create a kind of specialty bubble around themselves. . . . The literary historian specializing in early Elizabethan theater may not have much in common with a colleague specializing in Restoration drama, and will find himself reduced to conversation about the weather when encountering an expert on contemporary theater.

The unfortunate consequence of such specialty barriers is that knowledge, instead of being pursued in depth and integrated in breadth, is pursued in depth in relative isolation. Instead of getting a continuous and coherent picture, we are getting fragments—remarkably detailed but isolated patterns. We are drilling holes in the wall of mystery that we call nature and reality on many locations, and we carry out delicate analyses on each of the sites. It is only now that we are beginning to realize the need for connecting the probes with one another and gaining some coherent insight into what is there.

While the informational resources of the world have become so vast and the individual items necessary even in our own specialty have become staggeringly numerous, it is all the more necessary that we maintain some overview of that world we inhabit. Although all that can be accomplished here is to reaffirm once more with the strongest urging that a *general* curiosity is a necessary and inseparable part of a *specific* educational process.

Laszlo's advice is not intended for students alone; his words apply equally well to those with years of experience. Included in that general curiosity, and an important part of a scenographer's continuing education, is an active research into the work of other visual artists—not only those who work directly for the stage but also those who design for the cinema and for television. The cinema is an especially helpful adjunct to the education of student scenographers for several reasons. (1) Films, unlike most stage productions, do not appear in only one locale and do not disappear from view after a limited run. Their viewing life is usually long and, as with classic films and those with wide appeal or aesthetic worth, constantly reappear on television, in the showings of film societies, and increasingly on the shelves of book store chains. (2) The work done on most films and television releases (such as those available on "Masterpiece Theatre") is of a high quality and performed by expert artists and craftsmen. Cost and other limiting factors experienced in the live theater do not hamper most filmed productions to the same extent as the work done for the stage. (3) Detail is more important to the camera eye, since it often focuses closely on scenes or objects. For this reason, accuracy becomes an important factor in film; historical research has become extremely reliable in both filmmaking and television during the past forty years. (4) Since naturalism is and probably will remain the predominate style of production, many films become veritable living examples of a past age or of another culture. Some films, however, perform this function better than others and are of greater value to the student scenographer's understanding of other times. Tony Richardson's *Tom Jones*, for instance, is a more useful realization of another age than Stanley Kubrick's *Barry Lyndon* is, even though both show characters and locales in almost identical time frames. The reasons for this disparity are simple to see: in *Tom Jones*, the design approach and the actors' performances mutually aided one another. Director, performers, and supporting artists were all on the same "wave length," so to speak, and visual interest in the age did not supersede the dramatic needs of the script. The entire production was conceived, it could be said, *in the spirit of the time*. In *Barry Lyndon*, on the other hand, the focus of the film rested almost entirely on the visual evocation of the age; one could easily remember the stunning interiors peopled with beautifully dressed manikins who rarely shattered the mood with words or actions, the magnificent sweeping vistas through which the camera lovingly—but all too slowly—moved. With *Tom Jones*, it is possible to recall many individual scenes from the story; with *Barry Lyndon*, it is difficult to remember who was where or what really happened. Both works were beautiful in execution (and *Barry Lyndon* was certainly the more sumptuous of the two productions), but in *Tom Jones* we are able to understand better the peculiar atmo-

sphere of the early eighteenth century, while *Barry Lyndon* remained an entertaining stroll through a museum with animated figures not that different from those in Disney World. In short, one work had life, the other did not. Of the two *Tom Jones* is a better educational experience for the student scenographer than *Barry Lyndon* is.

Before leaving these thoughts on the scenographer's education it would be well to introduce a subject to which we can devote the briefest of discussions. The subject is, however, one of profound importance to all who work in the theater, since it relates to the essence of the theater experience. Although a full exposition of the points made below is not possible in this text, a brief encounter with the subject—the dual nature of theater—can be of value.

Students who undertake the study of any art soon come to realize that all arts have two major components in their makeup: the physical aspect (the craft part) and the metaphysical aspect (the philosophical part). The first part deals with the *How* of the craft; the second addresses the *Why* of the art.

The theater is an art whose subject matter is nothing less than the whole of human culture. Theater is the best measure of what we are; it is the perfect tool to assess our human capabilities as well as our all-too-human failings. It is by the tool of theater that the playwright can show us people such as Oedipus, Hamlet, Willie Loman, and Blanche Dubois: people sometimes greatly different from us but related to us as members of our human family. Although their sufferings and joys are unique to them, we must also acknowledge, as John Donne did long ago, that "no man is an island, each is a piece of the main, a part of the whole." As we watch them move through their often painful worlds, we begin to experience insights into the vicissitudes our own.

Understanding the relationship between that "real" world we live outside the playhouse and those many worlds we observe on the stage is the prime requisite of anyone working for the theater. Acquiring such understanding, however, is a difficult process; it is never fully accomplished, never completely mastered. Comprehending the ways these worlds interrelate and reflect one another has been the prime meditation of playwrights from the theater of fifth-century Greece down to our own time. In this century, perhaps no playwright was more obsessed with the interactions of world and stage than Luigi Pirandello; his play *Six Characters in Search of an Author* is an exploration of the mysteriously strange, often bizarre, guises adopted by that illusive thing called "truth." It was Shakespeare, however, using that introspective shadow of himself, Jacques, who voiced the definitive formula: "All the world's a stage and all the men and women merely players." This instance, of course, was not the only time Shakespeare linked the destinies of man to those of players. In *Macbeth*, he expresses the futility of human existence using a metaphor taken directly from the theater:

> Life's but a walking shadow, a poor player
> That struts and frets his hour upon the stage
> And then is heard no more. It is a tale
> Told by an idiot, full of sound and fury,
> Signifying nothing.

While all observations on the duality of stage and world are not so pessimistic—much of theater deals with the joys of living—the complexities inherent in relating what we do in the theater to the world we live day to day can be daunting to anyone attempting professional study of this art. While formal theatrical training will give the individual student materials on which to build an intellectual base, individual effort beyond formal education is also necessary. Foremost in that understanding must be the realization that the world of theater should always reflect the larger world that lies outside the walls of the playhouse.

The Fallacy of Self-Expression

Underlying all discussions concerning the possible paths toward a desired education is this most basic question: *How do I learn to express myself?* While this may seem, on its face, to be a perfectly natural question arising from a perfectly normal human desire, a closer investigation of this desire is warranted. It is an unfortunate situation that of all the arts and professions theater *seems* to be the one that puts the greatest emphasis on directly expressing the singularity of the individual. The prime requisite for electing any area of theater as a lifework, it is popularly thought, is a natural bent toward self-display in one form or another. At this earliest point, let it be said that this is a particularly dangerous attitude for the scenographer to hold; for while this popular image has been fostered by as many within the theater as it has by those without, those who commit themselves to work in the theater are soon disabused of this fantasy. The generation that grew up during the first third of this century, in fact, was shown in movie after movie that it was a simple step from a desire to perform to Broadway success; the only problem was—as Mickey Rooney (an iconic figure of the "show-off") would tell his small group of enthusiastic followers—"First, we have to get a barn," which in a remarkably short while was converted to an operational theater. From the intense desire to create theater to a slickly produced show (albeit still in the country and still in a barn) was a *fait accompli*, was all downhill. Those who designed the settings for these productions, being no less inspired by dreams of personal glory and admiring audiences who loudly applauded their work at every curtain rise, were part of the Hollywood vision that placed self-expression first and foremost among the reasons for becoming a person of the theater.

Doubtless, these early romantic attitudes are still an important part of the myth and mystique of "going into theater"; certainly this is still so in the American theater and probably most noticeable in college and university theater departments. But although inherent ability, an intuitive grasp of the dramatic, and an intense desire to show something to someone else are certainly prerequisites for choosing theater as a profession, they are just prerequisites, not a license to work in it. It would be well, therefore, to look more closely at this question of *self-expression* as the prime motivation in the selection of theater as a lifework. To assist in understanding why self-expression is not the lone goal of the theater artist, I have selected some voices other than my own to explain what is or should be a more useful attitude.

In *The Hidden Order of Art*, Anton Ehrensweig makes some important points concerning the confusion of artistic freedom and the blind indulgence that often passes for the artist's motivation:

> The old cult of free self-expression still lingers. . . . but it has thoroughly exhausted itself as a stimulus for the student's imagination. Once upon a time the slogan of free self-expression came as a liberation, carried along by the yearnings of the Romantics and later the Dadaists who chafed against externally imposed conventions and restrictions. The individual pitted himself against society. By disrupting and shocking conventional sensitivities he released in himself highly individual and potent sensibilities. By one of the many ironical turn-abouts in modern art, today self-expression has become a social duty forcibly imposed on the student by teacher, parents and the public alike. More ironically still, some students therefore feel greatly relieved if they are told that there is no need for them to express their personality and that any labored attempt to do so can only fail. Individual self-expression has turned into another social convention. If we were to formulate a new maxim that today could replace the platitude of free self-expression, it would be the opposite demand. Instead of straining too hard to discover his inner self, the student should objectively study the outside world. Because objective factors are alien to the inner self they are better able to act as extraneous "accidents" and so cut across preconceived and defensive cliches. In this way they will be able to tap hidden parts of the personality which have become alienated from conscious personality. Cool "alienation," then, has to fulfill the function which hot self-expression once filled. . . . The old psychological description and expression of inner states is replaced by a seemingly detached and objective description of man's outer environment. Somehow—and this is the paradox—our involvement with outer events is far better to express our real preoccupations than a direct attempt at looking inside ourselves or into the minds of other people.
>
> *Today the artist is involved with objective reality in order to reach his own self.* (Italics mine)

These words of Ehrensweig, although not directed to theater students per se, may come as something of a surprise but do apply to them as well. It is also quite possible that the student scenographer is better equipped emotionally to accept this reevaluation of the contemporary artist's motivational impetus than are some of his fellow students in the performing areas. Nor should it be difficult to comprehend that every art of the theater involves interpretation and pre-sentation of things discovered that are not completely original products of a single mind. We in the theater are required to perform not only a different amount of research than most other artists but a kind of research that many—painters, sculptors, printmakers—would consider secondary in importance and, at best, "copy work." Nevertheless, it is in the interest of all artists, despite their individual bents or media, to consider well, if they cannot completely take to heart, the words of Joshua Reynolds who, while he was speaking painting and drawing in particular, gave advice that cuts across the whole spectrum of creative work: "The greatest natural genius cannot subsist on its own stock; he who resolves never to ransack any mind but his own will soon be reduced from mere barrenness to the poorest of all imitations. It is vain to invent without materials on which the mind may work and from which invention must originate. *Nothing can come of nothing*" (italics mine).

In support of the sentiments expressed by Ehrensweig and Reynolds, Herbert Read, a twentieth-century critic sympathetic to creative artists, adds his own thoughts on this subject. Read forcefully points out the attendant dangers of the artist who is too concerned with demonstrating his own inner life while neglecting his larger social obligations. He says:

> The mistaken presentation of my point of view, of which I have myself been guilty in the past, is to describe art as *self*-expression. If every artist merely expresses the uniqueness and separateness of self, then art might be disruptive and anti-social. . . .
>
> Obviously the great artist who is not merely making something, like a carpenter or a cobbler, but expressing something, like Shakespeare or Michelangelo or Beethoven, is expressing something bigger than his *self*. Self-expression, like self-seeking, is an illusion . . .
>
> Society expects something more than self-expression from its artists, and in the case of great artists such as those I have mentioned, it gets something more. It gets something which might be called life-expression. But the "life" to be expressed, the life which is expressed in great art, is precisely the life of the community, the organic group.

Read comes very close in this passage to defining the attitude those who work in theater should have or attempt to foster. Of course, one might expect many artists to reject the admonitions we have just encountered; the painter working alone in his studio, the sculptor, or printmaker can say, "If I wish to disregard all social commitment in my art, who is to say I cannot do so?" And, indeed, who can? But theater artists are community artists even if much of their work is done privately. Still, even those most new to the theater have an intuitive understanding that their obligations go far beyond the simple wish to "to express myself and nothing else."

Let us add just one more voice to the arguments made here that the artistic vision of those in theater cannot be only an inwardly directed one. The noted psychologist Bruno Bettleheim makes a valuable point when he says: "The most fascinating dream, expressing the deepest layers of the unconscious, is at best clinical raw material. . . . At best it creates an emotional climate of the aesthetic experience to follow. It is a windup that remains an empty, misleading gesture, if no pitched ball is to follow. I am afraid that much of what we accept from students in our art courses is of this ineffectual nature; *it simply expresses, and fails to communicate*. . . . It is not the outpouring of the unconscious but rather the mastery of the unconscious tendencies, the subjection of creative ability to the greatest discipline which alone makes for works of art" (italics mine).

It is not uncommon, therefore, to find unique artists reaffirming that the objective world becomes increasingly indispensable to their continuing development. Brendan Gill, in an interview with the great cartoonist Saul Steinberg, reports that even this very personal artist has experienced a growing awareness that study of the external world is necessary for any truly creative process: "Nowadays, I draw from life," he [Steinberg] says. "Like the old masters, *as I grow older I become more and more interested in what is out there and not*"—with a forefinger he taps a graying temple—"*in here*" (italics mine).

The real goal of a sound scenographic education is to develop along with requisite skills an attitude that gives full realization to the fact that a scenographer is not an isolated specialist working apart and alone. Nor does the popular image of the solitary artist in the quiet of the studio struggling only with his own interior problems best fit visual artists of the theater. While much of the work of scenography must be done in the privacy of a studio, much more must be accomplished in the busy ferment of the theater and the noisy industry of its technical shops. It is very important, moreover, to keep in mind that the function of the scenographer is always part of something larger than just the successful completion of a personal effort. As British industrial designer David Pye (*The Nature of Aesthetics of Design*) writes: "Everything everywhere may be regarded as a component of a system. It is fruitless to consider the action of a thing without considering the system of which it is a component. This fact has special importance for designers in various fields because they tend to think of things separately and to design them separately. *We ought at least to remind ourselves that we are concerned with a whole system even if we are only able to effect the design of one component*. It is arguable that the locomotive engineers of the nineteenth century had more vision than the automobile engineers of the twentieth; for in the nineteenth century they conceived of the vehicle and its road as one system and designed them together" (italics mine).

Though Pye is speaking design procedure and theory in general, he draws our attention to the essential conditions of the scenographic process as it relates to theater as a whole. The system under which the scenographer works is also a comprehensive one, not a series of isolated problems to be independently solved.

If a great emphasis has been placed on the apparent dangers of self-expression as a motivating force in becoming an artist in the theater, this emphasis is, I strongly feel, an important and necessary precondition to anyone entering the field of scenography. It is imperative, moreover, that every student include in the educative process the continuing search for the reasons why certain directions are pursued. Nor should the fledgling artist give too much attention to the pursuit of originality simply to call attention to a supposed personal uniqueness. Once again the words of David Pye offer sound advice: "artists of little capability or uncertain vocation will take great care to make their work look 'different,' whereas those with any certainty in them will know that their work cannot help but look different from that of other people any more than their signatures can."

The Outwardly Directed Creative Impulse

The terms imagination and creativity rank among those words most difficult to define, most difficult to apply with any degree of exactitude. And yet the words *create, creative, creation,* and *creativity,* along with the words *image, imagine, imaginative,* and *imagination,* are constantly used by artists, about artists, and can be used to praise or damn not only artists but also students, teachers, politicians, and cooks; it is applied almost to every human activity from the painting of the *Mona Lisa* to the perfect poaching of an egg. Yet how often does anyone pause to examine what these words mean or to consider just in what situation they might be properly applied? While few artists before the twentieth century put their thoughts on creativity into written words, we now have greater access to them than in previous periods. Having such information, however, brings with it hidden dangers to working artists. As the poet A. E. Houseman tells us: "Meaning is of the intellect, poetry is not. If it were, the eighteenth century would have been able to write it better. . . . Poetry indeed seems to me more physical than intellectual. A year or two ago . . . I received from America a request that I would define poetry. I replied that I could no more define poetry than a terrier can define a rat, but that I thought we both recognized the object by the symptoms which it provokes in us." This calculated resistance on the part of artists to delve too deeply into the wellsprings of creativity is echoed by the sculptor Henry Moore. But here the artist balances his warning with words of advice that indicate that the thinking part of the artist's mind also plays a part in the creative process: "It is a mistake for [an artist] to speak or write very often about his job. It releases tension needed for his work. By trying to express his aims with rounded-off logical exactness, he can easily become a theorist whose actual work is only a caged-in exposition of conceptions evolved in terms of logic and words.

But though the nonlogical, instinctive, subconscious part of the mind must play its part in his work, he also has a conscious mind which is not inactive. The artist works with a concentration of his whole personality, and the conscious part of it resolves conflicts, organizes memories, and prevents him from trying to walk in two directions at the same time" (italics mine).

Consider for a moment these common questions:

What is imagination?

What is creativity?

Are the terms interchangeable?

In what part of the human being do these qualities reside? Are they in the mind alone or does the trained hand take on a creative power of its own?

Are either of these qualities a fixed quantity, an absolute invariable gift possessed at birth and destined to reveal itself in the lives of those who have it?

Can imagination or creativity be instilled in those not perceived to have it or in those who do not believe it within their ability to use?

Is theater an art independent of other creative arts, and if so, is it a creative one, or is it simply an amalgam of independent interpretive acts loosely gathered together within unclear boundaries?

Is interpretation a form of creative activity?

Can any act or set of acts shared communally be truly creative?

The list of questions is endless; the answers few. And yet all who work in the theater implicitly accept that what they do as a group does involve acts of creativity that have arisen out of imagination.

We cannot begin to answer in this text all the questions posed here, and while every argument we undertake will remain necessarily inconclusive, we will continue the time-honored tradition of discussing in great detail many things that cannot be proved. Imagination is, despite its ambiguous dimensions, a necessary tool of any creative process, albeit a tool we use in many instances without full knowledge of its operation. And is it not possible to conceive of any creative act that does not exhibit some evidence that imagination is the triggering force that sets it off. We are all but forced to accept the workings of the imagination blindly, but that does not mean we should ever set aside the questioning of the process entirely. In fact, it is through the constant questioning as to how these creative processes work that we can actively build imagination. Moreover, the most basic tenet of this book is that imagination is not a fixed quantity nor is creativity an exclusive preserve bestowed to the few by favorable genes; that creativity and the triggering mechanism of imagination are both capable of education and of growth. Still it is very possible to get caught in strange traps when we attempt to differentiate between that which is truly creative and that which is merely innovative. The astute eighteenth-century scholar Samuel Johnson made a telling point when, reviewing the book of a contemporary writer, he brought to the attention of the author that "your manuscript is both good and original—but the part that is good is not original and the part that is original is not good."

Shakespeare, who could lay claim to be among history's most imaginative and creative poets (and compared with his contemporaries one of the least innovative), often posed questions similar to those just asked. And while he always does so in the voice of a play's character, it is not difficult to perceive a personal voice behind the temporary mask. *In A Midsummer Night's Dream*, he gives Theseus this searching speech:

> Lovers and madmen have such seething brains,
> Such shaping fantasies, that apprehend
> More than cool reason ever comprehends.
> The lunatic, the lover, and the poet
> Are of imagination all compact.
> One sees more devils than vast hell can hold;
> That is the madman. The lover, all as frantic,
> Sees Helen's beauty in a brow of Egypt.
> The poet's eye, in a fine frenzy rolling,
> Doth glance from heaven to earth, from earth
> to heaven;
> And as imagination bodies forth
> The forms of things unknown, *the poet's pen*
> *Turns them to shapes, and gives to aery nothing*
> *A local habitation and a name.*
>
> (Italics mine)

Here Shakespeare clearly proposes that the work of the dramatic poet is to give hard edges to atmospheric promptings; to link the concrete image to the abstract, intangible thought. During the past three hundred years the dramatist has not modified essentially either his craft or its most basic tenet that no matter how sonorously beautiful the words may be, the real purpose of the text is to give perceptible form to "aery nothings." These words give the actor a list of instructions as well as a map of images by which a performance may be charted. The most important tasks in the theater are first to find and then to reveal on stage the tangible shapes and local habitations summoned up by the playwright's clues to those "forms of things unknown." It is possible to say, therefore, that scenography is a direct extension of the playwright's mind.

But what does this really mean to scenographers? By what means do they link their own creative imaginations to that of the playwright? More importantly, what do we owe to a playwright; for that matter what does a playwright owe us? Theater has always been a two-way street; and even so venerable a playwright like Shakespeare—gone from the world over three hundred years—is still our common fellow traveler on that road. Where, then, does the playwright's imagination end and where does ours begin? These questions need not be considered constantly, may be put from our minds most of the time; the craft of theater is, after all, mostly discovered in the doing of it. Still, it would serve us well occasionally to bring such questions out to see if we are any nearer an answer, an understanding. If you are persistent in your search for the roots of creativity and imagination; if you foster an inquiring mind as assiduously as you pursue your technical craft, you will in time realize that the asking of a question is often the best answer to it.

As we have pointed out earlier, there are numerous branches of art that do not require the involvement of others. The theater is not among these. A primary question the student of scenography should make every effort to answer is: *Do I want to pursue an art in which my work will always be incomplete without the work of others*? If there is any serious doubt, it is a fairly accurate indication that the wrong track is being pursued. If, on the other hand, scenography is chosen as a lifework, it would be well to always keep in mind that in our best service to those other artists of the theater, we best serve ourselves, best express ourselves.

If, then, our purpose in theater is one of communication (and I do not for a moment believe this in any way precludes a very personal expression on the part of the artist, simply an adjustment of priorities and self-realized purposes), what is the proper attitude to bring to this desire, the proper way to approach the problems inherent in this particular kind of communication? Let us step outside the limits of our own special art for a moment; a first step in our search could very well begin with some good advice from those concerned with the education and progress of students of another art: writing.

In *The Elements of Style*, a book by William Strunk, Jr., and E. B. White, the following passage occurs: "Young writers often suppose that style is a garnish for the meat of prose, a sauce by which a dull dish is made palatable. Style has no such separate entity; it is nondetachable, unfilterable. The beginner should approach style warily, realizing that it himself he is approaching, no other; and he should begin by turning resolutely away from all devices that are popularly believed to indicate style—all mannerisms, tricks, adornments. *The approach to style is by way of plainness, orderliness, sincerity*" (italics mine). At first glance, this seems to be saying that the first duty of the artist is to *express himself*. But, if we examine this instruction more closely, we find that when there is the realization that all any artist is ever doing is expressing himself, there are some ways of doing it that are better than others; ways that help the artist to say what he wants to say in the most forceful and, at the same time, the most meaningful way. Most important of all, this advice helps to point out the difference between genuinely attempted communication of all ideas and information that the artist has encountered and narrowly defined self-expression, which only seeks to explore the limited experience of the individual. Although these words deal specifically with those who seek to make the best use of words, the underlying good sense evidenced here can, with little loss in meaning, be applied to the art and craft of scenography. It could be said, moreover, that the spirit of this advice is identical to that which informs the art of the theater in general. In a real sense these words show the link between communication and creativity.

Let us now take a closer look at the motivating forces that influence the act of creation.

Rollo May, in his book *The Courage to Create*, takes a broad view of what those forces are and speculates on the mechanism that triggers them. He says: "Creativity must be seen in the work of the scientist as well as in that of the artist, in the thinker as well as in the aesthetician; . . . Creativity, as Webster's rightly indicates, is basically the process of *making, of bringing into being*.

The first thing we notice in a creative act is that it is an encounter. Artists encounter the landscape they propose to paint—they look at it, observe it from this angle and that. They are, as we say, absorbed in it. Or in the case of abstract painters, the encounter may be with an idea, an inner vision, or even a random image taken from the objective world that looses its customary familiarity when seen out of context. For the painter, the encounter may be nothing more than a response to the colors of the paint on the palette or the inviting rough whiteness of the canvas."

The scenographer has two basic encounters, as May defines the term: the first is with the stage itself—an "empty space" full of "loneliness," as Peter Brook characterizes it. The second encounter is with the text of the work to be put into that "empty space." The abstractness of each is of a totally different kind: the nothingness, which is, nonetheless, a physical quality of the stage, and the potentiality of the words, which give promise of an image but not the images themselves. These two encounters, then, establish the parameters of the scenographic art. May goes on to make another important point, a point that students of any art would do well to ponder.

The concept of encounter also enables us to make clearer the important distinction between *talent* and *creativity*. . . . A man or woman may have talent whether he or she uses it or not; talent can probably be measured in the person as such. But creativity can be seen only in the act. If we were purists, we would not speak of a "creative person," but only of *a creative act*. Sometimes, as in the case of Picasso, we have great talent and at the same time great encounter and, as a result, great creativity. Sometimes we have great talent and truncated creativity, as many people felt in the case of Scott Fitzgerald. Sometimes we have a highly creative person who seems not to have much talent. It was said of the novelist Thomas Wolfe, who was one of the highly creative figures of the American scene, that he was a "genius without talent." But he was so creative because he threw himself so completely into his material the challenge of saying it—he was great because of the intensity of his encounter.

These are observations that touch on the many doubts and anxieties that art students experience during their training but are unable to express. Uncertainty concerning the possession of ability and understanding of an art form often accompanies artistic growth: *Do I have talent or*—as May suggests—*do I have only talent?* and: *If I do have something more, how do I make the best use of my abilities?* Tomas Maldonado provides some guidance with these troubling questions:

Design is always an attempt to break with banality, a manifestation of originality.

Creativity, however, is also a notion which has been excessively abused in recent years. For many people education for creativity means education for self-expression. They maintain that creativity should be the result of a process of liberation from the inhibiting aspects of the personality. In other words any personality capable of expressing itself should be capable of creating. This is not true: no capacity for expression can replace the knowledge and experience required of a specific object. Of course the inhibited man is seldom a creative man, but this does not support the belief that people free of inhibitions are automatically creative people. Creation certainly is always an act of dissension, in some respects an act of revolt, but at the same time it is the result of an acquired instrumental skill.

Education for design has become a very complex task. We must train people capable of revolting against stereotyped ideas, but we must also equip them with the means to do this; otherwise the revolt is only declamatory. *Moreover, in most cases the act of creating is not something beginning and ending with an individual.* (Italics mine)

While Maldonado is speaking specifically about the training of industrial design students, his words directly relate to any students of design and have especial meaning for those students of scenography. It is particularly true of theater artists that any instructor in charge of their training must continually keep in the forepart of his vision the fact that scenography does not have its "beginning and ending in an individual."

Although we are emphasizing here an objective approach to the scenographic educational process, let us also realize that objective study of any subject does have certain limits, that the individual is at the center of the process if not the sole focus of it. Nor must we be mislead into thinking that the mastery of any art can be accomplished simply by the study and assimilation of abstract nonsubjective rules and principles; all education has an element that will always be made subjective by the individual's personal involvement with it. Every artist must take those rules and principles, in other words, and make them his personal property in the service of his personal vision. For example, it could be said that there is a "language" of form. This has a certain crude validity looked at objectively: it could be said that horizontal lines suggest rest, vertical lines suggest stability and strength, diagonal lines give a feeling of falling or dynamic movement; but these principles only have value when applied to specific design problems. More important, these principles may, in certain instances be used to reinforce precisely the opposite of their supposed inherent meaning. To believe, for instance, that curved lines always denote comedy and high spirits is to risk becoming convinced that all comedies must have settings composed only of curves despite any amount of internal evidence that points to the contrary. Lines, forms, textures, and colors can and do express emotional content, but it would be impossible to create precise formulas that prove this so. Interpreting a playwright's text into lines, forms, and colors will always be an individual responsibility.

Paul Rand, the noted graphic designer, makes some perceptive observations on the training of all visual artists:

The absence in art of a well formulated and systematized body of literature makes the problem of teaching a perplexing one. The subject is further complicated by the elusive and personal nature of art. Granted that a student's ultimate success will depend largely on his natural talents, the problem still remains: how best to arouse his curiosity, hold his attention, and engage his creative faculties.

Through trial and error, I have found that the solution to this enigma rests, to a large extent, on two factors: the kind of problem chosen for study, and the way in which it is posed. I believe that if, in the statement of a problem, undue emphasis is placed on freedom and self-expression, the result is apt to be an indifferent student and a meaningless solution.

Conversely, a problem with defined limits, implied or stated disciplines which are, in turn, conducive *to the instinct of play*, will most likely yield an interested student and, very often, a meaningful and novel solution.

Of the two powerful instincts which exist in all human beings and which can be used in teaching, says Gilbert Highet, one is the *love of play*. "The best Renaissance teachers, instead of beating their pupils, spurred them on by a number of appeals to the play-principle. They made games out of the chore of learning difficult subjects—Montaigne's father, for instance, started him in Greek by writing the letters and easiest words on playing cards and inventing a game to play with them."

This "love of play" that Rand alludes to must certainly be taken into account when we attempt even the most elementary understanding of the creative process; nor should we equate "love of play" (or *creative play*, which might be a better term) with the still-current term, *just playing around*. Creative play is an essential part of any creative process—nor would it be possible to put strict time limits on this process, since implicit in the concept of play is the corresponding freedom from imposed limits to time. But let us make the point here that also implicit in the concept of creative play is that serious approaches to creative problems are being employed even though these approaches may *seem* to be casual and undirected. Even the freest approaches to any form of play contain objectives in them, unstructured and "useless" as they might on the surface appear. Although all sand castles are destroyed by the incoming tide, the objective is to build the biggest and the best. This analogy is not as far-fetched as it might first appear: Is not the scenographer a builder of sand castles?—For permanence of physical structure is not the prime requisite of the scenographic art. The scenographer is a serious artist who must learn to use the insights gained from experiments that may to some seem frivolous activities. Creative play is, ultimately, not a temporary respite from scenographic problem solving but a seriously considered means of facilitating it.

Let us conclude this section by a brief discussion of a little-known principle that plays an important role in the creative process: the use of *unfocused attention* in problem solving. By unfocused attention we mean what psychologists call *undirected introspection*, which, like *creative play*, allows the mind to wander at will without the supervision of the conscious mind. This is a very difficult concept to discuss because its basic counsel is contrary to most of what we have been discussing so far; there is a real problem when the primary reason for this book's existence is to demonstrate a more or less rational approach to scenography and suddenly we are considering the possibility that sometimes one must find the way to stop thinking at all. But the advice we are entertaining here is not as paradoxical as it might first seem. Julian Jaynes, although speaking of a field where such an attitude would seem totally inappropriate, has something to say that just might prove valuable to those studying this book:

The picture of a scientist sitting down with his problems and using conscious induction and deduction is as mythical as a unicorn. The greatest insights of mankind have come more mysteriously.

[Even the greatest minds, he goes on to report, find their most significant insights when conscious direction is least in evidence.]

A close friend of Einstein's has told me that many of the physicist's greatest ideas came to him so suddenly when he was shaving that he had to move the blade of the straight razor very carefully each morning, lest he cut himself with surprise. And a well-known physicist in Britain once told Wolfgang Kohler, "We often talk about the three B's, the Bus, the Bath, and the Bed. That is where the great discoveries are made in our science." . . .

The essential point here is that there are several stages of creative thought: first, a stage of preparation in which the problem is consciously worked over; then a period of incubation without any conscious concentration upon the problem; and then the illumination which is later justified by logic. . . . *Indeed, it is sometimes almost as if the problem had to be forgotten to be solved.* (Italics mine)

It is important for the student of any discipline or any art to understand the series of steps that we call the creative process has essential features to it that extend beyond the bounds of both category and consciousness but not beyond the bounds of possibility. One last word to support what we have just encountered. In *The Cult of Information*, Theodore Roszak says this:

We can self-consciously connect idea with idea, comparing and contrasting as we go, plotting out the course of a deductive sequence, But when we try to get behind the ideas to grasp the elusive interplay of experience, memory, insight that bubbles up into consciousness as a whole thought, we are apt to come away from the dizzy and confounded—as if we had tried to read a message that was traveling past us at blinding speed. Thinking up ideas is so spontaneous—one might almost say so instinctive—an action, that it defies capture and analysis. We cannot slow the mind down sufficiently to see the thing happening step by step. Picking our thoughts apart at this primitive, preconscious level is rather like one of those deliberately baffling exercise the Zen Buddhist masters use to dazzle the mind so that it may experience the unutterable void. When it comes to understanding where the mind gets its ideas, perhaps the best we can do is say, with Descartes, "An angel told me." But then is there any need to go farther than this? Mentality is the gift of our human nature. We may use it, enjoy it, extend and elaborate it without being able to explain it.

The Scenographer's Role in the Theatrical Process

During the past four hundred years the role of the visual theater artist has changed greatly. Although graphic arts have remained the primary means by which ideas are formulated and communicated, skills in drawing and painting have assumed different emphases in different ages. Figure 20 gives a simplified overview showing how the need for these skills has modified over the years.

In today's theater any work intended for the stage progresses, however roughly, along the lines shown in figure 21.

While the playwright or composer might desire that the *initial impetus* (i.e., what he specifically wishes to say) is transmitted directly through these various levels, with the minimum of embellishment or alteration, it is easy to see that the nature of that communication will, by the very nature of theatrical work, change to some degree. This diagram, however, only indicates the *conceptual* nature of the scenographer's involvement with the production process. The *actual* task that he is required to perform in the working theater follows a pattern similar to this:

1. The scenographer attempts to form visual images during and after the reading of the play. (The wise scenographer avoids "seeing" the ac-

tion of the play on the stage, however, but tries to imagine the action of the text taking place in real world of the playwright's imagination, which is a much less inhibiting context.) Most of images gained from this initial reading are based on the internal needs (both explicit and implicit) of the text.

2. The scenographer then attempts to set these images on paper (both in plan and perspective) or in rough scale models. Pictures of intended settings are less helpful at this point than diagrams of action that will show a director the plans of movement and needed areas of floor space. Thinking diagrammatically helps both the scenographer and the director to clarify and give priority to the needs of the text.

3. The scenographer then attempts to combine diagrams and other visualizations into some related sequence or order by which effectiveness and appropriateness of ideas can be demonstrated to the director or any others involved in the production process. It is during this period of work that the visions of all the various visual artists are brought into phase with the vision of the director.

4. The scenographer must then make concrete plans and decisions so that his images can be rendered into actual stage forms and devices.

Up to this point, most scenographers are similar in their approach. After this point, their methods of work begin to take different paths, since at this level, designing becomes a more subjective and personal activity. Most production schedules follow, sometimes only roughly, a similar pattern of development. This plan, although different conditions within the producing organization do cause variations in it, usually corresponds to the basic outline found in figure 22.

The scenographer should always keep in mind that any theater design is conditioned by a number of factors that have little to do with the artistic merit of a particular design, important as that factor is. No scenographer, then, can plan a production without taking the following elements into consideration:

1. Budget available for building and finishing the setting and properties (and sometime costumes if one scenographer is in charge of the entire production).

2. Time available for construction, painting, rigging, and lighting the setting. (In the profes-

REQUIRED SKILL	HISTORICAL EMPHASIS (1656-1860-90)	MODERN EMPHASIS (1900-PRESENT)
1. ILLUSORY DRAWING BASED ON PERSPECTIVE SKILLS	ALMOST TOTAL	STEADILY DECREASING IMPORTANCE
2. ABILITY TO FASHION THREE-DIMENSIONAL CONCEPTS IN SCENIC MODEL FORM	LITTLE TO NONEXISTENT	STEADILY INCREASING EMPHASIS SINCE 1920S
3. ABILITY TO COORDINATE ALL ELEMENTS OF VISUAL PRODUCTION: COSTUME, LIGHTING, PROPERTIES, ETC.	ALMOST NONEXISTENT UNTIL MIDDLE 1990S	ALMOST TOTAL
4. MAKING OR SUPERVISION OF WORKING DRAWINGS AND SPECIFICATIONS	LITTLE (FLAT PAINTING EASY TO DUPLICATE BY SCENIC PAINTERS OF THE TIME)	STEADILY INCREASING EMPHASIS FROM 1920S (A CORRESPONDINGLY DECREASING EMPHASIS IS TAKING PLACE IN TODAY'S PRACTICE AS PROFESSIONAL SCENIC SHOP TECHNICIANS ASSUME RESPONSIBILITY OF TRANSLATION OF SCENOGRAPHER'S MODELS AND DRAWINGS DIRECTLY INTO WORKING DRAWINGS AND SPECIFICATIONS)
5. INTEGRATION OF SCENIC CONCEPTS WITH OVERALL MEANINGS OF TEXT	LITTLE OR NONEXISTENT	INCREASINGLY IMPORTANT
6. USE OF NEW TECHNOLOGY AS PART OF ARTISTIC PROCESS: FILM, TELEVISION, COMPUTER TECHNOLOGY, ETC.; COLLAGE, ASSEMBLAGE, DUPLICATION OF IMAGES MECHANICALLY	NONEXISTENT	STEADILY INCREASING EMPHASIS

Fig. 20. Chart showing scenographic drawing emphasis during past

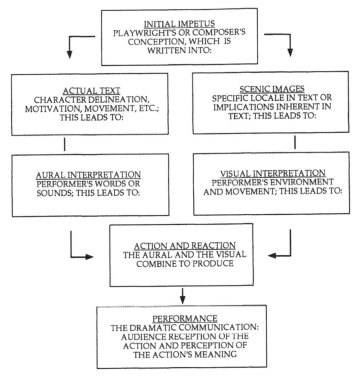

Fig. 21. Chart showing progress of stage work

sional theater, time very definitely is money; lateness in designs not only can cause added expense but in some cases can cost jobs or future commissions.)

3. The skill of the technical staff: carpenters, metal workers, painters, properties personnel, lighting technicians, and stage crew. (In the nonprofessional theater this is an area to consider carefully. Productions should be carefully tailored to the skills of the shops that will produce the design. There are very few scenographers indeed who do not realize that they are only as good and never better than the people who work with them and for them.)

4. The limitations of the theater plant where the production is prepared and those of the theater where the production will be presented.

It is very much part of the scenographer's job to be fully aware of all these factors during every step of the construction, painting, setup, and lighting of a setting; no scenographer can simply deliver the sketches and working drawings to the various shops and then forget about the production until dress rehearsals. Nor should the scenographer feel at the mercy of the above limitations; ingenuity in overcoming these limita-

tions actively builds the skill and prowess of the professional artist. But to ignore them can only lead to frustration at every stage in the preparation of a production. In order to fulfill the basic expectations of such a production plan, a competent scenographer should be able to give concepts in the following forms:

1. Rough and diagrammatic drawings that show intent in its most elemental visual form.

2. Finished scenic sketches that show intentions in fully accurate visual detail. While some scenographers do not choose to do so, any well-trained scenographer should possess the skill to include in a scenic sketch a graphic approximation of the effects of light and shadow one could achieve in the actual theater.

3. Three-dimensional models (either working models or painted exhibition models according to the desires of the director or other concerned with the production) that show scale representations of what is possible in the actual theater.

4. Mechanical working drawings from which the design can be realized in a scenic shop and brought to the stage as full-scale scenic structures. (Most working drawings are, however,

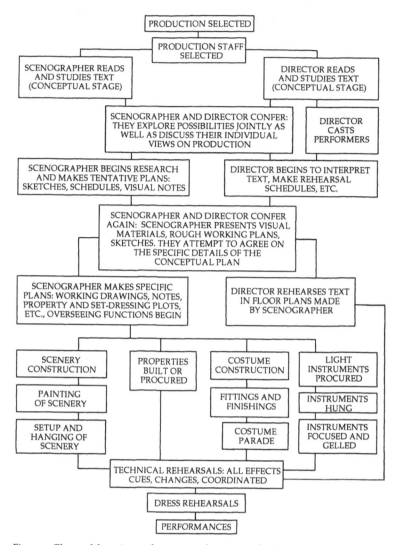

Fig. 22. Chart of functions of scenographer in production

redrawn by shop technicians, and it is wise to consult *before* making these to determine just what a particular shop wants or needs.)

5. Assemblages of visual materials that guide theatrical technicians to achieve accurately the specific colors, textures, forms, or finishes the scenographer cannot easily demonstrate in any of the above categories.

"Against Falsehood"
By John Bury

I became what would now be called assistant electrician to Joan Littlewood's Theatre Work-

shop. At that time in the 1940s we were on the road, playing in whatever halls we could find. We toured a set of black drapes, to create a nothingness, and an enormous amount of lighting equipment, with three dimmer boards.

It was there that I discovered the importance of light. Lighting is the most flexible scenery there is; you can isolate an actor, place him in a locale, create worlds of changing shape and size. I still think lighting is the key to making sense in the theatre; the audience interprets the set from what they can see of it. And the illumination of the actor, the way light falls on his face, can feed the audience's imagination. I remember after the war we did a documentary with Joan about various kinds of work, unemployment and so on. We had a completely bare stage, but the way the light was directed on to our actors—the glint of a furnace, the strong overhead light in a railway station—convinced the audience that they had actually seen these places.

After eight years on the road, we moved to Stratford East, and I had to face a really testing time. We were no longer in a fit-up world, with minimal elements of scenery. We were doing basic plays like Shaw and Molière, and we needed sets. At that time I did not think of myself as a designer; we worked with a succession of bright young designers out of art school. Often they were very good, and they certainly shared a set of intellectual principles with us. But both Joan and I felt that their sets were interposing between the audience and the real nature of our work, making an unnecessary comment on it. We pushed the sets around, turned them upside and back to front, but eventually we decided that I would have to try my hand at the job myself.

I wanted to work so that the set would grow organically out of the rehearsal process. We didn't fix anything before we began, but brought in elements—chairs, a table, doors, a window—as and where they were required by the action that came out of the work. We would start rehearsal with nothing but a heap of junk—odd chairs and windows, the scenery from the last production. When we had reached a workable set-up, I would move in to tidy up. But one thing I never did was to pretty things up. In my use of materials at that time, I was resolutely against falsehood. I wanted to use the real materials, not transmute everything into the fairytale unreality of canvas and scene-paint. We were running a theatre for people who would be put off by what I call decorative frou-frous. We wanted to show them reality on the stage. So we searched out paving-stones from the Council to cover the floor, we borrowed used stained tarpaulins from lorries in railway yard and nailed them to frames for our walls, we made walls out of brick, wood and plaster instead of painting them on canvas.

I can still remember, when I was trying to borrow an iron radiator to put on the stage, an old stage-carpenter saying to me "Laddy, you can't put real things like that on the stage, they always look wrong." Well, in his theatre of painted canvas they may have looked wrong, but I was searching for a theatre in which anything painted on canvas would see unreal. I had my own stage, my own workshop, my own set of overalls. If we wanted a set, we would collect the material, put it on the stage, push it around, pull it apart, nail it together again. It became an inhabitant of the theatre just as much as the actors. That way we made objects that grew out of the stage.

Well, success began to bring its own problems. In order to make enough money to keep the theatre going, we had to transfer shows to the West End, sets had to be built to schedule, actors were separated from the nucleus of the company. At one time we had three shows in the West End and one on tour, as well as keeping Stratford East going. Joan and the rest of us decided that the thing had served its purpose, that our next steps would have to be elsewhere.

After a couple of months I came to Stratford-upon-Avon, first as guest designer for various productions, then as associate, and now as head of design. It was a new world, very different: huge stage, the need for planning three months ahead, before the director could possible commit himself. How was one to preserve the flexibility we had achieved at Stratford East? How was one to find the precise texture of each play when the organic growth of a set was made difficult by having to be laid down so far in advance?

Because of the difference of scale, because Stratford-upon Avon is a repertory stage, where the sets are changed almost nightly, unlike Stratford East, where they take possession of the stage for a determined period and are then jettisoned, I had to reconsider my views on materials. When you ask actors or stage-hands to move scenery, it mustn't weigh a ton. I had to make real textures once more, but this time the plastics industry was expanding, and all sorts of synthetic materials, such as expanded polystyrene and the polyeurethenes, were coming on the market. This led to an entirely new function for the paint shops, creating surfaces rather than painting them. Surfaces which were the right weight, density and reflective index, in addition to the right colour. This was very exciting, and was the beginning of the route which led to the "world of steel" for the Histories last year. This distance I had travelled can be measured in this: if I had been asked for a world of steel in Theatre Workshop days, I would have begged and borrowed steel sheets. Instead we used sheets of copperleaf stained and treated with chemicals. But I was still light-years away from the omnipresent stage-painter, who would have said, "Steel, laddy? Right—a bit of white paint, a bit of black, a bit of silver—there's steel for you!"

In my first few sets for Shakespeare plays, I continued in the direction we had staked out in our Shakespeare production at Stratford East. Fluidity of scene was the keynote; make the action flow swiftly. So for *Measure for Measure, Macbeth, Julius Caesar*, I created an open platform which was an over-all statement, and allowed the director to play the scenes without the interruption of a single blackout. Within this there were a number of mobile elements—chairs, tables, and so on—which could be carried in by the actors in the rhythm of the situation. Incidentally, we've become very aware of the importance of scene-changing in the dramatic rhythm. The actors have to bring on their things in the right rhythm, and the stagehands must be rehearsed like actors. This rhythm-of-the-scene thing is very important; I've often noticed that if anyone has to move or work in the wings while a scene's being played, they can cut backstage noise almost to nothing if they're aware of and work with the rhythm of what's happening on stage.

By the time I came to work with Peter Hall on the Histories, I was already feeling that the open platform basis was constricting. It was too free, too bare; if you brought on a set of courtiers, they had to be grouped carefully, no one could sit down. So the basis of the Wars of the Roses set was two moving walls, which enabled us to change the area of the stage, to summon up (though not naturalistically) interiors, then open out to battlefields, hills, mountains, expanding or focussing as we wished. There was a definite gain in concentration, increased by our search for an image-object for every situation—a cannon, a council-table, a throne, a bishop's chair, the right hand-prop.

The same thing went for costumes. I wanted to take the fancy-dress out of costumes. But attempts to produce a "timeless" costume were failures—I think you nearly always end up with variants on the spacemen or superman-with-a-helmet image. What we try to do now is to remain true to the period in silhouette, but by use of tailoring techniques, choice of materials, modern parallels, to reduce the historical identity down to essentials, and to create a costume which is truly functional in telling us as much as possible what we want to know about the wearer. Again, in costume, it is essential that approximation and indication is avoided and the image must be precise and organic—in fact, they must be clothes, not costumes. An example of the attitude one is trying to combat is the girl I once interviewed for wardrobe work who said she could cut me Gothic style, Renaissance style, Restoration style, but when I asked her if she could cut a suit for a modern play, said no. Which makes you wonder how real her versions of Renaissance costume were. . . .

Now there is one big thing I would like to do. I want to create for this company an atelier of designers, all working together continuously to forge a true Royal Shakespeare style of design. I think it's possible this way to make something that is richer and deeper than the vision of one man. Designing should be able to work like the production of a play—the interplay between a director and the actors enriches his vision of the play, prevents it from remaining cerebral. In the same way there can be a team of designers who work on the same production, each contributing their special knowledge and gifts to the elaboration of a conception they all share. Equally, we must create a new race of craftsmen, who will bring their own independent contribution to the process, not simply do it the way a particular designer likes it done, as has so often happened in the theatre.

In this way, a company like the Berliner Ensemble, by creating a team and firmly searching for a distinctive style, has created over ten years a coherent and unified scenic language. Our way would be different of course, but we could do as much. It happens in other large-scale designing activities, like architecture, so why not in the theatre?

2

The Scenographer and the Physical Stage

Nothing is so beautiful as a bare stage: yet its loneliness and its openness is often too strong a statement and it must be enclosed. How? What objects should be put into this great void? The problem is always agonizing. Not too little. Not too much. What is appropriate?

—Peter Brook

Man has always been fascinated and disturbed by the perplexing and obscure phenomenon of space, which though it can be confined, is essentially boundless and intangible. A similar relationship exists between fantasy and reality, between conceptual and perceptual images.

—Heinz Bruno Gallee

Traditional Stage Forms

It is not possible to design for any theater without first examining the various physical forms the stage within it can assume. It is, perhaps, the first—in some ways most important—duty of scenographers to reconsider the possibilities that lie open to them when given a production to design. This is true for the smallest and simplest of theaters, as it is for the largest and most complicated of theater plants. Few scenographers have the opportunity (or need) to completely remake the stage and auditorium for one particular production, as did Norman Bel Geddes in the 1920s for Max Reinhardt's production of *The Miracle* or as John Napier has in the 1980s for the musicals *Cats*, *Starlight Express*, and *Les Misérables*. Still, most scenographers are more and more not content to accept as inviolate the flat floor and proscenium picture frame that still characterize most theaters today. They feel less inhibited about extending their settings (in many instances conceived of as scenic environments rather than static settings) into an area that for the past three hundred years has been given over exclusively to audience seating in new and radical relationships. It would be well to examine briefly, therefore, just what basic relationships between the acting area and the audience's viewing area are possible in theater today. For the most part, however, we will restrict our attention to the two kinds of theater structures the scenographer of today is apt to encounter: the open stage and the proscenium stage.

The Open Stage

In this book we are not so much concerned with the historical aspects of the open stage (although the scenographer should be aware of this form's development and of those open stage theaters built in this century like the Tyrone

Guthrie Theater in Minneapolis or the newer Swan Theater in Stratford-upon-Avon in England) as we are with the role the scenographer plays when working for the stage. Additionally, we should be aware how actors move through the space on such stages as well as how directors guide that movement.

Figure 23 is a diagrammatic representation of the elemental actor-audience relationship: from this relationship all theater springs. Established in the Greek countryside hundreds of years before the fifth-century B.C. theater we usually focus upon, it was then and remains still the most powerful of all actor-audience relationships. The lines of communication between the viewer and the actor are as direct as is possible in any theater form. It is little wonder that this relationship has been the prevalent one for many thousands of years, since it results from two very basic human traits: curiosity to know and desire to show. In this form of relationship all viewers have equal access to what is to be seen; the distance between actor and audience is also equidistant to the greatest degree possible, and the locus of the action is always as near to the individual viewer as is feasible. The immense popularity of the cinema has as its basis this fact: *The camera eye always places the individual viewer at precisely the point where experience of an event is at its optimum and moves that view as the event changes.*

Basically, movement on any form of open stage (and this includes theaters where audiences completely surround the acting areas as in figure 23) tends to be circular in nature. Directors find, because of the audience-actor relationship, that they must cause the actor (fig. 24A) to move in such a way that (1) she does not spend any appreciable time with her back to any one section of the surrounding audience, so that (2) when she is speaking, she is generally in a position that allows her to face both her partner (fig. 24B) and the greatest number of the audience at the same time.

The basic action that puts the actors in a favorable position to be seen and heard (although actors in this form of theater must often deliver lines with their backs to a large portion of the audience) is known as an "exchange." This movement (again basically circular) allows the actor on whom the focus has been placed, because he has lines to speak or actions to perform, to give over his position when the focus changes from him to another. Directors for the open stage find that they must also continually keep the actors moving in order to keep the audience's attention properly focused; the amount of physical action, therefore, in the average open stage production would be at least two-thirds as much again as in the average proscenium production (fig. 25).

At the same time, space on the open stage is almost always more restricted; that is, there just is not as much of it as there would be on the average proscenium stage, nor does the scenographer have access to the traditional offstage

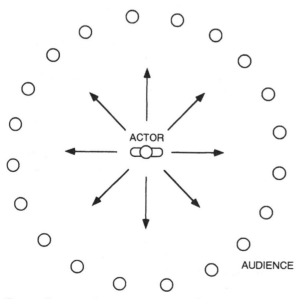

Fig. 23. Diagram showing elemental actor-audience relationship

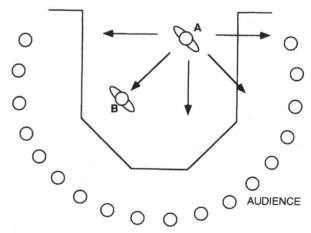

Fig. 24. Actor-actor relationship

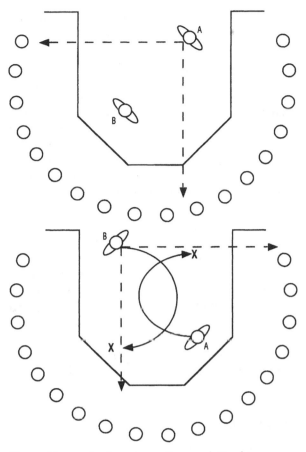

Fig. 25. Two-part actor-actor-audience relationships

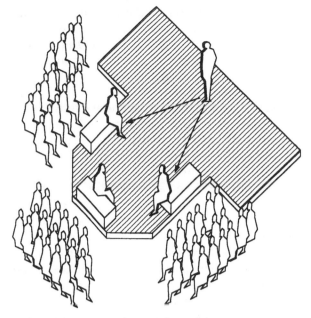

Fig. 26. Actor-actor-audience relationship

space most proscenium stages possess. The director and scenographer, therefore, must be expert in the use of this limited space. A director, for example, will often require the scenographer to provide sitting arrangements around the periphery of the acting area so that the speaking actor (or the one with the focus on him) can gain dominance through (1) height—he is standing, the one to whom he speaks is sitting, and (2) position on the platform—he faces the larger number of the audience, the one to whom he speaks faces up to him (fig. 26). We have already noted that the scenographer can and does affect the actor by restricting and channeling his movement; on the open stage it is imperative that the director and scenographer work closely together so that the available space is used most effectively.

Many actors like the open stage generally for several reasons. Being closer to the audience and being among them, not separated and isolated

to one side as they are in the proscenium theater, actors need not work as hard to secure proper effects, either vocal or physical. Their characterizations can be more natural, more subtle in interpretation when they do not have to project their words and actions over great distances as is the case in proscenium arch theaters with large auditoriums. At the same time, they are able to establish better relationships and more deeply motivated involvements with their acting partners, since they do not have to "cheat" toward the audience while trying to maintain the illusion they are relating to other actors on the stage. One of Stanislavsky's most desired reforms was to bring the attention of the actor more to the stage, to the objects on it as well as to other actors, and less to the audience. (It was a hallmark of nineteenth-century theater that the actor, no matter how realistic the intent of the play he was performing, almost always was more aware of the audience he was playing for than of the other performers on the stage. Stanislavsky did not want the actor to discount or ignore the audience, as he has often been accused; he merely felt that an audience would be more deeply engrossed in the drama if the actors themselves were.)

Even though the pendulum has swung from a naturalistic theater (the direction it was taking at the end of the nineteenth century) to a more theatrical one today, much of the open stage technique of acting and directing has now found its way onto the proscenium stage. More and more settings, for this reason, are "violating" conventions of the proscenium arch—that is, acting areas are being built across the curtain line and into the auditorium so that the performance of the actor can be more immediate than if it were contained wholly on the stage behind the arch line.

From the beginning of this century there has been a renewed interest in the open stage form. During the past four decades a number of theaters dedicated to this kind of stage have been built and most continue to draw audiences to them. The most successful new theaters built in this hemisphere have been, perhaps, those that exhibit the basic features of such a theater, even though there has been little attempt to reproduce exactly any historical open stage in detail. (The new open stage theater built on the south bank of the Thames in London will probably come closest to reproducing the kind of theater we think Shakespeare knew. At this writing it is still being designed.) The Stratford Theatre in Ontario, Canada, and the Tyrone Guthrie Theater in Minneapolis, Minnesota (fig. 27), are only two of the outstanding examples of new theaters built primarily to present works from the various ages of the theater and yet have been highly successful in accommodating modern plays as well. Some of the Guthrie's most popular presentations have been works by Chekhov, who wrote during his lifetime exclusively for a theater whose form and style are all but diametrically opposed to that of the open stage theaters of the past. Nevertheless, his plays not only have withstood the transfer from one form to the other but in many cases have greatly benefited from the advantages the open stage has to offer.

If one man were to be singled out as having popularized this type of theater in our own time, it would probably have to be Tyrone Guthrie; for a number of years he was one of the most successful directors working in the theater and many of his best productions were done on the open stage. Here is an article, "A Director Views the Stage," written by him in which he explains why the Min-

Fig. 27. Tyrone Guthrie Theater. Courtesy of *Design Quarterly* No. 58, Copyright The Walker Art Center

neapolis theater—the one named in his honor—was designed as it was.

In designing an auditorium, the prime consideration should be the relation of performer to audience. Since the middle of the seventeenth century when Italian opera took Europe by storm, theatres have been designed almost exclusively in the manner best suited to operatic performances. Such designs have a raised platform in front of which is a horseshoe-shaped auditorium, usually in several tiers of seating. Between stage and auditorium a great gulf is fixed, literally a pit, in which the orchestra plays. The stage of the opera house is further removed from the audience by a partition with a large hole through which the spectators view the performance. This proscenium opening is often decorated as a picture frame to enhance the illusion that the performance is a picture in which the figures magically move, dance, or sing. When the performance demands that the picture be changed a curtain falls and appropriate pulling and hauling prepares the stage for further surprises to delight the audience. When all is ready, the stagehands are replaced by painted mummers in fine raiment, and the curtain is raised. For many years I have worked in such theatres, and it never crossed my mind that a theater could or should be otherwise. When I was in my early thirties, I was hired to direct the Old Vic Shakespeare Company. Gradually it became clear to me that trying to put Shakespeare's plays into the conventional framework for opera was wrong. The plays had been written by a master craftsman for a theatre of altogether different design. It was certainly possible to adapt them to the requirements of conventionally planned theatres. It seemed more desirable, however, to adapt some common-place building than to adjust a masterpiece. As is often the case, the obviously sensible building plan was too expensive to execute. Yet, I realized that a more logical and easy way to stage these plays existed. It led to an examination of the whole premise of illusion which is the basis for the proscenium stage.

It has always seemed to me that people do not submit to illusion in the theatre much after the age of ten or eleven. They are perfectly aware that the middle-aged lady uncomfortably suspended on a wire is not Peter Pan but an actress pretending to be Peter Pan. . . . In planning the Tyrone Guthrie Theatre, it was necessary to decide whether the stage should be the conventional platform separated from the audience by a proscenium arch or whether it should be an open stage such as the Elizabethan theatre and the ancient Greek and Roman theatres. A third alternative was available. We might have asked our architect to create a flexible design which could adjust to both types. We rejected this, however, on the ground, that an all-purpose hall is a no-purpose hall—that insofar as a purpose is flexible, it is not wholehearted; that it was better to be firmly and uncompromisingly on one kind than to attempt to compromise between opposites which we considered to be theatrically and architecturally, theoretically and practically irreconcilable. We argued for the open stage for the following reasons: first, our intended program is of a classical nature, and we believe that the classics are better suited to an open stage than to a proscenium one. Second, the aim of our performances is not to create an illusion, but to present a ritual of sufficient interest to hold the attention of, even to delight, an adult audience. Third, an auditorium grouped *around* a stage rather than placed in front of a stage enables a larger number of people to be closer to the actors. Fourth, in an age when movies and TV are offering dramatic entertainment from breakfast to supper, from cradle to grave, it seemed important to stress the *difference* between their offering and ours. Theirs is two-dimensional and is viewed upon a rectangular screen. The proscenium is analogous to such a screen by forcing a two-dimensional choreography upon the director. But the open stage is essentially three-dimensional with no resemblance to the rectangular postcard shape which has become the symbol of the canned drama.

No claim is made that the open stage is better than the proscenium stage for every type of play. But, in our opinion, the open stage is more desirable for the kind of plays we propose to perform and the kind of project we propose to execute. (*Design Quarterly*, no. 58 [1963])

What Guthrie omits in the discussion of the reasons why his theater chose as it did is that not only are plays of the past best suited to the open stage but that almost all proscenium arch plays benefit from this form as well. For example, the Guthrie Theater is as famous for its Chekhov productions as it is for its Greek and Elizabethan works. Many works of the present-day theater, in fact, adapt well to the open stage. Figure 28 is a design for the Harold Pinter play *The Caretaker*, a work that takes well to open stage production. One cannot, however, use the same kind of thinking for both. Having different actor-audience relationships between the two forms means that the scenographer must conceive of the acting areas attuned to those differences. Notice, for instance, that the furniture is

Fig. 28. Design for *The Caretaker*

not arranged, as it would be in the proscenium theater, so as to favor any one direction (see fig. 31). And yet there is in this arrangement, casual though it may seem, a certain amount of planned orientation imposed on the actors working in this setting; when one sits on the bed (fig. 29A), or in the chair (fig. 29B), or at the table (fig. 29C), he naturally would be forced to face toward anyone in the general area of the center of the stage, the area where most movement is possible. Actor-to-actor relationships are thus strengthened (almost forced, one might say, upon the actors) by the placement of the furniture and the layout of the playing area.

As it has been pointed out, there is probably a great deal more movement occasioned by open stage productions than on the proscenium stage; the better the director, however, and the more skilled the actor, the less likely the audience will be able to perceive or be aware of the fact that the life they are seeing on this type of stage is much more active than that outside the theater or in the proscenium theater. For this and other reasons, then, the scenographer's task is often more difficult—if not more extensive—than when working in other stage forms.

The Proscenium Theater

In proscenium theaters, the audience is almost entirely isolated on one side from the action on the stage. The performance is therefore viewed two-dimensionally; that is, primarily as a picture. This analogy to paintings and drawings is often heightened in older theaters by the ornate frame often placed around the proscenium arch opening. This kind of relationship cannot help but force the scenographers to compose settings more pictorially than spatially. But what is even more detrimental is that this relationship cannot avoid separating an audience and the performers into two distinct groups. Lines of communication are, for the most part, in one direction: from the stage to the auditorium, from the actor to the audience. During the past century, moreover, the practice of turning down the lighting in the auditorium and increasing it on the stage has done much to make audiences more passive than during past periods of theater. In this form of theater, the members of the audience feel less called upon to participate as actively as they might in the arena situation or

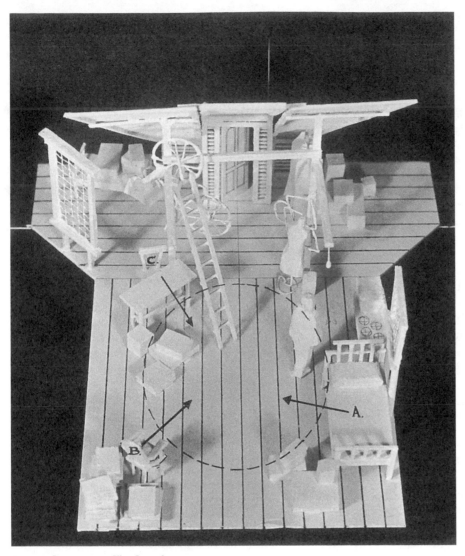

Fig. 29. Open stage, *The Caretaker*

while attending the open stage form of theater. There seems to be a willingness on the part of an audience to extend its attention more actively to the open or arena stage than in the proscenium arch theater. In any case, the proscenium arch does often act as a barrier to audience involvement and there can be little doubt that integration of audience and performer is at a minimum.

For some time now, and especially during the last half of this century, there has been a growing dissatisfaction with the proscenium arch theater. And if there is one trend apparent in present-day production practice, it lies in the abolition of strict barriers rather than in their construction. As a result, newer proscenium arch theaters are now built that allow the possibility of modifying the arch to differing types of production as well as making it possible to extend the stage areas more into audience areas. Much of the growing dissatisfaction with picture-frame stages stems from, and is in reaction to, the playwrights and producers who made a conscious attempt, starting in the late nineteenth century, to keep the stage and audience apart in separate units. What we observe during this period is a reaction of the more progressive playwrights (most of whom were championing a new wave of writing called *naturalism*) against what they felt was too much audience-performer fraternization. August Strindberg, one of the most vocal of this new generation, had distinct views on the subject and was instrumental in making the separation between stage and audience as complete as possible. He along with Stanislavsky in Russia, Antoine in France, and the Duke of Saxe-Meiningen in Germany eventually won out over the more theatrical approaches to producing plays, with the result that most of the dramas written since Ibsen have sought to present on the stage an illusion of life much as it appears outside the theater.

Even today the average audience member considers the proscenium arch theater as the true theater form; that other stage forms are simply quaint places where less important stage works are done. Starting in the 1950s, however, serious consideration of theater buildings that departed from this "true" form began to emerge. In 1959, the Ford Foundation Program for Theater Design initiated a program to study theater structures: what they were during the present time, and what they might be in the future. In 1962, the American Federation of Arts issued a catalog showing the results of scenographers working in close relationship with architects to formulate many of the new ideas in theater design that had been considered during the previous three years. This book, *The Ideal Theater: Eight Concepts*, represents the thoughts of a number of the best scenographers and architects of the time. Even though it has been almost thirty years since that book, much of what is presented there still has the power to provoke thought, even to stir controversy. One of the more interesting portions of the book is a number of statements by Arthur Miller concerning the proscenium theater. What he said then deserves our attention still and repays the time to review his remarks:

I have no doubt that plays are not being written just because of the limitations of New York's theaters. . . . You just can't write for these "shoe boxes" with the same ideas, with the same emotional scope, as you would for a (more adaptable) theater. . . . The New York theater is a limitation to the playwright at least to the degree that it is no inspiration to him—he is dragging it around on his back half the time.

. . . You can't hope to make one theater which is absolutely perfect for all kinds of plays. It's just a contradiction of terms. . . .

In some kinds of plays, the actors have to come and say, well here I am; but the proscenium says, here I am not. In fact, here you aren't.

The proscenium is a limitation for a hell of a lot of plays. . . . You see, the drama has become more and more a first person thing. Even such a really traditional writer as O'Neill started talking biographically as he grew older. There's subconscious analogy, I think, between the proscenium theater and the third person; here, the play is pretending to take place without any author; these people are supposed to be really talking to each other, and we are overhearing them. . . . You see, it's all a question of how much you're pretending that this isn't a play, or that this is a play—whether the emphasis is on the author or the actor—presentational or representational. The proscenium favors the latter . . .

. . . What we are trying to do now is make a theater of essences. That is, where an Ibsen would create the surrounding documentation of social existence (a new discovery—people weren't aware of themselves in society to the degree that they are now)—well, we take for granted that kind of documentation. So, when Ibsen would get to the essences at about the last third of each act—the first two-thirds being the setup for the social situation—we share an awareness of our situation to the degree that numerous plays can simply deal in essences. . . .

. . . You know, every flight from one form is always the attempt to fly into the most direct confrontation with the essence. You break up a form because its appurtenances keep you further and further away from the center. But then when you get into the center, it gradually begins to move out into the periphery again—and somehow you've got to get back into the center again. Time after time, scientists believe that they have reached the ultimate understanding of some process—then it turns out that there is a smaller world inside of the one discovered, a new path into a more recessed center always requires new kinds of documentation if the vision is to be proved to others.

What Miller would like to escape is the kind of theater that was during his period increasingly devoted to the use of literal scenery manipulated by highly complicated, antiquated, often cumbersome mechanisms. And yet since he spoke, many theaters have been built with mechanical abilities that far outstrip the possibilities of the theaters he knew. Whether we like it or not, the age of large elaborately equipped stages will be with us for some time to come. American theaters continue to rely less heavily on built-in stage mechanisms than do their European counterparts. Still, the most completely mechanized theater in the world today is the Metropolitan Opera House in New York City. It is interesting to note the reviews given the productions done in this house during the past twenty years. Critics have increasingly found that production (overproduction, in the view of many) has all but usurped the place performers used to occupy. Consider these strong comments:

At one time, Franco Zeffirelli was an opera director of artistic significance. His productions for Maria Callas and for Joan Sutherland in the 1950's showed off their great if dissimilar talents to advantage. His "Falstaff" at the old Metropolitan Opera House in 1964 raised staging standards there. For the last couple of decades, however, Mr. Zeffirelli's interest in opera has centered around the superficial and the trivial. As his new Metropolitan production of "La Traviata" showed conclusively on Monday evening, he is most charitably thought of nowadays as a fashion designer and interior decorator rather than as an opera director. . . .

Throughout the party scene at Violetta's place, scenery rose and fell, slid in and out, and doggedly followed the plot with distracting literalness. At least four complex scene changes took place in the first act alone (I may have lost count while absorbed in the watching the salon and bedroom come and go). Perhaps to take advantage of the turntables and other stage machinery of the Met, Mr. Zeffirelli allowed Alfredo to accost Violetta in her bedroom, thereby establishing her as an extraordinarily permissive hostess. . . .

In such a furbelowed, tasseled and bedizened production, the greatest singers would have a difficult time making an impression. . . . Wendy White, making her Met debut as Flora, disappeared in the scenery. No surprise: so did "Traviata."
(Donal Henahan, "At the Met, Zeffirelli on the Grand Scale," *New York Times*, 19 October 1989)

And yet no scenographer can avoid knowing well the machinery of the proscenium arch theater, or how one designs for it. Let us therefore, look more closely into what is involved in designing for this form of stage.

Regardless of the complexity of the stage mechanisms, the relationship of the audience to stage in proscenium theaters is approximately what we see in figure 30. Partly through necessity, but mostly from habit and practice, performers generally orient themselves directly toward the audience; this is also true for many

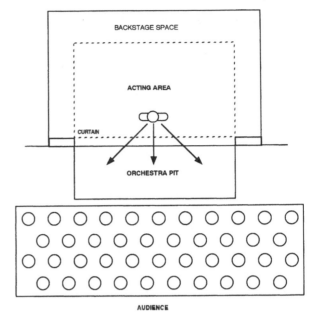

Fig. 30. Proscenium theater stage-audience relationship

scenographers who, often unthinkingly, orient furniture, important entrances, and scenic effects directly facing the arch opening (fig. 31). Although there is at times an attempt to disguise the practice, more today than in the past, movement—confined by the horizontality of the scenic elements of the stage—tend to be forced into corresponding patterns (fig. 32A). This horizontal relationship to the audience causes a cer-

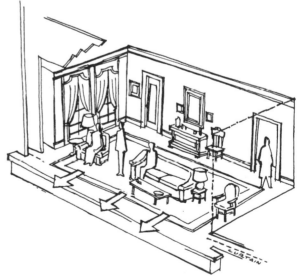

Fig. 31. Proscenium theater actor-audience relationship

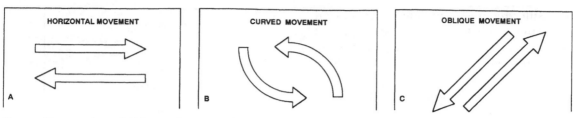

Fig. 32. Movement possibilities on the proscenium stage

tain strain on the performers, since they must orient both to the audience (to be seen and heard) and to each other (to maintain the necessary involvement with one another) at the same time. The three-quarter down position seems to be about the best compromise possible (fig 33A). During the past thirty years, however, directors and actors have become more bold and begun using the three-quarter up and full back positions as well (fig. 33B).

In this regard it is interesting to remember that when, in 1893, Strindberg wrote *Miss Julie*, he slyly complained about some of the restrictions we have just been discussing. In a preface to that play, he gave some of his views on current stage practices. Here are a few things with which he found fault: "Of course, I have no illusions about getting the actors to play for the public and not at it, although such a change would be highly desirable. I dare not even dream of beholding an actor's back throughout an important scene, but I wish with all my heart that crucial scenes might not be played in the centre of the proscenium, like duets meant to bring forth applause. Instead, I should like to have them laid in the place indicated by the situation. Thus I ask for no revolutions, but only for a few minor modifications. To make a real room of the stage, with the fourth wall missing, and a part of the furniture placed back toward the audience, would probably produce a disturbing effect at present."

Until recently the scenographer rarely (if ever) bothered himself with the problems and incongruities the box setting presented. Furniture was usually lined up so that the audience could reasonably see the actors use it, and in such a way that the actors could easily speak to the audience as directly as possible. Although few in the audience ever thought to question this arrangement, the characters in most plays, musicals, or operas spent most of their lives facing one direction in rooms with one wall missing.

It is more the common practice in today's production to rethink these arrangements of objects and the movement of performers; the theater has made some progress in this regard since Strindberg. We do see furniture with its back to the audience, or at least not lined up as it was

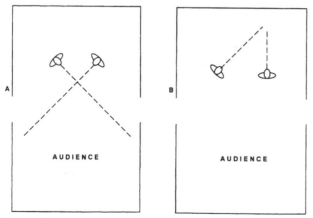

Fig. 33. Two-part actor-audience relationships on proscenium stage

in the traditional arrangements common to his time. Since the legacy of Stanislavsky and other naturalists is still a strong influence in our theater, both the director and the scenographer are trying to make the actor's environment appear more natural even if they often "cheat" furniture relationships toward the general view of the proscenium arch. In fact, there has been, on the part of directors and actors, a sometimes radical orientation of movement techniques used for the proscenium stage. (To cite only one example in this regard: when Charles Laughton directed a revival of Shaw's *Major Barbara* in 1956, during some of the longer "set" speeches in the first act, he seated two of his actors on a low bench directly downstage center with their backs to the audience; these actors became themselves, in a real sense, an extension of the audience. Later in the arsenal scene, at least five actors—at times more—performed most of the scene facing up toward the rear of the stage.)

Before leaving the subject of the proscenium theater let us review the standard elements one will encounter on such a stage:

Elements of the Proscenium Arch Stage
as Shown in Figure 34

1. Proscenium arch

2. Stage floor—(A) trap in stage floor (Opened here, closed when not in use.)

3. Apron (Wider in older theaters, increasingly narrower during second half of nineteenth century and during most of twentieth century.)

4. Offstage space (Often called the wings.)

5. Orchestra pit (In some theaters, slightly recessed under stage. In some theaters, such as Richard Wagner's Bayreuth, pit almost entirely under apron of stage.)

6. Back wall of theater (Usually contains loading doors.)

7. Grand drape (Often decorative, especially in theaters of the seventeenth, eighteenth, and nineteenth century. In addition to being lowered to make changes of scene, the grand drape can be lowered to change arch opening height.)

8. Main curtain (In many theaters this curtain can be either lowered from above or opened laterally from the side of the arch. Some curtains—such as that at the Metropolitan Opera in New York City—has the additional feature of being opened in a decorative arch fashion. This is accomplished by an elaborate set of lines sewn directly into the curtain itself.)

9. Second portal (This arch, usually black velvet or some light-absorbing fabric, comes after the main curtain; its purpose is to help mask off backstage and sidelighting arrangements.)

10. Gridiron (A number of supports suspended from the ceiling of the stage house, which allow scenery to be flown up and out of sight. Other features necessary to production—such as lighting instrument battens, curtain tracks—are also suspended from this gridiron.)

11. Fly gallery (Usually suspended some distance from the stage floor and where the lines attached to the flown scenery or other suspended units are manipulated after they have been counterweighted.)

12. A back drop (A large piece of material usually made of cloth or other flexible material. These units are temporarily attached to battens suspended from the gridiron and can be flown into sight or out of sight into the area immediately over the stage. Cloth drops usually have rigid battens at top and bottom, sometimes wooden but more often metal pipe.)

13. A cut drop (A piece of material like the back drop but cut to some decorative profile. If the pattern of the cut is extensive, netting or other transparent materials are put on the rear to keep the profiles from sagging out of shape. These units are also temporarily attached to battens suspended from the gridiron and can be flown into sight or out of sight.)

14. Cyclorama (Sometimes called a "horizont"—surrounds most of the stage area, unlike a sky drop, which is usually flat. The cyclorama is often part of a theater's permanent installment, not part of a temporary production's scenery.)

15. Scenic unit (Composed of flats, platforms, steps, etc. Temporary structures built for a particular production. Scenic units must be capable of being removed from the stage in short periods of time. Sometimes this is accomplished by building an entire setting on a platform wagon that can remove the setting to an offstage position while another setting takes its place. The Metropolitan Opera theater is equipped with a wagon stage on each side, one in the rear, and one on an elevator that allows an entire scene to

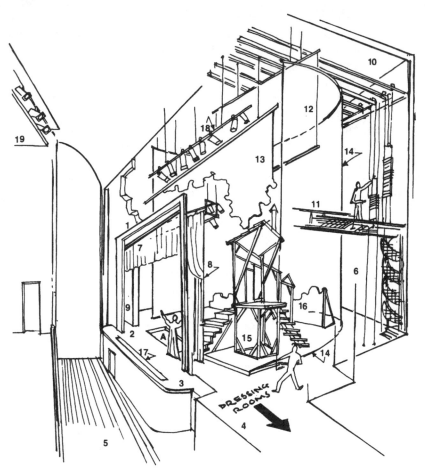

Fig. 34. Proscenium theater mechanics

be stored below the stage. All these wagon stages are controlled electrically. In addition to these, the theater has a large revolving stage built into the permanent floor.)

16. Groundrow (Scenic unit cut and painted to simulate a distant view: hills, houses, etc. Sometimes these groundrows are built as are cycloramas, semicircular rather than flat. At times they are constructed three-dimensionally in smaller than actual scale in order to give the illusion of distance.)

17. Footlights (Rarely found in most recently built theaters but a feature of most theaters built in the last two hundred years. When they are included in modern-day theaters, they are usually recessed and are able to be covered over when not in use.)

18. Light batten suspended from gridiron (These battens most often have attached to them permanent lighting connections that feed into

known circuits and are not used for anything else but lighting equipment. In some recent theater installations these battens have units that, when connected to lighting instruments, allows positioning and focusing by remote control, a feature that alleviates intensive manual labor while saving time. By coupling this technology to that of the computer the Metropolitan Opera theater is able to change a lighting plot from one production in their repertory to another in a short amount of time.)

19. Front of house lighting portals and positions (Usually built into the ceiling of the auditorium, although older theaters do not have them. They are in most cases self-masking and have protective wire mesh over the front openings to ensure the safety of the audience seated below. Generally there is more than one portal, and often there are portals built into or attached to the auditorium sides nearest the stage.)

New Stage Forms

During the last one hundred years numerous theories concerning the nature of theater art have challenged the old ideas as to what the theater art is and where it should be performed. While Richard Wagner was one of the first of those who questioned traditional theater forms and their systems of belief, many others were close behind. By the start of the twentieth century there were literally hundreds of theater artists clamoring to change the directions theater had pursued during the seventeenth, eighteenth, and for most of the nineteenth century. This was true for every country. A common desire infected the thought of countless playwrights, directors, actors, and especially visual artists who worked for the "old style" of theater: to abolish the standard forms of the stage, along with the accepted audience-actor relationships that existed in order to render the stage a more flexible instrument capable of confronting the spectator in a much more direct manner and with a greater impact than heretofore. Newer kinds of theaters were necessary, it was postulated, to express newer forms of theater. It was not possible for playwrights and their interpreters, it was felt, to involve audiences in theater forms of the past. While many of those, such as Stanislavsky, still relied on production techniques left over from earlier times, there were some who wished to break completely with practically all theater after that of archaic Greece. Perhaps the most articulate of this new breed was Antonin Artaud, a French poet and actor who left us a highly provocative document saying what he thought the theater of the future should be. In his book *The Theater and Its Double*, Artaud describes how the theater he envisions should be realized. Here are some of the basic requirements he proposes:

The Stage—The Auditorium: We abolish the stage and the auditorium and replace them by a single site, without partition or barrier of any kind, which will become the theater of action. A direct communication will be reestablished between the spectator and the spectacle, between the actor and the spectator, from the fact that the spectator, placed in the middle of the action, is engulfed and physically affected by it. This envelopment results, in part from the very configuration of the room itself. . . .

Thus, abandoning the architecture of present-day theaters, we shall take some hangar or barn, which we shall have reconstructed according to processes which have culminated in the architecture of certain churches and holy places, and of certain temples in Tibet. . . .

In the interior of this construction special proportions of height and depth will prevail. The hall will be enclosed by four walls, without any kind of ornament, and the public will be seated in the middle of the room, on the ground floor, on mobile chairs which will allow them to follow the spectacle which will take place around them. . . . The scenes will be played in front of whitewashed wall-backgrounds designed to absorb light. In addition, galleries overhead will run around the periphery of the hall as in certain primitive paintings. These galleries will permit the actors, whenever the action makes it necessary, to be pursued from one point in the room to another, and the action to be deployed on all levels and in all perspective of height and depth. . . .

. . . However, a central position will be reserved which, without serving, properly speaking, as a stage, will permit the bulk of the action to be concentrated and brought to a climax whenever necessary.

Artaud's theories have been widely accepted and put into practice in numerous instances especially during the past three decades. Peter Brook is only one of many directors who have been influenced by Artaud and at least one major critic, Jan Kott, has written extensively on his influences in present-day theater practice. Probably the most famous group to make use of Artaud's visions has been the Laboratory Theater of Jerzy Grotowski in Poland, who, in 1959, after becoming increasingly dissatisfied with the conventional theater—its purposes as well as its form—decided to create a theater of his own that, as Artaud did, broke with most theater practices established after fifth-century Greek theater. (In fact, Artaud decided to go back even further to archaic forms of ritual and spectacle that predate that period of theater.) While the theater of Grotowski has been essentially dormant from beginning of the 1980s, it has had a distinct influence on theater both in America as well as in Europe. The reason for this influence is that, unlike Artaud, Grotowski was one of the very first directors to successfully realize many of the ideas that Artaud had only theorized about.

Along with implementing new concepts of acting, Grotowski also abandoned traditional theater structures. Many of his productions take
place in locations selected specifically for individual project. A stage can be as small as a large
table around which no more than a few dozen
spectators are placed. In fact, each project is allowed to determine the number of people able
to see it at any one time. In many of Grotowski's
productions, the audience is fragmented into
small unequal groups and placed in spacial combinations in a larger space that has also been
broken into smaller acting areas of unequal size.
Figure 35 shows just such an arrangement for
Kordian, one of the productions in the Laboratory
Theater's repertory. In *Towards a Poor Theatre*,
Grotowski gives his reasons for completely dis-
avowing all stage forms and relationships as they
exist today. In the following passage taken from
that book, he gives the rationale for the position
he holds:

By gradually eliminating whatever proved superfluous, we found that theatre can exist without makeup, without autonomic costume and scenography,
without a separate performance area (stage), without
lighting and sound effects, etc. It cannot exist without
the actor-spectator relationships of perceptual, direct,
"live" communion. This is an ancient theoretical truth,
of course, but when rigorously tested in practice it
undermines most of our usual ideas about theatre.
It challenges the notion of theatre as a synthesis of
disparate creative disciplines—literature, sculpture,
painting, architecture, lighting, acting (under the di-

rection of a *metteur-en-scene*). This "synthetic theatre"
is the contemporary theatre, which we readily call the
"Rich Theatre"—rich in flaws. . . .

The Rich Theatre depends on artistic kleptomania,
drawing from other disciplines, constructing hybrid-
spectacles, conglomerates without backbone or integrity, yet presented as an organic art-work. By multi-
plying assimilated elements, the Rich Theatre tries to
escape the impasse presented by movies and television. Since film and TV excel in the area of mechanical
functions (montage, instantaneous change of place,
etc.), the Rich Theatre countered with a blatantly com-
pensatory call for "total theatre." The integration of
borrowed mechanisms (movie screens onstage, for
example) means a sophisticated technical plant, per-
mitting great mobility and dynamism. And if the stage
and/or auditorium were mobile, constantly changing
perspective would be possible. This is all nonsense.
. . .

No matter how much theatre expands and exploits
its mechanical resources, it will remain technologically
inferior to film and television. Consequently, I propose poverty in theater. We have resigned from the
stage-and-auditorium plant: for each production, a
new space is designed for the actors and spectators.
Thus, infinite variation of performer-audience relationships is possible.

Actually Grotowski has not created a new
theater so much as he has returned to that very
first relationship (shown in fig. 23) that began
theater, jettisoning everything accumulated to
that relationship between then and now. His
theories (which, if we accept his words at face
value, are more rediscoveries than original in-

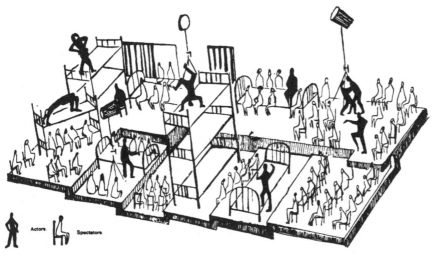

Fig. 35. Scenic arrangement for *Kordian*

ventions) and his experiments will undoubtedly continue to affect the theater of the future. Few who have seen and studied his work and his words doubt the depth of accomplishment or his sincerity of purpose. Still, it is probable that the inherent disciplines he demands and the methods he imposes on both actors and production—not to mention the smallness and specific kinds of audience he requires—will keep Grotowski's work always in the avant garde of theater and will prevent his theories and practices from ever being assimilated into the mainstream of the modern theater. There are many, in fact, who do accept the idea of a synthetic theater as a defensible aesthetic of theater, which, of course, Grotowski does not. One cannot escape or totally discount the traditions of the past one-hundred-fifty-odd years. This book is tacitly based on the supposition that synthetic theater (meaning here a theater that depends on putting together concepts and practices from a wide range of resources) is a defensible and viable attitude that will be with us for the near future at least, if not longer. But Grotowski has been of great service to those who do not fully espouse his philosophies; if nothing else, it causes us who work in the so-called Rich Theater occasionally to stop and take stock of what we think is important to our theater and what should be changed, what is necessary and what should be abandoned. Reading and thinking about how Grotowski views the theater could even send us back to reevaluate our most basic (usually unconsidered) beliefs. Perhaps it will cause us to once again consider Henry David Thoreau's great principle for all human activity: *Simplify, simplify, simplify*. It could even make us look through the complicated technologies of a *Starlight Express* to see the essential hollowness of its conception and purpose as well as the vapidity of its music and story.

If one salient point can be derived from the investigation of theater forms and actor relationships, it would probably be that no single point can be made. Quite possibly there is, for every single person who works in the theater, a single form as well as an accompanying philosophy that he or she feels most comfortable working in and with. We should always recognize that "best" for A may be acceptable (not first) for B and totally unacceptable for C. Who has the

ultimate right to make a final judgment that will decide this question of the "right theater form" once and for all? Perhaps each age gets—as Thomas Jefferson said of government—the theaters it deserves (a blessing in good times, a curse in bad). It is certain that scenographers training today will during their career encounter frequently and be confronted by the ever-changing virtues and shortcomings of many stage forms. One mode of thought should be avoided at all costs, however: that one kind of theater or that one stage form is inherently superior to another. Perhaps the only real point we should make here is that no single stage and auditorium could ever be expected to satisfy all the philosophies that exist concerning the physical theater. But we should hold as well the idea that it is the individual scenographer who can assist in the making of the best use of a particular theater form for a specific production.

The Scenographer's Areas of Influence

Few members of a viewing audience are critical of a production's scenery. When the curtain rises on a sumptuously decorated or highly detailed realistic setting, almost without exception audiences react with surprise and pleasure, following which spontaneous applause erupts. Even seeing scenic elements move—walls opening, platforms shifting position, solid objects mysteriously appearing or disappearing into the floor or into the space above the stage; almost magical accomplishments—give an audience visual delights akin to those encountered in childhood tales of magic and of adventure. Few of us are so jaded that we do not take pleasure in such spectacles; few who do not delight in having our eye dazzled and our minds teased by the visual transformations made possible by modern stage technology. And yet the scenographer of today must approach such possibilities with a firm understanding as to when spectacle is needed and when it is inappropriate. We need a means to assess when a production demands spectacle. More important, we need some principles that will tell us when we need to forego that formidable arsenal of technical machinery today's theater possesses. The natural curiosity most theater people have often tempts us to test the limits of a new technology rather than to seek out what real use it might have. For many years now we have had a safe way to fly Hamlet in for his first entrance. Few would deny this would be spectacular. Fewer still would ever consider this a reasonable thing to do even though the possibility exists. To confuse the entrance of Hamlet with that of Peter Pan, despite the gasps of delight that any audience would doubtless give, would be totally inappropriate to Shakespeare's intent.

It is not an unreasonable observation to make that a strong current trend in the producing theater can be summed up thus: *if it can be done, it should be done.* (And all too often this philosophy is followed with an unspoken caveat: It *will* be done.) For the truth of the matter is that during the past century the producing theater has found the electrical and hydraulic means of shifting large masses of scenery so quickly and silently that there is virtually nothing that a modern scenographer can design that cannot be built or moved easily in to or out of an audience's view. We have, it seems, all but forgotten Robert Edmond Jones's thoughtful warning that *machines are not a substitute for imagination.* As early as 1941—long before computer-driven scenery was envisioned—he took issue with the use of mechanistic scenic change simply to please an audience's desire for spectacle. Shakespeare, as you will recall from Chorus's speech in *Henry V,* had challenged his audience with the exhortation, *On your imaginary forces work.* Jones also believed that imagination should aggressively be pursued on both sides of the curtain. In *The Dramatic Imagination,* he devotes an entire chapter to considerations young scenographers should address. An important part of that advice is a warning concerning the unrestrained use of scenic technology.

A stage setting has no independent life of its own. Its emphasis is directed toward the performance. In the absence of the actor it does not exist. Strange as it may see, this simple and fundamental principle of stage design still seems to be widely misunderstood. How often in critics' reviews one comes across the phrase "the settings were gorgeous!" Such a statement, of course, can mean only one thing, that no one concerned with producing the drama has thought of it as an organic whole. I quote from a review recently published in one of our leading newspapers, "Of all the sets of the season, the only true scenic surprise was . . ." The only true scenic surprise, indeed! Every stage designer worth his salt outgrew the idea of scenic surprises years ago. If the critics only knew how easy it is to make a scenic surprise in the Theatre! Take two turntables, a great deal of—But, no. Why give away the formula? It is not surprise that is wanted from the audience; it is delighted and trusting acceptance. *The surprise inherent in a stage setting is only part of the greater surprise inherent in the event itself.* (Italics mine)

Probably both Shakespeare and Robert Edmond Jones would be morbidly fascinated by the technological developments that our modern theater has at its current disposal: *Cats, Phantom of the Opera,* and *Les Misérables* would not fail to capture their attention. Certainly they would take notice of vehicles such as *Starlight Express.* It would be interesting to know how they assessed the underlying material of these pieces. Would they, I wonder, attach any great merit to a work that consisted largely of a mindless plot filled out by thoughtless movement all accompanied by an overpowering assault on visual and auditory nerve endings?

It is well, therefore, that we consider as an important part of a scenographer's education the investigation of not only how a scenographer influences the visual aspects of a production but how those visual elements affect the others theater artists. The question has two parts: (1) *What are the basic categories into which the scenographer's work falls,* and (2) *in what ways do each of these contribute to the visual aspect of a production?*

As we attempt to analyze these influences into separate categories, we should also keep in mind that most scenographers do not approach a production in the manner we will here. How the scenographer does approach a production will be the subject matter of later chapters in the book. Here we are concerned with the *building blocks,* as it were, the scenographer uses, not the way they are assembled. Perhaps we should keep in mind Chekhov's advice to his friend Suvorin, when he sought to defend himself from Suvorin's complaint that Chekhov was remiss in his duties as an artist to be able to explain all that he did. Chekhov very wisely pointed out to him that "you confuse two things; *solving a problem* and *stating a problem correctly.* It is only the second that is obligatory for the artist. In *Anna Karenina* and *Yevgeny Onegin* not a single problem is solved, but they satisfy you completely because the problems are correctly stated in them."

We can profit by this advice as well; when working in the theater and when analyzing the production requirements of a particular play, we should be, as scenographers, first concerned with stating the problem correctly than solving the problem whose basis has not been thoughtfully considered. We should never think of *how* to fly Hamlet in before we have stated the *why*; that is, the need to do so in the first place. When we are at the point that we begin to consider what is needed for the production at hand (and assuming that we have stated and understood our premise correctly) only then can we begin to ask the question *what do we really need*. Unless we have a firm understanding of the basic categories of ways we can influence a production, we cannot fully understand which elements we need chose to solve our problems. Like good cooks, we not only need an ability to read a recipe but must have knowledge and feeling for the ingredients we use in our craft. For now, however, the ingredients of a design is our concern.

The Stage Floor

There is a great deal of soundness in the proverbial basic requirement for theater—three boards and a passion. When Peter Brook, in his book *The Empty Space*, states that "I can take any empty space and call it a bare stage," he is simply reaffirming that aphoristic definition of the theater. In the past, few designers for the stage gave much thought to this most important subjects. In this century we have come to understand that there is no better way in which the scenographer can serve the actor (and through him the playwright) than to provide an appropriately designed area on which he can perform.

Once, the stage floor was nothing more than just a floor, something to be walked upon but not to be considered to any great extent by itself. It was merely a neutral area with no definite shape or boundaries except those of the back and side walls of the theater. This total space was almost always rendered somewhat smaller by the placement of scenic units and masking units to hide those back and side walls as well as the mechanisms used to move the scenic units from backstage storage to audience view. As the scenographer became more involved with not only visual backgrounds for performers to be seen against but also the performer's possible actions on the stage, more attention was paid to this heretofore unregarded subject. Treatment of this area began to receive attention if not equal to that of the background, at least much more than in the past. Now, for many in the theater, this area has become the single most important element in the total design. The emphasis of scenography, once almost totally confined to the periphery of the stage area, has now all but given way to the treatment of the stage floor. Once only a simple horizontal plane (slightly tipped toward the rear wall in older theaters to facilitate the sight lines of an audience then seated on a flat floor), this area is now being fractured, extended, raised, lowered, and angled in literally every possible combination (fig. 36). To resolve the stage floor into appropriate acting areas is now for many scenographers (as well as directors) the first major step (some consider the most important step in the whole process of design) in planning a production. In figures 37 and 38 one can see just now different acting areas can be for two different productions done on the same stage.

The General Background

After the stage floor, the next area of design generally considered in that of the general background. This includes walls, backdrops, overhead units such as arches, foliage borders, ceiling (fig. 39). In one way, this is the least most important area, since performers cannot often relate directly to the general background; in another way it is an extremely important area, since items in this category tend to be the largest visual elements an audience sees. Because nothing can be seen without relationship to some sort of background, the scenographer must always carefully consider what the impact of the background will be on the performer standing before it.

Until the nineteenth century all theatrical performances were treated in an identical fashion; plays, operas, and ballet used settings that

Fig. 36. Design for *Oliver:* acting levels

had been designed only as pictorial accompaniment, much the same way, in fact, as incidental music for a production was written. Even today in the ballet we can see settings not unlike those used for all productions in the theaters of the seventeenth and eighteenth centuries. Here we see a large expanse of floor virtually unencumbered to facilitate the movement of the dancers. Even today scenery for the ballet is largely a matter of producing oversized paintings. Painters who have made their reputations elsewhere than on the stage are still routinely engaged to design works for this form of theater. During the heyday of Diaghilev's Ballets Russes all the major painters working in France were commissioned to design for the company. Nor were any of these artists required to think or create works in a manner contrary to their already established styles. This means that they do not really attempt

to work as the scenographer almost always does. All scenographers take it for granted that their function is to integrate what they design into the total production. The famous painter, on the other hand, is simply expected to present his persona as forcefully as possible; the success of such designs is largely measured on the ability of the audience to identify the painter from what is seen on the stage. Picasso was expected to remain Picasso. And it is a rare critic that ever complains of the situation as did Richard Buckle when he reported on the design of Salvador Dali for the ballet *Salome*: "It must be quite clear to anyone looking at . . . Dali's curtain and decor . . . that the celebrated Catalan illusionist does not design ballets—he allows dancers to take part in his painting."

The general background can be, therefore, at one and the same time, the least important part

Fig. 37. Design for *Home*: the floor as scenery

of the design to the performer (in terms of real use) and the most potent visual element in terms of what the audience sees. Performers simply cannot compete with a general background that is too bright or distracting. This area of design is potentially the most dangerous if not carefully considered. Adjustment of the general background in terms of color, light, and disposition of forms is critical in the scenographic process.

Specific Units of Scenery

These units may be part of the general background, but what separates them into a different category is that they may be, in fact often are, used directly by the actors and therefore become much more important to them. Doors, windows, platforms, steps, rocks, trees, and the like, can be used by themselves, that is, separated from their surrounding background, to create the sense of a particular place without the connect-

ing material—such as a wall—that would be found if the scene were completely realistic in conception. For instance, a room like the one shown in figure 40 can be defined simply by the placement of its architectural features (its specific units of scenery) and retaining the placement of its furnishings in a manner as if the actual walls were still there (fig. 41). Figure 42 shows a production for Henry Becque's *La Parisienne*. No walls connect the various units yet the room's form and period are easily comprehended.

Actors have an instinctive desire to relate to units of scenery in emotional as well as practical terms. For similar reasons playwrights have an equally instinctive urge to provide them for the actor to use. Windows and doors especially have always had a special symbolic fascination for both the playwright and the actor; it is a poor actor or an unimaginative playwright who does not seek out metaphorical possibilities in the physical elements of a play's scenic environ-

Fig. 38. Design for *A Midsummer Night's Dream*: acting levels

ment. These units provide, in fact, an invaluable means by which the actor can physically externalize hidden thoughts or motives. But in what way can the dramatic use of these elements be assured by the scenographer? A clue as to how this can be accomplished is furnished by these remarks of Katharine Kuh, an art critic and historian:

A window is to look through, both into and out of. Though often the symbol of an eye, it is not an eye, but a vehicle for light and for that volatile mirage we call atmosphere. A window is selective; it can frame nature in sweeping panoramas or in magnified close-ups. It provides access to inner visions more vivid than real ones. It can be nothing more than a blank, a vacant opening, or it can reproduce the unedited reflection of one's own image. Because windows imply secret revelations, because they are outlets to both the inside and outside world but, unlike doors, are rarely tangible passageways, they take on

Fig. 39. General background scenic units

Fig. 40. Drawing of setting

a variety of guises. Frequently exploited in art as compositional devices, they have come into their own only recently since Freudian discoveries infused them with new meaning.

Let us now see how these thoughts might aid the scenographer in work on an actual produc-

tion using Chekhov's *Cherry Orchard* as our focus.

In the last moments of the fourth act, Madame Ranevsky is leaving the home she has known and loved all her life. The room where she is—the nursery—has been stripped of most

Fig. 41. Specific units of scenery

Fig. 42. Setting for *La Parisienne*. Photograph by Don Drinkwater

of its possessions; only a few items of luggage remain and these too will soon be gone. Outside the windows of this room her beloved cherry orchard is being cut down, a sacrifice to progress and a signal that the old life she has lived heretofore is past, all its outward manifestations—the cherry orchard being the symbol of these things—vanishing. Soon even the house itself will be torn down to make way to a new cheap housing development. In a few moments she must walk out the door of this room never to enter again. What does she *feel* about the empty room once filled with life and promise, a place where so many happy times were spent? More important still, just what does she *see* as she looks out the windows overlooking the place where the orchard once stood? Most important of all, how can the scenographer aid the actress playing Madame Ranevsky to reinforce the un-

derlying emotions of these moments? How does the scenographer approach the design of those specific architectural elements so that an audience can perceive Madame Ranevsky's relationship to this place so dear to her heart? She has few words to show these feelings and those provided are relatively banal and insignificant. Of course, most of these problems must be left to the skill and art of the actor and the director. But the scenographer is not exempt from thinking in the same way as they do; the scenographer must be as much a part of the interpretation of these last moments as the actor or director. An indifferent scenographer could fulfill much of his obligation by searching out and reproducing on the stage a Russian nineteenth-century country-house window; this is a relatively easy thing to do. More is expected of the scenographer working in the theater of today. Directors expect the visual artists with which they work to also *see* the world through the eyes of the play's characters; scenographers should demand that of themselves. Moreover, not only must they see what is before them at that moment, but they must see with the eyes of their memory as well. In the first act of the play Madame Ranevsky's windows looked out on a happy contented life, while now they present a bleak and dying world. How does the scenographer make these things we have been discussing clear? Or can they be? Can a window or a door be designed that somehow helps both the actor and the audience to understand *something* about what is happening in the play's development? The questions we have posed have no definitive solutions. Still, they must be asked. Somehow they must be answered. Moreover, it is the asking of such questions (not necessarily the quick solutions to them) that separates the artist-scenographer from the scenic craftsman.

Let us take another instance in which a door becomes greatly important to the progress of the play and to the actor who must use it. In this case we are considering the design for the center portal (always in the Greek theater the entry to the protagonist's place of dwelling) in *Oedipus*. What size should the doors in this portal be, how big and how heavy? Of what materials should they seem to be? What physical effort should it cause the actor to open these doors? How, for that matter, does the door open; with what speed or what sound, if any? Do they open in or out? These are all practical questions and must be solved in technological terms. But there are other questions, questions such as those that occurred in *The Cherry Orchard*. Careful research will provide much of the information needed to satisfy the historical aspects of these questions. Consultation with shops and technical personnel will help the scenographer to implement his research findings. Yet after all the necessary research and technical data have been assembled, we are left with other questions, and these can be answered only by an understanding of the play. What are some of those considerations?

The doors we need to design have a practical use; but they also have another important function. While this portal is the entryway to the house of Oedipus, it is also, symbolically, the final door to the mystery of the plague that be-

sieges Athens, and it is behind these doors—the doors to his own house—that Oedipus finds the answer he seeks. How can these considerations affect the function of these doors or their appearance?

We can, for instance, make some artistic judgments in relation to the width and height of the arch that contains these doors; not only does it determine how big these doors will be, it will also have an effect on the spectator watching Oedipus, when he is seen in juxtaposition to it. We might ask in that regard, how large or high or thick this arch should be to be most effective, and what the relationship of the width to the height should be (fig. 43). While these are architectural considerations that can be addressed by period research, they are also visual considerations that influence the emotional response of the viewer. Once these decisions are made, we still have another problem to resolve—the quality of the doors themselves. For, like those considerations just mentioned, the treatment of the doors will also *say something* to an audience. What we have just been discussing needs some explanation. Let me use an example from my own past experience.

Several years ago a director of this play and I found ourselves discussing these very questions. At that time all he could tell me was that he wanted the door to Oedipus's house to be "the entrance to an 'unclean place,' that it it should be majestic, and "that hidden power lay behind the doors, but that dark and unclean things were also hidden there from the sight of men." He also spoke of the doors moving like "heavy oil in a dirty machine—slow and sluggishly—not lubricating the machine but clogging it." This is what he wanted the doors to show: *unclean, majestic, slow moving.* But at the end of the play, he went on, "this quality must be mitigated, in some way refined, made clear—the doors still majestic but now cleansed and bright." This, we both agreed, was a tall order. Since the doors could not be changed (it would not be desirable even if possible), they must be initially designed to incorporate the features of both desires, of both images—dark and corrupt, light and cleansed. And it was my job to make his verbal images concrete realities. The first step for any scenographer is having a clear statement of the problem at hand; that, I felt we had. Now

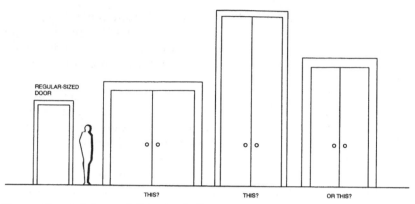

Fig. 43. Door height possibilities for *Oedipus*

it was time to go deeper into the play itself and find there some clues as to how the director's wishes might be accomplished. Knowing some history of the Greek theater and its traditional practices became the next level of investigation.

In the first part of the play these doors are seen in a dark world full of shadows and in the mists of early morning fires set around various parts of the pestilent-ridden city. As the morning light progressively brightens, the deepest shadows dispel. Greek plays actually did start, we are reasonably certain, during the first light of dawn and progressed into the light of full day. Audiences were in their seats before the sun rose, and the actual effects of sunrise were incorporated into the dramatic structures of many of the plays that have come down to us, *Oedipus* being one of those. There is, in fact, a similar progress from *darkness into light* in this play. The solving of the play's central mystery is fundamental to this dynamic image. Light, as all visual artists know, radically alters what it strikes if its source and tonality are also altered. Perhaps, we thought, this is the clue to fulfilling the director's images suggested to him in the text; the emerging strength of the light was also integral to the proper interpretation of the text, to the solving of the mysteries embedded there.

After much discussion, thought, research, experimentation, and more discussion, research, and further experimentation, we were able to arrive at a workable solution. The doors were designed that relied heavily on the properties of light (its ability, as we mentioned, to change color, direction, and intensity). The orna-

mentation of these doors consisted of massively carved entwined serpents in simulated antiqued bronze. At the beginning of the play these doors were lighted to capitalize on the three-dimensional qualities of the high relief, the side that the light predominantly struck was also more heavily "corroded"—finished to resemble the green oxide colors and textures of old weathered bronze. The other side (fig. 44A), which showed up during the later part of the play, was finished with brighter metallic colors. By changing the direction, color, and intensity of the light, it was possible to change both the tonality of the door and also to affect its dramatic qualities as well (fig. 44B). The undulating movements inherent in the carving of the coiling snake forms, as the source and intensity of the light changed, were forced back and flattened more into the background design of the doors. As these forms became flatter, they lost much of their dramatic power. As they changed tonality, they lost much of the feeling of corruption (unclean things) and the feeling of decay that had permeated the early moments of the play. We had been able to make the doors progressively match the progress of the play itself. That progress followed this pattern:

1. First part of the play—dark and heavily shadowed stage (Oedipus, literally and figuratively, "in the dark").

2. Middle part of the play—with the coming of the light (both physical and intellectual), the mysteries begin to resolve; the heavy snake forms lose their hard definition; their power lessens.

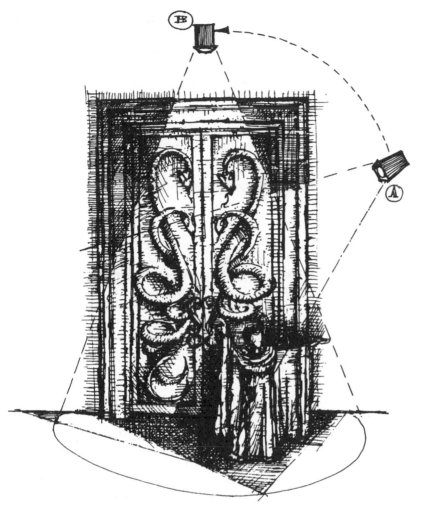

Fig. 44. Doors for *Oedipus*

3. Last part of the play—the light intensifies, all things become exposed to *the clear light of day* (the main purpose of all Greek philosophy); the palace of Oedipus, formerly an unclean place has been purged and, by Oedipus's understanding and subsequent actions, cleansed of the defiler.

When the final moment comes for Oedipus to emerge from the palace to announce the catastrophe within and to disclose the action he has taken upon himself (his blinding of himself and his decision to leave the city forever), what should we, the audience outside the door, feel? What emotions should we experience as the doors open? Does what we see on the stage at this moment (still carrying with us the memories of what we saw when the play began) in any way heighten our involvement with Oedipus and his

plight? Modern production theories are based on the assumption that we are very much influenced by those visual things that although they may work on us subliminally do in great part affect how we feel. The question has been, can scenographers in their work design specific units of scenery that not only have the necessary functional qualities to satisfy the technical demands of the production but can actually intensify the drama itself? For myself—and I am certain I speak for most professional scenographers working today—the answer is yes. Robert Edmond Jones observes in his book *The Dramatic Imagination* that it is only when the designer *thinks as a poet* that he truly serves the theater. This is the reason we must never dismiss the idea that while a door may be just a door or a window just a window, they might both be hidden accesses to something else; in the theater they usually are.

Furniture and Set Properties

These elements are one step nearer the actor, both in physical proximity and usefulness to him as an artist. Although there are only a few major categories of furniture that man has devised, there are innumerable variations and permutations on these basic forms:

1. Things to sit on
2. Things to lie on
3. Things to put other things on
4. Things to put other things in

Beds, sofas, tables, stools, chests, end tables, settees, desks, estageries, benches, book shelves, hallstands, bureaus, commodes, are but a few names in a long list that fall within these basic categories. But one should not overlook the point that in giving a particular name to a certain type of chair or a specific function to any piece of furniture, one is helping to establish the relationships these objects have to those who use them. Moreover, these differing names often help to establish the differing relationships between individual people or classes; the cultural as well as financial status of a person is often signaled by his possessions, and acquiring or retaining certain pieces of furniture ranks high in determining that status. Much can be told about the individual lives of people and how they view their positions in the world through a study of the objects we see around them.

The scenographer needs to foster a continuing interest in the ways human beings relate to their immediate environment as defined by their immediate surroundings. But this will not furnish a complete understanding without a working knowledge of the history of furniture. To be precise, this knowledge should include the following information:

1. Awareness of individual periods of furnishing as well as the relationship of one particular period to another
2. Styles that fall within individual periods as well as an interest in how that style was created or how it evolved within the period and into any periods that followed

3. Basic forms of construction and technologies used in the manufacture of individual pieces
4. Materials used during any one period as well as consideration of why particular materials were used or favored over others
5. Finishing materials (paints, varnishes, lacquers, gold-leaf, etc.) or specific treatments individual to a particular age (kinds and uses of waxes or specific techniques of buffing, etc.) or to a specific locale, along with consideration as to how these finishes or techniques influenced subsequent periods
6. An understanding as to how time and use affect both object and its finish is of particular concern to the scenographer, since often the effects of age and individual use are specifically detailed in a text's explicit directions or implicit needs
7. History of a particular piece of furniture or of its kind often reveals clues to the age in which it existed; quite often the spirit of an age lies in an understanding as to how those living in it related to the objects they selected

While contemplating the emotional impact or dramatic possibilities of furniture may seem far afield to an interior decorator, it is precisely this kind of speculation that points to the real difference between the scenographer and the interior decorator, who, while he needs an expert knowledge of furnishing as the basis of his work, can satisfy the demands of his profession only considering the categories just listed. On the other hand, the scenographer not only needs the information given there but must extend that information into many areas of human behavior— that specifically outlined by the playwright in his text—which the interior designer would find of no possible use. A key to the way in which the scenographer makes use of his knowledge of furniture can be found in *An Illustrated History of Furnishing* by Mario Praz. There he gives a significant clue as to how the close relationship that develops between man and those objects he makes or selects is used by the scenographer.

Dickens and Gogol have written about the capacity that objects have for expressing their owner. Podsnap's silver (in *Our Mutual Friend*) was characterized by a "hideous solidity." "Everything was made up to look as heavy as it could, and to take up as much room as possible." Twenty years before, in *Dead Souls*,

Gogol described Sobakevitch's house: "Tchitchikov looked around the room again and everything in it, everything was solid and clumsy to the last degree and had a strange resemblance to the master of the house. In a corner of the room stood a paunchy walnut bureau on four very absurd legs looking exactly like a bear. The table, the armchairs, the chairs were all of the heaviest and most uncomfortable shape; in short, every chair, every object seemed to be saying 'I am a Sobakevitch too!' or 'I too am very much like Soba-kevitch!'"

This is the house in its deepest essence: a projection of the ego. And furnishing is nothing but an indirect form of ego-worship. (Italics mine)

Praz's musings as to the interrelationship of furnishing to the lives of those who exist within the confines of particular places, then, is almost identical to the way in which a scenographer must think. The selection of a text's physical needs—among which furnishings play a significant role—becomes of crucial importance to the practice of scenography.

There are at least three distinct steps in the process of providing furnishings for the stage. These are:

1. Determining the needs of a scene: that is, analyzing the text to find the list of objects absolutely necessary to the action of the scene. But at this stage Gertrude's bed in *Hamlet* is no more concrete than is Maggie's bed in *Cat On a Hot Tin Roof*; it is generic in nature and we know little more than that a bed of some kind is required in both plays.

2. Seeking images from our outside research so that differences between Gertrude's bed and Maggie's bed can be determined: not only are these differences matters of historical period or geographical location alone, but also they require an understanding of how the characters use these beds as well as the playwright's hidden reasons—his *dramatic purpose*—for including them in the scene. In both instances the playwright had very different reasons for requiring such an object. In *Cat On a Hot Tin Roof*, the bed is crucial to the meaning of Williams's play; it is a battlefield where Maggie the Cat would like to vanquish her rival, the ghost of her husband's best friend. In *Hamlet* the bed is not involved in the action as much as in Williams's play; it is, rather, more a visual reminder of Gertrude's hastening too quickly to "incestuous sheets." In the Laurence Olivier cinema version of the play, however, the bed is used as the focus of the scene, its design carefully considered in relation to Olivier's interpretation of the scene. (In a 1990 Kevin Klein production of *Hamlet*, no bed at all was present in Gertrude's closet; the only furnishing in the room was a blood-red carpet. Much of the action that Olivier used in his production required the use of a bed; much of the action in the Klein production was performed by the actors kneeling, sitting, and rolling about on the the carpet.)

3. The scenographer must now do one of two things: (1) find the items needed or (2) make working drawings from research information. In either case, it is imperative that all the considerations mentioned above have an active part in the search for an existing bed or in the designing of the item to be made in the scenic shop.

No scenographer should ever take lightly this area of influence. We should constantly keep in mind another good piece of advice included in Praz's book, which is: "perhaps even more than painting or sculpture, perhaps even more than architecture itself, furniture reveals the spirit of an age." All scenographers might be well advised to follow this simple principle in their research into period interiors: Whenever seeking information concerning furniture or set properties, do not just try to find isolated pieces and objects but, whenever possible, find these items in images where they are shown being used.

A source picture such as the one shown in figure 45 is more helpful to both the scenographer and the director than a single object removed from its living context. As with a work of art, a good research picture is more than the sum of its parts. Furniture and set properties are far more necessary to the actor than either the general background (which he cannot use directly) or specific units of scenic architecture. But, as with this later category, it is possible to create a sense of place and period—its characteristic form and atmosphere—by careful selection and placement of furniture and set properties. In the arena theater and on the open stage, creating this sense becomes critically important to the scenographer's design, since furniture and set properties literally become the scenery.

It was said of Molière that he could place chairs on the stage so effectively that "they could

Fig. 45. Recommended source picture

almost speak." What does such a statement really mean? How can furniture "speak?" Does the placement of the chair in figure 46 *say* something to an audience? If one reads *The Physicists*, the play from which this image is taken, it will become immediately apparent what the placement of the chair means to the end of the play, the moment shown in the photograph. To the imaginative person this is not such a difficult concept to embrace. In the *Collected Stories of Tennessee Williams*, the playwright gives us an insight into how the creative mind often perceives the world of supposedly inanimate things:

This overstuffed chair, I don't remember just when we got it. I suspect it was in the furnished apartment that we took when we first came to Saint Louis. To take the apartment we had to buy the furniture that was in it, and through this circumstance we acquired a number of furniture that would be intriguing to set designers of films about lower-middle-class life. Some of these pieces have been gradually weeded out through successive changes of address, but my father was never willing to part with the overstuffed chair. It really doesn't look like it could be removed. It seems too fat to get through a doorway. Its color was originally blue, plain blue, but time has altered the blue to something sadder than blue, as if

it had absorbed in its fabric and stuffing all the sorrows and anxieties of our family life and these emotions had become its stuffing and its pigmentation (if chairs can be said to have a pigmentation). It doesn't really seem like a chair, though. *It seems more like a fat, silent person, not silent by choice but simply unable to speak because if it spoke it would not get through a sentence without bursting into a self-pitying wail.*

Over this chair still stands another veteran piece of furniture, a floor lamp that must have come with it. It rises from its round metal base on the floor to half a foot higher than a tall man sitting. Then it curves over his head one of the most ludicrous things a man has ever sat under, a sort of Chinesey-looking silk lamp shade with a fringe about it, so that it suggests a weeping willow. Which is presumably weeping for the occupant of the chair.

I have never known whether Mother was afraid to deprive my father of his overstuffed chair and weeping-willow floor lamp or if it simply amused her to see him with them. There was a time, in her younger years, when she looked like a fairy-tale princess and had a sense of style that exceeded by far her power to indulge it. But now she's tired, she's about sixty now, and she lets things go. And the house is now filled not only with its original furnishings but with the things inherited from my grandparent's house in Memphis. In fact, the living room is so full of furniture that you have to be quite sober to move

Fig. 46. Design for *The Physicists*. Courtesy of the Governors Royal Shakespeare Theater, Stratford-upon-Avon. Photograph by Reg Wilson

through it without a collision . . . and still there is the overstuffed chair.

The vision Williams demonstrates here is almost identical to that Praz reported earlier. For anyone working on a production of *The Glass Menagerie*, such factual information is helpful. (See "The Scenic Concept on Stage: *The Glass Menagerie*" in part 5 for further discussions of this play.) But far more valuable is the kind of imagination that imbues that so-called dead world with such a feeling of life. It is also this kind of imagination that triggers the imagination of other visual artists such as Edward Keinholz and causes him (in a strikingly theatrical way) to create an assemblage such as this in the collection of the Whitney Museum of American Art (fig. 47). We who re-create the worlds playwrights outline in words would do well to emulate the kind of vision that Keinholz exhibits and that Williams writes of in his eulogy to an overstuffed chair. Nor can the decisions we make in regard to furniture and set properties be underestimated in importance to the performer who, in many instances, has an instinctive desire to relate to his immediate environment in a highly personal manner. Jean Cocteau, although a man of letters, was, like Molière, keenly aware of the importance of furniture placement on the stage. "A chair," he once wrote, "badly placed on the stage is almost as dangerous as a trapeze insecurely suspended from the roof." While it has often been observed that young actors often blithely disregard their material surroundings (and in so doing give an audience the feeling that they don't really belong there), mature actors almost always take advantage of these surroundings to extend the scope of their characters. The veteran actor (or director) realizes that these objects can, as the French Dauphin of Eisenstein's *Ivan the Terrible* demonstrates (fig. 48), show something of what he is feeling and a great deal of what he is simply by the physical attitude he adopts toward the throne he sits in.

The scenographer should never forget that past ages had ways of seeing and ways of thinking that we living today do not share. These differences show up not only in the ways people think and act but in the ways they use things in the world about them. When scenographers use

Fig. 47. Museum construction: Edward Keinholz, *The Wait*. Courtesy of the Collection of the Whitney Museum of American Art, New York. Geoffrey Clements Photography, Staten Island

objects from past ages, such as furniture or other house furnishings, they, as well as the directors with whom they collaborate, must understand that our present-day attitudes toward these objects are not likely to be that of a distant time. Furniture, like all other artifacts from past times, exists in a context, a context that often has principles—often strict rules—concerning use. Moreover, these contexts, like all other human activities, change greatly as time passes. In *Home*, by Witold Rybezynski (a book that should be in the permanent libraries of all scenographers and directors), some of these important changes are discussed. Here is a brief passage from the book:

During the Middle Ages the prime function of the chair was ceremonial. The man who sat down was important—whence the term "chairman"—and his upright, dignified posture reflected his social stature. This association of the seat itself with authority has remained an integral part of European and American culture: we still refer to a judge's bench, or to being in the driver's seat. The movie director continues to have his name on a chair, even if it is printed only on canvas. There are even imaginary seats, like Chairs in Art History, or seats on the boards of corporations. . . .

Although chairs began to service more mundane activities such as eating or writing, the sitting position changed slowly. Throughout the Renaissance and the Baroque period, European sitting furniture, although it increased in quantity, accommodated what was essentially the erect posture encouraged by the earliest chairs. Even the domesticated seventeenth-century Dutch continued to sit stolidly in their straight-backed chairs, both feet planted firmly on the ground.

The ceremonial use of chairs is all but moribund today. Still, a few vestiges exist. In figure 49, a photograph taken during the coronation of Elizabeth II, queen of England, we see how precise the symbolism of ceremonial chairs can be. These thrones are used only for high occasions. They were not built for comfort but for state functions. What is interesting to note here, however, is the manner in which their height conforms to the dictates of royal protocol. Queen Elizabeth is the ruler of the British Isles. Prince

Fig. 48. Design from *Ivan the Terrible*

Philip, sitting beside her, is only a consort; his rank is below that of hers. Those responsible for the protocol which governs this ceremony have made certain Prince Philip does not sit higher than Queen Elizabeth. The actual variation between these thrones is quite small: to be precise the difference is approximately three-quarters of an inch. To accomplish this minute but all-important difference, a small block raises her throne to the higher level (fig. 49A). We can also see the difference if we draw a horizontal line across the tops of the two thrones. While we are apt to encounter few situations on the stage that reflect such precise thinking, we should be aware that those in the past or in different cultures do make distinctions we should be aware of.

Figure 50 shows a moment in the play *The Caretaker*, by Harold Pinter, as it was presented in an arena theater. (See "Scenography as a Physical Embodiment of Abstract Qualities" in part 5 for further discussions of this play.) The atmosphere of this room depends less on surrounding scenic units—with an audience seated on three of the four sides, actual walls could not, as in a proscenium arch theater, be used to reveal the nature of the locale—and more on the selection and arrangement of appropriate furniture and set properties. Casual as this arrangement appears the scenographer must use especial care in working out such an environment. Practically every moment of the play's dramatic action must be minutely considered and throughly understood if this room is to fulfill the playwright's internal demands or to accommodate the director's patterns of movement. Stanislavsky, both as an actor and as a director, considered the relationships of furniture and set properties to performing so important that he always put in his production notebooks many small sketches of proposed arrangements (fig. 52), which he later took care to realize on the stage (fig. 51). At the end of part 4 there is an extensive selection taken from Stanislavski's personal notebooks

Fig. 49. Coronation thrones

that gives a clear indication of the importance he placed on this subject.

Set properties, like furniture, can play important roles in a scenographic design. While in most instances these objects are selected to reinforce the period feel of the design, a particular item of set decoration can serve a greater function. In 1967, The National Theatre of Great Britain produced Chekhov's *Three Sisters*, directed by Laurence Olivier and designed by Josef Svoboda. Later the entire production was filmed in a studio version that duplicated the setting as it was seen on stage. (This version was produced by the American Theatre Film Festival and released in 1973.) While the basic settings were not realistic, the furniture and set properties were in period; these, although few, were carefully considered, both as to their placement and their dramatic purpose. One set property used in the setting for acts 1 and 2 (the same locale), was given a special function to perform. This piece was an ornate clock made in the likeness of a city cathedral; a building one might expect to find in some great Russian city. Ostensibly the clock

was simply a highly decorative but essential utilitarian item; no one ever actually wound it, called attention to it directly, or even acknowledged its presence in the room. To the casual observer, this clock would appear to be nothing more nor less than what it was: something that most drawing rooms of the period might have had and something any scenographer decorating this setting might use. Yet as the play progressed, this clock became an important "actor" in the drama. At one point it helped in a distinctly positive way to underscore one of the underlying themes in this play; that life passes most people by, that if there is any excitement or gaiety to be had out of it, it is always in some other place. For the characters of *The Three Sisters*, this better existence can only be had in a large city; in this case, Moscow. By combining the element of time (and consequently making it a constant reminder of its passage) with an image that also reminded this group of the glittering life they were missing, Svoboda created a potent symbol that made its point without intruding on the action of the play. One does not become aware of the clock's message directly; only at a certain moment in the play, in fact, is the audience required to take notice of this item of decoration, which occurs during a long pause when the clock slowly chimes out the hour. Isolated on its own high pedestal, this symbol of time passing and lives wasted communicated to the audience a subtle but clear message, one that reenforced the scene's moody atmosphere of purposeless lethargy. In the film version, this image became stronger than in the stage version. This moment happened when the camera slowly panned across the room and came to rest on the clock as it began to strike the late afternoon hour. When the camera stopped, the image was slightly out of focus. As the clock chimes continued, the image cleared to give the spectator a closeup view of this time-passing city-life symbol. There as no mistaking the message being sent to the audience; the point was clear and entirely communicated. Objects, as we have pointed out in our other examples, can speak; and what they say is often more eloquent and powerful than any words could ever be. In *A Sense of Direction*, William Ball warns how easily such messages can go awry when those who direct productions do not take care in their selection. Speaking of an-

Fig. 50. Scene from *The Caretaker*

other production of *The Three Sisters* he gives this advice:

One of the greatest errors directors make is what I call "breaking systems." This means that having established a pattern of systems, the director foolishly introduces a single detail that violates his own systems. Here is an example. I once saw a production of *The Three Sisters*. A great deal of effort was made to give it systems of authenticity. Nineteenth-century costumes, oil lamps, genuine military uniform, authentic crystal decanters, and period cameras were used. At the end of the first act, one of the actors presented a contemporary toy, a top, to Irina. By the chromium design and computerized buzz, the audience could easily see that the top was a creation of the 1970s. By using one contemporary toy, the director had violated his own systems authenticity, and all his work to achieve integrated naturalism in the first act was destroyed. That one moment of disbelief suddenly brought the entire act crashing to the floor. It is astounding how frequently, and with what apparent casualness, directors destroy their own systems.

It is possible for the scenographer as well—by careless selection or unthinking design of furniture and set properties—to affect a performer's function adversely. He can, for instance, cause the actor to sit in markedly different attitudes simply by varying the height of a chair a small amount in either direction from its normal dimension; a little too high or too large, the character may be perceived as insignificant or helpless (fig. 53, the ill-fated boy-czar, also from Eisenstein's *Ivan the Terrible*), a little too low or too small, he may appear oversized or awkward, as does the actor in figure 54. Of course, there are many times when such alteration is done on purpose to produce just such effects. This is the case in the two examples just shown. Still, there is a vast difference be-

Fig. 51. Scene from *The Seagull*

Fig. 52. Drawing for scene from *The Seagull*

tween the purposeful intention and the accidental result. It is not uncommon for actors to have
strong opinions concerning the furniture they
must use directly; it is doubtful if there is one
working scenographer who has not had many
confrontations with performers on this particular
issue. Although some might just be difficult to
work with and hard to please—perhaps because
they have been subjected to years of having to
cope with uncooperative pieces of furniture that
other scenographers selected or designed for visual effect rather than usefulness to the actor—
most realize that it can affect their performance to
such a degree and so directly that they feel it their
prerogative to ensure the scenographer does not
thoughtlessly hamper them.

Hand and Personal Properties

In the professional theater, properties are
most always classified into two rough categories:
set properties and hand properties. Responsibility for design or procurement of these items usually falls between two kinds of workers; set prop-

erties are almost always the direct responsibility
of the scenographer (working with a properties
master), while hand properties are sometimes
selected by the scenographer only in part, the
greater part being assembled by the property
master. There are even times when a hand property falls within the province of the costume designer. In a large production that requires numerous objects, the overlapping of these
categories must be carefully sorted out, or else
important things can fall between the cracks of
mutually exclusive responsibility.

In the amateur theater, properties are not
often given the attention they deserve. Too often
the making or procurement of them is relegated
to a person who, rather than considering each
item needed as a separate and integral objective,
tends to think of them only as a list of things to
be gotten as quickly and effortlessly as possible.
In theaters such as the Stratford, Ontario, Festival Company or the Royal Shakespeare Company and National Theatre in London, the properties are not only carefully designed (usually in
direct consultation with the scenographers of a
production) but are beautifully executed by
numbers of highly trained artisans. The conscientious property master finds out not only what
is needed, but how those things were used in
the past and will be used in the present.

It would be hard to overemphasize the importance of the role that objects play in human
communication. Use of things to reinforce verbal language is as old as mankind itself. The
practice is so ingrained in our daily lives that we
often point to, touch, or pick up objects that lie
near to hand in order to clarify those things we
cannot elucidate in words alone. Using objects
in this way can be a powerful means of persua-
sion. In many instances the thing used has little
value or meaning in itself. For those who

Fig. 53. Scene from *Ivan the Terrible*

watched the televised hearings on Un-American activities of the early 1950s, few will forget Senator Joe McCarthy's repeated waving of papers before witnesses and television cameras, papers he reported to be detailed lists of Communists who had infiltrated the U.S. state department. Later it was discovered that no such lists existed, that those papers were nothing but paper. Still, at the moment he made use of them, the effects were far-reaching and damaging to scores of persons, many of whom lost their job and reputations simply on the information they were reputed to contain. Playwrights no less than unscrupulous politicians know well the power of objects; in countless instances they use them in similar ways.

Robert Edmond Jones had a keen appreciation of the importance of properties. Jo Mielziner, another distinguished scenographer, recalls an incident that illustrates the care with which Jones approached the selection of objects to be used on the stage. In an article he wrote for the book of Jones's designs and drawings, *The Theatre of Robert Edmond Jones*, Mielziner relates the following story:

I recall that Arthur Hopkins' business manager very hesitantly and politely inquired of Bobby one day, "Is it necessary to have those eighteenth-century quills and sand shakers on the desk up-stage in the corner of the set? You must realize, Mr. Jones, that even the first row of the orchestra can't appreciate an

Fig. 54. Actor's use of furniture

object so small at that distance." Bobby turned and glared. "Do you think," he said, 'that only people on the other side of the footlights need exaltation? What about the actor? Surely he should *feel* the *sense of period* when working in this set?"

Unfortunately, all too few scenographers think as Robert Edmond Jones and far too many as the business manager. Not only is this attention to detail a quality most of the great scenographers do share, it is also a mode of thought that certainly should be cultivated rather than denied, as it often is even in the professional theater.

Just what is a hand or personal property? And just how does it get its power to move those who witness acts involving them? The simplest answer—although not all that easy to comprehend—is that a property included or implied in a dramatic text is the external focus of the actor's attention. In other words, the actor uses physical objects to expose what he is thinking about at the moment when the playwright provides no words to express the emotion or thought engendered by the scene. Often the most important moments of a play are those that take place in the silences between lines of written dialogue. In countless instances objects—a "prop," to use the more common term—is employed to make clear what no amount of words could. This is often a difficult concept for those who think that the only way a playwright communicates with an audience is by the use of words, and that by words alone the actors can convey the full meaning of the playwright's intent. But the concept is not as hard to understand if we see how actual properties are used in actual instances. Let us examine a few illustrations to show how this works.

In 1966 CBS Television produced a televised version of *Death of a Salesman*, using many of the original Broadway cast. In his subsequent review of the telecast Robert Lewis Shayon took especial note of one scene:

Television rarely sees exciting bits of acting, but there was one recently that could make a viewer start with a sharp intake of breath. It happened . . . during Act Two of the two-hour color production of Arthur Miller's *Death of a Salesman*. . . .

Willy Loman has been fired by his young boss. The aging salesman comes pounding hysterically into the office of Charley, his friend. Lee J. Cobb, playing Willy, finds Bernard, Charley's son, in the office. This is the school-grind, the anemic worm that Willy and his popular, athletic sons once scorned. Now Bernard is a successful lawyer on his way to Washington, carrying tennis racquet to play on the private courts of affluent friends. . . .

Willy desperately tries to maintain the old razzle-dazzle about his own son Biff's "big deal." Bernard offers him a cigarette from a large, gold cigarette case. Willy stops talking, stares at the case, takes it, holds it, closes it and passes it back—in a silent passage of torment, despair, and envy. . . .

The cigarette case is a symbol of everything Bernard has won in life—success, status, wealth—and a mocking sign of all that Willy and his two boys have failed to win. The pain on Mr. Cobb's face as his emotions overwhelmed him, the wordless eloquence of his baffled regard for that shining piece of rail that crushed his ego and pierced his boasting—were utterly communicated and shared. I think it was the production's finest moment. . . .

Yet afterward, scanning a reading edition of the play, I found no mention of the cigarette case and this bit of stage business. Seventeen years ago I saw *Death of a Salesman* during its original run on Broadway at the Morosco Theater. Perhaps the bit was done on the stage but I don't recall it. . . .

. . . Whoever suggested the bit gave the actor a rich opportunity and the viewers a rare experience. (*Saturday Review*, 28 May 1966)

Had Mr. Shayon gone to a book called *A Theatre in Your Head*, by Kenneth Thorpe Rowe,

he would have had his question answered. Included in the text is a section written by Elia Kazan, the play's original director, called "Notebook Made in Preparation for Directing *Death of a Salesman*." Among those notes is this: "(Bernard offers him a cigarette case. Willy takes it, examines it with awe, hands it back. Bernard opens it, offers cigarette, he shakes his head)." It is interesting to observe the economy with which the director puts down his thoughts about this particular moment. One can clearly see what the director had in mind. Did the playwright actually envision this moment played in this way as he wrote? Quite probably not.

It is interesting to note that many playwrights have taken particular care to specify exactly what the actor needs in the way of properties to make his motive clear. These are not always specified in formal stage directions (and for that reason are missed by those—such as the general reader or the literary student of a playwright's work—who are not expert in reading plays for the hidden clues to action they contain). Shakespeare, time after time, weaves into the fabric of a speech an object that would externalize a character's inner and deepest thoughts: the mirror Richard II dashes to the ground after reflecting on the image in it (and seeing there the folly of his own past life) is far more dramatic than anything he might say at that point; Yorick's skull in which Hamlet finally sees the ultimate observation that can be made on life, not the philosophical speculation of ceasing to exist expressed in words (he certainly does that up to this point) but in an actual piece of a human being he once knew and loved. Even Hamlet, who has a sentiment or word on practically every possible situation or event, is reduced to near speechlessness when confronted with this object that shows what death really means; the only word Shakespeare gives him at this moment is a barely whispered, "This?"

And yet while many playwrights do include directions in their texts (or by dialogue imply the use of objects not mentioned), directors often interpolate objects into the plays not specifically or implicitly called for by the playwright. To a certain extent, the director sometimes becomes the co-writer with the playwright. This is a condition that is often crucial to the process of interpretation, a condition most playwrights accept.

(For a further discussion of this aspect of theater production see "The Scenographers Relationship to the Playwright" in part 3.)

At times hand and personal properties cannot be strictly categorized; the more personal they are and the more integrated into the action of a scene they become, the more difficult it is to determine who is responsible for their introduction into a particular production. Another illustration that demonstrates this point can be found in Olivier's 1964 National Theatre cinema version of the *Othello*.

In the final scene of the play, Othello murders Desdemona. He believes his action justified but finds out that he has been duped by the treacherous Iago. After Othello realizes his error, he decides that death by his own hand is his only option. The play ends with Othello's suicide. The text's internal evidence reveals that his death is accomplished with a bladed implement of some sort. The exact size of the instrument is not specified: only that those around him did not know he had any kind of knife or dagger on him (Cassio says immediately after the act, "This did I fear, but thought he had no weapon"). There was a large sword in the room—it is with this that Othello wounds Iago—but this is taken from him after he strikes Iago. In this production concealment of any other knife would have been difficult, since Othello's robe was made of a light, almost transparent material. Nor would he have had any real reason to be armed when he comes to the room. It is clear from the text that Othello does not mean to disfigure her; his words specifically rule out disfiguring Desdemona in any way: "Yet I'll not shed her blood / Nor scar that whiter skin of hers than snow / And smooth as monumental alabaster—." How, then, does he kill himself? Even those who are familiar with this play and have seen many productions of it were shocked at the method Olivier chose. Olivier was famous during his career for the inventive ways he used the props given him. In this instance he employed a weapon that had been in full view of the audience from the first moments of the play. Why it was not seen was that it was concealed in an item of Othello's costume: a heavy metallic bracelet he wore on his right wrist. What the audience did not know was this was Othello's assurance that he would never be taken alive in battle; that he would

always have near to hand (literally) a means by which he could dispatch himself although disarmed of every other weapon. Figure 55 shows the moment before he plunges the small, but still effective, blade into his throat. This solution has, admittedly, worked well on the screen, but it was also an effective piece of business on the stage. I do not know if the decision to use this property was that of Olivier or someone else. This illustration does, however, demonstrate just how effective new solutions to old problems can be and how important properties are to even the greatest of actors.

Let us close this subject with an unusual tribute to the power of these frequently underestimated stage objects by reading a poem of an important twentieth-century writer, Bertolt Brecht. As a playwright, Brecht so thoroughly understood the dramatic power personal properties possessed that he felt compelled to record in poetic form the manner with which the famous Berliner Ensemble actress Helen Weigel went about their selection.

Weigel's Props

Just as the millet farmer picks out for his trial plot
The trickiest seeds and the poet
The exact words for his verse so
She selects the objects to accompany
Her characters across the stage. The pewter spoon
Which Courage sticks
In the lapel of her Mongolian jacket, the party card
For warm-hearted Vlassova and the fishing net
For the other, Spanish mother or the pottery basin
For dust-gathering Antigone. Impossible to confuse
The split bag which the working woman carries
For her son's leaflets, with the moneybag
Of the keen tradeswoman. Each item
In her stock is hand-picked: straps and belts
Pewter boxes and ammunition pouches; hand-
    picked too
The chicken and the stick which at the end
The old woman twists through the draw-rope
The Basque woman's board where she bakes her
    bread
And the Greek woman's board of shame, strapped
    to her back
With holes for her hands to stick through, the
    Russian's
Jar of lard, so small in the policeman's hand; all
Selected for age, purpose and beauty
By the eyes of the knowing

Fig. 55. Property used in *Othello*. Courtesy of the Kobal Collection

The hands of the bread-baking, net-weaving
Soup-cooking comprehender
Of reality.

(Translated by John Willett)

Costume

Although the practice of using another designer to create the costumes for a production independently of the scenographer is now common, the most desirable situation is for one person to control all visual elements of a production. Costumes, like properties, are all-important to the actor, since on the stage the way a character is dressed in large part tells an audience what that character is like. Every scenographer should be able to design costumes for a production as

well as know the fundamental practices of costume construction (fig. 56).

Robert Edmond Jones, a scenographer who always took responsibility for the entire visual design of a production, makes several excellent points about the kind of vision one needs to design costumes. Here are few of his remarks:

In learning how a costume for the stage is designed and made, we have to go through a certain amount of routine training. We must learn about patterns, and about periods. We have to know what farthingales are, and wimples, and patches and caleches and parures and godets and appliques and passementerie. We have to know the instant we see and touch a fabric what it will look like on the stage both in movement and in repose. We have to develop the brains that are in our fingers. We have to experiment endlessly until

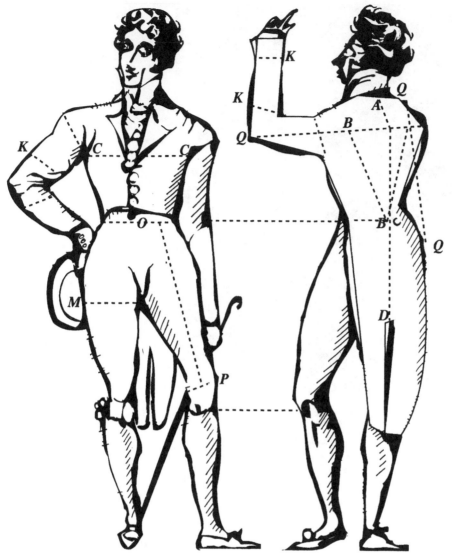

Fig. 56. Costume construction pattern

our work is as nearly perfect as we can make it, until we are, so to speak, released from it. . . .

A stage costume is a creation of the theatre. Its quality is purely theatrical and taken outside of the theatre, it loses its magic at once. It dies as a plant dies when uprooted. . . . Each separate costume we create for a play must be exactly suited both to the character it helps to express and to the occasion it graces. We shall not array Lady Macbeth in pale blue organdie or Ariel in purple velvet. Mephistopheles will wear his scarlet and Hamlet his solemn black as long as the theatre continues to exist. A Hamlet in real life may possess a wardrobe of various styles and colors. But in the theatre, it is simply not possible for Mr. John Gielgud or Mr. Maurice Evans to say, "Tis not alone my tawny cloak, good mother, nor customary suits of tender green."

While there is much good advice in these words, Jones's point of view is essentially a romantic conception of costume. But, then, so was his entire philosophy of theatrical design.

There have been in recent years, however, newer philosophies in theater that take a markedly different point of view as to what the role of costume is in on the stage. It would probably be more accurate to say that there are more points of view than were expressed in Jones's most creative period that spanned the early part of this century until almost the middle of it. Many of these trends have veered away from the romantic conception of costume design. More and more, dress for the stage is "selected" rather than designed, assembled rather than constructed, and many costumes are made from materials not invented until the second half of the twentieth century. It is now common practice to use clothes and accessories found in secondhand stores and attics rather than to construct costumes from new fabric that must be artificially aged and distressed. In some instances designers who are responsible for costumes that show the effects of great use and age will find their materials in old ready-made garments. These are then taken apart, recut into new patterns, and assembled into entirely new styles and periods. The shirt for the character of the Marquis de Sade (fig. 57) was recut from a water-stained crepe de chine ballroom gown of the 1920s, while the rest of his costume was constructed from sunbleached velvet rescued from the vaults of a theatrical warehouse.

Another noticeable trend in the design of costume during the past four decades has been the decreasing use of brightly colored and excessively elaborate costumes for period productions. Simplification in cut and profile as well as the use of heavily textured fabrics and other materials owes a great deal to the influence of Bertolt Brecht and the designers who worked for his theater, the Berliner Ensemble. Costume designers today often work within more limited color ranges; many of their tonalities are grayer in tone when compared with the technicolorlike hues of most productions during the early part of this century. It is possible, in fact, to trace this progressive muting of color by looking at films made from various time periods. If one looks at the films of the late 1930s through the early 1960s, there is a marked change in how color is used. Even between the stage version of *Camelot* and its cinematic remaking only a few years later, noticeable differences in costume philosophy are strikingly evident.

Along with newer concepts of tonality, there has also been a corresponding interest in synthetic materials, not only fabrics but plastics, metals, artificial fur, and both real and synthetic leathers. The introduction of fiber-glass cloth

Fig. 57. Shirt of Marquis de Sade

and strands, as well as other plastic impregnated materials that harden when exposed to chemical treatment, have opened up whole new vistas of possibilities in costume construction not feasible, not even dreamed of, even thirty years ago.

Costume designers routinely use paintings and drawings as visual guides for gaining information on a dramatic character's dress and outward appearance. It is not as widely known that they also use the work of other graphic artists as

source materials for their work, obtaining their
ideas as to character traits and behavior. Figure
58 shows the costume and makeup for Madame
Rosepettel, a character in *Oh, Dad, Poor Dad* by
Arthur Koppit. For this production the designer
used the work of two late nineteenth-century
French artists—Toulouse Lautrec (fig. 59) and
Henri Degas (fig. 60)—as inspiration for both the
costume concept as well as the basic "look" of
the makeup design. Working with the director,
the designer also influenced the actual performance of the play by bringing to the attention of
the director the stylistic possibilities inherent in
the original source materials. (This was also the
case in a production of *Marat / Sade* and another
production of *Krapp,* by Samuel Beckett; see part
4 for further discussions of how costume aids
the interpretation of a production.) There have
even been instances when a playwright will
model his characters directly from graphic images encountered in previous viewing experiences (see Michel de Ghelderode's letter in "The
Scenographer's Relationship to the Playwright"
in part 3).

 Along with all the technical advances in cos-

Fig. 59. Toulouse Lautrec print

Fig. 58. Costume for Madame Rosepettle

tume there has also been another development
that we should note before leaving this category.
This relates to the manner in which conceptual
imagery—most notably metaphor—is used in
the design of stage costume. In many instances
a designer will base a character's look on images
that lie beyond period detail verisimilitude. The
reason for this approach is to incorporate into
the dress of the character hidden clues to personality, purpose, or condition. One example
should suffice to demonstrate how metaphor can
be used in costume design.

 In *Romeo and Juliet* there is a short but important scene late in the play when Romeo, banished to Mantua, is brought the news that Juliet
is dead (she is not, of course, but he has no way
to know the truth). Before returning to Verona
where he intends to die beside Juliet, Romeo
seeks out an apothecary he hopes will provide
him the poison needed. Within a short while,
Romeo locates the shop of the apothecary. This

Fig. 60. Degas drawing

"An' if a man did need a poison now,
Whose sale is present death in Mantua
Here lives a caitiff wretch would sell it
          him."
O this same though did but forerun my
          need,
And this same needy man must sell it me.
As I remember, this should be the house.
Being holiday, the beggar's shop is shut.
What ho, apothecary!
          [*Enter* APOTHECARY.]
APOTHECARY: Who calls so loud?
ROMEO: Come hither, man. I see that thou are
          poor.
          Hold, there is forty ducats; let me have
          A dram of poison . . .
APOTHECARY: Such mortal drugs I have, but
          Mantuas's law
          Is death to any he that utters them.
ROMEO: Art thou so bare and full of wretchedness,
          And fearest to die? Famine is in thy
          cheeks,
          Need and oppression starveth in thy eyes,
          Contempt and beggary hangs upon thy
          back;
          The world is not thy friend, nor the
          world's law,
          The world affords no law to make thee
          rich;
          Then be not poor, but break it and take
          this.
APOTHECARY: My poverty, but not my will,
          consents.

character appears only once in the play; the scene in which he appears is short. Nevertheless, it is a crucial one to the play. The design problem here is to create a costume for the apothecary that provides clues to who the character is and how he fits in the action of the play at this point; to show clearly those three things mentioned above: *personality, purpose, and condition.* To better understand what these are, let us read what Romeo himself says about the man (the only information we have, in fact, that gives us the necessary clues to guide the designer):

ROMEO: Well, Juliet, I will lie with thee tonight.
          Let's see for means. O mischief, thou art
          swift
          To enter in the thoughts of desperate men!
          I do remember an apothecary,
          And hereabouts 'a dwells, which late I
          noted
          In tattered weeds, with overwhelming
          brows,
          Culling of simples; meagre were his looks,
          Sharp misery had worn him to the bones;
          . . . .
          Noting this penury, to myself I said,

Shakespeare gives many clues in the lines of this scene to the outward condition of the apothecary: poor in health as well as poor in dress. What is given in the lines is helpful in a general way. It is the designer's task, however, to find some image that not only shows destitution but the furtiveness of the character's manner. The reason he is in dire straights is hinted at by Romeo but not explained fully: that reason is so many have sought the same service, the sale of poison, that the authorities in Mantua have passed the death penalty on its sale. What these others wanted was a means of doing in enemies, not themselves, as was Romeo's purpose. It is evident that the apothecary is still in business; nor would it escape the modern-day audience that certain modern-day associations are present, most notably the comparison between him and drug dealers of the present time.

The designer now has to make some decisions: how to merge the physical descriptions of the character with the nature of his trade. The use of a metaphorical image aids in this process; in this case it allows us to think of the character in terms that play on our revulsions and fears. Let us adopt for our metaphorical image that of a rat skulking about the dark alleys of a city slum (fig. 61). Using this image we begin to imagine not only a range of colors and textures for the costume—heavy shaggy textures in mottled grays and dirty browns, grizzled matted hair, long skeletal fingers with broken nails, perhaps dark sunken eyes with *"overwhelming brows"* (Shakespeare's word for *overhanging*)—but for the actor's movement as well. Metaphor used in this manner connects clues in the text directly to our own experience; thinking in this manner is the real basis of all theatrical thinking. It should also be noted, moreover, that the most important purpose for using metaphor in the design process is not to make the audience overtly aware of the imagery employed but, rather, to give a focal point to our own creative thoughts while giving a sense of direction to our work. Using metaphorical imagery is one of the few practical ways to integrate into the overall context of the production characters who appear for a few brief moments and then vanish. Metaphorical images should, therefore, resonate in the subconscious parts of the viewer's mind, not thrust themselves into the forefront of attention. No one in the audience should ever say when the apothecary appears: "Ah, a dirty rat!" What they should *feel*, however, is an unease and apprehension as the brief desperate scene takes place and to feel some of Romeo's own pity and loathing for both himself and for the situation in which he finds himself. Figure 62 shows how a costume designer might incorporate some of these things just discussed.

If there is one major trend discernible in the progress of costume design during the past hundred years, it is this: the costume designer has become less and less just a dressmaker who supplies vaguely appropriate costumes and more and more a creative artist whose techniques, knowledge, and artistry have progressed far beyond just knowing how to sew a straight seam, cut a pattern, or dye a piece of cloth.

Fig. 61. Urban rat

Fig. 62. Costume for apothecary

The Scenographer's Relationship to the Director

In *Creativity in the Theater*, Philip Weissman writes, "no performance of a written work of art can be more than a single interpretation. The greatness of a director depends on his capacities to identify with the creator and to create in performance an optimal and original communication that enhances the author's creation without distorting it. A director identifies with the contents of the created work and interests himself in communicating its contents. He is more identified with the dramatist or composer than with the audience. " In an article by Harold Clurman called "In a Different Language," a director says this of his profession:

That action speaks louder than words is the first principle of the stage; the director . . . is the "author" of the stage action. Gestures and movement, which are the visible manifestations of action, have a different language from that which the playwright uses, although the playwright hopes that his words will suggest the kind of action that ought to be employed. The director must be a master of theatrical action, as the dramatist is master of the written concept of his play. . . .

It is rarely the director's intention to alter the playwright's meaning. (Of course this has often been done—consciously as well as unconsciously—and occasionally with very happy results.) But it is a mistake amounting to ignorance to believe that the playwright's meaning is necessarily conveyed by merely mouthing the playwright's dialogue and following his stated instructions. In a sense the playwright's text disappears the moment it reaches the stage, because on the stage it becomes part of an action, every element of which is as pertinent to its meaning as the text itself. (*Theater Arts* 34 [January 1950])

The philosophy of interpretation that underlies these statements applies not only to the director but to the scenographer as well. It also, in part, helps to clarify the similarity of purpose and artistic bond between them. Although their materials and techniques differ greatly, the aims of both are especially similar. In a successful collaboration, both personalities might very well be evident, but just as some aspects of observations are directed by thought and some by purely visual response, so it is with the director's and scenographer's contributions. One might say that the scenographer's role is to act as another pair of eyes to the director-mind. This relationship is not unlike that of different parts of a single human body; they are separated but not unrelated. What these different parts do are part of a single function: interpretation of the playwright's words. In a successful production, it is often impossible to separate these two influencing forces into individual contributions. That all too often the work of the director and the scenographer exist side by side with little or no relationship of one to the other is testimony to the fact that this desired collaboration does not happen automatically or effortlessly. In fact, the odds always seem to be heavily weighed against it.

Perhaps we should take a brief look at the development of this relationship between the modern director and scenographer. From the middle decades of the nineteenth century until the early years of this, the philosophical approach held to be the most advanced solution to making theater an important art was this: *one person had to be in charge.* Even today the most common perception of how theater works is that any successful production must come from a single person with a single viewpoint. Subordinate talents are, of course, needed to implement this singular viewpoint, but the power to make conceptual decisions must not be shared. For almost one hundred fifty years we have been largely under the influence of such theatrical visionaries: Richard Wagner (who first articulated the concept of theater as an integrated work of art), the Duke of Saxe-Meiningen (who insisted on accurately researched settings and costume), Gordon Craig (the father of modern scenography), and Adolphe Appia (who first saw the dramatic possibilities of electric light). All held a similar view of what theater should be: an institution that would not attain its rightful place in the world until it produced artists whose vision was uncompromising and whose word was law. In practice, none of these men ever completely attained this vision, but they were instrumental in the creation of a mythical creature— the omniscient super director—that still is a stock character in many films and plays that have theater directors as characters. In figure 63 we have a diagram that shows the route by which commands and ideas would be channeled down

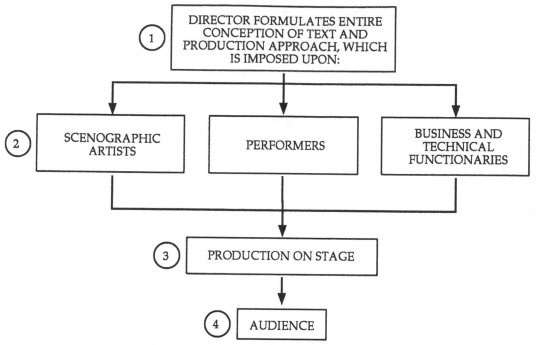

Fig. 63. Chart showing dictatorial approach to production

from the all-powerful director to an audience. Rudimentary as this diagram is, it does make clear that little give-and-take is expected or allowed.

It was not until the first decade of this century, however, that a man who fitted the desired description arrived on the scene. Max Reinhardt was the first of stage directors who came close to fulfilling the hopes of his nineteenth-century predecessors. Although there are many fanciful tales concerning Reinhardt and his style as a director, those who knew him best reported he was an eminently reasonable person who was exceptional in the way he was able to solicit the best advice of others, that his success was in large part due to the creative interaction of those he chose to work for him. Probably the only true superdirectors are those who work behind motion-picture cameras—the cinema director— and some few opera directors such as Franco Zeffirelli and the late Jean-Pierre Ponnel.

Reasonableness, quiet assessment of differing points of view, compromise—all elements of any sound directorial approach—make for good theater. Both director and scenographer must be, in the truest sense of the word, *reasonable* people. A more helpful diagram would be,

therefore, one like that shown in figure 64. This more nearly approximates the true path of concepts as they make their way from inception to a viewing audience. And the very first thing we see in this diagram is that any concept must undergo a series of steps, *all of which in some way alter the original intent.* As Tyrone Guthrie intimated earlier, compromise is the rule of the theater, not the exception. Far from being a limiting or negative process, new and original thoughts and concepts are brought about by such a progress. Furthermore, the continual testing of ideas by the process indicated in figure 64 better assures that needed changes to a production will be identified and accomplished. One should not forget, however, that concepts too quickly adopted often suffer two major misfortunes: (1) they never become completely integrated into the major design of the production, or (2) they cause the production to take a wrong direction, a situation that can subvert the intention of all concerned.

What we see in figure 64 is only a general outline as to how the director/scenographer relationship might work. It is an abstract plan and, like all abstract plans, is not based on the actual way any one director/scenographer team works.

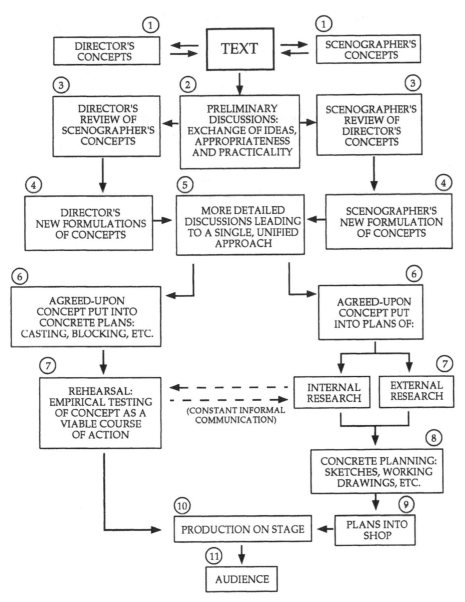

Fig. 64. Chart showing director's relationship to scenographer

It would be helpful to us, therefore, to listen to an actual director's thoughts on this subject. Here is William Ball's advice to directing students taken from his book, *A Sense of Direction*:

Design Conferences

Each director relates to his stage designer and his costume designer in a unique and personal way. . . .

In talking to the designers, it is important to begin discussion with a description of the general beauty. Leave discussion of mechanical details until a later time. In order to make the best use of the designer's creative imagination, it is valuable to begin by telling him what excites you about the play and why you find it beautiful.

In our early discussions, we agree on a metaphor. And [ask] designers [to] present ideas for the metaphors, such as photographs and paintings. It is essential that the director and . . . designers agree; there must be [an] agreement on the metaphor, because the metaphor will be a limiting factor [for] all . . . of us in the preparation of the production.

It is crucial that the director be specific in sharing his impressions. Be very open with the designers, tell them your secret thoughts about the play, tell them extraneous thoughts, thematic thoughts, impressions, dreams, resemblances, jokes. Tell them what the play reminds you of. Tell them in poetic terms, in dream terms, in casual terms, in peculiar terms. We take this impressionistic approach because the designers are listening for clues. We cannot be sure in advance what will awaken their imaginations, so we talk freely about our impressions. We talk generally and vividly about the peculiarities of the writing. We talk about the rhythm, the speed of the play, the movement, the color. We talk about every impression, and we ask the designers for their impressions of the play. And among this great salad of impressions, the director and the designers gradually find an image emerging that increases their mutual enthusiasm. . . . It is important to let them go home with their thoughts, allowing time for gestation and synthesis.

I always ask the designers to work in pencil and to come to me with rough sketches, because once a designer has done a completed rendering, replete with detail and color, it is almost impossible to get him to change anything. It is better that his ideas be expressed in many sketches so that we can work together on changes and modifications. . . .

Some directors are easy to please and use everything that is given to them by the designers. I tend to ask endless questions. "Will this coat have inside pockets? How many steps will it take to get upstairs? Will the risers be five inches, seven and one-half inches, or nine inches? Will the banisters bear weight? Will the door slam? With a wooden sound or a metal click? Will the sofa be cushy? Will the panes of glass reflect light? Will the walls wobble? . . . I tend to plague the designer about these details, partly to assure myself, and partly to be prepared to tell the actor all about them. I want there to be as few surprises as possible when the technical rehearsal date arrives.

What underlies much of the advice Ball gives to the student of directing is that the director must make the scenographer part of his own function. This philosophy is an apt one: the expert use of experts is perhaps the director's most important function in the staging of a production. This all but precludes the dictatorial approach discussed earlier. The only place one is likely to find the autocratic approach to production in evidence is where experts are in short supply; smaller college and university theater departments or community theaters are more apt to spawn the all-powerful director than would be found in professional companies.

It would be well that we now look more

closely into both the explicit and implicit assumptions the diagram in figure 64 makes. It is important that while such a plan as presented there is abstract and to some ideal, it still represents working philosophies more useful to the student scenographer than does the diagram outlining the dictatorial approach.

As Ball intimates in his remarks, he wants those scenographers working with him to understand his concerns and visions. Some directors, like Ball, are able to think in terms similar to the scenographer's (some, in fact, were scenographers before they became full-time directors; Franco Zeffirelli, quoted below, is such a director) and are able to speak the language of scenography, to make clear their ideas to the scenographers with whom they work. These directors, strangely enough, are often less dictatorial than those to whom scenography is a closed book written in a foreign language. Very few scenographers have not had the experience of working with a director who simply could not visualize in one scale—the working plans, models, sketches—what would eventually be rendered in another. And how often has been heard the complaint, "I didn't know that *that* was what it would really look like," or the defense, "I don't know what I want until I *see* it on the stage."

There are directors, though, and the number is increasing steadily, since theater schools have begun training directors and scenographers to work together, that are able to express their directorial concepts in images and words the scenographer can understand and make use of in his own search for a scenic concept. Most scenographers do not, I think, feel this is an intrusion into their private areas of creativity. As a matter of fact, it is not uncommon for a scenographer to become so involved in the problems of the director that he actually begins to direct himself. Take for instance the example of Franco Zeffirelli mentioned above; a successful scenographer who has become an even more successful director. Although, as we saw earlier, Zeffirelli has during the past decade received criticism for his increasingly elaborate productions, we can still benefit from his comments made during an earlier period of his career. Let us then, as with William Ball, listen to his thoughts concerning the visual aspects of direction. As you read, particularly note that he is unable to keep his "scenographer's eye" from determining much of the action in the scenes he describes.

You don't need many ideas (in directing a play), you need one. On that you work and the idea carries you if it's right. . . . [Each of his interpretations he reports is based on a controlling image, a core.] In *Cavalleria* [*Rusticanna*] I have always seen the core as a wide white street going uphill in a Sicilian village, that and the sky. At night the wind blows, and a tiny figure with a black shawl comes down running, closing under her shawl her pain and sorrow. It is the destiny of some Sicilian women. I built the set that way. The stage hands at Covent Garden can tell how fussy I was about the platform. The curtain goes up on the prelude. After that it's easy. You are on your path and you follow the consequence. What happens at dawn in Sicily? All the old women come to church. And so on. . . . For *Lucia* [*Di Lammermoor*], mine was the image of a woman shouting in a tremendous room, a castle hall, with her wedding veil covered with blood, crying and chasing her cries. How would a woman arrive at that point? How? I couldn't bear a kind of mechanical bird performance in the mad scene. It's a great tragic scene. (*Directors on Directing*, ed. Toby Cole and Helen Chinoy)

Zeffirelli is by no means—although in recent years he has become more so—only a pictorial director. He has in many designs demonstrated a strong commitment to the playwright's text as well as the scenic environment. Still, we see here a director reinforcing the concept that the correct scenic image is of great importance to a successful production. Zeffirelli does, in fact, use visual artists other than himself in his cinema productions. Much of Zeffirelli's motion-picture work clearly shows that both the director and the scenographer can, as separate creators, interest themselves in the other's function, as in the case of his 1966 *The Taming of the Shrew* and 1968 *Romeo and Juliet*.

Sometimes, however, although the scenographer and director may work in close harmony and understanding, the resulting collaboration is something less than artistically successful. Why should this be; how does this situation come about? It is easy to understand failure when they do not cooperate with one another. What possible explanation could there be for failure when these two do work together? Peter Brook, in his book *The Empty Space* touches on this matter and offers some thoughts from the director's point of view.

In performance, the relationship is actor/subject/audience. In rehearsal it is actor/subject/director. The earliest relationship is director/subject/designer. Scenery and costumes can sometimes evolve in rehearsal at the same time as the rest of the performance, but often practical considerations of building and dressmaking force the designer to have his work cut and dried before the first rehearsal. I have often done my own designs. This can be a distinct advantage, but for a very special reason. When the director is working this way, his theoretical understanding of the play and its extension in terms of shapes and colours both evolve at the same tempo. A scene may escape the director for several weeks, one shape in the set may seem incomplete—then as he works on the set he may suddenly find the place of the scene that eludes him; as he works on the structure of the difficult scene he may suddenly glimpse its meaning in terms of stage action or a succession of colours. In work with a designer, a sympathy of tempo is what matters most. I have worked with joy with many marvellous designers—but have at times been caught in strange traps, as when the designer reaches a compelling solution too fast—so that I found myself having to accept or refuse shapes before I had sensed what shapes seemed to be immanent in the text. When I accepted the wrong shape, because I could find no logical reason for opposing the designer's conviction, I locked myself into a trap out of which the production could never evolve, and produced very bad work as a result. *I have often found that the set is the geometry of the eventual play, so that a wrong set makes many scenes impossible to play, and even destroys many possibilities for the actors.* The best designer evolves step by step with the director, going back, changing, scrapping, as a conception of the whole gradually takes form. A director who does his own designs naturally never believes that the completion of the designs can be an end in itself. He knows that he is just at the beginning of a long cycle of growth, because his own work lies before him. Many designers, however, tend to feel that with the delivery of the sets and costume sketches a major portion of their own creative work is genuinely complete. For them, a completed design is complete. Art lovers can never understand why all stage designing isn't done by "great" painters and sculptors. What is necessary, however, is an incomplete design: a design that has clarity without rigidity; one that could be called "open" as against "shut." This is the essence of theatrical thinking; a true theatre designer will think of his designs as being all the time in motion, in action, in relation to what the actor brings to a scene as it unfolds. In other words, unlike the easel painter, in two dimensions, or the sculptor in three, the designer thinks in terms of the fourth dimension, the passage of time—not the stage picture, but the stage moving picture. A film editor shapes his material after the event: the stage designer is often like the editor of an Alice-Through-the-Looking-Glass film, cutting dynamic material in shapes, before this material has yet come into being. The later he makes his decisions, the better. (Italics mine)

Of course it is impossible to set down an ideal work plan that the scenographer and director could always follow to ensure a successful collaboration; too many factors exist, and these factors change from production to production. Certain principles, however, can be evolved (as both William Ball and Peter Brook imply in the statements we have read) that help keep open channels of communication.

Now let us proceed to a more detailed outline of some basic functions the director and scenographer directly share. As we have noted, the work of the director and the work of the scenographer moves on roughly parallel tracks. Both tracks, however, comprize eight levels of shared functions. These are:

1. *Reads texts.* Both read the text many times from various perspectives in order to determine the general outline of the narrative and way the language of the text serves the narrative.

2. *Analyzes texts.* Both make preliminary assessments as to how the intention of the text relates to the performer's physical requirements—properties, levels, spatial distances—and both attempt to determine how these relate to the performers' patterns of movement. Both also make preliminary determination of the play's eventual emotional background as described or implied in the text: perceived mood, color and tonality, times of day or year, weather conditions, qualities of sound.

3. *Interprets texts.* Both make individual judgments as to what direction to pursue but then must coordinate individual assessments into an agreed-upon plan of action: i.e., style of production, form of stage space, period to be adopted, level of reality to be attempted, attendance to performer's explicit physical needs, range and nature of images and metaphors to be incorporated into production.

4. *Research initiated.* Both gather images that embody metaphors or shows visual interpreta-tions of text's implications. Both search for documents, outside written sources and commentaries that support or explain selected images and text's requirements. Both assemble physical examples of tonalities, textures, images of objects required or to be interpolated into the production.

5. *Research assimilated and assessed.* Both make a unified presentation of all information gathered. At this point, however, the work of the director and the work of the scenographer begins to separate into specialized functions. While the visual records of the gathered ideas, thoughts, images, and metaphors selected will remain similar, the technical means of implementing them will begin to diverge. It is also during this period that a re-evaluation of all initial decisions and materials gathered thus far should be undertaken.

6. *Concrete planning.* Both begin to record (but in their own languages) the decisions and agreements reached. For the director this means making visual patterns of action (i.e., blocking notes and diagrams) along with precise notes of production needs. For the scenographer this means getting or making not only firm commitments to the stage for style of production, period details, physical requirements of setting, objects, costume (if the production is totally designed by one person), spatial relationships but also decisions as to the means of scenic change, agreement on quality of light for each scene (if production is not lighted by scenographer, which is the increasingly more common situation).

7. *Instruction to others.* At this point both undertake supervisory functions. The director works primarily with performers. The scenographer works primarily with scenic craftsmen: carpenters, scenic painters, metal workers, property makers. It is important to note that there must remain a constant communication between the director and the scenographer—as outlined in figure 64—in order to keep abreast of the many physical changes that accompanies all productions. Every professional theater worker knows that the best reason to make detailed plans is to ensure the time necessary to change them.

8. *Observation and refinement.* Both the director and scenographer must continually reevaluate both their own work and the work of those they supervise. For the director, this means refining patterns of movement or reblocking patterns not

viable, ensuring that themes and motivations are integrated with the performer's intentions and with the physical elements of the production. For the scenographer, communication with the director has a twofold obligation: (1) to assure that the physical elements of the production match the decisions made in point 6 of this outline and (2) to ensure that the various shops and craftsmen executing the physical production are aware of any changes made during the director's work with the performers.

This is the basic pattern of work followed in the translation of a dramatic text into a production for the stage. There will always be, of course, minor variations to the pattern; no two directors and no two scenographers work exactly alike. The pattern is also affected by the kind of producing organization involved. Nevertheless, the essential outline can be expected to remain roughly constant for all modes of production regardless of production type or size, or producing organization.

A few philosophical words are in order as we close this subject. In a scenographer's period of training, one frequently encounters directors who seem to possess total control over every aspect of any given production. In the professional theater, however, director and scenographer are more apt to consider each other as coworkers who are roughly equal in the interpretation of production's text. Each, ideally, has the primary intention of serving the best interests of the text. The master-subordinate relationship between director and scenographer is a rarity in today's theater. And while the director quite often is the first of these two to be retained, and, consequently, has started his conceptual work earlier than the scenographer, many directors make a conscious effort to "leave the door open" to the thoughts and concepts of the person who has been commissioned to design the production. This is because the intelligent director fully realizes that it is in his best interests to keep open and free channels of communication with other sensitive like-minded artists; a good director knows that an ill-considered design can irreparably mar an otherwise brilliantly conceived production. The best work on Broadway, in London, and, indeed, throughout the world gives testimony to the care with which directors forge alliances with "known quantities": Jo Mielziner

and Elia Kazan, Harold Prince and Boris Aronson, Peter Hall and John Bury, to name but a few examples. The discussions that take place when these artists meet are only productive to the extent that both enter with open minds. In *Creating Theater*, by Lee Alan Morrow and Frank Pike, Emily Mann says that *"a director can find a play through the designers. I like to get them into the process early. Even as a writer I've often found a play first through a designer."* While all working scenographers over the years will have their patience tested many times in many places, the professional theater is still a much more reasonable place than popular conception of it often allows.

During the remainder of this book the relationship we have been discussing should never be far from the reader's mind. Scenographers cannot perform their jobs successfully unless they find ways to cooperate with the directors with whom they work while still preserving their own artistic integrity. It often difficult but it can be done.

The Language of Space

In *The Concept of Action in Painting*, Harold Rosenberg says: "Action is . . . a means of probing, of going from stage to stage of discovery. If someone asks me a question, my answer will come from the surface of my mind. But if I start to write the answer, or to paint it, or to act it out, the answer changes. What is being done provides a clue to another thought."

The creation of static images is commonly thought to be the scenographer's primary function in theater; that is only partially correct. Scenographers do make visual images: sketches, set renderings, working plans, and numbers of other kinds of drawings. Contributing to the creation of active images on the stage is a better description of the scenographer's function. But, it is not possible to assess this contribution without an understanding of the kind of space he gives the performer to occupy. And the kind of space supplied depends upon how the playwright or composer regards its nature and what demands as to its use they have embedded in their written texts and musical scores.

Although concepts of space have existed throughout man's recorded history, it has only been during this century that any great attention has been given to the concept that there might be more precise meanings inherent in spatial relationships in the theater than heretofore imagined. (This kind of thinking, however, has been an integral part of Japanese art and culture for hundreds of years.) There is a much wider acceptance now, and especially during the last half of this century, that spatial relationships in the theater involve a more precise kind of language, a more reasoned approach than we formerly thought. The study of stage design has become largely the study of changing spatial relationships.

When we discuss space in the theater, we often assume a certain approach to the subject without sufficiently pinpointing the specific nature of that approach. We agree that there is a language of spatial relationships (and that they just *might* affect scenography), but we often do not seek further as to how this language relates to other elements of scenographic training: scenic sketching, the study of art history, or the understanding of stage mechanics. These subjects tend to remain isolated areas of study. Nevertheless even the least informed of present-day students seem to be aware of the implications of a language of space than were their counterparts a hundred years ago. But there appears to be a wide gap still between the recognition that such a language exists and the ability to make a knowledgeable use of it in a specifically predictable way. Few training in the theater today would not have some comprehension of what Peter Brook means when he says, "I can take an empty space and call it a stage." Very few, however, could adequately explain the meanings underlying such a statement or the philosophy that informs such a thought. And while I would expect many students of theater to comprehend Shakespeare's aphorism, "All the world's a stage, and all the men and women merely players," I would not really expect many to be able to specifically relate or explain Shakespeare's words to Brook's concept. And yet, simple as both the words and the concept are, I have often found that there is little understanding that Shakespeare and Brook have in common this basic philosophy: that the stage, no matter its restrictions or imperfections,

is a place set apart from everyday experience; that it is a kind of no-man's land but at the same time every-man's land—a place that is both limited in time and space and at the same time unlimited in time and space, a place where anything that can be conceived can be shown. A closer look into this special conception of space is the subject we now need to investigate.

First, we should define more carefully the kinds of space that can be perceived. But while these are to a large extent arbitrary designations—all of which overlap—it is to our eventual advantage to attempt an understanding of how our concept of these designations affects our thinking and work in the theater.

It is possible to categorize the modern-day conceptions of space in several ways. For our purposes, we will look at three of these: real, cultural, and scenographic.

Real Space

This is the kind of space we all live in day to day. Actually, what we call space is not a thing at all but simply the most convenient way of discussing the distance between objects and objects or objects and ourselves. The intensely exciting development of the ability to free ourselves of this planet with space vehicles has given such an emotional charge to the term *space* that the word has taken on a meaning that obscures the fact we are still only talking about relational distances, not a thing in itself. One of the most intriguing aspects of man's intellectual development is that he has come to regard certain relationships—and space provides a good example—as something tangible, when, in fact, it is simply the absence of the tangible that is our real focus. We have even begun to use the term *space* to describe certain stages of being that do not actually involve physical distance; for instance, it is not at all uncommon to hear one speak of *"exploring inner space."* Suspect as the term *real space* has become, however (and, of course, we must be aware that even such a designation is a contradiction in terms), our use of it here is necessary to bridge to a better understanding of the kind of space that Brook implies in his book and Shakespeare infers in his plays.

Cultural Space

During the past few decades we have seen a great interest displayed in seeking out information on the diverse cultures that inhabit this earth. This interest has resulted in a growing body of works that span a number of fields: archaeology, anthropology, religion, art, and, not least among these, theater. We have, as a world civilization, made tremendous strides in attempting to understand one another, to give respectful understanding of how we differ from one culture to the next, and to how national behaviors vary as we move from country to country. It is gratifying to note, moreover, that Western culture has made tremendous strides in freeing itself from the notion that there is an absolute hierarchy of cultural development directly linked to levels of technology and that Western culture (being the most technologically advanced) is the unquestioned apex of that hierarchy. This reassessment of the values of differing cultural views has given rise to an increasing number of studies that deal specifically with the social implications of the differences that occur as one goes from culture to culture. And one of the most important—and for the most part, most hidden—aspects of these studies is the way in which different societies give specific meanings to spatial relationships within that society. These studies have given a tremendous advantage to us not only in the understanding of other cultures but in the better understanding of the often questionable assumptions of our own. In our own culture we have always been aware that there were certain basic ways in which one group differed from another; these were often so visually evident that understanding got no further than observation of the fact. Nor did we ever question that most basic of assumptions that *familiar is good, different is bad*. While it is not possible to say that there is a universal lessening of parochial judgment, the willingness of many cultures to attempt an understanding of other points of view has led to a tremendous cross-fertilization in the arts. The theater in particular has greatly benefited by these exchanges. But then, the theater has always, in a very real sense, been a peacemaker; when Shakespeare affirms that "All the world's a stage," he is saying that we are indeed all different, but in our differences, much the same. He does not excuse or apologize for those differences, just draws our attention to their existence. Notwithstanding the fact that we must all come from somewhere, and are what we are precisely because we do come from a particular background, those who work in the theater should realize that just as their art spans time and space, they too should make the attempt to free themselves from the crippling effects of too limited a view of the world in which they live. Nor must they ever be so careless in the practice of their particular art to forget that as they deal with the dramatic literature of different cultures and different times, there will always be something missing from their work if they investigate only styles of architecture, periods of furniture, dress or utilitarian object and neglect to search out those aspects of cultures foreign to them that tell not only what was used and how but in what special (and spatial) circumstances.

Just how is this information to be gained? Where do we go to find instruction on this important aspect of a theater artist's education? A good start can be made by reading *The Hidden Dimension*, by Edward T. Hall, a work dealing specifically with the various ways different cultures approach spatial relationships. In this important study, Hall draws our attention to the difference between the traditional Japanese conception of space from the way it is perceived and used in European culture. He tells us: "The early designers of the Japanese garden apparently understood something of the interrelationship between the kinesthetic experience of space and the visual experience. Lacking wide-open spaces, and living close together as they do, the Japanese learned to make the most of small spaces. . . . In the use of interior space, the Japanese keep the edges of their rooms clear because everything takes place in the middle. Europeans tend to fill up the edges by placing furniture near or against walls. As a consequence, Western rooms often look less cluttered to the Japanese than they do to us."

(In Japan, Hall tells us later, the Japanese have even given a name for that which we perceive to be nonexistent: the *Ma*, which like our word space, is not actually the name of a thing but the designation of the particular space that exists between objects. In Japanese philosophy and in Japanese art—much of which is an exten-

sion of that philosophy—this distinction demands a respectful understanding and is therefore given as much dutiful attention as are the
objects that establish the boundaries of the *Ma*.
In the paintings of Cézanne—one of the founding fathers of twentieth-century painting and
both a student as well as admirer of Japanese
art—there is this same attention paid to negative
space and its inclusion as an important aspect of
composition.)

How an individual culture uses space, we can
begin to see, tells much about what the values
of the culture are. It is not possible, for instance,
to understand the London of Dickens's time—
nor Dickens himself, for that matter—unless we
also understand that it was not only an overpop-
ulated city but an aggressively social city in spite
of the often horrendously uncomfortable conditions experienced by its ever-increasing population. Gustave Doré, in numerous drawings, has
left us ample proof that although London was
bursting at the seams, that was exactly the way
the populace of the day wanted it; that the citizens of the place took every opportunity to be in
the streets with their fellow citizens. In the cinema version of Reginald Barth's musical *Oliver*,
based on Dickens's *Oliver Twist*, this understanding of how the inhabitants of London be-
haved was the conceptual basis of the film's choreography. If one wishes a better understanding
of Londoner's feelings concerning the utilization
of space during the nineteenth century, Henry
Mayhew's *Poor of London* is a source of information difficult to match. This four-volume work
(now available in a Dover paperback edition) is
an invaluable compilation of facts and commentary detailing the lives of numerous individuals,
groups, and social levels that coexisted in London during the middle and later half of the nineteenth century. All scenographers should be
aware of this important work, one of the principal documents to come to us from that age.

Scenographic Space

In an article, "Recent Trends in Scenery Design: Twenty Years of Scenography," Denis Bablet says this:

The French word "decor" is a conventional term
that we continue to use because habits are deeply

rooted, but it is an obsolete one. . . . The designer's
task is no longer to ornament or to embellish, to create
a shrine for the production. . . . the setting is today
an interpreter of the play, an actor. In many cases, of
course, it must still specify or evoke the scenes of the
action, but above all it acts out and reveals the action,
stresses or explains its meanings.

The first step towards making dramatic action possible is to create the dramatic space. A Mertz or a
Neher, a Svoboda, a Sean Kenny or an Acquart conceive, in agreement with the director, an organization
of the scenic space that is functional in relation to the
play, to the staging, to the actor and to the public.
They model a stage floor, they portion out acting areas, create different levels. They trace axes, prescribe
lines of circulation, in a word, *they establish a scenic
architecture of which each element becomes indispensable,
brings out the relationship that unites the characters, accentuates the signification of the actor's slightest gesture.* They
are creators of space. It is understandable that many
designers prefer to style themselves "scenographers,"
the term so justly employed in Central Europe. (Italics
mine)

We have arrived at the point where the term
space must be given a deeper more precise meaning, since the way we will begin to use the term
differs markedly from the way it is used outside
the theater. It is also at this point we must begin
the attempt to understand Peter Brook's first
sentence in *The Empty Space*: I can take any empty
space and call it a bare stage.

Tyrone Guthrie was once asked in an interview what his most precise definition of the stage
was. He answered: "It is whatever I say it is."
He was then asked: What do you you think
Shakespeare would say if asked the same question? Guthrie thought for only the shortest of
moments and then replied: "He would probably
say that it was whatever *he* said it was." The
interviewer then asked: Who would be right?
This time Guthrie did not hesitate: "We'd work
something out—we always have."

While these remarks were made with good-
natured lightness, they give, as Guthrie was
asked to do, a precise definition of what the stage
meant to him: it was, as he said, a place that
could be whatever he wanted it to be and—although he did not specifically say so—a place
where he had found it necessary to compromise.
One cannot help but notice that what Guthrie
said and what Brook says is remarkably similar;
in substance their philosophies are identical. The

stage is, for everyone who works on it, just such a place as Brook and Guthrie have defined. It is infinitely accommodating and must be accommodated infinitely. At the heart of all theater practice lies this Janus-like duality, this mysterious place that is every place and no place. Still, "It goes with the territory," as Willy Loman might say.

In Thornton Wilder's *Our Town*, we can see this duality clearly at work. The play begins as the Stage Manager walks onto a bare stage. It is his function to lead us through the past lives of various inhabitants of a small New England town. He does this by sometimes taking a role in the play, at other times standing outside time and commenting on what is passing and what has passed in the town's history. In his first appearance, however, his job is to locate for us just where he stands and where we are: "The name of the town is Grover's Corners, New Hampshire—just across the Massachusetts line: longitude 42 degrees 40 minutes; latitude 70 degrees 37 minutes." It is doubtful if any in the audience take this information at face value; who there would seriously wonder how far they had to travel to reach home after leaving the theater? What Wilder has done, through the character of the Stage Manager on that bare stage, is to establish the point that we in the audience are no longer seeing events in real space or in real time, but in a different element, a different kind of world that, most important of all, demands a different attitude toward space and time. He asks that we compromise—as Guthrie and Shakespeare and Brook also ask—with that so-called real world outside the theater in order that he be able to show us another *real* world: a world of the imagination that can transport us to anywhere at anytime to see anything. One should also note (a kind of paradox, if you will) that although the playwright has taken the greatest care to establish the setting of his play with precise measurements needed to locate a geographical point in that outside world, what he is really saying is, "You are now playing in my ballpark and I make the rules." Like Guthrie and Shakespeare and Brook, the playwright is, on a bare featureless plane with nothing else to aid him, *setting the terms of the bargain he wishes to strike with his audience.* Wilder is not unique in demanding such an understanding: many present-day play-

wrights feel that is an inherent right of the modern theater to use time and space in the freest possible manner, provided the purpose and understanding of this usage are not lost in the innovation. Nor do I believe this demand—despite an increasing use of scenic technology to create elaborate replicas of real things and places—puts an undue burden on the understanding of an audience; if anything, there is a growing awareness that spectators surfeited on television and cinematic reality actually welcome playing a more active role in the use of their imaginations.

It is also important for scenographers in today's theater to learn that while a great part of their day-to-day work depends upon subdividing that bare plane with the utmost care and accuracy, they should not forget that much of the real work of scenography lies in finding ways to assure that each scene of a production has set its own boundaries through its internal requirements. Just how this is done will occupy our thoughts during the rest of the text. For the moment, however, let us demonstrate one aspect of the principles we are examining in this section of the book. Let us also take note how a spatial relationship, having been established, can alter its basic nature as the time-space framework of the scene changes.

In Arthur Miller's *Death of a Salesman*, the play begins in real time and is to be understood as taking place in an actual locale capable of being found geographically. Although Miller does not give us the exact location of Willy Loman's house—as the Stage Manager does in *Our Town*—he does state that Willy visits various places in New York and Boston of his time (the early 1950s). It is certainly reasonable to assume, therefore, that this is Willy's selling territory and that he lives somewhere between the two cities. Miller also gives us, in his written stage directions immediately preceding act 1, not only a description of the house in which the main action of the play takes place but also information concerning the immediate surroundings: the back yard, the buildings that close in on his small lot. These specific directions (few of which are the original writings of the playwright but are, rather, the revised directions and descriptions applied to the play during and after its Broadway production) tell us two things: first, that the play is basically a naturalistic one, at least to the point that it deals with recognizable people experiencing actual situations in what we would call a *real world*, and second, that we cannot simply assume that that is the entire story; that within that framework of reality, some strange things might indeed happen; that time and place may very well lose its accustomed shape, form, and reality. This is, in point of fact, what does happen as the play unfolds. Within the first few pages of the play's text we see a bending of the laws of time and material; and it is the precise task of the scenographer to make this change of worlds not only evident to an audience but understandable. Jo Mielziner, in the original Broadway production solved the problems set by the playwright in the following manner:

1. Willy's entrance from the unseen garage is some distance (not the nearest) from the back door to the kitchen of his house (fig. 65A). To reach that back door, Willy must take the longest route to it (fig. 65B). Willy enters through a small trellis at the far side of the yard and starts the trek to the kitchen door. He walks slowly with some effort: this trip is in some ways a symbolic acting out of the many trips with the same heavy sample bags he has made over the years. But we can see even in this short walk that the years have taken their toll and that Willy is a profoundly tired man. The scenographer in league with the director has forced Willy to take the *longest possible path* in order to reach the necessary entrance to the house. (We should note here the scenographer and director have already established important conventions for this setting: that is, although the house has no actual walls to it, the actor cannot step onto the platform at any point without violating an established convention; he can only get into the house by going to the designated kitchen door.)

2. Once in the room—which in actuality is only some inches above the outside of the house—Willy's actions are restricted by the smallness of the kitchen area. (The actor could, of course, at any time he chooses, step off that slight level; he will not do so—until specifically given permission—because playwright, scenographer, director, and actor have agreed, walls or not, that area *is* the kitchen and that, seen or not, there are real physical barriers that cannot be violated. Acceptance of this convention, moreover, is an absolute necessity to the dramatic structure of this play.)

3. After preliminary conversation with his wife, Willy opens the refrigerator and removes a bottle of milk. The stage direction reads: *He pours milk into a glass. He is totally immersed in himself, smiling faintly.* As he does this he begins to talk to himself; his mind begins to wander

Fig. 65. Diagram showing movement pattern

back to a happier time, a time when he and his sons were on better terms, a time when he was not as old and tired; a time when he was still considered an important salesmen, a man to be envied and emulated by younger salesmen. Here the stage direction reads: *Willy is gradually addressing—physically—a point offstage, speaking through the wall of the kitchen, and his voice has been rising in volume to that of a normal conversation.*

4. A short while after Willy begins his interior conversation with the past, he rise and walks off the platform that has, up until this moment, had "physical" walls surrounding it. At this point, Willy, literally, *walks through the wall* into the backyard; but more important still, he walks *backward in time* (fig. 66C). Later in the play, he will not only go back into time but will step into another geographic locale—a hotel room in Boston—not merely his own backyard.

The actions just described and the spatial requirements made of them are extremely simple in concept and execution. What is important to note, however, is that a complex interaction of time, space, and movement was made with a minimum of physical change in scenery; at no time was it necessary to lower a curtain, revolve a turntable, or shift a wagon to effect the change or make the scene understandable to the audience watching it. It is doubtful if an audience of

a hundred years ago would have "read" the scene in the way that a modern audience does; modern-day audiences, whether or not they consciously realize it, have come to accept a whole set of stage conventions their predecessors would have found incomprehensible. It has been during that hundred-year period that the theater has once again found ways to actively engage an audience's imagination. It should also be noted that only through the close cooperation of the scenographer and director that such actions are rendered comprehensible to a viewer in the theater.

Tyrone Guthrie was absolutely right when he said that the stage is *what I say it is*. Shakespeare would be absolutely right if he, as Guthrie supposes, answered the same. What scenographers must constantly keep in mind is that it is their special task to aid both to determine just what they think that "it" is.

There is, however, one very important point that we should understand before we end our discussion of stage space. That is, that any truly workable understanding of the physical stage can only be arrived at through actual experience on the stage. When Peter Brook states, as we have already read, that he believes "that the set is the geometry of the eventual play, so that a wrong set makes many scenes impossible to

Fig. 66. Diagram showing movement pattern

play," he is, in actuality, bringing to our attention the vital hidden requirement of the scenographer's work: the kinesthetic understanding of specific playing areas for specific dramatic problems. Just what does that mean?

"Every little movement has a meaning all its own." Thus goes the lyric of a well-known song. The idea behind these words is not difficult to understand or comprehend; the thought is part of our consciousness, part of our everyday working social relationships with others, which is as applicable to the stranger as well as a friend. We do, in fact, "read" the movements of others and obtain messages from those movements—"body language" has become a popular description of such an understanding. Some of these messages are obvious and occur to us as conscious thought; others are intuited and are received subliminally as feelings. In all cases, however, we are aware that movement does, as the song points out, have meanings that are the result of purposeful patterns of action. And although not as easily seen or charted, these patterns, taken in a sequence of time, require a precise physical amount of space. These patterns do not usually, though, leave physical traces: the dancer moving in a large circle does not produce an actual circle on the floor. Nevertheless, in terms of time one can make the case that the circle does exist; first, in the mind of the choreographer who conceived of it and, second, in the understanding of the scenographer who must either provide the physical space needed or at least leave that space unencumbered with physical objects. This circle is an actual *shape* that although only perceived in time must be allowed for in space. This is what Brook means when he talks of "shapes . . . immanent in the text." Actors, much like dancers, create such shapes as they move through the enactment of a text. Just as it is important that the choreographer be able to *see* these shapes in the composition of dance, it is equally important that the scenographer—in tandem with the director—see in a written text the possible paths actors might take. Evolution of a total spatial pattern is the key to a workable floor plan for a particular play. The "sympathy of tempo," which Brook also seeks in his work with a scenographer very much involves the agreement of both as to the physical parameters of such a plan.

Now, it is quite possible that the entire work of a scenographer for a particular production can be done within the confines of a studio or at some place other than the actual stage on which the production will occur. But it is extremely important that the nature of that space be understood *kinesthetically* as well as *conceptually*. This sounds abstract, but it is actually a simple proposition in practice. What is meant here is that the scenographer, who has physically walked out the space on the empty stage where the eventual scenographic design is to be, before any scenic element has been conceived of or built for a particular scene, is much more able to conceive and design a specific plan, a specific place for actions immanent in, and appropriate to, the text to occur. If, on the other hand, spatial problems and actions suggested in the text are restricted only to oral discussions away from the site where they will be performed, then the understanding of the shapes immanent in the text will be at best arbitrary and tentative. As an example, consider this situation: someone wishes to know the exact distance between one point on a map and another. Looking at a topographical map of the area (which is analogous to a floor plan) will show exactly how far a mile is; and it is fully possible to determine where a hill is or where a stream might occur along a certain path of movement. But the person who has *actually* walked that mile, has climbed that hill, or has crossed that stream will have an understanding of that path the most detailed study of the map could not provide. The point is that the information is received kinesthetically, not conceptually, and is all the more valuable for having been experienced physically, not abstractly.

This analogy may seem strained; most scenographers simply do not have time or opportunity to "walk out" the stage in order to arrive at a kinesthetically experienced solution to the spatial problems a production poses. Nevertheless to fully understand those "shapes . . . immanent in the text," which Peter Brook thinks it important to do, then the practice is not an idle philosophical goal. And it it important to understand that this kind of activity is a real part of the training that every scenographer should seek out in early training and first experiences. As Jo Mielziner recalls from his own past: "I confess my unbounded delight in my early days at seeing my settings revealed by glamorous stage lighting after they were completed at dress-rehearsal time. I almost resented the prospect of actors standing between my picture and the admiring audience! . . . When I eventually realized how indispensable an imaginative, experienced stage director is to a production, *I began to read a script as though I were going to direct it myself. This did not turn me into a director, but it did make me a better designer*" (italics mine). Mielziner, subsequent to those early productions he recalls, did on many occasions meet with directors on the stages where productions were planned, and in many instances these topics of discussion revolved around the kinds of space they wished to impose on a particular production. The main point we should note here is that when a scenographer turns from the desire to create pictures—as Mielziner's words imply—to the desire to promote action in space, we can begin to glimpse the true relationship of scenography to the theater.

The scenographer should never forget, therefore, that during a performance of any work—play, musical, opera, or ballet—"empty" space is never actually empty but only unoccupied for the moment, that the necessary amount of that empty space is directly related to periods of time when it will be occupied. In sculpture there is a specific term given to a form or group of forms seen in motion. The accepted name for forms seen in motion is *virtual volume*: a three-dimensional shape that only reveals itself in time and movement. If time-lapse photography recorded any object over a period of time, the object at rest would appear considerably different from that same object in motion. (How the wires of a rotary egg-beater, for instance, appear to the eye when they rapidly turn is a good example of virtual volume.) The golfer in figure 67, for example, occupies only a small amount of space while at rest. The moment he takes a swing of the golf club—as shown in figure 68—he automatically increases his need for more space; his action defines the exact parameters of a new volume. Action, therefore, determines the specific amount and form of the space required. While not readily evident in the theater, actors—even performing the slowest or most static of dramatic works—require amounts of space that may not be revealed by any other means except by consciously predicting and combining *all* the kinesthetic needs of the individual performers into a plan. Since this plan can only be seen in time, it often remains unseen to those untrained to appreciate its implications. This kind of thinking

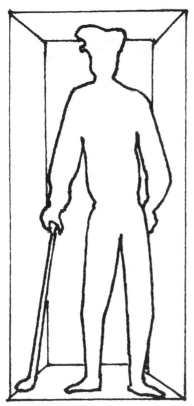

Fig. 67. Golfer at rest

Fig. 68. Golfer in movement

Fig. 69. Scene from *Crime on Goat Island*

is one of the great overlooked considerations in the thinking processes of those new to theater; they very well can see an acorn and can as equally well understand the concept that oaks grow from it; what is not fully grasped is the time frame that shows how the one gets to be the other. And it is precisely this process of performer-action-time-space that often eludes the most careful study of the most dedicated student.

The scenographer, then, is always required to consider both the total amount of space needed for a particular production and the precise shapes—determined by the virtual volume needed for each—into which his design will be divided. This is the real meaning of Adolphe Appia's statement that the scenographer designs with his legs, not with his eyes.

It is not difficult to discern the effect of the

scenographer's visual influence in a scenic environment such as the one shown in figure 69, *Crime on Goat Island* by Ugo Betti. What is not so obviously apparent is how one arrives at certain configurations of object in space. What gives the scenographer the insight to know not only what to include in these configurations but just what spatial relationships are immanent in a text? For almost every scenic environment is, so to speak, arrived at in reverse from life outside the theater; that is, the performers whose actions will be affected by the scenographer's work often come onto the scene *after* the parameters of the space are defined and the physical relationship of the objects within those parameters set. In many instances scenic environments are created before the director and actors arrive. Just how, then can the scenographer know that his decisions will mesh with the work of the director and performer? A partial answer—and probably the only thing that can be said—is that scenography is simply an extension of the directing process; it is not totally preposterous to see in the fashioning of an environment a direct link to performing.

Let us examine one last point before we leave this subject of spatial relationships on the stage. And that is that the scenographer exercises two basic influences on the stage environment: the first and easiest to comprehend is the physical influence. Out of the physical influence arises a second influence that could be categorized as psychological. While psychological influences will not be discussed until a later chapter, the purely physical influences should be mentioned in this section. These can be separated into four distinct categories and are as follows:

1. Floor pattern and level change (fig. 70A)

2. Objects directly used in the action of the production (furniture, seating possibilities, set properties, personal properties [fig. 70B])

3. Barriers that restrict and direct the flow of the performer's actions (fig. 70C)

4. Scenic elements and objects that have a visual influence on the audience but not a direct influence on the performer (fig. 70D)

These influences have all been discussed during this section of the text. They are shown here to illustrate how all are combined into the actual scenic environment.

There is an all-important fifth influence that does not fall within the purview of this text: light and the effects of light on physical form (fig. 71). It is in the use of light, moreover, that one sees the merging of physical and psychological influences. This subject, however, will be left to other writers and other books.

The stage, then, is not just a place where anything can happen but a place where something specific always does: the stage although free of any real time restriction is always in the active present tense. But every action on that stage is, or should be, a specific action to a specific purpose. Every little movement, as the song says, does have a meaning of its own. The role of the scenographer, in equal collaboration with the director and performer, is to fashion out of time and space the only place where the play-

Fig. 70. Spatial influences of scenographer

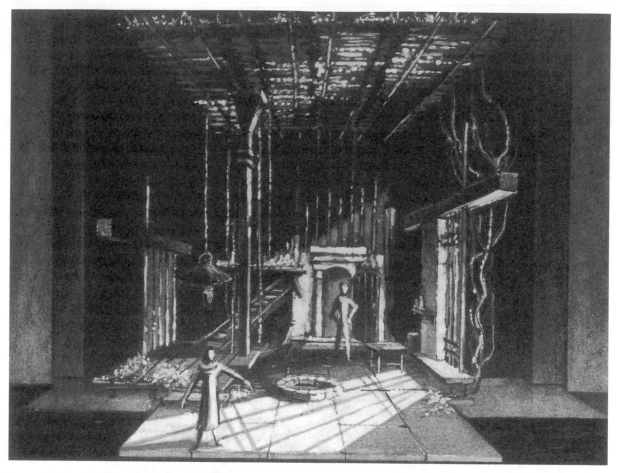

Fig. 71. Effect of light on three-dimension forms

wright's world can exist. And while we must always be aware that what we do as scenographers and directors must be rendered into exact physical dimension and form that may seem to stand apart from the "meaning" of the text, we cannot afford to dismiss or discount that "interior geometry of the play." Just what is a stage, one may ask? *Three boards and a passion,* is the aphoristic answer—which is to say, anything you say it is. The scenographer must never forget that size, shape, and arrangement of those boards must be given as much care as those things we later decide to put upon them. For every project we undertake, a strict attention must be given to sculptor Naum Gabo's astute words, "Space is a material by itself, a structural part of any whole." Scenography, in the final analysis, concerns itself with important questions such as how far Willy Loman must walk before he steps from his backyard into the past.

"The Building or the Theatre"
By Sean Kenny

[This article was written over two decades ago; since then Sean Kenny has died and the theater has changed in many ways. Still, his observations have an ability to provoke thought and begin discussion. His forceful words—often polemical—retain a freshness of expression that make them worth continued examination. I have, for these reasons, retained the article in the present revision.—D.R.P.]

The Theatre has become a thing outside of life. Too far outside. It's a mediocre, minority, closed-group activity. It has nothing to do with people having bread or finding things that are exciting. In economically developing countries, people are finding, for the first time, that they can have things other than necessities. They can go places, do things, that weren't available to them before. If the theatre is to be an art form of our time, it must take these new excitements of ordinary people and develop them into a new voice. A new voice: a new theatre.

People are deserting the old form, the old theatre, because it's rubbish. There's nothing to it. We have to forget about the eighteenth-century drawing room behavior and all that nonsense. Let's relegate Chekhov, Ibsen, and Shakespeare to their proper place: a museum theater that would show how things were written and done in the past; how dancers, singers, and actors can interpret a life, a situation, a problem of another time. In art, people take a seventeenth-, eighteenth-, or nineteenth-century painter and consider his work a comment on things as and when he saw them—not a comment on today. What we call Modern Theatre is Theatre of Yesterday. We go on using it because we've developed no alternative. It's as though there were no more movies and we kept showing Charlie Chaplin and the Marx Brothers, saying: this is good cinema and this is the only cinema.

Our civilization is becoming more and more a civilization of action. People don't want to sit down, like coy Victorians, to watch a semi-risque story and giggle. They want to take part; they want to do something; they want to shout, to answer back, to rebel and to acclaim. I think these people would want to take part in a new theatre, a theatre that would be theirs and theirs to enjoy.

They'd want to take part in a theatre that reflects what's really happening in this world. At the moment, we have culture salesmen, amateurs who peddle culture to the masses, proclaiming life is an extension of art, art is all. They say to the factory workers: this is what you've missed. But those characters in the factory are bored. What the hell do they know about Picasso? What do they care about folk-lorists or old musical instruments?

I'm not advocating a socialistic, comment-message-ridden theatre. I want a theatre of excitement. A theatre where you don't have to wear furs, eat chocolate, and read programs. A theatre where you can go and have a ball, where you can drink, where you can do what you bloody well like: dance and jump around and sing.

This theatre, like a baseball bat, would hit you over the head with ideas. It would offer new breakaways, show new break-throughs, suggest how there can be more to life. It would show us how to be more individual—not better, not good, but more individual; it would tell us how to release the emotions half-hidden within ourselves. It would be a place for man: for each and every one of us.

I realize this sounds anarchistic, but in order to prepare the ground for a new theatre, we have to break down all the old barricades, the old ways of doing things. We have to get rid of and destroy, once and for all, the victorian Birdcage. We have to destroy the idea that theatre is designers, is theatre managers, is committees, is directors, is buildings.

Theatre is simply a playwright and a group of actors who want to tell a story before an audience. It doesn't require a building. A building can be a great liability.

People who want to build a theatre think first of all of the structure. They don't think of the heart of the matter, the powerhouse behind it: the group of people who will be the theatre. At meetings of theatre people, everybody discusses the building and the stage as if theatre originates with these inanimate elements. They debate three-cornered versus four-cornered, five-cornered, in-the-round, in-the-square, or upside down. If we could find a good, well-designed stage, they feel, we'd have the answer. They are just evading the real issue: what is theatre, what does it talk about, what's doing in our world today? Tackling this does not require a building; any place would do, any street corner, any parking lot. If the people were inventive enough, they would send somebody down the street for a couple of beer barrels and a plank, and have him stand on it.

New theatres, in almost all cases, are not being built by the people. City halls are building them, and the structures they turn out have nothing to do with true theatre. They are badges of culture: symbols of how well we live and how well we conserve and publicize our culture. They are part of the prevailing cultural supermarket—and have no value to anyone but status seekers, people who put badges on their walls.

Speaking of myself as a designer, I don't think I set out to change the theatre or to make it into something different. I wanted to find out exactly what could be done with it, as it was and as it is, and how far it could be stretched. But the nature of a designer's role limits his ability to influence the theatre. He is an outside man; he is not and cannot be, too involved.

We designers spend most of our time arranging wallpaper, chairs, and settees, odd bits of things here and there, that are supposed to make some kind of comment on the story. But to me, design in the theatre is basically a waste of time. A designer can't change anything about the theatre as it is now, unless he stops being a designer and writes a story. Short of that, there is nothing more he can do in the existing theatre; he's just a prop man.

But the designer could do something for a new theatre. He could find a very good square, a good space where the theatre could begin again, where he would say to the actors and the playwright: here is a good place to tell your story in—not a building inside which you can tell it, but a place. It would be marvelous if this place could be found, but I suspect it will have to be different from what we have now.

The new theatre will begin almost as the old began; someone will go to a small town with a group of actors and give a performance. In the prairies, in the mountains, it doesn't matter. There, like a dance, or a song, or a ballad that evolves into a story, theatre will emerge. And it will attain real significance when it succeeds in attracting the people in the streets and the children.

Our best hope for a new theatre may lie in the children themselves, for children have an idea of excitement beyond themselves. If instead of erecting stages in gymnasiums, the schools were to give platforms, chairs and materials to the children and let them do whatever they want, we might hear the beginnings of a voice called theatre. The children, as they grow up, might suddenly discover that there is one particular way in which they speak best of all, a way important to us. Tomorrow's audience, tomorrow's playhouse, tomorrow's playwrights, could be born in the schools. Just find a thousand acres, plunk the children in the middle with wood, nails, canvas—whatever they want—and say: now, you speak. It might be worth trying.

My feeling on theatre design, on problem of visual concept, is this: to hell with national theatres, to hell with provincial theatres, and to hell with Lincoln Center. Let's just have airplanes, trains and buses, Let's have squares and fields, But let's not build reinforced concrete theatres until we begin to find out which direction, which way our theatre is going to go.

Theatre should be like a floating crap game. It should be able to change its arrangement, to change its environment, to change its whole influence in relation to the things around it. Reinforced concrete foundations are a yoke. They won't let you move; they won't let you change. We are building theatres at this moment, designed for the next 80 or 90 years—however long they stand up—that are impossible to change. We are forced to exist inside them; we have to behave inside the architecture. This can't be theatre. We need structures we can knock holes in; we need to be able to move walls out entirely. The trouble with our theatre today is that if you push out the walls, the roof will fall in.

If this is a beginning period, a beginning time, then we need a beginning shape, and the only thing that we can have at this time is some kind of space tent or something, so that we can move in whatever direction our new theatre wants to go.

We need frames that can be changed; we need places where people can find their own physical ease for watching, sitting, lying, standing whatever it is. We need a new kind of space into which a director and a group of actors and a playwright can come and say: well, we'll put a platform here, and orchestra there, some of the audience here so they'll look like the Roman soldiers we're short of. The entire space could be designed, for each particular performance, for each particular story. The entire space should be always fluid, always flexible. A space that you couldn't even call a theatre, because it wouldn't exist until those boys came in and started to do something. Only then would it become a theatre.

All a painter asks for is a clean white canvas. We need a clean white canvas place, in which we can begin to tell a new kind of story. There should be no architectural statements made before we begin, no statement at all. We can do anything with whatever media we want to use; lighting projection, sound, everything in the world. But first we need this new kind of space.

In the new theatre the designer would be part of a cooperative team altering the place to suit the play. In some cases the designer might say to the director and the actors: you don't need anything from me, you don't need anything for this play; just play it with two chairs—the ones you're sitting on right now.

And there are people who go in this direction, people like Littlewood, Wells, Guthrie, and Svoboda. There are lots of people who have ideas; individuals who really want to speak out, who want to reorganize, who want to adjust and say: let's go in a new direction. But control of the theatre is in the hands of the wrong people, the direction is in the hands of old critics.

John Whiting, while he was writing *The Devils*, asked me to help him place the scenes. The only thing I could say to John at that stage was—don't write *any* place. If you can, think in terms of a cinema idea, a television idea, because it should be possible to do anything, to create any place. It doesn't always have to be "enter down left and cross to fireplace"; these sorts of things don't have to happen in the theatre. And so a lot of the stage directions in *The Devils* simply come out: two men are walking, two men are talking. My advice to writers is to start where you want to; go ahead and write—the man jumps out the window onto the back of a white horse and the white horse, chased by ten more horses, runs away through the audience. There should be a freedom about writing for the stage. Why set handcuffs on the theatre?

Lorca said the theatre must impose itself on the audience. It has to; the reason we're doing it in the first place is for an audience, not for ourselves. We do it initially to make a life for ourselves, but we do it finally and eventually for an audience.

Any dissatisfaction that I'm talking about, anything I'm complaining about, is inside the theatre. The trouble lies not with the audience but with how *we* are doing it. We're not doing it well.

I know that design can help change the theatre, can help change direction. But all I can do right now is voice my frustration and say that it's no good. From now, on I refuse to work in the theatre as it is, unless to change its direction. I don't mean that tomorrow every theatre has to be popular or I won't work in it; I mean that its direction must change to have reference to me in our time. There are things happening in our time that ought to have something to do with the theatre and theatre with them. Tomorrow we'll be on the moon; we can't do Molière on the moon.

A good parallel to the problem of theatre design is: How do you design a church for 1967? Now, it would be impossible to design a church for 1967 without first examining how religion relates to life in 1967. You couldn't possibly just design a church. You would have to find out the *meaning* of religion in ordinary life, how it affects people, everyday problems, and excitements. It should be impossible to examine the idea of designing a new theatre without finding out what theatre has to do with everyday life, what place it occupies in the lives of people today. The question of place relates closely to the questions of the physical thing called theatre: the physical building, the space it stands in, where it is, how we approach it, how we go to it. We should all be concerned with asking and finding answers.

3

The Scenographer and the Written Text

For the poet, language is a structure of the external world. . . . he is invested by words. They are prolongations of his senses, his pincers, his antennae, his spectacles. He manoeuvres them from within; he feels them as if they were his body; he is surrounded by a verbal body which he is hardly conscious of and which extends his action upon the world. The poet is outside language. He sees the reverse side of words, . . . touching words, testing them, fingering them, he discovers in them a slight luminosity of their own and particular affinities with the earth, the sky, the water, and all created things.
—Jean-Paul Sartre, *What Is Literature? and Other Essays*

When I eventually realized how indispensable an imaginative, experienced stage director is to a production, I began to read a script as though I were going to direct it myself. This did not turn me into a director, but it did make me a better designer. It gave me a kind of inner eye, a necessity for all artists.
—Jo Mielziner

We learn language by applying words to visual experiences, and we create visual images to illustrate verbal ideas. This interaction of word and image is the background for contemporary communication.
—Allen Hurburt, *The Design Concept*

The Problems of Theatrical Communication: Words and Images

We have many reasons to be grateful to the Greek civilization that flourished in the fifth century prior to our common era. Not only did they give us the basis of today's theater, they also provided the best definition of the critical features of that institution we are likely to have. The Greek word *theatron* means *a place where things are seen done*. In the briefest space this definition gives us the essential features of all theater: an area—both physical and spiritual—set aside from all other activities where any human act can be observed as it transpires. The Greeks also gave us a logical system of concepts by which we can study not only their works but our own dramatic creations as well. For those who take it upon themselves to translate the language of one form of art into the language of another—and that is the basic task of all who work in theater—these precepts give a valuable overview of the nature of that translation. Here is a brief outline, along with the word designations used in that system of evaluation, formulated in fifth-century Greece:

Ethos: The perception or statement of the spirit that motivates a work

Pathos: The personal emotional response to a work

Logos: The reasons that result from contemplation of the *ethos* of the work and from contemplation of the *pathos* of the work

Taxis: The analyzing and placing in order the elements in the work into a logical structure

Lexis: The work made manifest in a language

These principles inform all we still do in today's theater. They are central to the philosophy we follow in the interpretation of the language of the playwright—the text—into the language of the stage. And while these general principles worked well for the conventions of the Greek theater, and generally are still applicable today, we need to seek more specific applications of those principles to serve our modern theater. These more specific applications are our present concern.

Interpretation of any dramatic text is dependent on an awareness of, and a sensitivity to these major areas:

1. The *time frames* within the text

2. The *spatial framework* of the text

3. The *visual assumptions* of the playwright as perceived in the language of the text

4. The *period* and *social background* of the playwright's world as perceived in the language of the text

5. The *period* and *social background* of the playwright's world as perceived from a study of materials found outside the text

6. The *playwright's underlying assumptions* as perceived from careful study of the language of the text

This listing of assumptions forms the conceptual outline—establishes the boundaries, so to speak—of any project whose purpose is to bring a specific play to a specific audience. The order of implementation, however, is not necessarily the order as given here. To be more accurate, these categories must be addressed more than once during the interpretation process. Although we will study these individual subjects in this text as if they could be accomplished point by point, in the actual world of interpretation the process would be multilinear rather than sequential and even that multilinear process tends to be circular in nature.

There is one guiding principle of interpretation that takes precedence over all other considerations. This is that the play text represents two basic worlds: a contained and limited world described by stage directions as well as introductory notes and a hidden often amorphous world compounded from the experience and imagination of the playwright. Conscious consideration of these worlds disappears in the performance of the play on the stage; an attempt to detect the motivational forces that brought the text into being rarely concerns most viewers in the theater. Nor should it be otherwise; audiences have no obligation to be concerned about the impetus of a play; nor should they be expected to give a second thought to the labor and research expended on the project they watch. It is not the business of the performer to draw attention to how difficult it was to understand his character or how hard he is presently working to make that understanding manifest. Nor is it the business of any of the members of a producing company to expose in any way the time spent to bring a work to the stage. The hallmark of a successful production is the seemingly inevitability of what is seen, heard, and ultimately understood. Yet behind that totality of effect lies an infinite number of decisions. For it is only in the vast mysterious storehouse of the playwright's experience—a place of strange occurrence filled with memories, fears, obsessions, unrelated images and half-perceived visions—linked by both coincidence and purpose, that we may come to know something of what the play is really about: what the words behind the words mean, how the visions behind the images he describes can be realized.

It is not very likely that the true dimensions of these worlds are completely known even to the playwright; introspection must have a large role in the writing of most plays. But enough playwrights have written or talked about the process to indicate that even the most gifted of playwrights tends to draw on the unconscious mind—that dark attic of half-remembered events and all but forgotten acquaintance—without conscious deliberation. Shakespeare was perhaps the supreme dramatic genius since the inception of our Western theater, but there is very little reason to believe that his intellect was even remotely equal to that of an Issac Newton or an Albert Einstein. Shakespeare's worldview is especially difficult to ascertain, since only the plays and a handful of poetry survives to guide us on a tour of his past. But notwithstanding the difficulty of dredging up materials from "the muddy past of his own dead sea," as the poet Dylan Thomas described the problem of a writer attempting an understanding of his life, much more can be found from any playwright's past than a casual examination of the problem would lead us to expect. Of course, it is no more possible to know the entire thrust of those forces that formed a specific playwright's consciousness any more than it is to recover a record of every minute of his life; and that is not the purpose of our study even if it were possible. Nor would it add appreciably to what we know or want to know. What we really need to discover are those solitary unmarked lighthouses dotted along the dark shores of a playwright's past. It would be wise to keep in mind W. H. Auden's advice that "to read is to translate, for no two persons' experiences are the same. A bad reader is like a bad translator; he interprets literally when he ought to paraphrase and paraphrases when he ought to interpret literally. In learning to read well, scholarship, valuable as it is, is less important than instinct; some great scholars have been poor translators."

Working for the theater can be frustrating; the communication of visual ideas in other kinds of languages—words, for instance, or technical specifications—does not always proceed smoothly between coworkers. Very often the director misreads the intentions of the scenographer; too often the scenographer does not fully grasp the points the director wishes to convey through the actions of the performers. Interpretation can never be more than subjective discussion; no one can ever say: *I am right and I am sure I am right.*

We are stuck with certain basic forms of communication. It is imperative, therefore, that we understand as clearly as possible the nature of those forms we do possess. But this understanding does not come of its own accord; we must train ourselves—and this is something that cannot be taught in any course of study—to comprehend the hidden currents that lie below the surfaces of communication; to understand the clues and keys of the playwright's thought as he expresses it through the medium of the printed word. Most important of all, we must learn to

be more accurate in the kinds of language we employ to inform others of those concepts we come to hold. In *Problems of Art*, Susanne K. Langer touches on this ever-present dilemma:

Whatever resists projection into the discursive form of language is, indeed hard to hold in conception, and perhaps impossible to communicate, in the proper and strict sense of the word "communicate." But fortunately our logical intuition, or form-perception, is really much more powerful than we commonly believe, and our knowledge—genuine knowledge, understanding—is considerably wider than our discourse. Even in the use of language, if we want to name something that is too new to have a name (e.g., a newly invented gadget or a newly discovered creature), or want to express a relationship for which there is no verb or other connective word, we resort to metaphor; we mention it or describe it as something else, something analogous. The principle of metaphor is simply the principle of saying one thing and meaning another, and expecting to be understood to mean the other. *A metaphor is not language, it is an idea expressed by language, an idea that in its turn functions as a symbol to express something.* (Italics mine)

Richard Leakey, the noted prehistorian, adds to this thought; he even goes so far as to entertain the real possibility that human beings have had the faculty of expression through the combination of words and images for hundreds of thousands if not millions of years. In support of this speculation he states that "creating and mentally manipulating images is a way of exploring your environment from the perspective of experience, and the sharper those images are in your head, the more effective you will be in exploiting that environment. *Words—arbitrary sounds that name specific objects or events—are superb tools for sharpening and manipulating images in one's own head, and for invoking them in someone else's*: book, storm clouds, black stallion, beautiful woman, handsome man, war—all these words may pluck images from your mind, *images admittedly that differ from person to person, because of both the diversity of the world and the diversity of individual experience*" (italics mine).

Thus Leakey draws our attention to the double-edged nature of communication: the incalculable ability to implant an image from mind to mind and the ofttimes immeasurable distances between the common understanding of those images. This is the heart of the problem that all theatrical artists face when they come together to discuss and plan a forthcoming production. Even the most basic questions recur time and time again: *How can we know when we have distilled the correct images from the text? Are we truly getting our point of view across to others? Are we understanding their points of view? How do we both know if we are interpreting the meaning of the text's words or usurping that meaning with visual images that distort rather than enhance their intent?* And simply as a personal concern: *How blindly should we follow the dictates of others? When should we take a firm stand, when give over?* Most important of all: *To what extent should we heed only our own judgments?*

These are doubts all scenographers of integrity encounter throughout their careers, not only during student days. They are not—although it may seem to be the case—simply promptings of the individual ego. These concerns rise from the constant awareness that the visual image and written language can very easily become adversaries on the stage. Certainly, the old expression that "one picture is worth ten thousand words" must not, much as we would like to believe it, delude us into thinking that the scenographer's work ever takes precedence in the producing theater. One form of communication cannot ever be an absolute substitute for another. (Nor should we as visual artists ever be so impressed with our own calling that we forget that the old adage, just quoted, required words to bring our attention to the fact that images do, indeed, have unique values.) It lies, then, in the constant awareness of the problems of communication that we have the best hope of solving those problems; and it must be kept ever presently in mind that the greatest danger in the producing theater is not that directors and scenographers do not talk to one another, but that each could be on the very best terms with the other and still not know just what the other had in mind. And the most devastating miscalculation both could make is to assume that one—the director—is responsible for the intellectual content of the play's text, while the other—the scenographer—is simply a visualizer of locales and verifier of period detail; in sum, an expert purveyor of "pictures." Since this condition can naturally arise from the necessary division of labor in the the-

ater, too often what we see on the stage is a production where the performers, guided by the director, tell one thing and the visual element within which they exist tells quite another. At best, a concerted message is not communicated; at worst, one aspect of the production tends to dominate (and sometimes cancel out) the other. The truth of the matter is that both the scenographer and the director must be vitally concerned with the relationships of all elements of a production; both must seek to reinforce the work and visions of the other.

Words and images are often linked in the theater and in the cinema. (Indeed, unless the spectator experiences a dramatic work with closed eyes, a relationship will be perceived whether one is intended or not.) Playwrights, directors, and scenographers operate on the basic principle that not only are such links probable but much of the work of all three depends on consciously manipulating those links. While it is not possible to make any precise set of rules or to give a precise formula as to how those links are made, it is possible to give examples from past works that demonstrate that such links do exist. Let us investigate several images which occur in a cinematic work frequently shown in film courses: Sergei Eisenstein's *Ivan the Terrible*.

Carefully examine figure 72. This picture is nothing less than an image of the vast power that Czar Ivan holds. Even without our knowing what is transpiring in the scene or what is being said, this image causes us to begin a certain train of thought, to begin an exploration of why the image causes us to feel a certain way. (If we are watching the film as it would be presented in a movie house, we would not have the time to study closely the linkage that Eisenstein made between image and the message the image is to convey; the image would react more with our subliminal levels of mind and less with our analytical and logical mental processes. The still photograph therefore gives us an opportunity, not possible when watching the moving film, to examine how an image is linked to a dramatic concept first conceived in words.)

It should be obvious even to the untrained eye that the seated figure—Ivan—seems to emanate a power that is lacking in the figure standing before him; even though the standing figure is visually larger and looks down on him, Ivan is

Fig. 72. Scene from *Ivan the Terrible*

clearly the more powerful of the two. Much of this perceived power results from the shadow boldly cast onto the wall behind both figures. (Also note that there is *no* shadow for the standing figure.) Ivan's shadow, however, plainly dominates the scene; it literally *overshadows* the man standing before him. Although not connected to him, it is a visible extension of Ivan's influence. While this image speaks to our imagination, even in the movie house our subliminal analytical mind begins to seek out connections: Ivan—the most powerful man in Russia—figuratively (and here, literally) casts a large shadow over his subjects. This thought probably does not consciously arise in the viewer's mind as he sits watching the film in the movie house; but the underlying meaning of the image, the hidden message, is clear. And it becomes even clearer when we closely examine the manner in which Eisenstein consciously manipulated the elements of the image: the spatial arrangement of

the figures, the objects they use, and the precise light in which they are seen.

Examine these elements more closely. In particular, give attention to the objects resting on the table in front of Ivan: an armillary sphere (an instrument for the study of the earth's relationship to the stars and planets) and, more important, a chessboard inhabited not with pieces of traditional design but with chessmen that closely resemble actual human beings. Also note that no opponent faces Ivan; he plays alone. Little imagination is needed to interpret the images Eisenstein has included in this scene, even though he does not call our direct attention to them as the action of the scene unfolds.

Now examine figure 73, another scene from this same film. Here we see that the entire setting is nothing less than a chessboard raised to human scale. Even the figures stand in positions on the checkered floor reminiscent of those on Ivan's small board. Here we have an image the

Fig. 73. Scene from *Ivan the Terrible*

reverse of that seen in figure 72. Actual human beings are pieces; in Ivan's study, chessmen resembled human beings. Doubtless these two images are somehow linked to the telling of Ivan's story. But how? And for what purpose does Eisenstein repeat the image of chess? Does he want us to perceive a relationship between these two images? As the plot of *Ivan the Terrible* unfolds, Ivan—the master player and manipulator of others—is outplayed and outmanipulated by others. Is this the simple meaning behind the imagery? Or is the purpose of these images, rather, to strike visual resonances similar to deep resounding bass lines in works of music? Did Eisenstein actually know the precise linkage between the story and the imagery he created in this film? It is quite possible that he did not propose exact meanings to the images he created; but it is certain that strong relationships do exist between the words and the images in this work, and that Eisenstein had to consider them.

It is interesting to note the path by which Eisenstein arrived at his visual conception of Ivan. This conception incorporated research images taken from historical images; but the formal research process was preceded by an earlier one that was almost entirely based on visual stimuli

that had nothing to do with historical fact. According to Eisenstein, he first "recognized" the crude profile of Ivan while looking at a rough sketch of trees that he had drawn from his apartment window (fig. 74). This was, he relates, the shape of the image he had been seeking for some time. (The sketch even carries a date: 24 October 1944.) Using this initial idea, he developed the sketch further into that shown in figure 75. Combining this drawing with photographs of John Barrymore as Mr. Hyde in the 1920 cinema version of *Dr. Jeykll and Mr. Hyde* (fig. 76), Eisenstein arrived at a final concept for the makeup that resulted in the image we see in figure 77. What Eisenstein does here is a common practice for most graphic artists. As Kenneth Clark points out: "all good artists, or nearly all good artists, seem to distort, or at any rate to re-arrange nature. . . . And as to Michelangelo, there's an amusing instance—he drew a figure of Tityus lying on a rock, and the form pleased him, so he turned the paper over and he traced the figure through and made it into a Christ rising from the tomb. Thus showing that even for Michelangelo a really coherent and expressive form wasn't a thing to be wasted."

Let us examine one last example that reveals

Fig. 74. Sketch by Eisenstein

Fig. 75. Sketch by Eisenstein

how this master scenographic artist worked. Figures 78 and 79 show preliminary sketches for a scene that was realized in the same film we have just been studying. Figure 80 is a still photograph of the scene as filmed. In this second image we see Ivan at the lowest point of his life: the death of his wife. Every element of the design of this image contributes to our understanding of the moment: the most powerful man in all Russia brought low before the majesty of death. All his power, substantial as it had been in the past, is at this moment nothing. Although Eisenstein's earliest training was that of a cartoonist, a maker of visual images that—in a sense—told a story without further explanation, he knew and deeply appreciated other forms of communication, especially that of written words. Almost all of his sketches for his theater and film projects had detailed notes attached that not only help explain the drawing but enhance its meaning. The work he has left us attests that in his mind these two forms of communication were indissolubly linked.

Reading the Written Text: Some Initial Considerations

Playwrights, no matter how abstractly they work, almost always conceive of their characters as springing from, and existing in, a specific set of circumstances, in a particular kind of environment; in other words, their people live in a world that is real enough no matter how strange and foreign that world may be. Yet in the playwright's art, many things must be sacrificed to the limitations of the play form. He cannot, as the novelist is able to do, give us detailed background data about the place where his characters live. (While stage directions can tell a certain amount, the playwright is still much more limited in this respect than the novelist; the playwright also runs the risk of having his directions ignored by producers, a liberty most novel readers would probably never consider.) In some cases this situation does not really concern him

Fig. 76. Makeup for Mr. Hyde

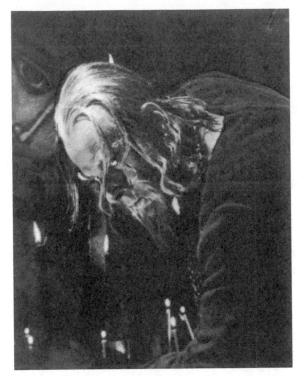

Fig. 77. Makeup for Ivan the Terrible

all that much; a study of practically any play-wright of the sixteenth or seventeenth century would bear this out. But when he does have definite ideas about the setting of his play, the playwright may find that the nature of play form is such that it restricts him almost completely to revealing this information to the audience in the theater through dialogue between the characters. Often we must piece out the necessary facts from oblique references. Even when the playwright does attempt to disclose pertinent information in stage directions, not only is he limited in space, he is powerless when others begin to interpret those directions to suit themselves.

Mordecai Gorelik maintains that one of the most creative acts a scenographer ever performs is the first reading of the play he is to design. First impressions may not always be workable or even accurate, but few will deny these first thoughts are extremely important and often make lasting marks on the creative mind, especially that part of the mind below the conscious level. Even though one's initial judgment may

be later amended or reversed, those first impressions still have some elemental effect, still have weight. To a young scenographer, the reading of a play he is to design is usually an exciting and pleasurable experience, and thus he cannot usually bring to the problems it presents a backlog of hackneyed solutions (nor often as much original imagination as he might like to believe). Later, as he reads more plays and designs more productions, he will begin to think in terms of former solutions; it is unavoidable. While this accumulated information and experience forms the basis of his knowledge and skill, it is not without its negative features; it can also be a danger to his continuing creativity. (Especially if he is seeking a "style" by which to identify himself.) This problem besets many artists in other fields, but it is especially true for those in the theater, where reliability is generally more trusted than creative originality. In the professional New York theater, for instance, more than one scenographer has been "typed" in much the same manner as actors: in the 1930s if one wanted a factory or rundown tenement building, Howard Bay was the scenographer to get; if an elegant interior was needed, no one was better

Fig. 78. Sketch by Eisenstein

Fig. 79. Sketch by Eisenstein

than Raymond Sovey, and so on and so forth. Still, to read the three hundredth play with the same kind of attention and response as one read the third is not possible even for the most creative scenographer. And yet, if he is to continue to develop new insights and renew his art with the passage of time, he must constantly keep this problem in mind. For, once the scenographer loses the sense of excitement and challenge that an unfamiliar play, or even a familiar one, can produce, it is almost impossible to create a living design for it.

Many scenographers have also indicated that they believe this first reading should be done with little regard to the mechanical workings of the theater stage plant. This is not surprising, since flats and backdrops and revolving stages have little place in the unlimited world of imagination. Important as the physical theater and its techniques are, they represent only the means by which the scenographer's visions are implemented, they should not be allowed to limit his thinking. It could be a great mistake by a scenog-

rapher to attempt visualization of the play on a stage during this important first reading. The world of imagination should not have a stage-right or stage-left orientation.

It might well be asked if all imagination—that process of seeing something in the mind—is not the same kind of activity. Perhaps it is in its most basic definition; but in the theater imagination must, by necessity, have a more specific function and more precise definition, especially when considered in relation to the scenographer's role. The methods by which imagination is brought to the stage, the very nature of it, differs greatly from how it is employed in poetry, painting, or music. This difference is a very practical one to the scenographer. In poetry or literature the object of the written word is most often to summon up images in the mind of a single person; the mind is the surface, the screen, on which these images find their form. No matter how vivid these mental images are to the individual, however, they are and always will remain a pri-

Fig. 80. Scene from *Ivan the Terrible*

vate "showing." No one can see these images but the person either reading the work or hearing it read.

The scenographer, on the other hand, does deal in imagery, but in a very special way. When he reads a play, it first exists, as with anyone else, only as a conceptual image or, rather, as a succession of images, since theater is, even in the mind, a time-space art and can never be, as a painting or piece of sculpture can be, seen all at once or contained in a single image. The difference between the function of the scenographer and the general reader of plays, who is accountable to no one for what he imagines, is that the scenographer cannot stop there; he must create an outward manifestation of the images he perceives. His job is dependent on how well he is able to do this.

The business of the scenographer, then, is to make visible what at first exists nowhere but in the mind, and, difficult as this may be, it is complicated by the fact that he must also include

in his visions those of the director and—when he writes specific directions in addition to the play dialogue—those of the playwright, bringing into some union what must be, at first, numerous incomplete and divergent ideas and points of view. But, to repeat, these images are set in motion, if not actually called into being, by the words of the text. While there seems to be less and less respect for the sanctity of the written script (most playwrights deplore the professional theater's treatment of their scripts—see *The Seesaw Log*, by William Gibson, for one author's view on this subject—but find they are all but powerless to do anything about the situation), most scenographers and directors still attempt to present this text as they think the author would wish to have it interpreted.

But the scenographer of the mid-twentieth century has become less a reporter of the external appearance of environments and more a synthesizer of environmental qualities and, at times, a creator of totally new ones. *Waiting for Godot*, for example, requires the scenographer to provide a landscape that exists no place on earth; it is, rather, a landscape of the mind he is asked to create. Nor is this play unique in this respect. The scenographer has been required more and more to create not only places that were or could be found outside the theater but also places that never could exist anywhere but in a theater.

The translation of words into images, subjective as this activity is, is the scenographer's primary purpose in the theater. It is the performance of this function that allows him to consider his contribution as a service on the same level as that of the director and actor. Yet student scenographers often have difficulty in explaining to others initial feelings and verbal reactions to the pervading qualities they perceive in the scripts they are studying. Moreover, they tend to be too general in their descriptions of what and how they feel concerning mood and atmosphere, too fuzzy in their thinking and ability to communicate these impressions to another—the director, for instance. And for this very reason, they actually miss a great deal in the script they would not miss if their communication skills were more refined. Ideas conveyed in words can and do produce concrete directions and results. Now, perhaps it is too much to ask of the scenographer, especially in his formative and training period, to be able to paint word pictures of what he "feels"; nevertheless, attempting to find exact and specific words that somehow summon up images in the mind is a necessity, not only for dealing with others who are concerned with the visual aspects of the production, such as the director, but for himself as well; it helps him recognize what he is seeking when he does begin to search for objective correlatives of those abstract impressions and feelings. One of the very first things I ask of students in classroom discussions of their design projects is that they give the rest of the group the qualities of their selected plays in words that contain visual clues. At first they find it difficult; the words they often select are usually too abstract and general. (The real source of their difficulty lies in the fact, however, that they don't really think such an exercise is "serious.") Often the student will employ words like "colorful" or "old." When he is questioned further (and sometimes goaded), he will begin to narrow down his vision and bring a sharper

focus to what he is trying to say; *he has to think about what he is thinking about*. He is forced to be less diffuse in his description and more specific. After some discussion he finds he can be much more precise in making others understand what he means. He also finds, as he does this, that his own understanding gains depth when he tries harder to make his feelings clear to others. After each student is subjected to this form of cross-examination, sometimes an ordeal, they almost all begin to see (from being on both sides of the fence—the one who explains and the one to whom something is being explained) that certain words are better than others, that some have more value, are more specific and precise than others. For instance, *tinseled, sleazy, rickety, translucent, iridescent, mossy, gritty, metallic*, are better than *colorful, heavy, dark, old, rich, grand*. Eventually the scenographer must make good the impressions and images he summons up in his discussions of his design concepts, but he should let himself range over a wide spectrum of possibilities during this phase. Notice how Robert O'Hearn, the scenographer of the Metropolitan Opera production of Richard Strauss's, *Die Frau ohne Schatten*, gives his ideas (in the 17 September 1966 issue of *Opera News*) on how he came to select the particular ideas and impressions he eventually incorporated into his designs:

Die Frau ohne Schatten is one of the most difficult of operas to design, since it takes place not only in a fantasy world but in three fantasy worlds. It has not one but two stories to tell: the fairy-tale one we see and hear, and a very elaborate philosophical one running neck and neck with it. The real meanings are purposely hidden and the clues confused, so the designer must venture on a detective hunt. . . .

. . . We decided that *Die Frau* should be placed in no specific country. Rather, the design should reflect the mood and meaning of each scene and world: a bluish icy-cold, glassy, jeweled world for the Empress, a warm red-earthy world of men for the Dyer and his steaming vats, a black-and-silver world of iridescent rock and winglike forms for the spirits. Also, water— physically and symbolically, the water of life—is important from the first utterance of the Nurse on and should be shown as shimmering light reflections from water, fountains and a tremendous real waterfall for the apotheosis. . . .

In plot and mood the second act goes from light to darkness, the third from darkness to light. For the third act I planned a rainbow progression, starting with black and purple for the grotto and going through blue to green to yellow green to golden yellow for the final burst of daylight and humanity.

. . . The architectural-research and mulling-over period. This meant dispensing with tempting Siamese and Indian temples, turning instead to enlarged photos of microscopic organisms and minerals, studies of jewels and branched quartz. We searched for unusual materials—transparent plastics, oily iridescent surfaces. . . .

The important Dyer's house went through about ten versions, from a darkly real Japanese interior to a sculptural abstraction something like the inside of a broken clay pot (or womb?) lit by a volcanic fireplace. In other words, relevant forms based on nature superseded real period detail to bring out the basic motives. The veined texture of the curved walls was suggested by a photo blow-up of the eye of a frog.

. . . I tried to use in the model the unconventional materials of the real sets: plastics, crushed glass, jewels, crinkled metal-foil surfaces, etc.

The Scenographer's Relationship to the Playwright

When the English playwright David Storey was being interviewed by a reporter of the *New York Times* concerning his new play *Home*, his answer to a familiar question that many playwrights are asked was this:

REPORTER (*to Storey*): What do you say to people who ask what your play is really all about?
STOREY: No idea.

While this may seem a flippant reply to such a question, even a paradoxical one, more than one playwright has answered just such questions in much this way. Do they really not know what they are doing or what they have done, or is there something else, a deeper more profound meaning that touches on the nature of playwriting itself behind the words of this reply? What does such an answer mean, moreover, to the scenographer attempting to understand the purpose and scheme underlying the playwright's creation? Should he, for instance, always take the playwright's written directions at face value or should he be free to interpret them?

Friederich Dürrenmatt, in discussing his function as a playwright, has written down some

of his thoughts concerning what he means to do and what he actually, in the end, does accomplish when he writes a play. Here is a brief extract from an essay called "Problems of the Theatre" (translated by Gerhard Nellhaus) in which he comments on his work and what that work "means":

For me, the stage is not a battlefield for theories, nor philosophies and manifestoes, but rather an instrument whose possibilities I seek to know by playing with it. Of course, in my plays there are people and they hold to some belief or philosophy—a lot of blockheads would make for a dull piece—but my plays are not for what people have to say: what is said is there because my plays deal with people, and thinking and believing and philosophizing are all, to some extent at least, a part of human nature. The problems I face as a playwright are practical, working problems, problems I face not before, but during the writing. To be quite accurate about it, these problems usually come up after the writing is done, arising out of a certain curiosity to know how I did it.

What I am concerned with are empirical rules, the possibilities of the theatre . . . the artist indeed has no need for scholarship. Scholarship derives laws from what exists already: otherwise it would not be scholarship. But the laws thus established have no value for the artist, even when they are true. The artist cannot accept a law he has not discovered for himself.

. . . Scholarship sees only the result; the process, which led to this result, is what the playwright cannot forget. What he says has to be taken with a grain of salt. What he thinks about his art changes as he creates his art; his thoughts are always subject to his mood and the moment. What alone really counts for him is what he is doing at a given moment; for its own sake he can betray what he did just a little while ago.

Here we have the playwright stating clearly and explicitly the idea that he, along with all those who read his play, find meaning in this work only *after* it is done; meaning is not necessarily a conscious goal the writer pursues at the time of creation or works out according to a preconceived plan. But, he also points out, with the completion of the writing, his work is done; *he is under no obligation to explain it further.*

What, then, do those who take the playwright's work and produce it on the stage owe him; in particular, how closely should the scenographer follow the playwright's wishes, assuming he can discern them in the first place; and just what is the scenographer's role in relation to the written text of the play?

There are no easy answers to these questions, nor is it possible to ever answer them finally; the nature and scope of the scenographer's task changes with each individual script. And it must be pointed out that though the scenographer and playwright are both creative artists, their raw materials, their purposes—even though they are attempting to produce a unified work—cannot be compared to any great extent. The biggest difference between the two, however, lies in the fact that the scenographer, though not a "scholar" in the sense Dürrenmatt uses that word, is always engaged in a form of research that in many ways resembles scholarship; he is not, usually, creating something completely new and original on his own. He is, in fact, an interpretive artist whose product depends largely on how successful he is in digging out meanings and information the playwright has hidden in his work and may even be unaware that he did so. It is a paradox that a production staff (of which the scenographer has become an increasingly important member) must sometimes consciously come to know more of the playwright's subconscious purposes than he himself might have been aware of were he directly confronted with the information.

Of course, no single rule can be formulated that will satisfy all situations regarding the obligation of the scenographer to the playwright; the obligations imposed on the scenographer in the name of interpretation vary too greatly from script to script and from scenographer to scenographer. And while there are scenographers who have designed productions without actually having read the script, the more common fault is *not* not having read it but not reading it with any degree of perception. It probably would not be a gross exaggeration to point out that there are far too many scenographers working today who think their job is finished when they have satisfied the most basic physical demands of the play's written directions: providing a door when a door is called for, a window because the script "says so." But even though Dürrenmatt seemed to imply that how his plays were to be produced or interpreted was not necessarily his business, he has had at least one occasion to reprimand a number of scenographers who apparently, in their zeal to make a distinct contribution to the "Interpretation" of the play, did not conceive of the design as he would have it. (This is a common fault in many playwrights who have occasion to be around a production of their play; more than one scenographer has noted that the author is perfectly willing to accept any solution in production just so long as it happens to coincide with what he wanted in the first place.) In an afternote to *The Marriage of Mr. Mississippi*, the author feels impelled to issue this warning to the scenographer of any future productions of the play: "Many productions, no doubt misled by the text, have made the mistake of using scenery that was too abstract. Since, among other things, this comedy is 'the story of a room,' the room in which everything takes place must at the beginning be as real as possible. Only so will it be able to disintegrate. The unreal and fantastic may safely be left to the text, to the author."

In all fairness to Dürrenmatt, though, in this case he has touched on a valid point. As a matter of fact, this note might very well have been written by Ionesco for his play *The Bald Soprano*, which has often received much the same treatment. Although the play is an example of what has come to be known as the theater of the absurd, since it takes a nonsensical approach to dialogue and situation—a characteristic feature of this form of theater—the author asks for (even though most scenographers have not taken him seriously) a typical English room in a middle-class home. And what most scenographers do not realize is that that is exactly what he meant, that the force of the play (its effect, at least) greatly depends upon the contrast of unreal dialogue against a very real physical background. The scenographer, in both cases, should, as Dürrenmatt points out, resist doing the playwright's work for him.

In the foregoing note, Dürrenmatt sounds a little upset with the scenographer. But what of the other side of this situation: How does the scenographer feel about his obligations to the playwright? Few have either the skill or inclination to make their views on the subject known in print; the playwright's way with words does give him a certain advantage in this respect. However, not many scenographers seriously question the right of the playwright to expect to be interpreted correctly; most would agree that

that is what they try to do. Still, most scenographers resent the prevalent unspoken assumption that he is nothing more than a highly skilled servant to the playwright; he feels he has a right to expect certain concessions from this playwright (even though he may have been dead hundreds of years), as well as being obliged to him. Sometimes, however, scenographers do express in print their "gripes" with playwrights; Peter Larkin in *The Ideal Theater: Eight Concepts*, for instance, raises some serious questions concerning the present-day writer who has become too dependent on the cinema technique of writing. Here is what he said:

The writer starts theater.

The author also is a victim of the movies. As he writes his play, he cuts and pans with a vengeance, where before he strove mightily to stick with the classic unities of time and space. . . . I attended not long ago a meeting at the Ford Foundation in which our finest playwright bawled all the designers out for our prehistoric, creaking old theater. Why were there no new techniques available to him? It is true our professional theater hasn't got answers for that. He placed the responsibility on the architect-designer's head. . . . You cannot develop what you believe to be an undiscovered wonder drug and then go looking for a new disease. Designers must not design stage sets but stages, architects not theater buildings but theaters; and playwrights must stop writing movies and write in a new way for theater.

While Larkin's remarks concerning this particular point may be less warranted today than they were even ten years ago, we now have playwrights who, in their search for the new and original, are creating works that rely greatly on multimedia production. It is possible that many of them are creating works that might be better realized in some other medium, the cinema for instance. These playwrights, in their infatuation with the exciting possibilities of projections, slides, closed-circuit TV systems, and filmstrips, often rely on the scenographer to "make it all work." These techniques and mechanical contrivances, although legitimate in themselves and often interesting to an audience, in many instances become mere gimmickery, masking a lack of genuine creativity and originality on the part of the playwright who makes heavy use of them in his work. All too often it is the scenogra-

pher who ends in making the pertinent and definitive statement rather than the playwright he ostensibly serves; this is simply because the playwright has done nothing much more with his script than write out a blank check for those in charge of the physical production to fill in to whatever amount they choose. Few scenographers really desire this situation, no matter how satisfying personally such opportunities can be.

And yet playwrights vary greatly one from the other in their concern with how their works will be scenically realized on the stage. But it has only been during the last hundred years, approximately, that any have bothered themselves with the problem at all. During this century, however, we have had a rather extensive spectrum of writers who range all the way from writing complete directions into the scripts (as George Bernard Shaw did when he felt that internal guides and clues were not explicit enough to secure the proper interpretation of the script) to the author who apparently couldn't care less how his play is produced in the theater. A great deal of the difference lies, quite probably, in the individual writer's personal view of his function in relation to a producing situation. While some feel the "trappings" have little permanent influence on the worth of their play, others have done all within their power to have the final word as to how it will be viewed by an audience in the theater.

Perhaps a truer, more realistic attitude of the playwright toward the producing theater (and one that most scenographers and directors implicitly act on) has been voiced by Michel de Ghelderode in a letter to a prospective director of his play *Escurial*. Here is a part of that letter:

You don't have to take into account the wishes and advice of its author, who has been living, for a long time, a solitary life far removed from the theatre. There are several ways *Escurial* can be played. Yours will be the right way; the style you give it, the incantory state you project upon it, will suit your temperament. These things escape me—they no longer belong to me: the play is yours and it is your obligation to bring it to life either from the inside or the outside depending upon the intensity of the reality or dream. That is your marvelous domain. I am not part of it. The stage is where you, in turn, become the creator. Everything I would tell you is suggested in the text: the cruel and hallucinatory aspect of this action is contained in the description of the decor and characters. The only thing that could be useful to you is this: *think of painting*; this play is painting become theatre. I shall explain. I was inspired to write *Escurial* after I saw two canvasses of the Spanish School at the Louvre. An El Greco and a Velasquez on the same wall and not far from each other (this was in 1925–1926). El Greco inspired an anxious, haggard, visibly degenerate, pulmonary "King John"—in brief, a beautiful, clinical specimen. El Greco's brush brought forth a terrible, disquieting, unforgettable character—and I dreamed of him! Velasquez inspired a magnificent dwarf, swollen with blood and instinct. To bring these two monsters together was all that was needed. The play was the outcome—and its plasticity captivated you as did its peculiarly intense and spasmodic tone, its sudden modulation—the voices once again became human. Yes, everything is painting: gestures, attitudes, miming, parades, I can't think of anything else to tell you. (Bettina Knapp, trans., "To Directors and Actors: Letters, 1948–1959," *Tulane Drama Review* [Summer 1965])

But while some playwrights have, as de Ghelderode did in this instance, completely abdicated to the scenographer and director the re-

sponsibility for the realization of their play on the stage, others have been very specific in their desires concerning the production of their work. Eugene O'Neill, at least on one occasion, even went so far as to visit a power plant in order to make a sketch of its interior and equipment to give the scenographer Lee Simonson so that he would more nearly obtain the effect O'Neill wanted for his play *Dynamo* (fig. 81).

Few playwrights ever go quite this far; at best the practice has limited application. Most scenographers would not take kindly to a script that came with exact pictures of the playwright's wishes. Most playwrights actually count on the scenographer's collaboration as an artist with ideas of his own; while there have been many occasions where authors have been dissatisfied with the production of their plays, few would want the responsibility for it themselves.

The playwright is often more helpful to the scenographer when he stays within his own province; O'Neill is much more useful when he is less specific visually and makes his wishes known in

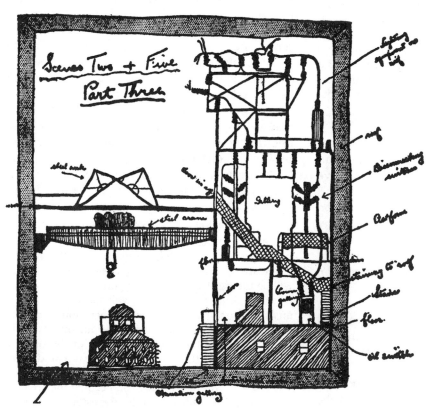

Fig. 81. *Dynamo* sketch by Eugene O'Neill. Courtesy of Mordecai Gorelik

terms that, while they guide the scenographer in certain paths, inspire him to make a contribution on his own. Read, for example, his description of the play's locale for *Desire under the Elms*:

The action of the entire play takes place in, and immediately outside of, the Cabot farmhouse in New England, in the year 1850. The south end of the house faces front to a stone wall with wooden gate at center opening on a country road. The house is in good condition but in need of paint. Its walls are sickly grayish, the green of the shutters faded. Two enormous elms are on each side of the house. They bend their trailing branches down over the roof. They appear to protect and at the same time subdue. There is a sinister maternity in their aspect, a crushing, jealous absorption. They have developed from their intimate contact with the life of man in the house an appalling humaneness. They brood oppressively over the house. They are like exhausted women resting their sagging breasts and hands and hair on its roof, and when it rains their tears trickle down monotonously and rot on the shingles.

This leaves something for the scenographer to do; the playwright is saying, "Here is the way I feel about this place. These are things I think are important for you to consider when you begin to design an actual structure where the characters of my play must live. And I don't feel I am encroaching on your art if I tell you about it. But, it is up to you to find a way of putting these thoughts and suggestions on the stage; at the same time it allows room for you to exercise your own art too."

Words: The Source of Theatrical Action

The most common mistake a young actor makes is to miscount the number of steps needed in a simple exchange of dialogue; that is, not to realize just how many separate, although related, parts are actually present when one speaks a line of the play's text and a second actor replies with another line. The most common mistake a young scenographer makes is to think that the actor is the only theater artist who needs to know how to *read lines*, that is, to obtain information from character interpretation when that information is not explicitly written into the text. The ability to extract useful information concerning place, time, spatial relationships, and the specific emotional charge (mood) from character analysis alone is crucial to the functioning of the scenographer. The visual form of the scenic environment and the subjective meanings embedded in the text can only be approached through the study of a play's characters. They are mutually dependent. Shakespeare always began a play in *exactly* the spot where the action had to begin and at the *last possible moment* that that action could begin. His great skill as a *maker* of plays has often been overshadowed by his genius with words. But the scenographer can never forget that although actions seem to arise from words, the opposite is more true: words arise from the impulse to action. Words came into being to extend, modify, and sometimes prevent physical action. Words are not substitutes for actions; they are logical outcomes of often unformed or unconscious thought. In the theater, the word is the secret key to the physical environment the playwright needs; before we study in detail how the playwright weaves subjective purposes into objective facts, we must clearly understand the purpose of a dialogue and how it is put together.

Let us take two lines spoken by the servants from the two feuding houses in the play *Romeo and Juliet* and see what even a short examination of them will reveal:

ABRAHAM: Do you bite your thumb at us sir?
SAMPSON: I do bite my thumb, sir

If one does not know this play, it is next to impossible to make heads or tails of this one exchange of dialogue. Taken out of context, as has been done here, these lines are nonsensical; nor do they give any information that relates to the story of *Romeo and Juliet*. It is doubtful if two of the finest actors in the world could make sense if given these lines alone and told to act them out in a meaningful way. Read in the context of the full script, these actors would be able to determine the meaning of the lines and be able to give them a proper interpretation on the stage. And it is the scenographer's duty to be able to read these lines alone in his studio and find out much the same information that those actors would in their studying the parts for presentation on the stage. There is an even more important reason, it could be demonstrated, for the scenographer's deeper understanding of these lines than that of the actor's: these two lines have a significance that might be missed by anyone but the most astute of Shakespearian scholars. The significance of these two seemingly casual lines lies in the fact that they are the very first words an audience hears, words that not only demonstrate the animosity between the two warring factions (after all Shakespeare, through the voice of Chorus, *told* us about the feud) but *show* the exact beginning of a new level of conflict that will at the end of "the two hours' traffic of our stage" terminate in the death of the two lovers. Shakespeare is casual in his introduction of this conflict; he does not say "Well, folks, you are now going to see just how fights get started, and how even those on the edges of violence cannot remain unaffected." But this, as we shall see as we follow the progress of the conflict in the play, is exactly what does happen; and it is at this precise point—the meeting of two insignificant and lowly characters—that the final conflict in the story begins, casual as that beginning may at first appear.

While the actors are only required to act out that moment of the play's story without comment of their own as to what the lines they are performing "mean," the scenographer, like the director, must comprehend the significance of that moment in larger terms. He, unlike the performers, must concern himself with this question: Since we assume that Shakespeare picked the proper place, the proper time, and the proper characters to begin this story, how best can we take up his leads and bring them into the physical theater so that they become part of the actor's world, not a separate world of their own that may or may not support their work. The answer lies in knowing the play in the same way as the actors; in fact, knowing *more* of play than they are required to know. It would not be exaggeration to say that the scenographer, unlike any other interpretative artist of the theater, must be able to read a play in three separate and distinct, although not unrelated, ways: first, as the actor reads it; second, as a director reads it; and third, as the scenographer reads it. The first of these readings gives him a subjective view of the world of the play; the second, an understanding of the

pattern and flow of movement; and the third, the visual environment he must fabricate to support the first two.

Now, however, it is time to consider more closely our original charge against the young actor (which we doubtless will find that the young scenographer shares): the inability to fully appreciate the exact nature of dialogue and the information often concealed in it.

The Hidden Steps in Dialogue

Any text of any play is only half a work; no text is ever more than half a work, and some texts are even less. So it follows that any two lines of dialogue, as those just quoted from *Romeo and Juliet*, are no more complete in part than is the text they come from complete as a whole. And it is precisely because of this that audiences still come to the theater; they come there to see the work *begun by the playwright* (even the work of so great a playwright as Shakespeare) *brought to completion as they watch*. When those two lines of dialogue are spoken before them, audiences are given—although they should not be consciously aware of it—not two lines of words but a continuous informational process that has other steps to it. In order for this informational process to be successful, moreover, those steps must be well understood by all those artists involved in the interpretation of the play, not simply those most in evidence, the actors.

In any two continuous lines of dialogue between two actors we should expect to find four distinct—although not consciously perceived by an audience—steps. These are:

Step 1. Impetus
Step 2. Written line of text
Step 3. Reaction
Step 4. Written line of text

But, what does this outline really mean; and just what do the words "impetus" and "reaction" have to do with the acting out of dialogue? Let us take these same four steps and look more closely at what they involve.

Step 1 (Impetus). Actor A—Abraham in our example—has a thought. This thought may originate in his own mind, or it may be a reaction to something just said to him or some action done to him or one he has just observed. (Abraham's thought originates from Sampson's gesture; until this moment he was walking along with his fellow servant more or less minding his own business when out of the blue, as it were, a gesture is made in his direction. At least he *thinks* it might be directed toward him, but he is not absolutely sure of this. An impetus may even originate as a result of something *not* said or *not* done directly, as it is in this case.) In any case, only after a thought is formed—no matter how quickly or how illogical can he go on to:

Step 2 (Written line of text). Actor A gives vocal utterance to the substance of his thought. What actor A says is a direct result, we can see, of what took place in step 1. It does not matter if the information conveyed is thought directly verbalized or changed to suit the purpose of the character as actor A perceives that purpose; what is important to note is that step 2 is not possible until step 1 is finished. Step 2 may be so quickly accomplished that thought and line almost seem to tread on one another; but, no matter how quickly, step 2 *must* follow step 1. Not realizing that that all-important first step is there often promotes the young inexperienced actor's desire to get his line out quickly so as not to forget it. The character Flute in *A Midsummer Night's Dream*, when he is playing Thisby, has precisely the same trouble; in rehearsing the play to be given before Theseus and the court, the play's director, Peter Quince, points out to him: "Why, you must not speak that yet . . . You speak all your part at once, cues and all." Although Flute is clearly a figure of fun to Shakespeare, he is just as clearly based on every actor—both then and now—who does not know that speech without impetus is essentially *thoughtless.*

Step 3 (Reaction). The second half of an exchange of dialogue begins when actor B—Sampson in our example—hears what actor A has said. Actor B then repeats the exact same process as actor A in step 1; actor B must form a new thought (although based on words or actions he might have himself initiated) before it is possible for him to go on to:

Step 4 (Written line of text). Actor B gives vocal utterance to the substance of his thought (perhaps, like actor A, altering this thought to suit his interpretation of the written line he must speak).

This process, then, so often mistaken for line of text followed by line of text, does have, as we have seen, more steps to it than at first appears. This observation may seem too obvious to take the time to point it out; but any amateur production will provide literally hundreds of examples that demonstrate how this seemingly simple common sense approach to acting is often aborted or omitted altogether. *Nor is this process as carefully studied in the scenographic design class as it should be.* While it may seem that knowing the elements of dialogue is only the actor's responsibility, ignorance of the process just described makes the scenographer's profession all but impossible.

Dramatic dialogue is, as we have seen, primarily a cause-and-effect process depending on questions to keep the process in motion. Very few who have not studied the principles of either playwriting or acting realize just how much of dialogue is nothing more than a string of questions and answers; it is only in the didactic (teaching) or a thesis (message) play that we find characters making any significant number of outright statements or posing only rhetorical questions. (Which means that one character alone may very well spend much of the time completing all four of the steps just examined; the conflict that arises from two separate characters asking and answering questions, on the other hand, accounts for both the interest an audience has in plays where real questions are posed and answered and the ofttimes lack of interest they show in plays which merely reveal a playwright's opinion.) The question—either explicit or implied—is the fuel on which the drama runs. The primary skill of the playwright does not consist in presentation of thoughts or philosophies directly to an audience as much as it is to raise questions *about* thoughts, philosophies and—most important of all—*actions of his characters.* And we must further realize that all questions are not of the same kind; those of the playwright must be forward moving (and must also contain implicit action from which the performer may extrapolate movement) and not be circular, which would keep the play in a holding pattern: that is, "What are you doing?" "What do you think I am doing?" "Why won't you tell me?" "What would you like me to do?"

The skill of play interpretation depends upon an ability to work backward. That is, contrary to human communication outside the theater, where an impetus always precedes speech (although not always a conscious or thoughtful process), the pages of a script contain only the results of an impetus, not the causes of those results. The second part of the process we examined above—the verbalization of an impetus or a thought—is rarely given by the playwright (and when it is given in a stage direction or as a note near the line, many a director and actor consider this as a failure on the part of the playwright to write "good" dialogue). This kind of information, although not at all uncommon in the plays of twentieth-century playwrights, is almost totally lacking in plays of the past. Nor would it be possible for any playwright to provide a complete subtext (to give this information its modern name) without becoming an entirely different kind of writer. If a playwright did provide a text complete with *subtext*, it would no longer be a play; the playwright would, perforce, become a novelist. Let us, for the moment, entertain the thought that Shakespeare did provide those intermediary steps in his written play; he could not avoid, then, writing in his text something very much like this:

ABRAHAM *thinks*: (What in the hell is that guy doing biting his thumb? Doesn't he know just how insulting such a gesture is? Is he stupid or is he out to start a fight? Don't these Capulets ever learn their lesson? Well, in any case, I just can't let this insult pass without saying something.)
ABRAHAM *speaks (with narrowed eyes and steely voice)*: Do you bite your thumb at us, sir?

Shakespeare would not, of course, nor any other playwright, take the time for such nonsense. This entire subtext may very well flash through the mind of Abraham in a split second; in fact, remembering past encounters of the same sort may cause him to react instinctively. But the point to be made is that as reasoned out above by Abraham, instantaneously reactive as he might well be, *something* was going on in the space that preceded his words, and that *something* is all important to the acting out of Abraham's part. Nor does that *something* only contain information indicating the proper vocal response an actor playing Abraham should adopt. Volume, rhythm, speed of delivery, tone of voice—

important as those clues might be—are not the only items of information to be found in these hidden steps. The actor must also deduce what actions must be employed to support any vocal response. The most important aspect of acting, therefore, begins *before* a line is spoken; that is where the spark of acting must take place. It is within these unspoken spaces that information needed to say the line with the appropriate emotion or the intended meaning must be found; and it is also within those same spaces that a performer finds the necessary action that gives support to those emotions. Shakespeare shows himself acutely aware of the interrelationship of written text and implicit movement when, through the character of Hamlet, he says: "Suit the action to the word, the word to the action; with this special observance, that you o'erstep not the modesty of nature. For anything so overdone is from the purpose of playing, whose end, both at the first and now, was and is, to hold, as 'twere, the mirror up to nature." He stresses especially the relationships we have just outlined: *action to word, the word to the action*. Nor does he imply, as many even today would defend, that all an actor has to do is, as I have heard a director instruct a cast, "just make sure to say all the lines—the rest will take care of itself."

The scenographer, like the actor, must look carefully at not only what is written on the page before him but what is *not* written there. And, just as the accomplished actor realizes that for every line he sees written on the script before him, there is an accompanying thought that has embedded in it a clue to action. Even when these clues tell that an actor does not move or does not speak immediately (i.e., when the clue says, *Do nothing!*), we still must find that information out from those spaces between the lines. It is just as important, therefore, for the scenographer to study these spaces as diligently and in the same manner as the actor. For it is there he will find the necessary information to give his own work form, usefulness, and direction, which it cannot ever have without that consideration.

The primary attitude the scenographer must adopt and foster is this: once we have understood what a character is thinking and feeling, we are able, with a much more reasonable assurance, to begin to understand the needs of that character in terms of movement; and by progressively charting those needs for movement, we begin to have a clearer view of how much space is necessary to accommodate those movements on the stage. This can never be found without an intimate knowledge of what transpires in those silent spaces between the spoken lines of a play. Although this information could be passed on by others—the playwright through specific directions, the director through precise requests— the modern-day scenographer is not relieved of the responsibility to find out as much of this information on his own before he begins the long process of communication and compromise that accompany every production of a theatrical work.

It is true that just the lines of a text can give information. But it is more important to realize that even the most beautiful or profound words strung out in flawless lines are no more than retaining walls for something that the lines themselves do not possess. The professional actor must, in order to continue to practice his profession, learn this most elemental principle of the theater. But so must the scenographer. The old and often-repeated observation that the sensitive person is one who can *read between the lines* is the most important prerequisite for any artist who works for the stage.

The Hidden Objective World of the Playwright

Action, as we have seen, lies hidden between the lines of a text. However, meanings of a scene also often lie hidden in images to which the playwright has responded in ways other than intellectual. The everyday world around us with its myriad visual experiences deeply affects all of us; we all have had our minds formed and our minds changed by what we see. Vision is the primary means to understanding; it is our ultimate language that lies beyond all verbal systems. And yet it is a common fallacy—a fallacy shared by most outside the theater and many within it—that intellectual thought expressed in written words is the only concern of the playwright. It is true that the written word is the playwright's primary tool; it is not, however, the primary source of his inspiration no matter how

eloquently he is able to use that tool. The great playwrights have always known that the image and the object are the most elementary carriers of meanings and messages. And it constantly escapes most of us just how many times a playwright "hides" his most important messages in those images and objects. Most important of all, we who work in the theater must come to realize, and then to make the best use of the fact, that the text we inherit is not the first product of the playwright's mind but only the result of a step that preceded it: his confrontation and interaction with those images and objects he encountered in his own experience. It would seem that these first experiences would be lost forever to us, that the text is the only means to his thoughts. For the most part, that is true. But it is much more possible, than it would appear at first glance, to dig out the reasons why his work is written and to understand the elements that channeled it in certain directions. Although this sounds like work more suited for a Sherlock Holmes than a scenographer, it relies on—as Agatha Christie's famous detective Hercule Poirot states—"putting the little gray cells to work." Detection of hidden clues and motives lies at the heart of reading dramatic texts.

Playwrights, then, are no less susceptible to the great world of experience than the rest of us. And their response to the visible is no less important to their work than it is to the scenographer. The important difference is, however, that we as scenographers are responsible for finding and bringing to view those images after they have been reduced to words and incased in thought. It would be helpful, therefore, in this section to examine instances either of how images promote the playwright's work or of how the scenographer gleans from those words images he believes to have been instrumental in its creation. One example, first, of just what we mean when we speak of an image promoting a written work.

Pretty Baby is a film directed by Louis Malle. Its subject matter is Storeyville, the notorious red-light district that flourished in New Orleans during the first two decades of this century. The story ostensibly concerns the photographer L. J. Bellocq who, much like Toulouse-Lautrec only shortly before, gained his inspiration from making photographic images of prostitutes in their everyday surroundings. Malle was less interested in a strong narrative than in capturing the feel and flavor of a colorful time and presenting a mysterious figure—Bellocq—in a more understandable context. But did the concept of this film spring forth as an intellectual desire to show the everyday life of a famous house of prostitution or to expose the motivations of an eccentric artist? I think not.

I am, rather, reasonably certain that Malle's most important impetus to create *Pretty Baby* was in direct response to the photographs made by Bellocq in 1912; undoubtedly they played a seminal role in the decision to make such a film. Viewing these photographs could lead to the speculation that they were even instrumental in the casting of the performers in the film, in particular Brooke Shields.

While we may realize that the cinema is a more image-oriented medium, it does not detract from the fact that the film *Pretty Baby* did not merely use Bellocq's photographs to bolster the period research for the work; *they are the reasons why the work exists.* Nor should this singular instance blind us to the realization that all writers have just such a "hidden world" from which they not only draw but from which, on occasion, their work actually springs. (See Michel Ghelderode's letter above in "The Scenographer's Relationship to the Playwright.")

The playwright often reveals his most important messages through the use of objects. Properties are often employed by a playwright and (sometimes interpolated by the director) to make a point that he would not be able to make with words or actions alone. In point of fact, it is not uncommon for the most abstract thought or for the most dramatic moment in a play to occur after there is a lapse in action or dialogue and to be transmitted to an audience through the use of a "prop," to use the vernacular of the theater. Of course, it is not the scenographer's job to tell the story of the text by the use of either scenic environments, independent images, or properties. But it is his obligation to know just how these objective forms work and the reason why the playwright introduces a certain object at a certain moment in the scene.

The relationship of the stage property to the performer's role is the most overlooked element of directing, acting, and scenography. Very few students of acting know just how important that relationship is and to what extent it directly affects the performance of a role; very few scenographers fully appreciate how important their contribution can be to this area.

Properties can be, and often are, the impetus of a thought that cannot be expressed in words, the embodiment of an emotion that cannot be described but can only be demonstrated. Properties are, to be more precise, often the "point" of the scene to which no word or combination of words—no matter how finely written—can add. Moreover, a property can precipitate a major turning point in the development of a plot line or can begin a wholly new direction in a play. It is even possible that a property can be the single most important element in a scene and that the absence of it would cause the plot to come to a dead stop. To explain more fully what is inherent in such strong statements as these, let us take a familiar scene from a familiar play that will show just how important these things called properties can be to the progress of a dramatic work.

In *Hamlet*, there are many allusions to death. Hamlet's preoccupation with the subject is unrelenting; his mind is never far from some aspect of dying. He talks incessantly of what death is or what it means; his speculations are many and profound. And yet there is only one moment in the whole play where he comes face to face with the full realization of what it means to be dead. It is a moment that reduces this most talkative of pessimists to near speechlessness. It is a moment during which words all but fail; and yet an audience watching the scene knows precisely what is being "said." And it is a property that makes the entire scene not only possible but meaningful. Let us look at the words that surround this moment:

HAMLET: How long hast thou been a grave-maker?
CLOWN: Of all the days i' th' year, I came to't that day that our last king Hamlet o'ercame Fortinbras.
HAMLET: How long is that since?
CLOWN: Cannot you tell that? Every fool can tell that. It was the very day that young Hamlet was born—he that is mad, and sent into England.
HAMLET: Ay, marry, why was he sent into England?
CLOWN: Why, because 'a was mad. 'A shall recover

his wits there; or, if 'a do not, 'tis no great matter there.

HAMLET: Why?

CLOWN: 'Twill not be seen in him there. There the men are as mad as he.

HAMLET: How came he mad?

CLOWN: Very strangely, they say.

HAMLET: How strangely?

CLOWN: Faith, e'en with losing his wits.

HAMLET: Upon what ground?

CLOWN: Why, here in Denmark. I have been sexton here, man and boy, thirty years.

HAMLET: How long will a man lie i' th' earth ere he rot?

CLOWN: Faith, if 'a be not rotten before 'a die (as we have many pocky corses now-a-days that will scarce hold the laying in), 'a will last you some eight year or nine year. A tanner will last you nine year.

HAMLET: Why he more than another?

CLOWN: Why, sir, his hide is so tanned with his trade that 'a will keep out water a great while, and your water is a sore decayer of your whoreson dead body. Here's a skull now; this skull hath lain in th' earth three-and-twenty years.

HAMLET: Whose was it?

CLOWN: A whoreson mad fellow's it was. Whose do you think it was?

HAMLET: Nay, I know not.

CLOWN: A pestilence on him for a mad rogue! 'A poured a flagon of Rhenish on my head once. This same skull, sir, was Yorick's skull, the king's jester.

HAMLET: This? [Takes the skull.]

CLOWN: E'en that.

HAMLET Alas, poor Yorick! I knew him, Horatio, a fellow of infinite jest, of most excellent fancy. He hath borne me on his back a thousand times. And now how abhorred in my imagination it is! My gorge rises at it. Here hung those lips that I have kissed I know not how oft. Where be your gibes now? Your gambols, your songs, your flashes of merriment that were wont to set the table on a roar? Not one now to mock your own grinning? Quite chapfall'n? Now get you to my lady's chamber, and tell her, let her paint an inch thick, to this favor she must come. Make her laugh at that.

It might be well for anyone studying this scene (or the entire play, for that matter) to take a moment to consider just how valuable this kind of scene is to an interpreter and to see just how much information Shakespeare places in scenes of this nature. If one carefully examines the chro-

nology embedded in the gravedigger's garrulous ramblings, it will be found that he outlines the entire timeframe of Hamlet's life and at the same time shows how that span of time relates to the activities of both his father and his father's arch rival, old Fortinbras. Figure 82 is a chronological diagram showing this information and how the significant points in the history relate to the plot of the play. Such information is vital to anyone who wishes to gain a comprehensive view not only of the individual events that take place in this play but how those events relate to the actions to specific scenes. Being able to visually see the flow of time greatly enhances the ability to understand the progress of the plot.

Now let us return to the main focus of this scene.

Before this scene, death has crossed Hamlet's path many times, but always at an intellectual distance. This particular scene, however, is different; it is at this point in the play that Shakespeare causes Hamlet to cross death's path. In point of fact, the progress of the play's action makes it impossible for Hamlet to avoid doing so, since the playwright has set the scene in a graveyard and a fairly active one at that. Shakespeare has, we will see, taken extra pains to manipulate very precisely the threads of the plot so as to make a precise point: to bring home to Hamlet in the cruelest, most forceful way just what the reality of death is; not its abstract understanding but its actuality. In this scene Shakespeare does not tell Hamlet *about* death, he *shows* him what it really means not only to be bereft of the vital spark of life but to be dissolved once again back into crude elements. And in order to accomplish his aim, he sets up Hamlet so that the lesson will have the maximum impact. Look again at the lines of the scene just quoted; consider just what Shakespeare has, as a playwright, done up to the point where we have taken up the thread of conversation. These are the actions he has crafted into the preceding text:

1. He has caused Hamlet to come home to the palace via the backyard, as it were. Hamlet, not wanting to call undue attention to his escape from Claudius's plotting, returns by the most inconspicuous way: the back door. (If the king's plan had worked, in fact, Hamlet would not be coming back at all.)

2. He causes Hamlet to come onto the scene

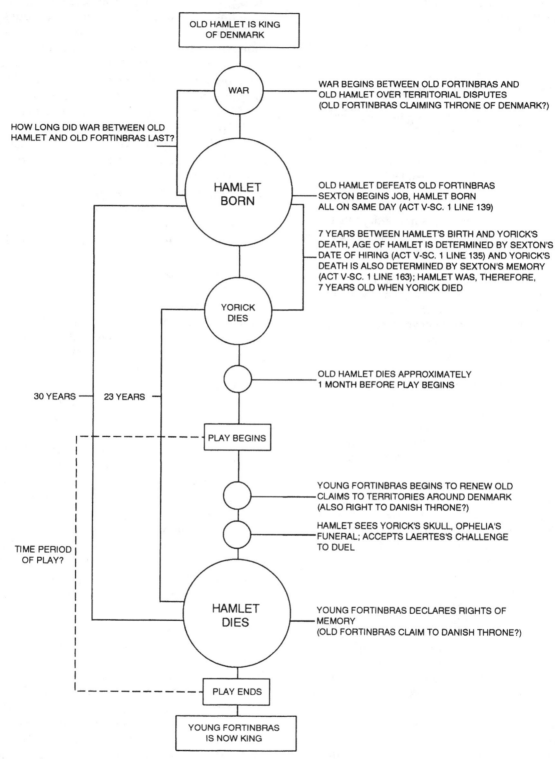

Fig. 82. Chronological chart of Hamlet

just at the exact moment when a gravedigger (whom Shakespeare calls *Clown*) is preparing a new grave. (A coincidence?) Hamlet, of course, having been out of the country and out of touch with the events of the court, could not be expected to know for whom the grave is being dug. The digging, therefore, means little to him, since he does not at this moment have any reasons to suspect that the gravedigger's job has any connection to his—Hamlet's—concerns.

3. He causes the gravedigger to be a fairly jovial person who, despite his grim calling, is not above singing happy songs while he does essentially sad work. (Comic relief; but for what purpose?) The fact that this digging is disturbing the final resting place of others buried in earlier graves (bodies were simply wrapped in shrouds and indiscriminately placed in the earth with little regard as to earlier burials) means little to the gravedigger and, probably, less to Hamlet. In sum, what Hamlet sees on his walk across the castle graveyard is simply a man at work who is apparently enjoying what he is doing; a man who is just doing a job in much the same way as he has done for years; a man no different from the other functionaries who keep the palace in repair and in working order.

4. He causes Hamlet to begin a bantering conversation with the gravedigger, which centers around the abstract facts of death and the eventual disintegration of the body once it is dead and placed in the ground.

5. He causes the gravedigger to call attention to one particular skull he has just tossed out of the grave in which he is working. Shakespeare gives the gravedigger a very special question for Hamlet: "Whose do ye think it was?"

Hamlet answers nonchalantly (thinking, quite probably: *How in the world would I know whose skull this one is out of so many that have been buried here?*") It is at this point that Shakespeare plays his trump card; brings all the coincidences of time, place, and personalities into a single devastating point: "CLOWN: . . . This same skull, sir, was Yorick's skull, the king's jester."

Hamlet is all but speechless. The only word he can utter (and quite probably it is a long moment before he can bring himself to speak even that) is "This?" The gravedigger's only reply is, "E'en that." Hamlet takes the skull in his own hands and begins his now famous (and often misquoted) lines: "Alas, poor Yorick! I knew him Horatio."

This is the point, then, where Hamlet has been shown exactly what it means to be dead, it is a moment when all the fine words about the philosophical import of mortality are forgotten in the presence of the awesome thing he holds not more than a foot away from his own face; it is the moment when words all but fail and a physical object becomes the focus of the drama; it is the moment when a "prop" holds the meaning of the play in a way that no amount of words could hope to rival.

Once Hamlet recovers from the initial shock of finding out to whom the skull belonged, he gives a fairly accurate picture of how it appears to him; the description is graphic and sharp; it is certainly not the kind of skull one might expect to find in a medical school—clean, complete, and almost white. This skull, on the contrary, not only has earth attached to it but may also have remnants of the decayed flesh of its former owner still adhering. It is, as Hamlet obliquely tells us, a sickening sight; "my gorge rises at it." (In other words, he says, it almost makes me throw up.) It is far from the antiseptic sort of skull a medical school might possess. It is, rather, a hideous unclean thing, and yet (another of Shakespeare's crafty coincidences) it is the sole remaining part of someone Hamlet once knew and loved very much. This is what makes this encounter so particularly dramatic and powerful; a moment ago it was just one skull among many, and now it is the skull of Hamlet's dearest childhood companion. He relates how it was Yorick who, when his father and mother apparently had no time for him, cared for and entertained him. It is, in fact, the only other skull—aside from his own father's—that could move him so powerfully; it also makes him see so clearly just how much time takes away from both the dead and the living. And yet, Shakespeare is not finished with this property, nor is he through with the twisting of Hamlet's deepest emotions. How, one may ask, can you go further than to place in Hamlet's hands the only skull that could shock or grieve him most? It is a difficult feat, but Shakespeare accomplishes just that.

Just before Hamlet's thoughts and attentions are diverted in other channels, he recovers both his composure and his humor sufficiently to make these remarks: "Now get you to my lady's chamber, and tell her, let her paint an inch thick, to this favor she must come; make her laugh at that." This, of course, is a reference to two things; first, it is a direct reference to Ophelia, and second, it obliquely refers to a taunting remark Hamlet made to her earlier in the play: "God gives you one face and you make another for yourself" (i.e., all women are two-faced). It is also a reference to the use of makeup as an attempt to make a woman more attractive; Hamlet challenges her, in other words, to use her talent for deceiving to put flesh back onto Yorick's skull—to give it life again—a challenge to which he knows she cannot but fail. His remarks show he is still bitter about the abortive nature of their love affair and that, even in jest, he expects little from her.

What Hamlet does not know, of course, is that the grave over which he and the gravedigger have been talking and making jokes is meant for Ophelia and that even now she is being brought toward it. (Another of Shakespeare's cruel but necessary coincidences.) He will, all too soon, learn of Ophelia's suicide, but at the moment it is simply part of the ironic web Shakespeare is weaving about Hamlet. The skull, then, is the impetus of a cruel remark that Hamlet will, in a matter of minutes, come to regret.

So we see that this one property, so familiar to theatergoers for hundreds of years, is, actually, the pivot of this very important scene. It not only causes the thoughts of Hamlet to go deep into the past but also foreshadows both immediate and later events in the play. It is, in a word, so integral to the meaning of *Hamlet*, that the play would be considerably less powerful if it had not been introduced. Our question, then, is just what does Hamlet hold in his hand? It is a skull, of course, and a particular skull at that. But what is the precise nature of the skull Hamlet sees and touches? And is this really an important question to ask?

I think it is. I also think it demonstrates how exactly the scenographer must visualize a text and the detail to which he must hold himself responsible. It is very easy to say that a skull is just a skull and most likely not too different from any other skull. But this is not so, or at least it should not be so. This property carries a very

great meaning with its use; for the scenographer, the care with which it is visualized and prepared must be considered. It is very much part of the playwright's hidden world and very much our responsibility to ensure that even so small a detail of the production must be directly supervised or delegated to those to whom one skull is not just the same as another. What does Hamlet see, then, when he holds this property in his hand? What goes through his mind? And, most important of all, how can this skull be treated to provide the maximum impetus to the actor using it?

Over the years interpreters have lost much of Hamlet's direct reaction to the horror of encountering such an object; they have, instead, allowed the poetic diction of the words to overshadow the immediacy of the actual event, thus making description (much as the Greek theater did) substitute for showing what Shakespeare intended. In a word, they have abstracted the content of the scene and in so doing have lessened its initial force. Even usually careful filmmakers have not paid the attention to this detail it deserves. Some of this inattention is evident in the 1964 USSR film version of *Hamlet* (fig. 83). The skull that this Hamlet holds is as clean as any in a medical school classroom (fig. 84). While Hamlet can with this particular skull ruminate on the *concept* of death, he is not reminded of the more difficult acceptance of the *facts* of such a state; they would remain, as stated before, abstract. Certainly he has little impetus to remark that "my gorge rises at it." Any actor holding this sterile bone object has little motivation to ruminate on the slow decay of the body, a subject Shakespeare has taken great pains to describe. All one sees here is rather sanitized final result possessing little of the horror of human flesh eaten away by worm and decayed by time. What the actor holds here is simply a clean relic that carries little of the memory of a loved human being. One might say that the actor is denied in this instance an opportunity to experience thoughts and feelings that would not surface when viewing a clean, white skull. More important, this skull contradicts the very precise description that Shakespeare causes Hamlet to make; this is not the skull that smells of decay or could make a viewer think of throwing up. And yet, that is exactly the kind of skull Shakespeare

Fig. 83. Scene from Russian film of *Hamlet*

wanted Hamlet to have placed in his hand: a physically disturbing thing to cause equally disturbing thoughts.

It would not be inaccurate or facetious to state that Yorick is a character in the play *Hamlet* and, moreover, an important one. Like the dead Polonius, he is "a . . . counsellor . . . most secret, and most grave." To a large extent, we are given more factual information about him than we are told of many of the other characters in the play. While he does not come onto the stage in actuality, he does "appear." Of course, he is long dead before either the action of the play in general or the scene in which he figures as a character. But appear he does, and although only a very little piece of him is present, the play would be infinitely poorer if that piece were not there.

Shakespeare brings Yorick into the action of the play for a very special purpose: he is the messenger who finally gives Hamlet a satisfactory answer to his most obsessive question—what it means to be dead, and perhaps more important still, what it means to live. Quite probably, the message Yorick gives is not the one

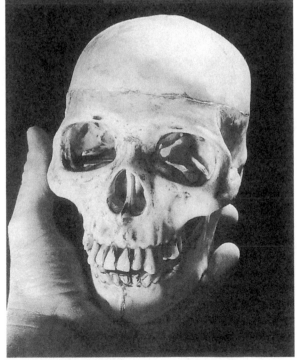

Fig. 84. Medical school skull

Hamlet would hear had he the ability to choose. Nevertheless, after the first horrifying shock, he does confront and then accept the facts of death with all their consequences. Nor would it be exaggeration to say that from this precise point on, Hamlet's chief concern is to put his affairs in order while awaiting the inevitable. Yorick's message is simple, clear, and final; Hamlet no longer questions what death is, he merely prepares for it. Would not the skull in figure 85 better relay that message?

Not to consider the "design" of this one important property—the skull of Yorick (fig. 86)—is tantamount to forgetting to provide a costume for an important character in a production. Small though this property is, and familiar as it has become to audiences in general, it does make such a powerful point in the play that we should consider precisely how it should appear both to the actor and to the audience. Our study of this property's use and features draws attention to an important underlying principle of the scenographer's art: *No detail is beneath active consideration nor outside the scope of direct attention*. This observation, though not a new one, must constantly

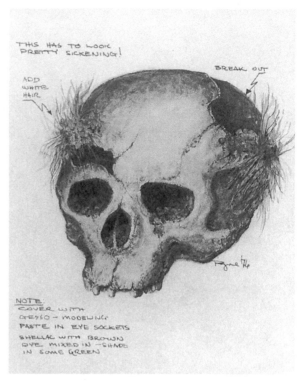

Fig. 86. Design for skull of Yorick

be kept in mind. Robert Edmond Jones always required of those in charge of creating or selecting properties that they use great care in their construction or take special care in their procurement. He was, throughout his entire professional career, intensely aware of even the smallest details in a production; he knew, as an artist working with other artists, that those elements of a design that affect the performer directly must be treated with care, with respect, and perhaps most important of all, *with imagination*. Once, a stage manager remarked that the set-dressing Jones had requested for a period play was "too small to be seen from even the front row." Jones replied, "Do you not think the actor needs exaltation too!"

What we have just discussed may seem to be an unusual amount of time and thought expended on a single, fairly small property that is used once and then almost immediately forgotten in the course of subsequent events. But I hope the twofold point has been made: that this object comes from that highly important "hidden world" in the playwright's imagination, and that the smallest details of that world deserve careful

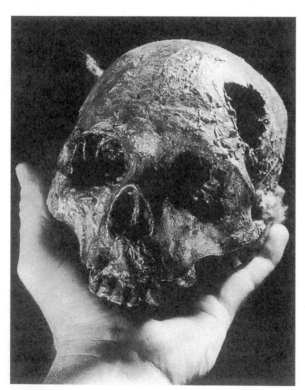

Fig. 85. Skull of Yorick

consideration. It is, I believe, important to stress just how much the scenographer must concern himself with those smallest of details in the overall planning of a production, and that he must give especial attention to those timeworn moments of the drama that we think we know through familiar repetition but of which we have all but lost sight and understanding.

Is it really the scenographer's function to consider so completely a piece no more than six inches in any direction with as much care as it is to concern himself with a backdrop eighty feet wide? The answer to this question is obvious to the artist.

Detailed Analysis of a Text: The Church Scene from Gounod's *Faust*

The first steps in designing for the opera are not unlike the approach to any other scenographic project. Study and analysis of the text usually take precedence over any other activity. There is a basic difference, however, between the text of an opera and most other scripts. Reading the libretto alone can be an uninspiring experience, since much of this text only becomes meaningful when it is amplified and underscored by the musical accompaniment. In opera, words and ideas, because they are not easily heard or understood when sung, are generally much more simple, repetitive, and straightforward in utterance, with the greater part of the emotional or poetic feeling left to the music. Still, this text must be as carefully studied as any playscript. It is gratifying to note, however, that modern operas have placed an increased emphasis on the libretto, with the result that many of these newer works have more literary merit than has been the case in the past.

Faust, by Charles Gounod and based on Goethe's drama of the same name, is an opera that belongs to the late-middle period of the romantic era, a movement that held the artistic world in its sway from approximately 1830 until well into the present century. Opera has yet to completely escape its influence (although as an art form it is not entirely alone in this respect) and probably will not as long as works written during the romantic period are still performed. At the present time, it is not possible to say just how long that will be, but it would seem that these works will be with us for some time to come.

In the Gounod *Faust*, much of the original legend, so powerful dramatically in the Goethe version, has, unfortunately been weakened and obscured by the excessively sentimental attitudes of the period. (In Germany this particular opera is generally advertised not as *Faust* but as *Marguerite*.) In the production we will examine here, it was decided early in the various conferences that precede such an undertaking to consciously counteract some of this gross (or that which seems gross to us now) sentimentality, which, while attractive and perhaps persuasive to audiences a hundred years ago (the first performance was in 1859), might prevent a present-day audience from easily accepting it. This, by the way, is not meant as apology for the composer and the librettist; it is, rather, an attempt to recover some of the original force and meaning they intended and did, apparently, achieve in the earlier presentations for audiences whose tastes were more in sympathy with the style and period. This, perhaps, is the most defensible reason for updating the period of a work: to expose the form and meaning that lie beneath the often antiquated surface of its original mode of presentation.

The decision concerning period, therefore, became the first and most important consideration for all those responsible for the look and "spirit" of the opera. The time period was not, however, to be exactly pinpointed but, rather, to be treated with a certain amount of conscious anachronism. (German scenographers, especially those who have worked for Brecht or have been influenced by his philosophies—Teo Otto and Caspar Neher, for example—have adopted this particular attitude toward design in general for a number of years.) This time period was to be placed roughly during the first years after World War I; a period, it was felt, that would contain some elements that might reflect attitudes found in the original legend and buried below the surface of the opera. *Faust* has a number of situations and acts of violence that are all but completely hidden under the patina and guise of conventional romanticism. Carnal love, disillusionment, betrayal, revenge, murder, and insanity are all part of the story's web; the church scene itself is a short but intense study in the horror possible in a mind cruelly tortured to the point of madness. It was with this attitude in mind that the production was approached; it was to be an exploration of the dark world that lay beneath the surface beauty of the music.

This was the period, then—the aftermath of a great war with its disillusionments, its sense of dislocation and destroyed values—in which the opera was to be set. It was also decided to use a trio of German expressionist painters—Nolde, Kirchner, Kokoschka—as a visual focal point, a point of reference and departure, and to consciously make certain scenes (the church scene for one, the Walpurgis night scene for another) expressionistic in nature. Some of the specific reasons why and how this was done will be discussed later in relation to the church scene.

For the moment, let us examine this question of consciously using a certain style, in this case expressionism, as part of a scenic concept. To use expressionism at all in the theater can be a dangerous course for the scenographer to pursue, although it is a style popular and widespread, especially in university theaters. The term actually implies the way one (and only one) person sees the world, with whatever distortion that personal view entails. When we look at an artwork done in this style, we are seeing precisely what the artist wants us to see. This is his view, his outlook; it is subjective and personal. As perceived by the artist it may appear distorted, since it is, by definition, a highly singular way of seeing. But while this singular vision is the prerogative of an individual artist creating an individual work, it is, with few exceptions, not a workable style for the scenographer, since an audience is rarely required to experience a scene through the eyes of one artist only (or one character as in Elmer Rice's *Adding Machine*). It is not entirely fair for a scenographer to impose an intensely personal subjective view on a play and, consequently, on an audience.

In the church scene, however, it was felt that an expressionistic approach was not only possible but desirable; that we are asked to see through the eyes of one person—Marguerite—and that what we see is a distortion of reality. In other words, although the general principle that

expressionism may be in most instances a dangerous course of action for the scenographer, in some cases it might be the right and proper one.

Let us take a closer look at the composition of this scene. Here is a synopsis. (In actual production, this scene is almost always played "in one"; this means that there is a larger scene set up immediately behind it hidden by a backdrop or curtain. In *Faust*, the scene that follows this one [the square scene in which Valentin, Marguerite's brother, has returned from the wars] was originally intended to precede the church scene, but it has become traditional to perform it afterward in order to give more emphasis to the famous "Soldiers' Chorus" and the death scene of Valentin.)

The interior of the cathedral. Organ music vibrates softly as Marguerite enters, kneels, and begins to pray. Suddenly the voice of Mephistopheles calls harshly that she must not pray ("Non! tu ne prieras pas!"). As Marguerite cowers in terror, a tomb opens and Mephistopheles stands before her, thundering that the devils in hell are clamoring for her soul. Marguerite cries out in horror and bewilderment. The choir behind the scenes chants of the awful Day of Judgment ("Quand du Seigneur le jour luira"). As Marguerite prays, Mephistopheles again proclaims her doom, then vanishes. She faints with a piercing cry as the curtain falls. (Milton Cross, *Milton Cross's Complete Stories of the Great Operas*)

In most productions of Faust, the appearance of Mephistopheles is unquestioned; he simply appears, says what he has to say and then disappears. In the present production, where and how he appears were the cause of much discussion and debate. Finally, it was decided that he did not just come to the church, he was brought there. By whom? There is only one other person in the scene—Marguerite. How does she bring him into the church? In her imagination. While the world where she is, the church, is real, what she is experiencing in it—the confrontation with Mephistopheles—is not necessarily real. What we, the audience, see, therefore, is what she is imagining. The scene is actually a hallucination, a product of a mind that is slowly losing its grip on reality, not an actual supernatural occurrence as it has usually been played heretofore. We, the producers, felt this would be more acceptable to a modern-day audience. But what does this mean to the scenographer? How can he and the director use this concept? Most important, how can this idea be made clear to an audience?

Usually this scene is not presented very elaborately; often it rates nothing more than a narrow horizontal passage of space in front of a painted drop that masks a larger scene behind it. But actually, it is a key scene in the drama of the opera and deserves more attention than it too often receives. Yet since it is a short scene and occupies an unfavorable position in the flow of scenes, great care must be taken that it does not become too cumbersome and difficult to set or strike. This was the main problem in the actual realization of the set on the stage, and the solution to the problem demanded great care in planning, precisely because it had to be done quickly.

If there has been one major development or trend in opera production during the past eighty years, it has been the attempt to make the staging more acceptable on the realistic level. Even in the often grotesque and fantasy world of opera, audiences seem to be demanding greater skill both in the presentation of character and in the design and execution of the scenery used in opera production. And yet much of present-day opera scenography is still inspired by middle and late nineteenth-century settings. But, what was almost exclusively created in flat two-dimensional terms then, that is, in painting, is now being built in three-dimensional form. What was then represented in a series of flat wings, backdrops, and groundrows—all artfully painted—have now become complex and practical structures.

Before we go further, let us examine the text more closely in order to get some idea of the form the church scene takes in relation to the physical actions it requires. Questions and notes accompany this text and were made by the scenographer as he studied the scene for possible clues to its design. (It would also be helpful to anyone studying this particular problem to listen to the passage on the recorded version of the opera.)

Faust: Charles Gounod
(Translated by Peter Paul Fuchs)
Act IV. Part I—Scene 1, The Church
(Time: Approximately, 10 Minutes)

Actual Libretto	Scenographer's Notes
	1. Curtain rises on first bars of organ solo (13 bars after music begins). Stage very dark and shadowy.
	2. Marg. enters immediately after curtain starts to open.
	3. Marg. kneels at holy fount, dips fingers in water, crosses herself, rises, goes to another place, and kneels. (All this agreed upon with director.)
MARG: Dear Lord, to this poor sinner wilt Thou be Forgiving who would in Thy mercy confide.	
MEPH: [4] No—you are not to pray, No—you are not to pray! Strike her heart with misgiving, Spirits of dark, rush to her side.	4. Voice only—where it comes from unknown to Marg. or audience.
CHOR: [5] Marguerite!	5. Voices only—unseen. From behind or below? (*Problem*: Where is chorus to be put so that the chorus master can see the conductor?)

Actual Libretto	Scenographer's Notes

MARG: Oh, what voices!

CHOR: Marguerite! [6]

> 6. Figure of Meph. appears at this point. It should slowly emerge. Quality of light around him should be different than that around Marg. or in church proper. Meph. should be, literally, "king of shadows." Not fully revealed, his appearance should have the effect of a snake peering out of a pit. (How?)

MARG: Who is calling? I'll die!
Oh Heaven! [7]

> 7. Perhaps she has risen when first hearing the voice and sinks down at this point. She needs something to hold, some support?

MEPH: [8]
Think again of the past,
When, protected by angels
Your pure heart knew no evil,
When in church you knelt,
Singing praise to the Heavens,
In heavenly song.
Here your lips would pronounce childish
Prayers
In a voice filled with innocence and love.
You would feel in your soul your dear
Mother's caress
And blessing from above.
But now these sounds that you hear
Are the demons of hell, claiming loudly
Their right.
This is the voice of your conscience,
The voice of damnation,
Freed by the dark of the night.

> 8. Meph. reveals himself more. His movements should not be too hampered or confined. His position should not be level with Marg. but higher so that he can dominate most of the scene (fig. 87).

MARG: Lord! Who frightens me so,
Whisp'ring words in the darkness? [9]
Heavenly Hosts! What Voice of terror
Grips at my heart?

> 9. She can't see him. (Why?)

CHOR: [10]
Once the clouds are torn asunder
There will be eternal thunder,
And the world will be blown to dust.

> 10. Another chorus, different in quality from the first Orchestral accompasniment sounds like winds high in the air. (Possible change of light to help localize this chorus in different place, higher than first?)

MARG: No more, no more!
This holy song sounds even more appalling!

MEPH: No! The Lord has no mercy for you.
For you the stars will soon be falling.
Go—go!

CHOR: How shall I face my creator,
Where procure an arbitrator,
When the guiltless tremble with fear?

Actual Libretto

MARG: Ah—this song is harsh and depressing!
I'm caught in a prison of gloom. [11]

MEPH: Goodbye to feasts of love,
Past are joys of caressing.
You'll go below! Your fate is doom!

MARG: My Lord. [12]
O Lord, do not spurn the contrition
Of souls gone astray.
Show their sins forbearing remission
With one gleaming ray.
With one gleaming ray.
O Lord, do not spurn the contrition
The contrition of souls gone astray.
Show their sins forbearing remission
Show their sins forbearing remission,
With one gleaming ray!

CHOR: [13]
O Lord, O Lord do not spurn the contrition
The contrition of souls gone astray.
Show their sins forbearing remission
Show their sins forbearing remission,
With one gleaming ray, one ray!

MEPH: Marguerite! Be accursed! [14]

MARG: Ah! [15]

CURTAIN

Scenographer's Notes

11. "Prison of gloom." Can the walls of the church have a closed-in, prisonlike aspect? Narrow, confining—no exit (fig. 88).

12. This is the main part of the scene, the highest points it reaches both dramatically and musically. Marg. is borne up by her prayer and the sheer sound of the orchestral accompaniment. She needs to be supproted visually at this moment. Almost as if the clouds part momentarily and a ray of sun strikes her.

13. This section for chorus is simultaneous with Marg. last passage.

14. He pronounces a judgment on her as if in a court. (Is this scene a trial? What could support the image of trial or courtroom?)

15. She collapses under the weight of the sentence. The darkness rapidly falls again.

The scene, then, is fairly simple in structure; Marguerite comes in, kneels, prays, is tormented by the voice of Mephistopheles, prays again but is apparently not heard, collapses, curtain.

However, there is something that informs the scene and gives it its particular horror; wherever she turns, she cannot escape. She even calls the situation a "prison of gloom." She has come to the church for comfort—she gets, instead, torment. This is, perhaps, the key to the design of the scene: whenever she seeks one thing, she receives just the opposite. This is a clue, but only a start. Now, her actions must be more carefully analyzed and noted.

Let us picture this church in its simplest form; a stone structure not well lighted. The time of day, according to Mephistopheles, is night and Marguerite remarks about the darkness of the church itself. Her first action, after entering the church, would be to receive holy water (the original text has her doing most of the scene from this place). If we could see this action, it might look like what is shown in figure 89. First action: she goes to holy-water fount, kneels, and crosses herself (fig. 90). Second action: she rises, goes some distance (?), kneels again, begins to pray (fig. 91) probably in front of some object of devotion (?). (In some productions, the curtain does not rise until after the organ passage just before she begins to sing. It was felt, however, she would have more opportunity, if the scene started immediately with the organ music, to

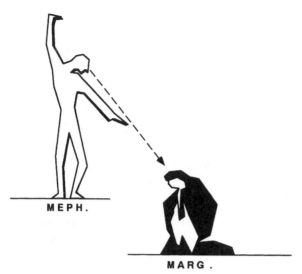

Fig. 87. Action by Marguerite

show her emotional state better by being seen
coming into the church instead of merely being
discovered there.) Now let us sum up what we
know to this point:

1. Situation as of this scene—Marguerite,
abandoned by Faust, alone, since her brother is
at war, has come to the church to ask forgiveness
for succumbing to Faust's advances. (All this we
know from study of the complete opera.)

2. The church to where she has come—she
probably has not gone to a main part of the
church. In disgrace, she wishes to hide, so has
picked a time of day when not many people are
likely to be there (night, according to internal
evidence). The church is dark and full of shadows. By what illumination do we see her? What

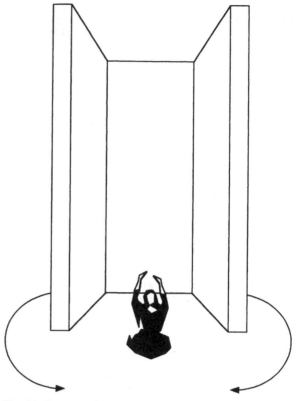

Fig. 88. Diagram of walls

is the source of light—windows, votive candles?
In any case, the walls and ceiling of the church
are likely to be lost in darkness.

3. After the preliminary ritual (the holy water), she goes to some other place and kneels. It
is in front, no doubt, of some religious object.
The Christ figure is usually given the most prom-

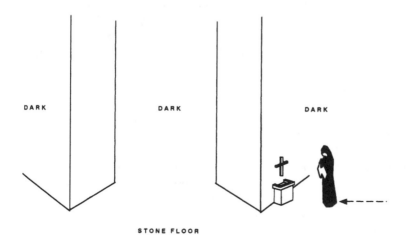

Fig. 89. Church essentials needed for actions

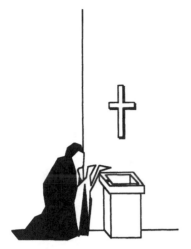

Fig. 90. Action by Marguerite

inent place, over the altar. She wishes not to be conspicuous, so perhaps goes someplace other than that most important area in front of the main altar. Let us assume she goes to a Madonna figure in order to pray *through* her to God, even though in the text she address Him directly.

She is now ready for the main part of the scene, the prayer, the confrontation, and the collapse. In the synopsis, Mephistopheles appears out of a tomb. And, even though this is a direction in the original work, this is only one of the many ways his appearance has been staged. Sometimes he appears in a column, sometimes behind a scrim wall, sometimes, as in a 1950s revival at the Metropolitan Opera, not at all—just his voice was heard. Our problem at this moment is, therefore, where will he appear?

Earlier, it was said that this scene would be done expressionistically, through the eyes of one character, that character being Marguerite. And the decision was made that it was she who would bring Mephistopheles into the church in her imagination. We also have assumed that wherever she turns, she is confronted by him.

A basic relationship suggests itself at this point. It might be diagramed in this way (fig. 92): (1) she enters church; (2) she kneels in prayer for forgiveness; (3) if successful, she is free to go forward from this point. This diagram is a combination of concrete actions and a conceptual goal (a desire to be forgiven). But she is intercepted by Mephistopheles and her path blocked. At this point her progress is checked; she can go no farther (fig. 93). A more detailed plan of this

Fig. 91. Action by Marguerite

confrontation might look like figure 94. (This also shows a level difference that increases the "power" of Mephistopheles).

But, as of now, nothing stands between Mephistopheles and Marguerite: the scene demands concealment for him—at least at first—and some object for her to direct her prayer to, to focus on. The figure of the Madonna, suggested earlier, would serve both these needs. But just how would this serve both? In her torment, Marguerite has turned to prayer for relief. It is to this Madonna she has come to seek remission of her transgressions. Yet, instead of forgiveness, she is reminded by the voice of Mephistopheles of her sins and is taunted with the promise of damnation. She has turned to the Madonna figure for help but apparently receives just the reverse of what she seeks. This is another key to the design: a perverse response to her prayer—a metamorphosis of good into evil.

It was agreed upon between the director and the scenographer, therefore, to make whatever seemed, at first, like one thing become just the

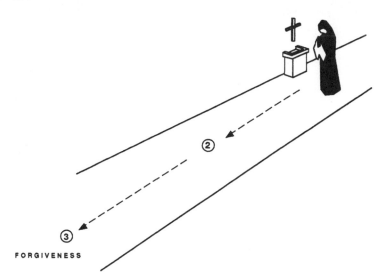

Fig. 92. Action by Marguerite

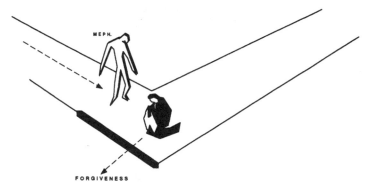

Fig. 93. Action by Marguerite and Mephistopheles

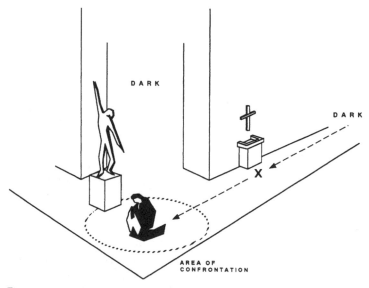

Fig. 94. Action by Marguerite and Mephistopheles

opposite of what it had appeared to be. If she prayed to the Madonna, then, this figure must in some way become what it was not. Finally, it was decided that the Madonna figure would not actually change into Mephistopheles but, rather, would provide a place for him to hide behind and from which he could emerge when it became necessary for him to be seen. (In the actual presentation of the scene, he was made to appear, at first, as part of the robe of the figure and, after his first words during which he is not seen at all, to slowly detach himself from the main body of the statue. Marguerite, on the other hand, was instructed never to look directly at the figure or at Mephistopheles but to seem as if she were seeing [or hearing] the scene only in her mind. By directing her attention not to an actual object, she could better show that she was, in fact, going mad from the accumulative effect of guilt and grief.)

It is now time to begin to explore the other visual elements of the scene in more detail. The actual place where she spends the most time in this scene and the light sources were the next two questions to be studied. First, let us examine her playing area more closely. After she kneels and begins her prayer, Marguerite is fairly well limited in possibility of movement; actually, she is stuck in one place for the greater part of this short scene. But not only must this position be visually effective, it must also be favorable in terms of sound. Possibilities for use of this confined area, therefore, became important to the performer. The idea suggested earlier that this scene has similarities to a criminal trial, plus the fact that the church would almost certainly have altar railings around the various religious sta-

tions, made it desirable to have a structure that would both aid the singer and create a scenic unit. For these reasons, then, a railing was devised that would help define the space and, at the same time, would provide something for Marguerite to use directly in the action of the scene. (There are moments when she very much needs something to hold on to, to provide support.) Since this rail served in a symbolic function as well as a practical one, it was designed to enclose Marguerite in the manner of the European prisoner's dock, but shorter, since most of her scene is played from a kneeling position (fig. 95).

The statue, because one of its functions was to provide a hiding place for Mephistopheles, had to be fairly large. It was decided to overscale it, that is, make it much larger than any such statue one might find in an actual church. (Again, the expressionist point of view was adopted: during this scene, the things to which Marguerite directs her attention loom larger to her than they might under different circumstances. The figure of the Madonna, therefore, becomes an overpowering symbol of refuge at first and later, in her distorted vision, an equally powerful reminder to Marguerite that Heaven may be denied her.) It was also designed so that the Madonna looks above and beyond the place where Marguerite kneels; she is, in fact, *overlooked*. Actually, Marguerite is more in the shadow of the statue than addressing it directly. This brings in the question of light source in the church. Where does it come from, what are its qualities?

Several possibilities exist for light motivation.

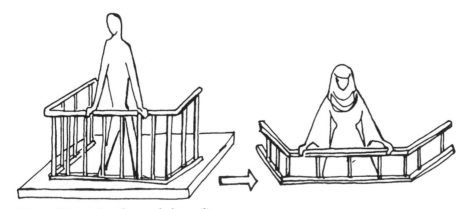

Fig. 95. Prisoner's railing and altar railing

The windows are stained glass and would give patterns of light that could emphasize or suggest the fractured planes of color that one finds in expressionist paintings. But it is night and little light would be coming through the windows from outside. What light does exist, then, in the church and around the various statues? The most prevalent source would be, at night especially, from votive candles lit by supplicants. They do not, moreover, give out much light; the church could still remain mostly in shadow. The light from the votive candles also suggests another means by which the scenic concept may be reinforced, especially if they are in the small red glass receptacles as is often the case. Let us suppose, therefore, that these candles will be our motivating source of light; they would probably be placed on a stand in tiered rows. Research reveals something like figure 96.

There is not time for Marguerite to light a candle (or really a need), so perhaps it should be placed somewhere out of her direct path. Since she is in the shadow, the light in her area quite possibly should be kept on the cool side; on the other hand, the votive candles in red glass holders would give off a firelike glow (which would have to have auxiliary light from lighting instruments—with red mediums—so that this area will be bright enough; the candles alone

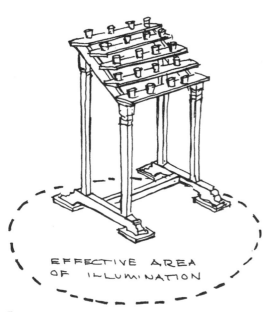

Fig. 96. Votive candle rack

would not provide nearly enough light or exactly the desired color). The stand was placed on the opposite side of the Madonna from the area where Marguerite spends most of the scene (fig. 97).

We now have two general areas of light: a red one near the place where Mephistopheles appears and a cool one where Marguerite kneels. The votive candlestand in this position also helps in another way; it further supports the plan to make the ordinarily religious objects of the church take on perverse uses. Although these candles are lit to honor the sanctified dead, when Mephistopheles appears, the flickering quality of the light and its red color become reminiscent of hellfire (especially if the light in this area is intensified as he emerges from the shadows of the statue).

It is about this time in the scenographic process that all the design elements and action plans must be brought together. At this stage the scenographer should be able to make drawings that not only will show pictorial and decorative possibilities but will take into consideration the spatial needs of the performers as well. Many scenographers also make a practice of including in these drawings (usually small and quickly made) pertinent notes. Figure 98 is such a drawing. Approximately two by three inches, it is only meant to be a crude indication, not a complete or final drawing; it is not uncommon for a scenographer to make several dozen of these small sketches, most of which are discarded quickly.

From this point on (and the point at which we will leave this example), the scenographer's work becomes increasingly more technical and specific. Ways must be found of putting these crude products of the imagination in more useful physical form; working drawings must be made, the builders and craftsmen in the shops supplied with detailed information, and their work carefully overseen. A thousand decisions must be made scrutinized, and, if necessary, changed or discarded. It is all the more important, then, that a firm scenic concept be evolved before the technical phase is reached so that the scenographer is provided with a firm base from which to work and a security of purpose so that his imaginative vision is not lost in the hectic world of production (fig. 99). There are seven scenes in *Faust*; our concern has been with only one of

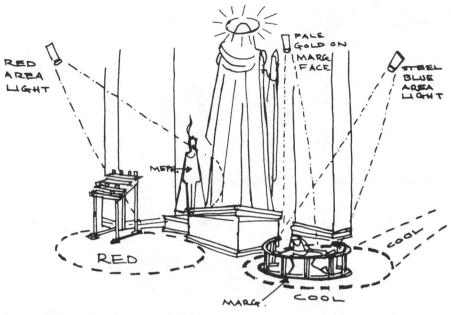

Fig. 97. Warm and cool areas of light

that seven. In a multi-scene work, however, the scenographer must think of the production as a visually integrated total, not as a series of independent nonrelated designs. He may, for instance, choose common visual elements or a range or colors that are repeated in a number, or all, of the scenes. He is almost certain to find that a playwright or composer has consciously—although sometimes intuitively—constructed every scene so as to contain clues that aid in the

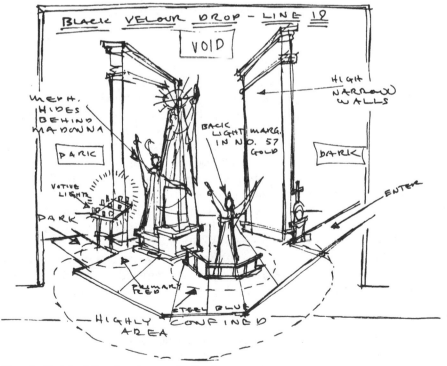

Fig. 98. Sketch of the church scene in *Faust*

Fig. 99. Model of the church scene in *Faust*

realization of not only that particular one but also others as well. How does this affect the scenographer's overall scenic scheme?

In analyzing the text of the church scene it was necessary to follow closely the train of Marguerite's thought; it was through her remarks that we obtained valuable clues to the scenic environment. She believed, at the beginning of the scene, that she had come to a place where solace and peace of mind could be found. By degrees she finds it is something entirely different from what she expected. In fact the church has become a "prison of gloom." In order to produce the desired mood, the qualities of a prison were emphasized—heavy stone walls, unrelieved with any softening detail or ornament—instead of those of a church. At the end of the scene she has been tried and found guilty of a moral crime, and she believes damnation to be her fate. In the final scene of the opera, however, she has committed an actual crime—the killing of her child by Faust—and has been put in a real prison. The question the scenographer must answer is, then, how do these two different places—the church and the prison—visually relate to each other? Or should he draw some sort of visual comparison? Quite probably he should and in so doing strengthen the unity of the production. (Actually Gounod's dramatic scheme contains a fairly obvious equation concerning these two scenes: Marguerite finds in the church, condemnation; and in the prison, salvation.)

Here is the very last part of the libretto. It describes what is supposed to happen to the prison at the very end of the opera.

FAUST: O Marguerite!
MARG: What blood is that which stains thy hand!
    [pushing him away]
    Away! Thy sight doth cause me horror!

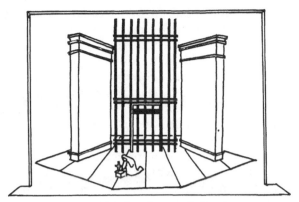

Fig. 100. Design of the church scene in *Faust*

MEPH: Condemned!
CHORUS OF ANGELS: Saved! Christ has arisen!
   Christ is born again!
   Peace and felicity
   To all disciples of the Master!
[The prison walls open. The soul of Marguerite rises toward heaven. Faust gazes despairingly after her, then falls on his knees and prays. Mephistopheles turns away, barred by the shining sword of an archangel.] End of the Opera.

Whereas the church was a prison, the prison now becomes the portal to heaven. In the production under discussion it was decided to make these two scenes strongly linked; the walls of the church would also be the walls of the prison, only certain details would be changed (fig. 100).

At the appropriate moment in the score, this is what took place on the stage (fig. 101): first, the prison grillwork was flown out (fig. 101A); second, the surrounding black velour maskings were also flown out (fig. 101B); and third, the walls pivoted outward (fig. 101C), revealing a golden stairway leading into a blindingly bright light at the top of the stairway (fig. 102). As Marguerite slowing ascends the steps, Mephistopheles slinks away into the few shadows left on the stage.

"La Môme Bijou"
By Brassaï

[Playwrights do not operate in vacuums; they are part of an actual world, and that world invariably permeates both their thought and their work. It is rare, however, that we are privileged

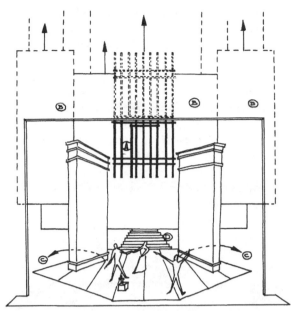

Fig. 101. Diagram for the scene transformation in *Faust*

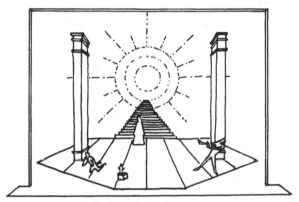

Fig. 102. Design for the finale in *Faust*

to know the primary source of a playwright's inspiration, even more rare to be shown the actual person upon which a dramatic character is modeled. Such sources and persons do exist; few playwrights invent without external inspiration despite the fact that characters in a dramatic text are almost never exact replicas of those originals. But, for the most part, these sources remain obscure and inaccessible to all but the most dedicated researchers. The general playgoing public rarely is aware, and there is no compelling reason they should be, that such and such a character has a prototype in the playwright's past. In the following short article we have the opportunity, however, to encounter just such a primary source. This opportunity is afforded us by a particularly well qualified observer: a photographer who is also a sensitive and imaginative writer; a man who both captures an image on film and then proceeds to comment on that image in evocative and informative language. I have included this article and a photographic image (fig. 103) taken by him of the article's main subject (both from *The Secret Paris of the '30s*), since it forcefully supports the contention that playwrights often do, indeed, have a hidden world from which to draw even their most exotic and imaginative characters—D.R.P.]

One winter night in 1932 around two in the morning, I went into a small bar in Montmartre, the Bar de la Lune. The first figure I made out through the cloud of smoke was that of an ageless woman who was sitting alone with a glass of red wine in her hand. Her dark clothes glittered strangely. Her bosom was covered with an incredible quantity of jewelry; brooches, lavaliers, chokers, clips, chains—a veritable Christmas tree of garlands, of glittering stars.

And rings! She wore more than a dozen—two on each plump finger, crammed on up to her knuckles, which were entwined in the fake

Fig. 103. Photograph of La Môme Bijou. Photograph by Brassaï

pearls of the necklaces she had wrapped like bracelets around her wrists.

I was struck by this fantastic apparition that had sprung up out of the night, like an entomologist by a rare and monstrously beautiful insect. I discovered what had to be the queen of Montmartre's nocturnal fauna.

"You don't know her?" the bartender asked me, surprised at my astonishment. "It's La Môme Bijou—Miss Diamonds. Once she was rich and famous, led the good life. When people still had carriages, she rode in the Bois de Boulogne in her barouche. . . . Now she lives on charity, she reads the customer's palms . . ."

Fascinated, I devoured her with my eyes. Miss Diamonds was a palette come to life, refined. The dark mass of her old-fashioned black velvet cape, ragged and torn, shiny in spots, topped off with a moth-eaten fur collar, her black evening dress in the style of 1900, all silk and lace, brought out the greens, purples, pale pinks, the nacreous colors of fake pearls, the glitter of paste jewelry, of fake rubies, fake turquoises, fake emeralds. The palette of Gustave Moreau. . . . Her face, with its white clown make-up, was softened by a green veil decorated with roses.

And yet—behind her glittering eyes, still seductive, lit with the lights of the Belle Epoque, as if they had escaped the onslaughts of age, the ghost of a pretty girl seemed to smile out. Had Miss Diamonds really been a demi-mondaine, a younger sister to Cléo de Mérode, Liane de Pougy, La Bell Otero, Odette de Crécy—all dear to the heart of Marcel Proust—or had she walked the streets from the Moulin Rouge to the Place Pigalle, going from bar to bar, from one dance hall to another, one body to another, as some of the patrons of the bar told me? I wanted to know about her life, to have her tell me her memories. Where did she live? Did she sleep in a four-poster bed hung with veils and lace, or did she sleep on a pile of rags? Would she show me her old photographs, the proofs of her gilded past? It was too late to strike up a conversation with her. I took only three photographs, but I intended to return another evening. Alas, I never saw Miss Diamonds again.

One morning, after my Paris de Nuit had come out in 1933, Miss Diamonds put in an unforgettable appearance at my publisher's office. Swathed in her tawdry finery, outrageously made up, she created a panic. Removed from her surroundings, deprived of the night's complicity, revealed in the light of day, she was monstrous. "You published my picture in your book," she shouted threateningly. "You printed nasty things about me. Do I seem to be 'escaped out of a nightmare of Baudelaire'? Do I! Me, a nightmare? You'll pay for it!" And she refused to leave until the publisher had paid her for her "insult."

Jean Giraudoux's The Madwoman of Chaillot, written in 1943 during the Occupation and first performed on December 21, 1945, at the Athenee, dragged Miss Diamonds out of the shadows. At the time, she was thought to have been the inspiration for Giraudoux's play. And since it was also performed in London and New York, she became world famous. "I remember her well," Joseph Kessel wrote on the day following the premiere. "You used to see her at dawn in Montmartre, when the night gave rise to fatigue and hallucinations. She would suddenly turn up in some brasserie on the Boulevard de Clichy or in a delicatessen on the Place Pigale, and no one would pay much attention. They were used to her, she was one of the night people, one of the troubled. Men in the bars would buy her sausages and red wine to get her to tell her stories. Every morning she was drunk, and she never laughed. A horrible, fascinating old woman, on the brink of madness, on the brink of decay, she had an indefinable air of grace, of love . . ."

Miss Diamonds wasn't the only model Giraudoux had. There was another madwoman, the Madwoman of Alma. And the play's heroine, Aurelia, was a mixture of these two eccentrics. Unlike Miss Diamonds, the Madwoman of Alma was an extremely rich woman, and not an ex-courtesan. She could sometimes be glimpsed around the Place d'Alma, laden with baubles, necklaces, semiprecious stones, feathers, bows, and velvet ribbons, with a scarf of Valenciennes lace around her neck, her head wrapped in a cloud of tulle. Indifferent to the passers-by, she would stroll along majestically under her lace parasol like a sleepwalker. If Miss Diamonds is better known than the Madwoman of Alma, it is because of my photographs, which were used in designing the play's costumes, whereas no picture exists, that I am aware, of the Madwoman of Alma.

Thirty years later, in 1963 at the Menton Palais du Louvre, we were hanging the photographs in my show which had been exhibited earlier at the Bibliothèque Nationale; I had included my photographs of Miss Diamonds, and it had appeared that morning in a Nice newspaper. Suddenly, an old man, still vigorous and neatly dressed, came into the Palais and asked to see me. "Sir, are you the author of this photography? When I opened my paper, I got quite a shock. So you knew her! I wanted to know, because in my younger days, I was Miss Diamonds' lover . . ."

A miraculous encounter. Would I finally learn the true story of Miss Diamonds? "It was a long time ago," my visitor told me. "I could tell you so many things . . ."

Unfortunately, the installation was not finished, and I excused myself promising the noble old man that I was immensely interested in his story and that I would visit him in a few days. Visibly disappointed—he was trembling with eagerness—he presented me with his card and left.

I kept my word. But when I got to his hotel, one of those old, dilapidated Menton palaces dating from the time of the Grand Dukes, and mentioned his name—Dumont-Charterêt—I was met with dismay at the desk. Delays, consultations, phone calls. After a long wait, the concierge asked me, "Are you a member of the family?"

"No," I said, "but Monsieur Dumont-Charterêt wants to see me. We made an appointment on the telephone. Would you please announce me?

"I'm sorry, sir, but that's impossible . . ."

"Impossible? Why?"

"Monsieur Dumont-Charterêt has just died. He died suddenly yesterday afternoon. I'm sorry, sir."

My aged gallant carried his secret with him to his grave. And so I will never know the true story of Miss Diamonds.

4

Creative Research in the Theater

Like Architecture, the theater is receptive to all the other arts, indeed it could hardly exist without recourse to several among them, but it does not consist of any of them in particular.

—Etienne Gilson

The Greatest natural genius cannot subsist on its own stock; he who resolves never to ransack any mind but his own will soon be reduced from mere barrenness to the poorest of all imitation. It is vain to invent without materials on which the mind may work and from which invention must originate. Nothing can come of nothing.

—Joshua Reynolds

Investigation and Interpretation: The Dual Role of the Scenographer

All research, regardless of its subject or purpose, requires of the researcher two primary abilities: the ability to investigate and the ability to interpret. Too often those we designate as *artists* are tacitly exempted from the first activity in the mistaken belief that investigation is an occupation more suited to police detectives, social workers, ambitious journalists, or literary scholars. On the other hand, interpretation is considered a matter of personal feeling and artistic insight, both of which lie beyond scrutiny. In the theater, however, whether we direct plays or design scenic environments, these two areas often overlap. They are, in fact, different aspects of the same activity. That this interrelationship is often slighted in the educational stages of a scenographer's development or, at best, given slight attention, is the primary reason the present book was written.

It would be well for us to begin with a close look at these two words—*investigate* and *interpret*. Here are brief definitions of the words themselves as found in most dictionaries:

Investigate: To observe or study closely: inquire into systematically: to EXAMINE OR SCRUTINIZE.
Interpret:
  1. To explain or tell the meaning of: EXPOUND, ELUCIDATE, TRANSLATE
  2. To understand and appreciate in the light of individual belief, judgment, interest, or circumstance: CONSTRUE
  3. To apprehend and represent by means of art: show by illustrative representation: bring (a score or script) to *active realization* by performance (Italics mine)

It is not difficult to see that the activities that accompany these definitions are certainly not synonymous; *to investigate* has a more rational, logical purpose behind its meaning than does the phrase *to interpret*. But do not be misled into the mistaken conclusion that these activities do not overlap in significant ways; nor should it take much understanding to realize that both run on the same fuel: *the question* or, to use the term we will adopt in this book, the *informed question*. Moreover, the structure of any investigation or interpretation is determined by the nature of the questions posed. As Heinrich Engel, the noted German architect, observes: "The idea of any study is best understood and consequently best pursued when expressed through a series of questions. *For the question is not only the origin of all intellectual endeavor of man but also, if precisely formulated, indicates the sphere that encircles the answer*" (italics mine).

In its most elemental form, the dramatic text is simply a long list of questions—an investigation, if you will—clothed in the guise of dramatic dialogue. Those who come to the theater want answers to what they see on the stage. Their concern may range from "What is the meaning of life?" to "What is going to happen in the next five seconds?" Curiosity may kill cats but it keeps an audience's attention alive. Often, unlike the investigations of a Sherlock Holmes, these answers may not come as verbal explanations. The "answer" on the stage may very well come in the form of a revealing image. Actually the theater's most satisfying answers tend to be those that *show* us a resolution rather than *telling* us anything in words. But dramatic texts do not come with accompanying pictures; words are all we have to guide us. How, then, do the words become those affecting images? What steps must we must take in order to bring those images into being? That is the focus of our book. In order to understand how the word on the page becomes an image in the theater, we need to comprehend something that frequently escapes conscious attention: the first reading of the play.

There is an important first principle concerning the reading of any new or unfamiliar play that most theater artists through experience come to understand; a principle many practice faithfully to keep that all-important inner eye clear of the hidden dangers of habit. That principle is: *The first reading of any new or unfamiliar play should be done for enjoyment only; no other purpose need be considered.*

Simple as this proposition seems, the underlying advice becomes increasingly difficult to follow as experience accrues. Since the greater part

of any theater research technique consists of stripping away the emotional color of a play's text in order to get at its underlying structure (i.e., untangling the web of questions that chart the play's development), it might seem time wasted not to begin the intense analysis of the text as soon as possible. But in this very eagerness to understand the hidden structure and the concealed meanings, the playwright has willfully or unconsciously placed there, such a reader may abort many important subconscious processes, processes that might never be recovered in subsequent readings. Expert readers have long known of this danger. Samuel Johnson drew attention to the fact that "what is read with delight is commonly retained, *because pleasure always secures attention*; but the books which are consulted by occasional necessity, and perused with impatience, seldom leave any traces on the mind" (italics mine).

This is good advice; still, it is often difficult to follow in the busy world most of us live. Nevertheless, impatience is the common enemy of any good research regardless of the field in which it is done.

Is it possible for the experienced director or scenographer to read a play with a mind cleansed of all past encounters with the stage? Probably not. A new play, unless it closely resembles or mimics some earlier work, often presents fewer problems in this regard than a familiar one. And while any new work may remind the experienced director or scenographer of previously read works, its unfamiliarity often helps to keep minds open. And yet is it possible that many experienced directors or scenographers can approach the rereading of *Hamlet* as if for the first time? For many of us who live with an intimate knowledge of this play, and have done so not only for years but for decades, the answer is *not entirely and never entirely*; the more experience encounters, the more experience colors what is known. For most theater artists even the new rapidly becomes tainted with experience gained from the old. Naturally, expertise in any activity must rely heavily on that residual stain of past experience and accomplishment: that is the basis of a seasoned director's or scenographer's effectiveness. Still, the very thing that renders us effective and reliable carries within it the possibility that our work may become, as

Hamlet says of his life, increasingly "flat, stale and unprofitable."

The problem is not insurmountable; it is manageable if considered early in the scenographer's development. There are methods of overcoming the hidden dangers of bias as well as overcoming the blind reliance on past "tricks of the trade." This brings us to a second principle to consider. This is: *As you read—either a new play or a familiar one—put your imagination in the same world as the playwright's.*

The playwright's text almost always takes place in a real world, fantastic as those worlds sometimes are. Almost all texts describe people, places, and things as if they might be encountered in the world outside the theater's doors. *Stage right, stage left,* and *the curtain falls,* all are applied to a play *after* the play is conceived and recorded. These and similar directions are part of the working world of the theater; they are mechanical necessities that have little to do with that seminal world of the playwright's imagination. The best playwrights, Shakespeare, for example, have little difficulty in bridging these two worlds; often the seams between the two are undetectable; in many instances Shakespeare himself commented on the curious relationship between that world of imagination and the world of the practical stage. But he was never in doubt that the first must come before the second: that the play of the imagination precedes the play in the theater. And it is this that we who must read plays for our instruction and as part of our profession must constantly keep in mind as we undertake our investigations and interpretations into those imaginary first worlds of the playwright. It is only to the extent that we keep our minds free of the prejudicial information of past experience that we will remain free to absorb—both consciously and unconsciously—the original elements of a new work or come to understand the still to be discovered secrets of those most familiar to us. The eventual shape of a production will, of course, rely on the nature of the logical questions to which we subject the playwright's text. But it is in those first attempts to *feel out* the play's emotional undercurrent and subtext, paying as little regard to the technical workings of the theater as possible, that we will make our most important discoveries. The key to all good research, whether as a director or as a scenographer, lies in our ability to make that all-important first reading as an *absorbing experience* as possible.

The Active Eye: The Role of Research

In *Walden,* Henry David Thoreau made this complaint (which I am certain he was more than willing to endure its continuance): "Who placed us with eyes between a microscopic and telescopic world? I have the habit of attention to such excess that my senses get no rest, but suffer from a constant strain."

Every visual artist bears this same burden. Moreover, it is a burden that he must seek to make greater as his art matures. The eye is traditionally considered as something that is acted upon; passive until something strikes its view. The visual artist must, however, have a somewhat different philosophy as to how his eye works and, more important, how to make it work better for him. Of course, we must constantly be ready to receive and process the random image; the encounter with the unexpected is one of the great joys of art. But we must always have as the most basic tenet of our artistic philosophy and practice that the artist's eye is *active*; that, to use an extremely old phrase, we must "cast an eye" over the entire world we encounter if we are to keep the ravenous appetite of our artistic imagination fed.

There can be little doubt that man's most comprehensive sense is vision; while his other senses add to and qualify much of what is perceived through the eye, the ability to gather information and make evaluations through this sense alone has been tantamount to his survival as a species. The eye is also of primary importance to the construction and understanding of any communication system or form of culture. While vision has been important in many systems that transmit direct information, serious study of those messages that cannot be directly perceived (or perceived fully at a glance) is a fairly recent concern. The most prevalent mistake we have made as members of separate cultures is to accept without question the erroneous assumption that all human beings see alike; even the speculation that different cultures might see differently has been until very recently almost completely ignored. Although the mechanics of optical reception are similar in all human beings, little attention has been given to how groups with individual characteristics see. Now, however, we are becoming more and more aware not only that different cultures see differently, but that members of single culture cannot be said to see alike. This also brings us to another important point: the difference between seeing things directly and reading visual situations in the light of past visual experience; that is, seeing what we expect to see, not necessarily what is there.

When we say we *know* something, it means that we have become aware of some piece of information or the connection between two or more pieces. Encounters with new information occur constantly, often without conscious effort on our part. Formal education is nothing more than purposefully putting oneself in the direct path of facts or theories while at the same time making a conscious effort to comprehend the content or effects of those facts or theories. This much is easy to understand. What is not so apparent is the way—actually, ways—we absorb the content of what we seek to know; for *knowing* something involves more than simple confrontation and memorization of facts and theories. Additionally, different forms of information must be acquired in different ways.

Gaining information (with the attendant goal of knowing the content) has four general paths. These are:

1. *Things seen.* In *The Science of Mind*, Kenneth Klivington says this: "All sensory systems serve a similar purpose, to bring information from the outside world into the brain. The general patterns of their organization are also similar, but there are some important differences. In each case a sense organ receives a signal: sound in the ear, light in the eye, and so on. It translates this signal into the language of the nervous system and sends the resulting message coursing toward the brain. . . . *One of the most studied senses is vision.* Scientists have carefully unraveled the connections of brain cells in the visual system and have studied how they respond to light, so we have many clues about how the brain takes visual images apart. *What is particularly elusive, however, is how the brain puts the pieces back together, turning two-dimensional patterns of light on the reti-*

nas into our perception of the visual world" (italics mine).

2. *Things read.* We have just discussed the difference between raw seeing and that piecing together of elements into shapes and objects. There we observed that things seen by the eye and processed through the brain cause the mind to create unified patterns out of separate elements: that is, lines form shapes, shapes form objects, objects form patterns, patterns form facts, facts form theories, and finally theories give rise to *meaning.* On a rudimentary level, the meaning of anything results from searching patterns for likenesses and differences, then ranking those likenesses into complex orders and patterns.

3. *Things perceived.* Independent patterns when considered together can cause the mind to seek connections that do not actually exist. When, however, a number of elements that have no logical connection are linked together into a pattern, meaning can also emerge, since the mind—as we have noted—both actively and subconsciously seeks to impose a pattern even where none exists. The most logical of patterns has synaptic gaps over which the mind must leap in order to grasp a meaning. In the most complicated of patterns (and plays, novels, poems, paintings, music, are subject to this condition), there are unavoidable holes and gaps that the mind must cross if understanding of the pattern is to be accomplished. Intuition is an important element of perception in the knowing process; intuition is the assumed *reason* in the French aphorism, *The heart has its reasons that reason knows nothing of.* It is primarily through the act of active intuition that the actor finds meaning in his lines and that the scenographer finds reasons for his setting.

4. *Things kinesthetically experienced.* In his advice to the players in act 2, scene 2, Hamlet lays especial emphasis on relationship of physical movement to written text. He says, "Suit the action to the word, the word to the action . . ." Even four hundred years ago those who made theater a profession knew well the vital link between subjective thought and objective action. Stimuli encountered *directly through actions of the body in time and space* are not only crucial to learning processes but are often the key to under-

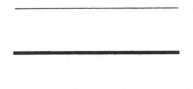

Fig. 104. Diagram of visual
elements

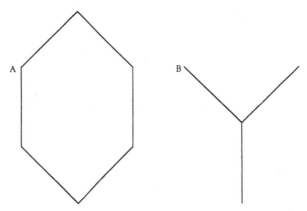

Fig. 105. Diagram of visual shapes

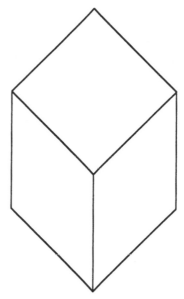

Fig. 106. Diagram of visual form

standing a fact or a theory. It should also be noted that only through kinesthetic action do all aspects of knowing come into play. The kinesthetic action brings into synthesis patterns seen, patterns read, and patterns perceived. All performers are aware of this way of learning. Theater designers are less attuned to the role that physical action plays in the production process. Understanding that kinesthetic action does have a direct impact has been commented upon by past designers. Remember Adolphe Appia's words—noted in an earlier section of this book— that "a designer designs with his legs." Add to that this advice of Robert Edmond Jones that "we have to know the instant we see and touch a fabric what it will look like on the stage both in movement and in repose. *We have to develop the brains that are in our fingers"* (italics mine). Both attest to the role kinesthetic action plays in theater art.

All vision is not of the same kind or order. It is important for any whose profession is based on visual perception to understand the distinction between *seeing* an image and *reading* an image. For instance, the objects in figure 104 are called lines. The same holds true for those objects in figure 105A and figure 105B. When lines are combined as shown in figure 105A and B, shapes emerge. These objects can now be upgraded from the status of a collection of lines into that of shapes with specific names. Figure 105A has a definite name: a hexagon. Figure 105B is more subject to interpretation, since it resembles the letter Y. But it is not until we combine these two shapes that we advance to another level of vision. Figure 106 is the combination of the two shapes and as a result of that combination takes on a different aspect. Our mind has not only combined the individual line elements into shapes but has also combined the

shapes into the image of a box perceptibly three-dimensional. The mind has stopped seeing individual units such as lines and has begun to form those abstract separate elements into associative forms; in this case, a box or a cube. In a very real way we have stopped *seeing* elements and have started *reading form*. Despite the fact that the box or cube is only a combination of the same line elements in figure 104, our eye has unconsciously assembled these forms into a meaningful whole. We no longer see the lines, only the box. (This, by the way, is the basis for the aesthetic aphorism that *a work of art is more than the sum of its parts. We literally loose sight* of the individual elements at the same time as we gain a vision of the whole.

The ability to work backward from wholes to elements is crucial to the work of any visual artist. This ability is not a natural one since our brain insists on working the other way: it always puts disparate elements into patterns as the initial step to comprehension. The mind cannot abide ambiguity, and it uses its instrument of perception—the brain—to incessantly scan all within its visual field to constantly assemble disparate parts into meaningful wholes. An important feature of all visual processes is that even when meaning is absent, the mind supplies the deficiency. It imposes patterns on what is perceived until a meaning—no matter how tenuous—emerges.

So insistent is the mind to put into order what it receives from visual stimuli that often it accepts as fact an image it knows cannot exist. For example, the "object" shown in figure 107 appears to have three tines leading to a base. But if one looks closely at the base, only *two* tines begin there. This object could not exist in reality. As a drawn image, however, a clever arrangement of lines makes the impossible appear possible. The ambiguity of this figure is processed by the mind by alternating between the acceptance of the three tines when focused on them and accep-

tance of the two tines when focused on the base. These figures demonstrate that mind will find consistency and order even when it knows that what it perceives is a logical impossibility.

In addition to the mind's capability to make sense of ambiguity, there is another major way it processes visual information. This process is called *completion* and is sometimes called *closure*. Completion is the ability of the mind to bring disparate elements into a pattern or a whole. It is similar to what we observed in the object above in that the purpose of the mind here is to finish out what it perceives to to missing. Figure 108 shows what appears to be a white triangle superimposed onto three black circles. There is no triangle, there are no black circles. There are only three small irregular forms (fig. 109) strategically placed that produce the illusion of a white triangle. Again, we see evidence of the mind *reading* information beyond the limits of what the eye actually perceives. The ability of the mind to find continuity when it does not exist, to create whole

Fig. 108. Diagram showing white triangle

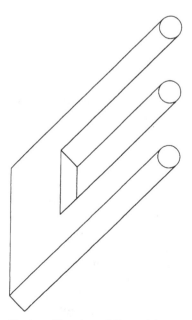

Fig. 107. Drawing of illogical form

Fig. 109. Diagram of individual units

images from incomplete parts, is a crucial part of every visual artist's understanding and education. It is also an essential tool in the practice of scenography. Scenographic designs in today's theater rely on the minds of audiences not only to complete whole images from isolated details but often to *read into* those fragmentary images meanings that support the action of the production or the sense of the text. Settings such as that shown in figures 42 and 110 clearly do not represent factual reality as encountered outside the theater. Few spectators seeing such an arrangement on the stage would have little difficulty accepting performers behaving as if they were living in an actual structure. A cardinal condition of theatergoing is—has always been— a willingness to substitute symbolic representation for the common perception of reality.

The act of seeing, it is evident, is not as simple an activity as one might first believe. Even in the perception of the most uncontroversial of visual events—as we see in the illustrations above— there are a distinct, although related phases. Visual experience is progressively built by these steps that are continuously and, for the most part, unconsciously performed by every sighted individual. Although much we perceive is unconsciously processed, visual artists can never take their seeing abilities for granted or believe their visual training is ever complete. To a degree not required from most other individuals, the scenographer must search for those elements of an image *that evoke meanings and information that lie beyond recognition of surface features*. The scenographer, unlike the casual observer, must be an especially active looker, not simply a passive receiver of visual stimuli. The formative stage of any visual artist's training is not unlike that of the biologist who carefully dissects into constituent parts a specimen in order to understand more clearly the relationship of those parts to the living whole. While it is never possible to understand that whole merely through inspection of parts, our understanding is, nonetheless enhanced if we become familiar with the elements that make up the whole. Let us now expand on the ideas encountered above as we begin to relate these and others to the purposes of scenog-

Fig. 110. Setting for *A Streetcar Named Desire*

raphy. The basic steps involved in all visualization are as follows:

1. *Visual sensation.* Any visual stimulus has an immediate effect on the brain, but all sense stimuli are interrelated to the other senses. (When we see a cut on another person, for instance, quite often we experience a definite perceptible sensation in our own bodies. Looking down from great heights can also produce reactions in parts of the body that cannot be said to be purely visual responses.) The stronger the initial visual sensation, the more quickly are we forced to a second response:

2. *Thinking.* Upon seeing something, the mind begins immediately to fit the visual sensations it perceives into rational contexts. This process attempts to relate new visual sensations to past patterns of images and experience. (We speak of "making sense" to describe this process. We also use the phrase "at first glance." Both of these indicate the natural inclination to fit any visual experience into an understandable pattern, which does happen for the most part instantaneously; this process is so quick, in fact, that very strange sensations are often glossed over in the process. The visual artist must train himself to slow down this assimilation process; otherwise he will often miss that very creative process that is summed in that other hackneyed phrase, "like seeing it for the first time." This is often the visual artist's most important task: *seeing the familiar as if it were for the first time.*) The thinking process almost invariably leads to a third response:

3. *Feeling.* The residual effect of both the sensation and the immediate conscious assessment of what has been visually experienced leads us to a stage wherein we have "made sense" of the visual response. Having "made sense" of our reaction implies that we now have some emotional response and, as well, added to that visual response. (Familiarity with an image or set of images can, however, be so familiar and so frequent that this emotional response becomes atrophied to the point of being nonoperational—witness the effect of violence to which we are subjected in the cinema and on television. While many would debate its ultimate effect on our actions, few would deny that violence perceived in these media produces little emotional reaction beyond casual recognition.) While all of these

first three responses are taking place, a fourth—and perhaps a simultaneous—process is happening:

4. *Intuition.* This is the unconscious assessment of the image in terms of past experience and quite possibly an unconscious understanding of how this image might relate to future experience or action. Here we do not speak of "making sense" but, rather, of *sensing* something not immediately available to the conscious mind. It is quite possible that no awareness is present at all in the conscious levels of the mind, that the various sublevels of the mind are recording the visual event or relating it to other images stored there. This storage process cannot take place, however, without the objective image being present (although images already stored can, of course, summon up others not actually physical). This is, quite possibly, the best reason for the artist to expose herself constantly to images with no apparent need for their immediate use. Dylan Thomas, an unusually sensitive poet to things visual, often spoke of his formative years when he went about "with my eyes hanging out." It is this attitude that all visual artists come to espouse in time; it is, however, an attitude of which the evolving artist must become intensely aware before she can appreciate the need to train her eyes to work independently of directed intention.

Seeing and intuition are inseparable parts of one another. Nor is intuition the exclusive prerogative of some while denied to others. No doubt some persons are more predisposed to intuitive reasoning than others; but this does not rule out the possibility that it can be nurtured and strengthened in those who feel a positive need to do so. The investigative mind cannot, however, confine itself to that often very narrow band of rational and logical thought that often declines to acknowledge any solution to a problem outside its own boundaries. No artist, certainly not the scenographer, can afford to discount the powers of intuition or the pursuit of its attainment. Henri Cartier Bresson, a great artist whose primary medium is photography, says this concerning the role of intuition in his own work:

There is subject in all that takes place in the world, as well as in our personal universe. We cannot negate subject. It is everywhere. So we must be lucid toward what is going on in the world, and honest about what we feel. . . . Subject does not consist of a collection of facts, for facts in themselves offer little interest. Through facts, however, we can reach an understanding of the laws that govern them, and be better able to select the essential ones which communicate reality. . . . Composition must be one of our constant preoccupations, but at the moment of shooting it can stem only from our intuition, for we are out to capture the fugitive moment, and all the interrelationships involved are on the move. In applying the Golden Rule, the only pair of compasses at the photographer's disposal is his own pair of eyes. . . .

I believe that, through the act of living, the discovery of oneself is made concurrently with the discovery of the world around us which can mold us, but which can also be affected by us. A balance must be established between these two worlds—the one inside us and the one outside us. As the result of a constant reciprocal process, both these worlds come to form a single one. And it is this world that we must communicate. . . . For me, content cannot be separated from form. By form, I mean a rigorous organization of the interplay of surfaces, lines, and values. It is in this organization alone that our conceptions and emotions become concrete and communicable. (*The Decisive Moment*, Photographs by Henri Cartier Bresson)

These words, by a photographer, apply equally to those who work in other visual worlds. But, as Henri Cartier Bresson also advises us, "It is essential to cut from the raw material of life—to cut and cut, but to cut with discrimination." The scenographer, as with all visual artists, must learn to make the power of intuition a working tool by which that raw material is gathered and processed.

Perhaps every creative person, artist and scientist alike, can take hope from the words written in a decision handed down by the U.S. Court of Customs and Patent Appeals a few years back. Part of that finding reads as follows: "Invention isn't always the offspring of genius; more often, it's the result of plain hard work; sometimes it arises from accident or carelessness; occasionally it's the happy thought of an ordinary mind; and sometimes invention is simply the product of sheer stupidity."

All students of scenographic art must give long and careful attention to the ways they visually perceive the world as well as to consider how they shape the vision of those who see their work. Let us leave this subject with these words of the nineteenth-century painter who shaped much of the vision of the twentieth-century artist Paul Cézanne: *Time and reflection change the sight little by little until we come to understand.*

Scenographic Vision

We often hear the expression, "To the trained eye"; it denotes that the person possessing such vision is able to perceive information that is not at first apparent or readily accessible to the casual untrained observer. A doctor can often predict, for instance, certain types of internal diseases or disorders simply by observing the color or discoloration of the skin alone; the farmer can, by look and feel of soil, appraise its value for growing certain crops, as well as predict an expected crop yield; dozens of professions rely on the ability of an individual to give precise evaluations from quick surface investigations of objects, materials, or mixtures: a calculated "guess" that will, at a later time, be borne out in proof. This vision, this "trained eye," this insight, while it may exist without antecedents or understandable reason in some—a Mozart or a Beethoven or a Leonardo da Vinci—is not an inborn trait for most individuals; it is a faculty which must be rigorously pursued and then carefully nurtured. The scenographer must, like every other trained professional, learn to use the natural sensory equipment he has in ways and at higher levels of perception than even the most sensitive or intuitive member of an audience could imagine; the work of the scenographer is, to a very great extent, a visual medium through which the vision of others must pass; an audience sees through the eyes of the scenographer, since he both rationally and intuitively selects what they view. Moreover, he controls not only what they see but also the context in which they see it. The objective vision of the scenographer very much determines the subjective reality an audience perceives.

The innermost nature of the theater depends upon the use of imagery. But, just as all imagery is not of the same kind, all the purposes to which imagery can be put in the theater are not similar. Basically, the purpose of imagery is to make the nonvisual elements of the production more effective. Philosophically, imagery is based on the assumption that in the theater things or acts directly seen have a greater effect than things or acts described or reported. Perhaps the ancient Greek theater's practice of reporting acts of extreme violence or catastrophe would lend support to this contention; while one could show the effects of violence—Medea's dead children, Oedipus's blinded eyes, the head of Pentheus after he had been torn apart by his mother and her followers—it was felt that showing the actual act would be too strong a vision for the audience to support. Since that period, of course, such restrictions in the theater have been disregarded, although the question concerning the showing of violence is still being hotly debated, especially as it relates to television. In any case, there can be no doubt that what is seen is many times more affective than what is described. The scenographer is, of course, an artist who constantly deals with images. But, just how often do we consider precisely the type of images we use daily or the import of the various levels of imagery we often employ unthinkingly? For not to consider these questions is, in part, to relinquish an important part of the control we as scenographers are given.

It is taken for granted that the scenographer works to be effective; that is, the training and inclination of the scenographer are toward the production of predictable and intended results. Yet a scenographer may be very effective and still not be an artist of the theater. A setting or scenic environment may be basically appropriate, workable for performers and may, indeed, even create an atmospheric mood. All these elements might be present in a design, and still something will be lacking when the total work is presented to an audience.

What we speak of here is not the skill to be *effective*, which, it should be expected, is the prime purpose of disciplined training, but the ability to be *affective*. While these words may sound similar, in fact they are often used interchangeably, they are far from being the same. It is, moreover, in the power to be affective that the scenographer contributes his own special art to the theater. It could even be said that scenography is largely the ability *effectively* to promote predictably *affective* images on demand. It is, more important still, in the construction of af-

fective images that the undercurrents of a production are given form and direction. While the rational faculties of the scenographer must be under his strict control in order to create these supporting images, they will, to a very large extent, lie beyond completely rational explanations and definitions. An affective image is one, in the final analysis, whose full import must be experienced in terms beyond verbal exposition, its perceived meaning lying outside the most careful attempt to "explain" that import. And yet careful analysis is the most basic of the scenographer's tasks: analysis of a production's meaning in terms of text, imagery, physical needs, and audience perception. It is paradoxical (if not downright contradictory) to say, on the one hand, that a scenographer must know every step in the production of an environment as it relates to both the conceptual meanings of a stage work and its physical construction and, on the other hand, to affirm that this work can involve images that cannot be logically or rationally explained. Yet when we cross that illusive line from craft to art, our certainties as to intention and results often become less tangible. It is, however, when we cross that line that we must also begin to speak of levels of the mind that, although not completely clear in outline, do operate in positive and productive ways. It is when we venture into these areas where the truly creative processes begin to operate that we must begin to trust other systems that, for want of a better phrase, are out of our control. And it is in the acceptance that such systems do, indeed, exist and work for us in a positive manner that we make our most important step toward becoming that artist we aspire to be.

Most simply put, the scenographic process is an interlinked network of skills, historical understanding, sensual perceptions, love of dramatic action, deep appreciation of the power of all manners of language, and a willingness to probe all levels of the mind of oneself and of others. It also means a firm commitment to a life of self-examination rather than one of self-expression.

To be *effective* is within the powers of almost anyone who is willing to invest the time for the accumulation of required skills; to be *affective* is to acquire skills beyond those purely mechanical, the most important of those skills being the ability to *see*. Perhaps, therefore, the greatest error the beginning scenographer can make is to assume without question that once those mechanical skills of the craft are mastered—which, indeed, must be done, or no further progress is possible in any direction—the natural and unique imagination we are all endowed with will supply any other minor requirement: that one can automatically draw upon an inexhaustible spontaneous natural store of imagery out of past experience that will supply the form and detail necessary for the effective design of an appropriate scenic environment. Nothing is further from the truth. But why is this so?

For our present purposes, the answer lies in the nature of man's vision. Let us repeat it once again: the most important skill for any student of the visual arts is to develop the ability to see. While this sounds too elementary for comment, too simple a requirement, in practice it is not as simple as it seems. And the reason it is not a simple matter is that theatrical vision requires not one but two distinct types of seeing. One vision addresses itself to the world of the objective; the other vision must deal with the world of the illusive subjective—a world that often is hidden from purely objective (if such a thing exists) vision and investigation. It is not uncommon for mature scenographers to speak of an "inner eye." This is not simply a poetic or mystical expression. What they are referring to is a real and necessary part of their working technique; an attempt to describe the kind of vision and understanding all visual artists must develop. Seeing is the subject of the following section, but it is to that subjective "inner eye" that the most of our attention must be directed. And while it is impossible to assure that every student of scenography will in time come to possess or make use of such a vision, we must discuss this area of artistic training at least to the point that we can assure to all that such a vision is a practical necessity for working in the theater.

Robert Edmond Jones once said that "stage designers are born, not made." A great part of what he means by that statement has to do less with natural selection or cultural background than with the particular ways certain natural predispositions are channeled into the theater. But the callings of destiny aside, just how does the vision of the scenographer differ from the vision everyone else possesses? Or is there a differ-

ence? Are not 20/20 or corrected vision and a certain level of manual dexterity the only real requirements for the pursuit of any visual art? Increasingly, I feel, the answers to these questions must be *no*.

We cannot ignore the growing evidence that each human being is, indeed, a truly unique entity; that, similar as we sometimes appear to be to others who either look like us, dress like us, sound like us, or have the same basic cultural background, we all possess individual minds that may altogether contradict the most identical of surface similarities. Even identical twins can have distinctly separate and basically different ways of perceiving the world. We do not, as the timeworn phrase might lead us to think, all congenitally "see eye to eye." And this can be especially true in the manner in which we encounter the visual world about us. Gordon Rattray Taylor draws our attention to some observations that directly affect our old notions of human vision; more importantly, he raises a distinct challenge to the idea that all sighted people see the same objective world.

Some authorities have asserted that no thought is possible without imagery, but that is almost certainly false. It was Professor Bartlett, at Cambridge, who in the course of studying memory, came to the conclusion that people fell into two distinct groups: visualisers and verbalisers. The late Dr. Grey Walter . . . brought a little more scientific accuracy to the subject when he estimated, on the basis of the brain waves he studied, that fifteen per cent of the population think exclusively in visual terms, fifteen per cent exclusively in verbal terms, while the rest employ a mixture. . . .

Visualisers find it hard to form abstract concepts and find it difficult to communicate with verbalisers. . . . verbalisers tend to operate in a domain of concepts which have, all too often, only the vaguest relevance to the real world. I suspect that many lawyers, legislators, bureaucrats and administrators have the same defect.

Few of us like to admit that we do not see immediately and perfectly. The truth of the matter, however, is that even the most perfectly sighted person sees selectively and, at best, imperfectly. This can be demonstrated very simply by the following quick test. Look at the caricature of Abe Burrows, coauthor of *Guys and Dolls*, by

Al Hirschfeld shown in figure 111. Question: Just what did you *see*? If you said, "I see a line drawing of a man wearing a two-button jacket, a plaid vest, a figured tie, glasses, and smoking a cigarette," you would be right—but only half-right. The image also contains other items of information that have been purposely hidden in this relatively simple drawing. To be precise, it contains not only three hidden things but the clue to the number hidden. Now go back and look at the lower right side of the image; there you will see the name of the artist and a number beside it; the number is the clue. The clue to what, you ask? The clue to the number of times Hirschfeld has included the name of his daughter in the drawing; it appears three times. And where are those names? That is the game he has been playing with his fans for many years. The

Fig. 111. Abe Burrows, by Al Hirschfeld. © Al Hirschfeld. Drawing reproduced by special arrangement with Hirschfeld's exclusive representative, The Margo Feiden Galleries Ltd., New York

name of his daughter is *Nina*. Now, if you go back, it will take very little time to decipher the puzzle. It is easy to solve the mystery once you know that there is something to be found in the lines of the drawing; once alerted to the possibility of "hidden things" in the drawing, our vision is *actively directed* toward seeking out just what those things are. This *actively directed vision* is a necessary requirement for the practice of any phase of theatrical art, not just that of scenography. It should take very little time or effort to find that Hirschfeld has incorporated into the bends of the elbows and at the base of the ear of the figure the name "Nina"; being part of the design and sharing the same qualities as the other lines, the name becomes, however, very much like Poe's purloined letter—all but invisible to the *undirected vision*. Having once *seen* these names *as names*—not abstract lines representing cloth in a sleeve—we can never look at this drawing again without seeing them. In short, our vision has become *instructed*. And yet, those who do not know the "secret" of the drawing rarely see those names without being similarly instructed. This has nothing to do with native intelligence or perfect vision; it does very forcibly point out that intelligence and perfect vision must sometimes be directed toward a goal.

This simple test should bring home the observation that few of us do see immediately and with perfect understanding that which is seen; reception of an image and perception of that same image are not always in phase. It is especially sobering to realize that the vision of the scenographer must be trained to "see" when helpful clues, such as the ones Hirschfeld supplies, are few or more deeply hidden in the images we must use for theatrical work. Rest assured, however, there will always be similar "mysteries" inherent in the visual materials that scenographers use in their work.

Let us pursue this problem further; let us admit to ourselves that *seeing* of any kind can be *directed* and *deepened* by influences that have nothing to do with visual images. A picture is, it has been sagely observed, worth ten thousand words—and perhaps no number of words can ever adequately take the place of the image or make it as apparent to the mind as the image itself does. And yet, as another wise person once pointed out, *it took words to make that observation apparent*. There is a principle every scenographer (indeed, every theatrical artist) must be aware of that words can directly affect images; that the most profound statements the theater affords are a direct result of this interaction.

When Hamlet, in act 3, scene 4, is admonished by the ghost of his father to be less harsh in his indictment of his mother, he finds to his surprise that what is perfectly apparent to him in a visual sense is neither apparent nor visible to her:

HAMLET: Do you see nothing there?
QUEEN: Nothing at all, *yet all that is I see.*
(Italics mine)

The scenographer's vision is much like the sight of Hamlet; it sees both with a special intensity and with a special purpose. His mother's vision, on the other hand, has serious blind spots in it precisely because it is an unquestioning act. She sees only what she expects to see, making no attempt to see further. This is the prime mistake no artist can afford to make: *seeing that does not question what is seen is uninformed, and vision uninformed is vision impaired.* In the simplest terms, not only must all artists possess a keen outer eye that perceives shape, form, color, texture, and spatial relationships, they also must have an equally sensitive inner eye. The artist's vision is at once objective in the analytical sense as well as subjective in the most symbolic sense. The kind of seeing we speak of here is not, however, a matter of idiosyncratic vision—a strictly personal view such as the one practiced by the German expressionists immediately following the First World War—but a vision capable of interpreting forces and meanings contained in an object or image that escapes the superficial or cursory investigation of the untrained eye. Like Hamlet, one must be prepared to receive and perceive information that will always remain invisible or incomprehensible to others such as Hamlet's mother. It is a common mistake to think that if one can see at all, one can see it all. The Queen does not see the ghost, therefore it does not exist—at least for her; but everyone in the audience knows that he is there, that it is a necessity that he be there. Theatrical vision, then, is the sight Hamlet possesses. But, having

said this, just how does one go about getting this unique vision?

Artists cannot develop their abilities to any significant degree without two very important characteristics present in their nature: (1) they must have a natural curiosity about the objective world in general, and (2) they must have an intense need to know the facts concerning particular situations beyond the common perceptions of reality. They must have, in short, a complete vision, reflective in nature but fed by objective stimuli. Scenic seeing is, essentially, the development of the eye so that it "thinks" as well as sees; to be able to "see" in more than one time dimension and, most important of all, to be able to distill from the obvious surfaces of the material world that which is dramatically poetic. For as Herman Melville has taken care to point out, "poetry is not a thing of ink and rhyme, but of thought and act, and, in the later way, is by any one to be found anywhere, when in useful action sought." The fact that the messages the scenographer sends through the medium of design are often not meant to be perceived by conscious perception does not in any way weaken the point that he must be perfectly aware of what those messages are and strive to incorporate them into material form.

Our first question concerning the development of scenic vision as opposed to just "seeing" might very well be this: Does not everyone with 20/20 vision, regardless of culture or background, see the same thing when looking at the same thing? The answer, all questions of natural intelligence left aside, is unequivocally and absolutely no they do not. The next question, invariably, would be, If not, why not?

This is a question that all beginning visual artists have, and usually, they do not seriously entertain the idea that they do not see all there is to be seen. It is a difficult pill to swallow for beginning artists to be told by their instructors or by more advanced compatriots that being able to "see" is a time-consuming and difficult undertaking. Usually the explanation of why this might be so ceases with the statement. But in fact, there is no one reason why the young artist does not "see" all that his more experienced counterpart does; there are many. Of all the reasons, time and exposure to the objective world are the largest, most important factors; not only does experience of the world teach us to see more, but the constant questioning of the very act of seeing is a necessary part of the artist's visual development.

Let us begin this search for understanding by looking at a famous sixteenth-century painting: *The Ambassadors* by Hans Holbein, painted in 1533 (fig. 112). Examine the picture for the information it contains; it is not difficult to inventory the visual contents of the painting: two men, both in costume of the day (although one is dressed in academic garb, not in court dress, as is the other figure). They stand at either side of a two-tiered open case that contains representative instruments of all the arts and sciences of the time. We see, in short, a factual record of two famous men, and we can infer, by the painter's juxtaposition of them to the objects included, that they are not only figures of breeding and position but inquisitive men of intelligence and accomplishment. Their grave but open faces, their ease and poise, their familiar relationships to the accouterments of learning, combine to

give the viewer a message; a message not difficult to understand even some four hundred years later. And yet in this most meticulous rendering of objective reality, the artist has also included a strange object that defies rational explanation. Holbein, who in all of his other works scrupulously copied the outward appearance of reality, has, in this painting, introduced an irrational element that, in one sense, cannot be part of the total picture and, in another sense, cannot be separated from it. This "thing," which starts from the lower left of the painting and sharply cuts across the floor, is nothing less than a human skull; but it is painted in such a distorted manner that its true visual form cannot be grasped until the onlooker assumes another physical viewpoint that distorts the rest of the picture (fig. 113). Both views cannot be seen at the same time; both, in other words, cannot be understood at the same time; both do not belong to the same painting—and yet they can in no way be separated. Why did he do this? Several

Fig. 112. *The Ambassadors*, by Holbein. Courtesy of the National Gallery, London

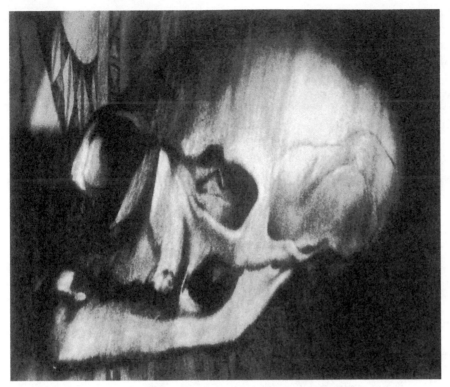

Fig. 113. Detail from *The Ambassadors*. Courtesy of the National Gallery, London

ideas present themselves—but we cannot ever know for sure if our explanation for this strange work is the correct one (assuming in the first place that there is, in fact, a "correct" one). Any explanation cannot be entirely verbalized, entirely satisfactory; this painting will, quite probably, remain something of a provocative mystery.

This painting has been included here not for its value as a work of art nor because it presents a tantalizing visual mystery. Both are true. It is here in this text because it serves as a visual touchstone as to how the scenographer employs his own special vision. In *The Ambassadors*, Holbein gives a mystery to be sure; but he also has done much of the "work" for us. All we have to do is to assume the two different positions and the two different images will emerge: the real and the phantasmagorical. But that is really not the point to which we should bring our attention; having approached the picture from those two viewpoints, having seen the images in both, we are left not with an "answer" but with a question: *What was Holbein getting at—what was he trying to say?* And, even more important than being a tantalizing question, the fact that he forces us to

move physically in order to make any sense of this work is a valuable lesson for the scenographer to learn. The image engages our attention but does so in a particularly dynamic way; we must do more than passively "see," we must actively work to bring the image into focus. Physically changing our viewpoint is required to understand this work at its most basic level: mentally changing our point of view is every bit as important and must be pursued in a similarly active way. It is an unsettling thought that we cannot or should not trust our ingrained and comfortable modes of perception, that we do not, as Hamlet's mother, see all that is. But it is with just such an acceptance of this situation that real progress in the art of scenography begins. The images we confront in our research do not, as with the Holbein painting, come equipped with such readily accessible clues; nor are there numbers, as with Hirschfeld's drawings, to tell us precisely the entire stock of hidden things. We must, as an integral part of our artistic work, seek these hidden factors out by less direct means, more difficult searches. As with the Holbein painting and the Hirschfeld caricature, there are ways of finding help and we should be aware that such aid does exist. Let us examine another image: a photograph taken in Toledo, Spain (fig. 114). Before reading any further, take a long look at the building in this photograph.

Now, ask yourself these questions: What did I *see*? What does this image project to my immediate vision? Is there anything *hidden* in the picture, any *quality* or *fact* I am not seeing or understanding? These, it must be granted, are difficult thoughts to entertain, since the question must almost certainly arise: *But just what am I looking for in the first place?*

Go back and look at the picture again. This time, however, ask yourself these questions: *If I were designing an environment that required elements from this locale—Mozart's* Don Giovanni, *for instance—what could I use from this image? What elements are appropriate; what would I choose to ignore? Does this picture tell me anything I need to know about Spain itself?*

These speculations do not give hard information; they do, however, begin an extremely important process: they cause us to change our focus from what is simply observed in the image to what exists in this particular image that can

Fig. 114. Photograph of a Spanish building

be used for a specific purpose. This line of thought is, by its very nature active rather than passive; our senses are alerted to the possibility that *something* or *some things* are included in this image that are appropriate to our specific purposes—the setting for *Don Giovanni*. But what?

Robert Edmond Jones very likely had just such questions when he began his initial speculations concerning the design of *The Birthday of the Infanta*, a work performed at the Manhattan Opera House in 1922. He had, of course, several years earlier visited Spain and had seen firsthand much of the visual material he would need to incorporate in the design. But did he simply copy details from the sketch book we know he carried throughout that country; did he simply check out research materials from the New York Public Library? It is quite certain he did look at and study many images from numerous sources; it is also just as certain that he did not stop his investigation of the design possibilities when he had found a "right" picture to copy from. We do not have either his written thoughts or his reported speculations on this project. What we do have, however, is a review of the design Jones created as that design appeared in performance. This review, moreover, reveals a great deal about how Jones studied the information contained in that material.

Here is how Stark Young, who reviewed the first performance of *The Birthday of the Infanta*, reacted to what he saw on stage: "No where in Spain have I seen buildings like these. But I have seen in Spain that character of sterility, of color and mass. I have seen that barbaric and cruel barrenness of sheer walls emerge, though any amount of rococo and baroque or plasteresque ornamentation had been superficially laid on to soften the aspect of it. . . . The character of Mr. Jones' setting, then, perfectly expresses the Spanish instinct, into which the actuality of the buildings has been translated by the artist. But that is not the important point just here. So far they have indeed become art, it is true, but not necessarily the art of the theatre. The important thing to be said here is that this is not architecture in Spain or anywhere else, but a translation of architecture into theatre terms."

Once more go back to figure 114. Certainly the picture you now see is different from the one you saw before. "Barbaric and cruel barrenness," "superficially laid on," "the Spanish instinct": Have not these qualities become apparent to you in a manner that was not evident when you first examined the photograph? Is it now relatively easy to perceive that while the blind copying of details could give a certain "Spanishness" to the design, it was necessary for Jones to *understand the import* of what he did select? If he had only copied a building from Spain, it is doubtful that his underlying thoughts and feelings would have been projected to Young. Robert Edmond Jones was an artist who could and did make an active effort to distill from the mass of what he saw the precise forms, colors, and textures needed for a precise purpose. He possessed and used his inner eye.

It is very possible that you will never again be able to see either an image of a Spanish building or the actual architecture of Spain without the words of Stark Young in some way guiding your vision. It is also possible that your understanding of the architecture of other countries will become more discriminating precisely because you now have a kind of architecture with which to compare it. It is not difficult to comprehend the principle put forth here: that there is always more to any visual experience than at first appears; that it is very possible that while a picture is worth ten thousand words, words can add to the worth of that image. But, once having articulated this principle, it must be said that it remains only an abstract thought that must be reexamined and reproved every time it is brought into play. And that is why "scenic seeing" is the core of the scenographer's art; he can never take for granted that he has reached some absolute level of expertness where this vision is an automatic response to anything that comes into view. As Frederick S. Wight points out in *The Object as Self-Image*, "A man-made object has a way of revealing itself to be something else than it at first appears, and then that revelation proves to be a cover story, and the whole process of undraping the truth is a disturbing one, subject to unaccountable blockages." This is true for the scenographer's research whether he is examining a photograph or a drawing or looking at something in its actual context, as Jones did when he toured Spain. We must constantly force our minds to change their points of view much in the same way Holbein forces us to change physically our viewing points; otherwise we will always be on the outside looking only at the surface of things.

Before leaving this discussion let us take another "test" to explore how that inner vision that scenographers use works. To facilitate this, let us construct a short outline of questions that allows us to catalog our impressions and thoughts.

First, examine the image shown in figure 115, a photograph of a French fourteenth-century church facade sculpture. Viewing this image alone some impressions are bound to occur. Now examine the image in figure 116; this image shows the constructing of a dinosaur in the American Museum of Natural History in 1916. As with the illustration of the Spanish building seen in figure 114, this picture seen in isolation elicits few questions or allows few observations to rise to the surface of attention. When the two images are compared, however, the situation alters; although the two have little connection or relationship other than their present juxtaposition, certain comparisons and analogies unconsciously begin to form in the mind. Curiosity is aroused; imagination springs into action; chains of associations begin. What are these associations; how does the examination of one image affect what is perceived in the other? How does one, then, track the mind as it explores the random thoughts that arise from such associations?

Fig. 115. Fourteenth-century sculpture

Fig. 116. Photograph of dinosaur skeleton

These questions and others like them form the basis of our investigative technique. Such questions—which one can easily see have few "logical" answers—are addressed by simple investigative procedures that include the following:

1. Listing all visual correspondences: that is, *What visual qualities of one image are similar to visual qualities in the other? What visual relationships of form, line, texture, are alike?*

After this phase of the exercise proceed to the following:

2. Listing emotional crossovers: that is, *What qualities of the sculpture alter your feelings about the skeleton of the dinosaur? What attributes of the skeleton do you perceive in the sculpture?*

Now begin to think how these thoughts and visual observations might be used in a design for a production. Consider how would you combine the two images into stage structure? Begin to make small sketches showing how you might use the visual qualities of both images in a single image. You might begin, at the same time, to consider what specific plays or musical works could use such imagery. (While this is backward to the usual way a scenographer works, this kind of *creative play* is not only pleasurable at times, it can actually break creative blocks when working on specific projects.)

Let us take one last test of vision.

While it is a sound principle to seek out the help of those highly knowledgeable or expert in their fields—as we did when we read the remarks of Stark Young concerning the architecture of Spain—it does not relieve the individual viewer from using his own vision to question the vision of others. *An inquiring vision is also a skeptical vision;* even the wisest and most astute scholars can misinterpret what they see or what they *think* they see sometimes making mistakes in visual interpretation. One example is sufficient to show how this can happen.

Figure 117 shows the sixteenth-century portrait of Thomas More painted by Hans Holbein. In his book *Thomas More*, Richard Marius uses this picture as a springboard for an interpretation of the predominant character traits he believed More possessed and that he, Marius, thought Holbein captured in this painting. Here is a partial account of what he says: "The stupendous Holbein portrait done about 1527 shows us in part a conventional pose, a man who aims to

Fig. 117. Portrait of Sir Thomas More

look the part he plays in the world wearing the golden chain of Tudor knighthood—dignified, sober, wise. But no other Holbein portrait shows a figure so brooding, *with so much on his mind, with so many things to do that he must hold a little book with both hands as if to keep himself from jumping up and going back to work*" (italics mine).

Closely examine this portrait for yourself. Do you agree with Marius's interpretation? What he reports seems reasonable enough; if you read the rest of passage quoted as well as the rest of the book, what he relates about the picture makes good sense. One would have to agree that what he puts forth here seems to be both true and convincing.

There is, however, only one real problem with this interpretation: that is, that *the author is in error reporting what he sees.* For More is *not holding a book but, rather, a folded piece of paper;* moreover, this piece of paper is held by one hand alone, not by two (fig. 118). These, one must admit, are two rather insignificant points; they do little or nothing to detract from the import of this fine biography, quite probably the best written during the past fifty years on this impor-

Fig. 118. Detail from portrait of Sir Thomas More

tant historical character. Still this does not alter the fact that mistakes in seeing were made. These are enough for the careful researcher to question any other observations Marius makes that deal with specific interpretations made from examination of visual research materials.

We have taken time to show how words cannot only explain images but can actually alter radically the perception of those images. A short codicil, then, should be added to our basic principle: *When you seek out the dwellings of other opinions, make sure you do not check your own eyes at the door.*

While "tests" of this kind we have been taking may seem to have no *real* purpose, the speculations and discoveries we make doing such exercises bring into focus two important principles of creative visual research: (1) *That scenographers must assemble many images in order to set the forces of the imagination into play;* (2) *that a strong element of skepticism accompany any research of any kind.*

The noted scientist Linus Pauling gives us good advice to accompany our research chores when he advises that *"in order to have a good idea you have to have lots of ideas"*. I would add to that thought in advising that the element of play—as discussed earlier in this text—is also a necessity in good research technique. All visual artists, scenographers not least among them, in time come to realize that *all good research is a serious form of play,* that the element of puzzle solving is an important component in the process of designing for the theater.

Imagination, it is clearly evident, is not a fixed quantity. It is not something you "have or don't have," are born with or born without. Nor is it

a randomly acquired human trait like freckles or red hair or blue eyes. It is, rather, the active combination of an ability to see, in the manner just discussed, individual attitudes (both conscious and unconscious) and—most important of all—the active employment of mechanical skills to serve the imaginative processes of the mind.

In order to feed the voracious appetite of the imagination, the scenographer must maintain an active awareness of the artwork of the past. To some extent this need can be supplied by course work in art history; but this approach can at best only supply a limited knowledge and understanding. Only if the interest is constant and the pursuit lifelong can an understanding of the past be gained or professionally used. In large part, knowing exactly what to take from that extensive body of work is the business of scenography. The extent to which direct use is made of precise forms or specific works is, however, a matter of judgment, and that illusive quality we can only inadequately call "taste"; but using a criteria of complete originality for the evaluation of the worth of an artwork has been, and remains today, contrary to the most basic practices of all past artists regardless of their individual art. Only in the twentieth century have we given innovation and originality such a high place in our judgment as to what is "good" or "bad" art; these are standards, we should also note, that are being substantially called into question as the only viable means by which to assign value to an artwork.

In a lighthearted moment, William Faulkner once observed, *"Immature artists copy—great artists steal."* While this is a humorous remark (but, nevertheless, a view that Faulkner is not alone in holding) that obviously overstates the case, it does point to an important truth concerning a continuing interrelationship between contemporary artists and their past counterparts. And while few would suggest we always blindly copy the work of the past, we should seek its guidance when appropriate. Faulkner's remark can also mean that the past's accomplishments are not "off limits" to us; the student of this art must come to realize (as the mature scenographer is constantly aware) that what we term past is also a name for a living heritage meant to be used as well as studied. Nor should reverence for that which is gone immobilize us from making the best use of that which has survived. A good example of the principles that arise from the assimilation of the thoughts just presented can be demonstrated by examination of the 1971 production of *Antigone* designed by Douglas W. Schmidt for the Vivian Beaumont Theatre in Lincoln Center (fig. 119). Schmidt used an original source for his design with a minimum of change: a section of a frieze from the Great Altar at Pergamon, a Greek work that dates from approximately 180 to 160 B.C., now part of the Staatliche Museen, Berlin (fig. 120). But, while he has retained the basic forms and design of the original fragment, he has found it necessary to incorporate a detail from another section of the same work in order to give completeness to his own work (fig. 121). This was made necessary, in all probability, by the different context in which the basic design ideas appear; that is, from museum fragment to theatrical setting could not be a simple one-step job of copying. The addition of the shield detail was, it is obvious, a conscious act

on the part of the scenographer, which demonstrates that unthinking duplication of another's work was not the only act performed. The exact reason why Schmidt incorporated that detail quite possibly was an intuitive one, but nevertheless, it indicates that the scenographic mind was at work. Use of historical materials in this manner is a legitimate part of the scenographer's function; moreover it is a creative use of visual research materials. The greatest playwright in our language—Shakespeare—was not above borrowing ideas and plots (and occasionally a line of text from another playwright) from any source of information to which he had access.

The direct use of these original materials is not so much the question as is how they are used. While we cannot formulate strict rules as to how these materials should be used, it should expected that the exact manner will change from scenographer to scenographer; one should expect to see similar "steals" incorporated into the same works in differing ways. For instance, while the Vivian Beaumont Theatre production

Fig. 119. Setting for *Antigone*, by Douglas W. Schmidt. Courtesy of Lynn Pecktal. Photograph by Arnold Abramson

Fig. 120. Detail from the Great Altar at Pergamon

used actual three-dimensional building materials (the panels were sculpted from Styrofoam
slabs), another production of this same play,
shown in model form in figure 122, used a projected image of statue from the same country and
period, but from the British Museum in London.
Similar sources do not determine similar results;
there is always ample opportunity for "originality" even in the most obvious cases of "stealing"
as these two examples have shown.

(Note: The British Museum allows anyone
who wishes to do so to make photographs as
they tour the various halls; this practice is one,
however, that not all museums or galleries observe, although slides and other pictorial materials are usually available from their own retail
shops. Picture galleries are more apt to restrict
photography than those museums that house
less perishable artworks such as sculpture; flash
photography will, like sunlight, alter the pigmentation of a painting over a period of time.
Any scenographer who visits these important
storehouses of the past should make it an ongoing practice to seek out and note those images
that are personally most affective. It matters little
if these images are for a project in the making
or simply those that accidentally stand out as

Fig. 121. Detail from the Great Altar at Pergamon

Fig. 122. Model for *Antigone*

a unique viewing experience unrelated to any specific purpose. Not only does this activity aid the scenographers in their day-to-day work, it is the most successful way to extend and deepen that understanding of the entire history of art in a manner that a limited course in a particular subject could never hope to do. Seeing these original objects as they really are—that is, not reduced in scale, changed in color or made flat, as seeing them in books cannot help but do—plus the habit of consciously collecting these images will, in time, prove to be an invaluable personal resource that can be drawn upon for ideas unforeseeable when these images were first secured.)

Theatrical Thinking

All work in the theater starts as an idea, a concept without physical form. The image we see on stage is no exception. However, it would be a mistake to believe that the transition from an idea or a feeling to a finished design is a single step; many steps, in fact, intervene, and the process is complex and multifaceted.

Probably the most often asked question of any director or scenographer is, Where do your ideas come from? The real answer is quite simple: everywhere. But explaining the answer is somewhat more difficult, and the entire process can never be fully revealed (and some aspects of the answer remain shadowy even to the scenographer himself). Nevertheless, while it is true that scenographers obtain what they need from literally everywhere, it is difficult to dispel the myth that the individual artist relies primarily on an intangible property of the mind we like to call *imagination*. What is difficult to explain to anyone is that while imagination is required in the practice of any art, its real role in the creative process is to *select*, *judge*, *reject*, and *synthesize* the materials found in the research of external facts and images. As the eighteenth-century painter Sir Joshua Reynolds wisely reminds us: *"The greatest natural genius cannot subsist on its own stock; he who resolves never to ransack any mind but his own will soon be reduced from mere barrenness to the poorest of all imitations. It is vain to invent without materials on which the mind may work and from which invention must originate. Nothing can come of nothing."*

All artists—including those who work in the theater—are included in this important dictum. *Even the greatest minds*, is no idle phrase; for some our own century's most important theater figures have relied heavily on the work of not only those who lived in the past but their contemporaries as well. Bertolt Brecht, certainly one of the greatest innovators of the twentieth century, often used the work of others in ways that might surprise those who believed that his plays sprang full-blown from the esoteric levels of his own individual imagination. One example—although not unique in the career of Brecht—should reveal the somewhat blatantly direct manner in which the creative mind works.

In his part-folk, part-modern parable play, *The Caucasian Chalk Circle*, Brecht required that the setting for the wedding scene in part 3 should include a small enclosure that during the playing of the scene would gradually fill up with festive guests. In figure 123 we see the setting designed by Karl von Appen for the original Berliner Ensemble production. As a production photograph of this scene shows, the characters literally fill this structure from wall to wall (fig. 124). Brecht meant the scene to be a comic one and instructed his scenographer accordingly. But what very few in the audience watching the play knew was that the visual source for this scene was a sequence in the 1935 Marx Brothers motion picture, *A Night at the Opera* (fig. 125). This is where Brecht got the inspiration that was crucial to the designing of the setting for the scene. Doubtlessly von Appen also found it necessary to do other research; research that provided him images such as the one shown in figure 126, a painting by the early

Fig. 123. Scenographic sketch for *The Caucasian Chalk Circle*

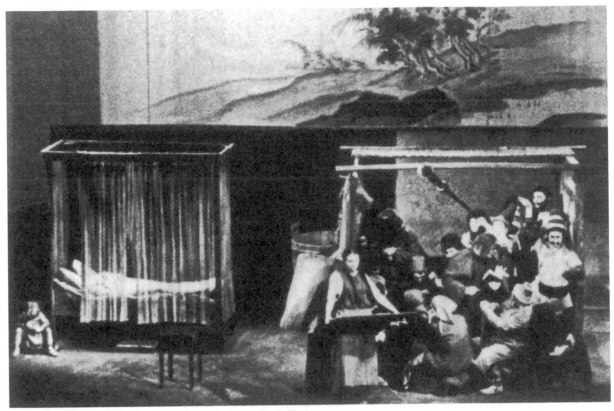

Fig. 124. Production photograph for *The Caucasian Chalk Circle*

fifteenth-century Flemish Limbourg brothers for a book of hours (a private prayer book of the period). This kind of historical research is also necessary to support the time period during which Brecht set his play. But the fact remains that the real impetus for the scenographer's design came from a 1930s Hollywood farce. Brecht was one of the first in the modern theater to demonstrate to us that ideas may come from *any* period and from *any* source as long as they are used to support the playwright's dramatic concepts. Since Brecht and his scenographers first formulated the theatrical philosophy of *conscious anachronism*, this mode of thought has become one of the most widespread practices in the staging of plays and the design of scenery and costume. There are very few scenographers working today who have not designed productions using this approach.

It is interesting to observe in figure 124 how closely Brecht, in his actual staging of the wedding scene in *The Caucasian Chalk Circle*, took the positioning and grouping of the performers

suggested by the scenographer in his scenic sketch. This does indicate that while the initial idea of the scene was Brecht's, he allowed others to aid in the development of that basic idea in production; in fact, Brecht himself often wrote that he counted heavily on his scenographers to flesh out his sometimes sketchy suggestions.

Let us examine another external source that was in great part responsible for a design on the stage. Figure 127 shows a setting for David Storey's play *Home*. Here we see a frankly theatrical, almost abstract stage arrangement; but this design is an almost direct copy of an image found outside the theater in the actual world (fig. 128). And this is the very photograph the scenographer used in his research for the play: a long narrow path in an English park with its final destination lost in the distant winter fog. This image was not decided upon immediately but only *after* the director and the scenographer began a search for an image that was first suggested by another literary work that graphically summed up many of the thoughts and feelings

Fig. 125. Scene from *A Night at the Opera*. From the MGM release *A Night at the Opera* ©
1935 Metro-Goldwyn–Mayer Corporation. Copyright renewed 1962 by Metro-
Golden–Mayer, Inc.

Storey wrote into his play—a sonnet by Shakespeare.

That time of year thou mayst in me behold
When yellow leaves, or none, or few, do hang
Upon those boughs which shake against the cold,
Bare [ruin'd] choirs, where late the sweet birds
    sang.
In me thou seest the twilight of such day
As after sunset fadeth in the west,
Which by and by black night doth take away,
Death's second self, that seals up all in rest.
In me thou seest the glowing of such fire
That on the ashes of his youth doth lie,
As the death-bed whereon it must expire,
Consum'd with that which it was nourish'd by.
This thou perceiv'st, which makes thy love more
    strong
To love that well, which thou must leave ere long.

There are literally no limits to the ways a
scenographer can use his findings, as the setting
shown in figure 129—a French production for
the play *Rabelais*—demonstrates. Here the scenographer took his entire inspiration from a single
image in a medical textbook printed during the
period that Rabelais actually lived (fig. 130). This
image was then reproduced on the stage as a
grossly enlarged structure that was variously
used as a banquet table, a platform, and for numerous other purposes as the play progressed.

Rarely, however, does the scenographer literally reproduce any image in its entirety on
the stage. More likely, elements of the original
source will be used selectively. While the design
for *Cat on a Hot Tin Roof* (fig. 131), owes its inspiration to the image shown in figure 132, the
source was used primarily as a suggestive cata-
lyst to the imagination, not as a literal guide for
naturalistic reproduction.

It is easy to see that a scenographic idea often
has strange history and that an idea or an image
for a scenographic design rarely comes from one
source alone or from one branch of arts exclusively. It would be more accurate to say that

Fig. 126. Fifteenth-century Flemish painting

what finally appears in the theater is an amalgam of *all* human activities, all arts and crafts, and is gleaned from all possible research sources. The main point to be observed here—and we will in later sections of this book explore more deeply this question of the sources of imagination—is that in the initial stages of seeking out a beginning point for the creation of a scenographic design, there is really no limit to the images or ideas available to the scenographer for his use; nor should the scenographer ever arbitrarily restrict his search to those from his own mind or to those of the playwright. It must also be remembered that it is the imagination's chief function to synthesize images from the outside world into physical realities on the stage that best serve the total production, not to demonstrate the scenographer's artistic prowess.

When, after some image is found or a visual idea occurs to the scenographer, a number of options lie open to him as he begins to put these ideas into physical form. Many scenographers assemble sketches and images onto collagelike boards before proceeding with actual three-dimensional experimentation. On the other hand, the scenographer may begin his work directly with actual three-dimensional materials—found objects, boards and papers, wire screening and meshes, cord—without any prior graphic work. But, as the student scenographer will probably discover very early in his study, the development of most ideas into scenographic form means that a great deal of both kinds of work—graphic and three-dimensional—must take place; that rarely does one kind of work ever take entire precedence over the other, and that often the

Fig. 127. Scenographic sketch for *Home*

one kind of work invariably leads to the other and then back again much in the way one plays leapfrog. By that I mean that rarely is any artwork a straight-line activity with clearly defined steps, one following the other in a strict order of cause and effect. Scenography, like all other artwork, tends to proceed in stages, each made up of differing (not always predictable) forms of experimentation. A sketch might precede an experiment on the model stage, or it might just be a graphic record of what is assembled there. But it is also possible that that sketch might, in turn, cause the scenographer to alter on the model something suggested by the sketch. And this process may take place dozens of times before a viable solution to a design problem for a particular scene finally occurs. The scenographer will doubtlessly find that as he works on project after project, it becomes increasingly difficult to separate his work into neat self-contained steps. The professional scenographer must be expert in all forms of artwork and must continually develop that outer eye that can capitalize on the rich visual world surrounding us all.

Fig. 128. Image for *Home*

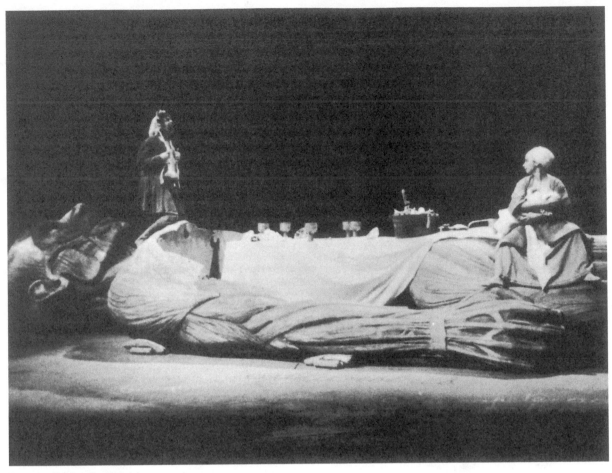

Fig. 129. Setting for *Rabelais*

I would not like to leave the impression that all scenographic design is simply a matter of finding a striking image to copy or the cannibalization of the creative work of others; obviously that is not so. The imagination is also capable of visualizing original concepts—although almost always based on some aspects of the objective world—from which a design will develop. Before the actual work on a production begins, before the scenographer starts his own experimentation or the director begins to rehearse his performers, most productions are thoroughly discussed so that certain agreed-upon intellectual and visual directions will be correctly charted. Often the scenographer and the director working together—using the written images of the playwright or the librettist—will create their own imagery; imagery they believe will best serve that of the text or libretto. Read, for instance, these words of the noted British scenographer John Bury concerning the Royal Shakespeare Company's *Wars of the Roses*, a group of Shakespeare's related historical plays that were performed as a unit:

The Wars of the Roses was designed in steel—the steel of the plate armour—the steel of the shield and the steel of the broadsword.

In this hard and dangerous world of our production, the central image—the steel of war—has spread and forged anew the whole of our medieval landscape. On the flagged floors of sheet steel tables are daggers, staircases are axe-heads, and doors the traps on scaffolds. Nothing yields: stone walls have lost their seduction and now loom dangerously—steelclad—to enclose and to imprison. The countryside offers no escape—the danger is still there in the iron foliage of the cruel trees and, surrounding all, the great steel cage of war.

The costumes corrode with the years. The once-proud red rose of Lancaster becomes as a rusty scale

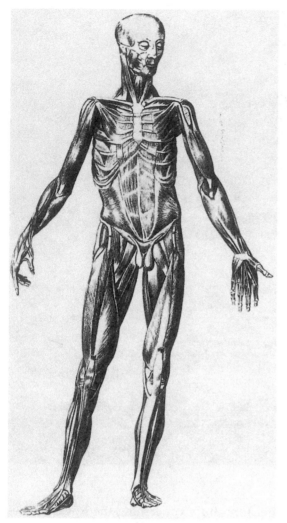

Fig. 130. Seventeenth-century medical drawing

on the soldiers' coats; the milk-white rose of York is no more than a pale blush on the tarnished steel of the Yorkist insurrection. Colour drains and drains from the stage until, among the drying patches of scarlet blood, the black night of England settles on the leather costumes of Richard's thugs.

Certainly, the mature scenographic imagination is at work here even though what is discussed is nothing more than a list of materials, objects, and literal descriptions of the effects of war and the passage of time. Most certainly this imagination depends entirely on the quality of the research that precedes any planning of a production. Visual research in various guises forms the underlying structure of this book.

The Nature of Research

No matter how creative the individual director, no matter how clever the scenographer, no aspect of theater art can be pursued without frequent recourse to research in some form. In the producing theater the importance of this multifaceted, many-leveled activity should not be minimized; it is as important that both the director and the scenographer be adept in finding appropriate source materials that will aid them. They must know as well just what and how much to take from those sources. Yet there is a vast difference between mere research—that is, finding something that relates to the text's requirements in a vague way—and creative research, which seeks to find *exactly the right thing* for that particular production of that particular play. As the great French critic André Malraux stated, "Genius is not what it encounters but what it annexes."

The simplest form of research is satisfied with superficial representation of period style or detail alone. Many hundreds of costume films made during the past seventy years attest to the unthinking manner that research can be done. In many of these works what we see is a world that superficially *looks* like a particular place at a particular time but does not persuade us that the picture is a true depiction of the spirit of the time or representative of the cultural climate it seeks to portray; ostensibly *accurate* in detail but unconvincing as a whole. Creative research concerns itself more with the *evocation of a past time* than it does with the literal replication of it. Research is only useful to the extent it assists the director or the scenographer to clarify the underlying themes of a production or to elucidate for a modern-day audience a play's oftentimes obscure text. Simply to reproduce a picture of a past age is not the purpose of the theater. Museums do that much better than the theater can. Creative research makes it possible, however, for interpreters to show a present-day audience considered syntheses of living cultures distilled from collective pasts. The theater allows us—to borrow an apt phrase from the poet W. H. Auden—*To break bread with the dead.*

Yet how does one know what to select, and how does he know what he selects is *right*, is

Fig. 131. Scenographic design for *Cat on a Hot Tin Roof*

useful to the purpose just stated? For out of a world of possibilities, there must finally be a limited number of selective judgments made, definite choices that preclude all other possibilities; definite choices that will push the text in one direction or another, slant the meaning of the words in the text. What test of use or criterion of selection should we adopt in our search for these *right* things? Any form of interpretation, of course, has its attendant dangers. John Kenneth Gailbraith reports that as George Bernard Shaw grew older, "he became less and less interested in theory, more and more interested in information." Gailbraith goes on to say , "I now pick up magazines and leaf through them looking for articles that are rich with facts; I don't care what they are. Evocative and deeply percipient theory I avoid. It leaves me cold unless I am the author of it myself. My advice to all young writers would be to stick to research and reporting with only a minimum of interpretation."

Should the director or scenographer heed this advice? Is there anything in the experienced attitudes of a Shaw or a Gailbraith that would apply to the kind of research we do in the theater? This is a question all researchers must consider if not resolve. Let us attempt, therefore, to be clear as to just what are the *goals* of the kind

Fig. 132. Ruined plantation house

of research that goes beyond simple annexation of superficial detail.

As a basic outline of intent these aims could be listed:

To explore
To find
To distill
To understand
To choose
To assemble
To show

These goals outline the work all researchers do. Keep them in mind as we progress from subject to subject in the remainder of this text. Precision of intent should inform the work of both director and scenographer alike. A short example as to what is meant by this phrase *precision of intent* should suffice.

Several years ago a student selected *Hamlet* as a project to design; the scene where Polonius is stabbed through the curtain (called an *arras* in Shakespeare's time) in the Queen's bedchamber was under discussion. The basic task for the class was to consider what a director and scenographer would agree upon as the design of this curtain; what would be appropriate in terms of historical research, and what would be useful to the director's concept of that particular scene. The student was questioned about what factors would influence his decisions in the making of a design specification for the curtain. "Well," he said impatiently, "I haven't picked one out yet or designed it. Just a tapestry." He was asked if his selection of this tapestry—or his design—might in any way help reinforce the director's work, or if it would possibly tell something *about the Queen's character*; something that might allow the director to bring to the attention of the actors something about the purpose of the scene itself. After all, as a character in the play, she might have had some influence on the way her bedchamber was furnished. What sort of things does she select. What does it say about her tastes? Or is it not possible that somehow this tapestry might subtly underscore, even intensify the feelings of the audience who will witness the cold-blooded murder of a harmless old man as he hides behind the hanging? The student thought about these possibilities. (He also admitted that he had not considered the selection of the rooms' furnishings in any detail, certainly not very carefully.) Finally he came to the conclusion—although it took some time and further research to arrive at a new understanding of the scene—that although the tapestry need not be greatly symbolic in any way, consideration of those questions could help him recognize the right tapestry among the several examples he found.

Let us now examine some of the basic purposes that lie beyond simple satisfaction of a text's basic needs.

The Purpose behind Theatrical Research

Everything man fashions—his houses, works of art, the clothes he wears, the tools he makes in order to create the objects he needs or wants, even the institutions that mold his social life—speaks a silent language not easily comprehensible and has a story to tell that superficial investigation will not reveal. Simple research will isolate these things so that they may be named and categorized; creative research, on the other hand, not only does this but also deals with their interpretation and meaning—it hears and translates that silent language into practical information. The theater artist—no matter whether his job is to instruct the actor or design their costumes or create the worlds they live in— must learn to see *through* the surface of things, as opaque as that surface often is.

Remembering Robert Edmond Jones, Jo Mielziner draws our attention to just such an artist:

I recall the time when Jones was supervising the execution of the stage setting for the seventeenth-century Spanish room in *The Buccaneer*. A week earlier he had completed his design, and on this particular day the crew of fine artists in Bergman's Studio was executing the set on the paint frame below Jones's studio. Bobby couldn't bear the idea that they would think of their work as simply the job of executing a large painting; so he scurried out with me to gather up bits and pieces of what he called "living things" which related to the setting: a lovely antique bench of the period with the patina of age and the beauty of line that he loved so much; a swatch of antique yellow satin, with some black lace and a huge artificial red flower; a yard or two of heavy gold lace; one lovely Spanish Renaissance tile. These things he placed on the floor beside the setting on which the painters were at work, because Jones wanted—for himself and for all who were working with him—to be conscious of the relations of this painting to its final achievement and appearance on the stage. . . .

Robert Edmond Jones could be described as a dreamer, but he was also a doer. Idealist he was, but certainly he cannot be dismissed as a mere visionary. A prophet, yes, but at the same time a most practical craftsman. (Jo Mielziner, "Practical Dreams," in *The Theatre of Robert Edmond Jones*, ed. Ralph Pendleton)

This, then, is the crux of our problem when we endeavor to do more than mere literal research. As Jones wrote in 1941, "we may fairly speak of the art of stage designing as poetic, in that it seeks to give expression to the essential quality of a play rather than to its outward characteristics." Although these words come from a time that had a view of theater somewhat different from the one we profess today, the essential truth and good common sense of Jones's view still applies, is still valid. In the final analysis, creative research is a means to the poetic art of scenography that Jones felt was so important. What he sought then, although much has changed in theater since, is still basically what we seek now, what we as scenographers still attempt to do.

John Ruskin, the noted nineteenth-century art critic, once wrote: "Great nations write their autobiographies in three manuscripts, the book of their deeds, the book of their words and the book of their art. Not one of these books can be understood unless we read the two others, but of the three the only trustworthy one is the last" (Kenneth Clark, *Ruskin Today*). It is an accepted principle of most historians that all activities of an age reflect either directly or indirectly the spirit of the time. Music, philosophy, religion, and political theory, as well as architecture, sculpture, and painting, all exercise influences one on the other and interrelate to such an extent that the theatrical use of any one element cannot help but call a knowledge of the others into question. Not even so great an artist as Michelangelo, despite his personal genius and singularity, can be fully understood without consideration of his close working relationship to the church and the doctrines of the day. Nor could the church itself be fully understood without examining its relationship to the secular, political milieu of late Renaissance Italy. To comprehend the visual image of a period along with the myriad facets of that image—and this is the scenographer's ultimate aim—he must also understand the forces that had molded the people who in turn determined the character of the age in which they lived. It is a common fault of young scenographers to limit their research into a period too narrowly; the veteran artist seeks his images and concepts from behind the surfaces, from the obscure, out-of-the-way nooks and crannies of the past. Simple research, that which stops at surface examination, can be carried out by the most uninterested of workers; creative research, that which goes into the deeper layers of what is being examined and seeks to understand more than a cursory glance can reveal, is a highly personal activity and the necessary business of an artist; discovery of a fact may be important, but understanding and interpreting the forces that created that fact is essential if the resultant findings are to have any real worth to the scenographer. It was precisely in this area—the difference between these two ways of approaching research—that the scenographers of most nineteenth-century productions fell short. They were more than conscientious and meticulous in reproduction of historical detail, but contemporary drawings and early photographs reveal that what they produced would have been more serviceable for Madame Tussaud's Wax Museum than for a living theater. Accuracy of detail alone is not sufficient to ensure that the contemporaneity of the past can be evoked.

In speaking of the craft of poetry, Dylan Thomas once pointed out that "the best craftsmanship always leaves holes and gaps in the works of the poem so that something that is *not* in the poem can creep, crawl, crash, or thunder in." Creative research is not altogether unlike this; often a scenographer feels he is looking for something (having read and studied a playscript or libretto), the nature of which he is not quite sure. Often the most knowledgeable and experienced scenographer cannot with absolute certainty always know just what this unknown quantity is until it is found. And it is quite possible that he overlooks what he needs by looking too hard. As Jean Dubuffet, the French painter has noted:

I am obsessed by the idea that there is something both false and unprofitable in looking at things too closely and too long. It is not normal for a human being to stare at objects for the sole purpose of inspecting them and making an inventory of their constituent parts. Such a position in our relation to them seems to me to destroy completely (if not to empty them of all content) the mechanisms of communications that exist between man and the objects around him, the way he perceives them and the way they affect him. Man sees things without trying to see them. While he is looking at one thing he sees another as though obliquely. . . .
. . . I must say my feeling is—always has been— very strong that the key to things must not be as we imagine it, but that the world must be ruled by strange systems of which we have not the slightest inkling. This is why I rush toward strange things. I am quite convinced that truth is strange; it is at the far end of

strangeness that one has a chance to find the key to things. (Peter Selz, *The Work of Jean Dubuffet*)

What Dubuffet is saying (and he is certainly not the first or only artist to realize these hidden forces that influence any art form) is that awareness is never a completely logical or "conscious" process, that there are, indeed, other ways of being aware, ways that directly influence what an artist produces but that are neither under conscious control nor, for that matter, always predictable. This is an important point to understand when we begin any research for any purpose: that specific task-oriented projects must take into account an entire spectrum of "awareness." As Gordon Rattray Taylor points out in the *The Natural History of the Mind*: "Of all the problems which arise in connection with the notion of 'mind' the most difficult is the fact of consciousness itself. Consciousness is often defined as awareness—awareness of self and of the environment—but this does no more than substitute one word for another, since we are equally unable to explain the subjective aspects of awareness. . . . *consciousness is not a single entity but varies in kind as well as degree*" (italics mine).

What this means is that we must learn to cooperate with our own minds (and to give way at times to inner promptings that seem to defy our "logical" sense of rightness); to create within our own selves the climate for the fullest utilizations of all levels of our consciousness, not merely that top layer that we have heretofore called *awareness*. In short, we must learn (and more important, put to use) the meaning of Dubuffet's words: "it is at the far end of strangeness that one has a chance to find the key to things."

But what do these words mean to the scenographer? Is this type of research valid, this philosophy of vision acceptable or usable to him; is it even employable in the practical world of theatrical production? Yes, it may very well affect the manner is which the scenographer approaches his research chores. And yet this does not mean to infer that research is wholly an intuitional activity, or that the scenographer merely goes to the library or his files methodically examining everything in sight until some psychic bell rings; there are methods and principles of research that will both expedite much of the guesswork and still leave room for the "strange systems" alluded to by Dubuffet to do their work. As Ben Shahn, another famous painter, has pointed out in his book *The Shape of Content*: "The subconscious may greatly shape one's art; undoubtedly it does so. But the subconscious cannot create art. The very act of making a painting is an intending one; thus to intend and at the same time relinquish intentions is a hopeless contradiction, albeit one that is exhibited on every hand."

What Shahn says about painters applies equally well to scenographers; one must trust his intuition to a great extent but never use intuition as an excuse for not digging into a problem of research. It does little good to tell the novice scenographer that in twenty years the task of locating useful material hidden away in libraries and museums may still be difficult but not as difficult as it is today; for the professional scenographer never outgrows the need to perform research in the practice of his art. It is obvious that experience will ease the difficulty in finding appropriate source materials; but the process becomes neither entirely automatic nor ever anything less than a chore. For the student the problems in learning to perform scenographic research are real and substantial. And while there has been a veritable explosion of printed materials that should make the job of finding information easier, this profileration has in many ways made the job of research more difficult than ever. So, if it is not possible for us to say *where* to find information, we can, at least, point out a few guidelines that may be helpful in learning *how* to approach this all-important subject. Let us begin by examining how the *element of chance* affects the process of research.

The Role of Chance in the Creative Process

Creative research is as much an attitude as it is a specific goal-oriented pursuit. These attitudes often are products of accidental experience, not conscious thought; linear research technique is not always the most productive. At times, when we are least looking for a specific

answer to a particular question we accidentally *happen* upon information that may instantly illuminate our understanding, even causing us to abandon long-held preconceptions. Accidental encounters may even provide information relating to questions of research we have yet to discover. We cannot discount the mysterious side of research procedure.

In my own experience such encounters frequently occur. For example, during my student days, while spending an afternoon in London's Victoria and Albert Museum, I chanced across information that substantially altered my previous understanding of the past. Having no purpose in mind with the exception of avoiding a late winter storm, I found myself idly wandering among cases of costume accessories and period jewelry. One case contained objects that appeared to be unusually long hatpins. Too large and too ornate for hatpins, I was puzzled about their use. Although of French origin, they were owned by upper-class and aristocratic English women during the first half of the eighteenth century. The names of these objects were unfamiliar. Asking a nearby attendant for further information he replied, "Lice stickers—the only way to get to them out when the hair was done up a few months." This isolated fact—revealed in the pragmatic way it was—sharply focused the curious double standards of another age. Questions that had unconsciously accumulated in my mind concerning this time instantly became clear. Soon I was to design a production set in the period these pins were made and used. At that moment my mind was far from the project. My attention was not on the characters I would in a few months have to house and clothe. The words of the museum attendant shocked me. I already knew that all European countries, especially France and England, placed great emphasis on outward refinement of dress during most of the eighteenth century. I also understood that class and status demanded that its members maintain styles that identified as well as separated them from lower classes. Yet until now my concerns with the period reached no deeper understanding than that which the casual eye perceives from words and images in books dealing with the period. With all my art and social history studies I did not differentiate between museum exhibits and living worlds of the past. While sure of the exact dates and period features in Fielding's *Tom Jones* or Sheridan's *School for Scandal*, I was less sure how people of the time lived day to day. I had read Pepy's diaries that revealed the age immediately preceding this one and was also familiar with Samuel Johnson's writings and Boswell's anecdotes. While I had much information at my fingertips, I now realized I did not really *know the people themselves*; that although I was intellectually familiar with the *name* and *look* of what they wore, knew precisely what they sat on, had considered the places they frequented both "in the season" and out, I did not have a living image of everyday life. With all the information at hand I still possessed little understanding as to how those living then felt or thought. I did not know, I realized, *how they lived from day to day*. Yet here—in a glass case only inches from my own hand— was an object that another hand two hundred fifty years ago used for specific purposes, purposes that gave me such an empathetic feeling that I found myself involuntarily scratching my head. Never before do I remember an instance where the past so forcibly engaged my imagination. As I examined the object before me, I began to perceive the concerns of eighteenth-century daily life—not only the constant need to dispatch vermin from hair but also the deeply felt need "to be in fashion." I began to understand that one must not only seek out specific dates and pictures of past ages but must find ways of knowing the people themselves in ways museums and collections of objects can in no way show. Knowing from earlier study that cleanliness beneath expensive dress and excessive makeup was not a dominant concern of the time, I sensed that my twentieth-century revulsion to the unsavory aspects of the period acted as a barrier, an opaque screen, preventing me from accepting that these people actually lived in a world not that different from today. Leaving the museum I had no firm design concepts in mind. I felt better prepared, however, to believe that the early eighteenth century had existed; that I might—with diligent study and help from other revelations—come to understand it better.

Months later, I began work on the *The Beggar's Opera*, John Gay's eighteenth-century ballad-opera (a work that Bertold Brecht would adapt in the twentieth century and rename, *The Three-Penny Opera*). My research began attempting to recall those feelings experienced in the Victoria and Albert Museum. It also included examination of materials I gathered from other museum visits while in London from Sir John Soane's house—which is not so much a museum as it is a private house open to the public. There I had encountered another important "key" by which to enter this period: the paintings of Hogarth. Of especial value to my current project were a series of paintings—which Hogarth also issued as prints of drawings—called *The Rake's Progress*. Not only did these works show many visual details in the appropriate time period that concerned my project, they even dealt with the same class of people who people *The Beggar's Opera*. Little effort was needed to see links between the world Hogarth painted and the world Gay wrote about. Another idea occurred to me at this time. "Now," I thought, "since they— Hogarth and Gay—lived in the same period, did they *know* one another?" A little research revealed they did. This led to a further thought: since they knew each other, they must have known other writers and artists. *Who were those others?* With this simple question, a chain of associations began. My research now took on aspects of investigative reporting.

As a result of these speculations, two kinds of material began to accumulate: (1) Visual materials—such as Hogarth paintings and prints, images of items, furnishing, clothing, crafts—from everyday life and (2) written materials garnered from those living at the time who had recorded their everyday experiences. Beginning with Hogarth's images and Gay's words as "letters of introduction," I began to "call" on their friends and acquaintances. The circle was wide and varied; among the group, however, several stood out. One in particular addressed many of the visual and written descriptions I had assembled. Jonathan Swift—the Irish writer who lived in London for most of his life—recorded particularly vivid (at times savage) descriptions of the life one might find in London during the first half of the eighteenth century. From his writings alone it was possible to obtain a coherent picture of the period; and it was he more than any other who gave me entry to the time of *The Beggar's Opera*. One instance—although many exist—as to how the process of combining word and image to gain a picture of a past age should suffice.

Along with the many images collected for detailed notes on furnishing, costume, properties, and the like, was the Hogarth print shown in figure 133. This print records a moment in the daily life of a group of itinerant actors. The focal point of the picture is a woman who could serve as visual information for several of the characters in *The Beggar's Opera*: Polly Peacham or Lucy Lockit among them. The title for the print derives its name from this person: *The Strolling Actress*. If one carefully examines the picture, many distinct items are evident. The drawing is so animated and specific that it is possible to speculate on individual personalities and relationships of those shown. Now, since the drawing is accurate—the eye of the artist being highly selective in the detail included—what more can any scenographer wishing factual information hope to find? In not this visual record sufficient to show us *how the people of the time lived*, since we can see clearly *how they appeared*? This is the juncture of research where Swift is able to enhance perceptions of what is visually evident, a demonstration as to how *words and thoughts* change attitudes as to what is *seen*. Swift wrote the following poem in 1731:

A Beautiful Young Nymph Going to Bed

Corrina, Pride of *Drury-Lane*,
For whom no Shepherd sighs in vain;
Never did *Covent Garden* boast
So bright a batter'd, strolling Toast;
No drunken Rake to pick her up,
No Cellar where on Tick to sup'
Returning at the Midnight Hour;
Four Stories climbing to her Bow'r'
Then, seated on a three-legg'd Chair,
Takes off her artificial Hair:
Now, picking out a Crystal Eye,
She wipes it clean, and lays it by.
Her Eye-Brows from a Mouse's Hyde,
Stuck on with Art on either side,
Pulls off with Care, and first displays 'em,
Then in a Play-Book smoothly lays 'em.
Now dextrously her Plumpers draws,
That serve to fill her hollow Jaws.
Untwists a Wire; and from her Gums
A Set of Teeth completely comes.

Fig. 133. Hogarth print, *The Strolling Actress*

Pulls out the Rags contriv'd to prop
Her flabby Dugs and down they drop.
Proceeding on, the lovely Goddess
Unlaces next her Steel-Rib'd Bodice;
Which by the Operator's Skill,
Press down the Lumps, the Hollows fill,
Up goes her Hand, and off she slips
The Bolsters that supply her Hips.
With gentlest Touch, she next explores
Her Shankers, Issues, running Sores,
Effects of many a sad Disaster;
And then to each applies a Plaister.
But must, before she goes to Bed,
Rub off the Dawbs of White and Red;
And smooth the Furrows in her Front,
With greasy Paper stuck upon't.
She takes a *Bolus* e'er she sleeps;
And then between two Blankets creeps.
With Pains of Love tormented lies;
Or if she chance to close her Eyes,
Of *Bridewell* and the *Compter* dreams,
And feels the Lash, and faintly screams;
Or, by a faithless Bully drawn,
At some Hedge-Tavern lies in Pawn;
Or to *Jamaica* seems transported,
Alone, and by no Planter courted;
Or, near *Fleet-Ditch's* oozy Brinks,
Surrounded with a Hundred Stinks,
Belated, seems on watch to lye,
And snap some Cully passing by;
Or, struck with Fear, her Fancy runs
On Watchmen, Constables and Duns,
From whom she meets with frequent Rubs;
But, never from Religious Clubs;
Whose Favour she is sure to find,
Because she pays 'em all in Kind.
    Corinna wakes. A dreadful Sight!
Behold the Ruins of the Night!

A wicket Rat her Plaister stole,
Half eat, and dragg'd it to his Hole.
The Crystal Eye, alas, was miss't;
And Puss had on her Plumpers p———st.
A Pigeon pick'd her Issue-Peas;
And *Shock* her Tresses fill'ed with Fleas.
　　The Nymph, tho' in this mangled Plight,
Must ev'ry Morn her Limbs unite.
But how shall I describe her Arts
To recollect the scatter'd Parts?
Or shew the Anguish, Toil, and Pain,
Of gath'ring up herself again?
The bashful Muse will never bear
In such a Scene to interfere.
Corinna in the Morning dizen'd.
Who sees, will spew; who smells, be poison'd.

This often savage, ultimately devastating portrait details the daily life of a person that not only Swift and Gay probably knew well, but that Hogarth quite possibly often drew or painted. But can one glean the particulars of this life from the evidence of Hogarth's drawing alone? The clues are there, but the image is a sanitary one compared to the images Swift draws in the mind of the reader. While it is painful to imagine what Swift records, if one reads *The Beggar's Opera* carefully the description rings true. We even are warned early in *The Beggar's Opera* of the kinds of people we are soon to meet: in the prologue a beggar directly addresses the audience telling them not only what the play is about but who they will see. Among the types—all from the lower and criminal classes of London—are thieves, highwaymen, pickpockets, fences, murderers, prostitutes, pimps, many bearing the colorful names that surfaced during Shakespeare's time and earlier: jades, trulls, trollops, queans. But, as the beggar says: "All is human." After reading Swift's poem, we are not likely again to see Hogarth's paintings or prints in quite the same way.

A twofold principle of creative research can be formulated from the kinds of experiences encountered above: (1) that creative research is a continuous process frequently subject to the vagaries of circumstance and chance, and (2) that imagination is not a fixed quantity of chosen individuals but an ongoing bargain artists make between eyes and mind.

How, then, can one be trained to know precisely the ways to gather an often diffuse body of fact, image, and opinion? This, in brief, forms the basis of the question students of scenography most often ask: *Where do I find the answers to questions I may not know how to ask?* While this may seem to be a nonsensical question on the surface, it presents a real problem in research: finding factual materials that satisfy intuitional needs. One of the more bizarre aspects of such creative research is that often a scenographer will discover the answers to these needs purely by accident—*by chance.*

This statement is not as illogical as it might first appear. Principles can be fashioned that take into consideration the random nature of researching needed materials. Moreover, there are many who have sought to know just how these principles can be made operational. Among the clearest expositions of this fascinating problem is a study by James H. Austin. In his book, *Chase, Chance, and Creativity*, Austin provides a good understanding of the ways chance can be put to work for anyone engaged in searching out answers to problems that appear to have no straightforward solutions. Here are some comments from his book:

What is chance? Dictionaries define it as something fortuitous that happens unpredictably without discernible human intention. Chance is unintentional and capricious, but we needn't conclude that chance is immune from human intervention. Indeed, chance plays several distinct roles when humans react creatively with one another and with their environment.

Chance I is the pure blind luck that comes with no effort on our part. If, for example, you are sitting at a bridge table of four, it's "in the cards" for you to receive a hand of all 13 spades, but it will come up only once in every 6.3 trillion deals. You will ultimately draw this lucky hand—with no intervention on your part—but it does involve a longer wait than most of us have time for.

Chance II evokes the kind of luck Charles Kettering had in mind when he said: "Keep on going and the chances are you will stumble on something, perhaps when you are least expecting it. I have never heard anyone stumbling on something sitting down."

In the sense referred to here, Chance II is not passive, but springs from an energetic generalized motor activity. A certain basal level of action "stirs up the pot," brings in random ideas that will collide and stick together in fresh combinations, lets chance operate. When someone, *anyone*, does swing into motion and keeps on going, he will increase the number of collisions between events. When a few events are linked together, they can then be exploited to have a fortuitous outcome, but many others, of course, cannot. Kettering—was right. Press on. Something will turn up.

. . . As we move on to Chance III, we see blind luck, but in camouflage. Chance presents the clue, the opportunity exists, but it would be missed except by that one person uniquely equipped to observe it, visualize it conceptually, and fully grasp its significance. Chance III involves a special receptivity and discernment unique to the recipient. Louis Pasteur characterized it for all time when he said: "Chance favors only the prepared mind." . . .

. . . Chance can be on our side, if we but stir it up with our energies, stay receptive to its every random opportunity, and continually provoke it by individuality in our hobbies and our approach to life.

While these observations do not give exact formulas for accomplishing creative research—nor can anyone answer all questions concerning the role of chance in the artistic process—they give positive reinforcement to the principle of "keep going." As the comments of Austin infer, research is an activity to be approached in the spirit of adventure; we should neither be afraid of the paths where our research might lead us nor be hesitant to follow what may seem at first glance a frivolous direction. To paraphrase the old French aphorism: *creative research has its reasons that reason knows nothing of.*

While not possible for any interpreter to unearth every reason why a playwright wrote a certain line in a certain way or to seek out in every instance the exact cause why a character says certain words—in many cases, the playwright may not consciously know all these reasons himself—the search for useful information must continually go forward. That is what interpretation means. If we constantly keep in mind that there are always many more facts to be found in a text than will be found, then our anticipation of finding that information will make us—as Austin thinks—more active searchers. As a result we will increase the probability as well the certainty that more will be found. On the other hand, when we blindly accept the words or directions of a playwright strictly at face value with no further scrutiny, we decrease our ability to get to those levels of a text that reveal the playwright's deepest concerns or his

hidden worlds. Chance, as we have seen, is not a fixed operation immune to human intervention. It can be prompted; an active belief that this is so will help us to capitalize on information that comes by the most indirect route.

Let me cite one more experience when my path accidentally crossed that of a playwright to show how this accidental encounter greatly aided my understanding of the environment necessary for the play.

At the beginning of *A Streetcar Named Desire*, Blanche du Bois comes to live in New Orleans with her sister, Stella. The house in which Stella and Stanley—Stella's husband—live is a cramped, run-down structure at the edge of the Old French Quarter (see "Environment in the Scenographic Process" in part 5 for further discussions of this subject). A few days after Blanche arrives Stella plans an outing for Blanche and herself to a well-known restaurant. She is aware that Blanche not only is ill at ease in her new surroundings but actually feels threatened by the situation in which she finds herself. Believing that a night out will lessen the shock of Blanche's recent displacement, she tells Stanley of her plan:

STELLA: Oh, Stan! (*She jumps up and kisses him which he accepts with lordly composure.*) I'm taking Blanche to Galatoire's for supper and then to a show, because it's your poker night.
STANLEY: Well, isn't that just dandy! How about my supper, huh? I'm not going to no Galatoire's for supper!

Later that night the two women return; before entering the house, this exchange takes place.

STELLA: The game is still going on.
BLANCHE: How do I look?
STELLA: Lovely, Blanche.
BLANCHE: I feel so hot and frazzled. Wait till I powder before you open the door. Do I look done in?
STELLA: Why no. You are as fresh as a daisy.
BLANCHE: One that's been picked a few days.

Once again, Blanche must enter the claustrophobic house, a microcosm of that world that both oppresses and frightens her; a world so different from the environment in which she and Stella grew up. The crude and vulgar character of the house, as well as the area that surrounds it, is an inescapable reminder that Blanche has seen better days, more "genteel" surroundings. Stella, on the other hand, has not only adjusted to this world but finds it is entirely suitable to her real nature even though it is the antithesis of the past life that Blanche champions (all the more fiercely now that it has vanished).

Shortly after they go in, Blanche meets Mitch for the first time. She immediately perceives that he is not of the same rough disposition as the other poker-playing friends of Stanley. She attempts to form a closer relationship with him, to draw him out, since she instinctively feels his shyness and sensitivity.

MITCH: You are Stella's sister, are you not?
BLANCHE: Yes, Stella is my precious little sister. I call her little in spite of the fact she's somewhat older than I. Just slightly. Less than a year. Will you do something for me?
MITCH: Sure. What?
BLANCHE: I bought this adorable little colored paper lantern at a Chinese shop on Bourbon Street. Put it over the light bulb! Will you, please?
MITCH: Be glad to.
BLANCHE: I can't stand a naked light bulb, any more than I can a rude remark or a vulgar action.

In the context of the play, every remark made in the scene seems natural; every word is unremarkable in its casualness: people talking to one another about nothing much in particular. Yet hidden in these aimlessly spoken lines lie deep insights into Blanche's nature and character. The playwright has, although the clues are carefully masked, supplied us with almost everything we need to know concerning the character of Blanche and how she views the world that she now finds herself. He has done one thing more that would, probably, escape the attention of anyone who did not personally know the city of New Orleans or had not had the *chance*, as I later did, to discover how intricately motivated those casual exchanges of dialogue. I had read this play many times; I believed I detected most of the possible meanings behind the text. It was not until I had moved to New Orleans, however, to work in the theater in the French Quarter that I realized how intricately Williams wove actual

places into the actions and emotions of his characters in this play or how much a part the city itself plays in all his works, both dramatic and literary, or how important the city is to this play in particular. My realization as to just how specifically the atmosphere of this unique city is captured in the text of *A Streetcar Named Desire* happened in a flash of insight and occurred the first time that I—as Blanche did—went to Galatoire's restaurant to dine.

I knew of this famous restaurant both from its reputation as well as from personal recommendation of many friends. Although they had also informed me that this was the place many native New Orleanians preferred to more famous names associated with the tourist trade, no one thought to give me indications of its physical description—or of its particular *atmosphere*. Nor was I at the time thinking of either the play *A Streetcar Named Desire* or of Blanche du Bois. However, upon entering the front door both immediately leapt to mind. My first words were, "My God, how did she stand it!?"

What I had encountered in that first moment was this: a large single room constituted the main part of the restaurant; the walls were painted a stark white, and around the room were large wide mirrors—the entire area brightly lit from hanging lights; there were numerous "naked bulbs." The emphasis here, it was quickly apparent, was on food served with efficiency—and ample light to see what you had ordered. Later, as I recalled that moment, I began consciously to fit my own spontaneous reaction to the information the playwright provides in the text. What follows is, in a more or less orderly and logical presentation, what I came to understand about the place *to which Williams sent Blanche* on her first outing in New Orleans and, most important of all, why he chose it out of all others. First, let us venture some speculations as to why Stella acts in the manner she does; that is, makes the choice of Galatoire's:

1. Stella—who is unlike Blanche in almost every way and, more important, is actually considerably younger than Blanche despite Blanche's "little white lie" that Stella is the older of the sisters—takes Blanche to the restaurant she considers to be the best: Galatoire's. Her reasons have nothing to do with considerations

of the restaurant's atmospheric qualities or decor but, rather, with the quality of the food served there.

2. Stella—neither excessively vain nor yet at the time of life when age is a real concern—does not consider that her sister is morbidly sensitive to the passing years and is, consequently, extremely apprehensive at being seen in a bright revealing light. In actuality, as with most relatives, Stella hardly *sees* her sister at all; certainly she does not see her as a middle-aged woman. For Stella, the bright light holds no sinister aspect; nor does she appreciate the light's threat to the youthful illusion Blanche seeks to maintain. Stella does not realize that she is taking her sister to the *one well-known restaurant where Blanche would be most self-conscious and tormented*: Galatoire's. With its glaring light and mirrors that reflect one's image back at every turn, this restaurant would be the one to avoid at any cost; as it is, we can easily understand that the experience is a veritable nightmare for Blanche. And can she really say to Stella: *Let's leave—here everyone can see how old I really am!* No. She is caught. Is this selection of this particular restaurant calculated or only coincidence? Probably elements of both are present; certainly the element of chance came into the play as I walked in the same door as had Blanche (or, to be more accurate, as had Tennessee Williams). There is no doubt in my mind, however, that Williams had picked out of his own experience the one place (perhaps unconsciously) where Blanche would suffer the pangs of being viewed under the worst of conditions. But while this decision of the playwright could very well have been "accidental," it does, in point of fact, begin a chain of events—of reactions, more specifically—that are central to the progress of the play's actions and absolutely essential to the play's dramatic force.

3. Blanche—on her way back to her new "home"—buys a Chinese paper lantern. This act is certainly motivated by her earlier encounter (not mentioned, however, until her return from the restaurant) with the hanging light in the room where she is forced to live; but it is also possible that it is motivated by her recent experience at Galatoire's. (And it was only *by chance* that this possibility occurred to me.) Her real reason for getting the lantern, ostensibly an im-

pulse purchase, is to modify the harshness of the "naked bulb" hanging in the room where she must spend an unforeseeable time to come. But it is also possible that the purchase was spurred by the desire to prevent insofar as possible a recurrence of the Galatoire's experience. We can easily deduce that Stella is blithely unconscious of the effect that strong white light has on aging skin (and is also something of a less-than-dedicated housekeeper, since she has apparently never made the effort to provide a shade for the bulb), and that Blanche feels compelled to take immediate steps to keep any light in her vicinity under strict management in the future. (It has already been established that she will not come outdoors until after the sun has set.) While Blanche's lantern is seemingly a modest gesture toward making the room more attractive, it has a very practical self-protective motive at bottom: to screen out the age-revealing qualities of the "naked bulb." (And you can be all but certain that the color of the lantern she picked was pink: the same color that hides best those small lines that herald the approach of old age; it is also, coincidently, the color of the theatrical media that aging actresses demand as a standard provision in their stage performance contracts.) At every step of these apparently unimportant events we can see the playwright's hand pulling hidden strings. As Chekhov remarks: *If a pistol is introduced in the first act of a play, it must be fired before the play is finished.* So it is with Blanche's Chinese lantern; put up to mask the harsh light, it must be removed before the action of the play ends.

4. The chain of actions continues. The purchase of the lantern gives Blanche an opportunity to seek—with all the antebellum charm she can muster—the aid of Mitch to put it up. She only met him minutes before; still she does not miss the opportunity to involve him in the seemingly insignificant—but incalculably effective—modification of her living space. More than that, she uses the event to cast the first thread of the web in which she hopes eventually to catch Mitch. Not only is it an extremely masterful stroke on the part of Williams's craftsmanship, it is a virtual necessity to the fabric of the play that the *same person who puts the lantern on the light must also be the person who will eventually tear it*

off. Mitch, in a very real way, is made part of Blanche's destruction (and to a lesser extent, his own) in the intricate pattern of cause and effect that innocently began with Stella's decision to take her sister out to have a good meal. Nor does this pattern reach its eventual end until late in the play when a stormy scene takes place between Blanche and Mitch, after which he rips the fragile lantern from the bulb and brutally holds her face up to the harsh white light. In a sense, he returns Blanche to the "real" world that does not understand or tolerate her mysterious avoidance of the light. In figure 134 we see the climax of this scene in an unusually forceful image; it shows well the dramatic power of this moment. Such an outburst as recorded here cannot be achieved only at the last moment; it is the result of causes that have been building from the very first moments of the play, from that time, perhaps, when Stella took Blanche out for a good meal (see "Time Frames in Dramatic Works" in part 4 for further discussions of this subject).

Much of what has just been said is, of course, interpretative; conjecture, speculation, and plain

Fig. 134. Scene from *A Streetcar Named Desire*. Photograph by Joe Scherschel

guesswork have been the foundation of statements that are, at the very least, personal points of view. Do such suppositions really aid in the work of the scenographer? I think they do. Moreover, I can affirm that my own work is made more meaningful (if not easier) by such research. Chance, in this case, did provide many valuable clues to a deeper understanding of certain hidden motives that related directly to specifically written actions. Let us, however, for the moment cast some doubt on this process; or rather, let us raise a possible objection to the value of such an admittedly time-consuming and *chancy* way of working.

The question then might arise: Since the restaurant where Blanche is taken for that stressful dinner is not an actual part of the action seen on stage, why consider this tangential information at all? What possible difference does it make to know where she spent an uncomfortable evening? The general answer to this question is that *anything* that gives a more thorough understanding of any character in a text is a positive aid in understanding that character's physical environment (whether or not that environment is ever to be shown in its entirety). But a more specific response to such a question is this: Knowing exactly the contexts of a character's "offstage" experience can contribute extremely profitable information about how the onstage environment should be considered; for it can be taken for granted that the playwright did consider just such encounters as well as the consequences of those encounters. Nor is it outside the scenographer's ability to discover these useful pieces of information. This line of investigation is, admittedly, oblique in nature; it is, however, relevant to the total research inquiry and should be undertaken seriously. For instance, it seems reasonable to me—and not a difficult feat of investigation to have performed—that Blanche bought the delicate paper Chinese lantern required in the acting of the play not simply as a passing whim *but as a direct response to her exposure to the merciless white light she experiences in that particular restaurant the playwright causes her to go.* And I am very certain that it was Williams's exact purpose that this restaurant—rather than a more romantically lighted one where she could safely hide her age in the shadows of discreetly shaded lamps or candlelight—should be the one to which Stella, who is thinking only of the quality of the food and not of the atmosphere, would unthinkingly take her sister. The playwright does not, of course, ever have time or opportunity to include in the play's text every indication of the hidden geneses of actions and words; but it would be extremely shortsighted of any interpretative artist working on this text not to realize that such information exists and is often possible to unearth. If we, as scenographers, doggedly pursue the reasons leading to the actions of characters—such as the seemingly insignificant and impulsive buying of a cheap paper lantern—we are much more apt to "know" the atmosphere and physical parameters of their environments. In the case of Blanche, such considerations not only tell us the kind of situation in which she finds herself but also indicate the small ways in which she seeks to change her physical environment to suit her own desperate needs. The hanging of a cheap paper lantern over a "naked" (her words) light bulb may seem the most casual of actions, but this one act is integral to the development of this play; without it, the highly charged scene between Mitch and Blanche in the latter part of the play cannot take place. It is imperative that *he* rip off that lantern and expose her again to the merciless white light (in exactly the same manner as she was exposed in Galatoire's). In a very real sense Blanche begins the play with an offstage experience that shows her just how important it is to preserve the increasingly fragile illusion that she is still young. Her ability to maintain this illusion is eroding rapidly, which the playwright shows us by the integration of this seemingly insignificant object into the mainstream of the action. When Mitch does tear the lantern off the light (which he had carefully put on earlier in the play), Blanche's last reserves are shattered; her despair and anger at the unrelentingness of age explode as we saw in figure 134.

The deep searches we must make into the structure of a text are not simply to verify the exactness of background locale or period accuracy but to seek out the very nature of the playwright's world, the innermost character of his concerns, intentions, and—not least—his obsessions. While the visual arts of the theater ostensibly rely on the information we find in period research and the simulation of form found in the observable world outside the theater, that information must be subjected to a scrutiny that lies beyond purely aesthetic judgment. We who interpret that information must also think in much the same way as the archaeologist, psychologist, and social historian. More important, our methods of approaching texts in the theater are not unlike those puzzles Sherlock Holmes or Hercule Poirot have repeatedly found so fascinating. We—like them—must look closely at the facts as they surface; our "little gray cells" must probe as deeply those mysteries of character and circumstance the playwright sets before us, knowing all the time that the facts we encounter in a text for the stage often mask complex and all but undiscoverable human motives and actions.

It is relatively easy to make exact replicas of past works; architecture, costume, furniture, crafts, all can be simulated in today's scenic shops with amazing verisimilitude and accuracy. It is, however, considerably more difficult to restore a living meaning to those works if something else, something more, does not accompany that expert copying of detail. But this something more is precisely the task of the scenographer; he alone is given the great responsibility of assuring that that former life will become part of the physical work of selection and simulation; he, more than any other artist of the theater, is given the charge to *link the playwright's world of words—no matter how distant in time or different in nature from that we call "real"—to the actual world of the stage.* To find exact information that illumines the look and feel of the New Orleans where *Streetcar* takes place is important; to understand the particular life of Blanche, Stella, Stanley, and Mitch as they live in it requires stepping beyond the bounds of archaeological tourism.

Nor would it be stretching the point to say that the New Orleans in which Williams sets his play is seen in two distinct kinds of physical light that essentially determine the particular nature of this particular play: (1) the warm romantic glow of candlelight and Chinese lanterns and (2) the harsh glaring light of an unpretentious restaurant or a naked bulb in a cheaply constructed dwelling in an unfashionable part of the city. These two qualities of light are as integral to the interpretation of this play as is the adversary relationship of Blanche and Stanley or the desperately hopeful relationship between Mitch and

Blanche. Both must be played out in certain qualities of light that stem from the physical world Williams had witnessed in actual life and from the world of the play that he constructed for the characters of his imagination. We will see later how important qualities of light are in another Williams play *The Glass Menagerie*. There light becomes an important part of the play's dramatic structure, so much so that not to carefully consider what role it plays is to seriously jeopardize the meaning of the play. The director's and the scenographer's task is to bring onto the stage environments where the battle resulting from the clashes of character and light are clearly evident to those watching. This understanding of the play in the terms just set forth does not make itself readily apparent to the eye of the casual seeker; it must actively and carefully be sought out from many sources, many of which are difficult to find. But that, of course, is the function of the scenographer: to be an active and informed eye, not simply a mechanically recording one. My own understanding of this play was fortuitously aided by several accidental encounters with the exact place where Williams sent Blanche and her sister to dine. I also lived and worked in the place where the playwright chose to set his play. Still, one cannot rule out other possible ways of obtaining the same information we have looked at here. I have not related this experience—or any other, for that matter—to demonstrate my unique vision or to boast of my singular good luck. I merely wish to affirm that such encounters do exist and happen to every artist who is active in his art. Such information, such encounters happen to all artists constantly; it is how they obtain the raw materials of their art. All artists must be *lucky* or they would soon cease to be artists. Perhaps what we call "lucky" is simply another name for the necessary activeness of creative research.

Before leaving this subject to attend the more practical chores of research let us pause for a brief word of warning. It is very possible for artists to be too intellectual in their research of a project. Part of the task in becoming a good theater researcher is to know the difference between useful information and the frivolous speculation. There is a real and vital distinction to be made between the seeking out of information useful in re-creating the playwright's world and

the often fruitless overextended academic exercise. You can, in other words, *think too much.* (Although I cannot remember too many instances of this pitfall surfacing in my own classrooms.) Ivor Brown, in his entertainingly helpful book *How Shakespeare Spent the Day*, neatly pinpoints the kind of speculation that hinders an interpreter's insight and understanding instead of aiding it:

What curious discoveries are made by the probing and learned academic mind! For example, in *The Question of Hamlet*, Professor Harry Levin of Yale, who has carefully read his way through the deterrent jungle of Hamlet literature and can tell us in brief what the scholars have told us at length down the centuries, decides at one point that "Hamlet is reenacting the classical Eiron, the Socratic ironist who practices wisdom by disclaiming it. More immediately, Shakespeare was dramatising the humanistic critique of the intellect as it had been generally propounded by Erasmus." Of the "to be or not to be" soliloquy Professor Levin writes: "Such is the doubter's model of dialectic which leads him back—through complementary semicircles—to his binary point of departure. This is the question, *esse aut non esse*, which metaphysicians from Plato to Sartre have pondered. . . . The ontological question becomes an existential question and the argument lifts from metaphysics to ethics." One can imagine that Shakespeare, confronted with a commentary of that kind, would have torn in bewilderment what hairs may then have been left on that exalted head when he was reaching middle age.

Two Primary Approaches to Research Technique: External and Internal Research

If one draws a line through the middle of nineteenth-century theater, it is possible to gain a reasonably accurate understanding how philosophies of production before and after circa 1850 changed (see p. 194, fig. 136). Before the middle of the nineteenth century those responsible for staging theatrical works showed little consideration for historical accuracy. Those who worked for the stage showed scant concern for any of the following:

Historical facts: dates, periods, verifiable facts

Fig. 135. *A London Street*, by Gustave Doré

Cultural awareness: customs, mores, religions, beliefs

Artistic accuracy: dress, crafts, pictorial symbolism

Geographical awareness: borders, coastlines, climate, flora, fauna

Archeological knowledge: dates, periods, styles, artifacts

These areas were not considered worthy of deep investigation. From the beginning of western theater (the Greek theater of the fifth century B.C.), verisimilitude was never a serious concern. During and after the middle of the nineteenth century, however, attitudes changed radically. A new principle of interpretation emerged that profoundly affected how playwrights conceived their characters and how actors approached the playing of them. Briefly this principle holds that characters on the stage should be presented as actual people living in a real world, a world that mirrors the one outside the theater. A philosophy was also adopted that not only should these characters be shown in their own time but in visual contexts compatible with historical fact as

revealed by research. The present-day theater still operates within the basic principles of interpretation established during the middle of the nineteenth century. For instance, when plays such as *Abe Lincoln from Illinois, Amadeus,* or *The Private Life of Henry VIII* are produced on the stage, one can expect these productions to accurately reflect a careful research of the period in question. While naturalism as a style of production only briefly dominated the theater during the early part of this century, the philosophy of both playwrights and interpreters is still based on perceivable reality. A sense of actual place, a sense of chronological order, and a sense of believable events occurring for the first time permeates most works seen in the present-day theater.

Plays written before the nineteenth century—whose characters are not conceived of "real" persons, such as Molière's Miser or Shakespeare's Puck—when produced today must now be considered in ways that would have never occurred to producers of earlier periods. The question of "doing a production in period"—a term that would have been incomprehensible to those working in the Elizabethan theater—is now routinely asked. Producers today freely choose periods other than those during which the play was written or out of the period in which the playwright originally set his action. So far, I know of no production of *Hamlet* set in the twenty-third century A.D. but it is only a matter of time until one will appear. Such a production would be more defensible than imposing that century on a production of *Amadeus* or *Long Day's Journey into Night.*

The characters a playwright includes in his play may or may not have historical models. Even when characters do not have real-life counterparts, in many instances there are good reasons why they should remain in contexts the playwright intended. Although Lady Macbeth retains a persuasive reality in times and cultures other than that Shakespeare intended (as Kurosawa proves in *Throne of Blood,* a successful adaptation of *Macbeth,* set in medieval Japan), Blanche Dubois, on the other hand, is irrevocably tied to her own particular period and place. In most of Tennessee Williams's plays, the sense of time and locale is so integrated into the sum and substance of the work that it is all but impossible to consider these characters as universal symbols. Like flies in amber, their setting is inseparable from their meaning. As with the Elizabethan concept of the Great Chain of Being, where everything in nature had its own place and function, all unchanging and unchangeable, there are some characters who cannot—at least should not—be pried from their niche in time. When dealing with the past, or when considering the period and style of a production, common sense—that all-too-often uninvoked state of mind—must be our guide; Mozart in a Star Trek spacesuit or even Abraham Lincoln in a miniskirt is a factual possibility on the stage; no law of theater prohibits it. Still, one hesitates even to voice the idea.

In this section we will list a number of general principles of research in outline form. These principles are intended for the student with little experience in scenographic research. As the student scenographer grows proficient in the craft of theater design, approaches to research will alter significantly. Creating personal methods of research grows in tandem with other skills. No two scenographers work in the same manner for long, nor does the individual scenographer work the same way during the span of a career.

Here principles of research will be divided into two basic units: external research and internal research. The first category will include those elements of information pertinent to, but not actually found in, the written script. The second category will deal with items of information explicitly stated in the text or gleaned from close investigation of it. This division, of course, will result in some overlapping of materials; in addition, the need for research will vary considerably from script to script. A large part of the scenographer's research—especially the visual aspects of it—are comparatively easy to understand for the beginning scenographer. The understanding of what lies below the surface details of historical or unfamiliar artifacts, or comprehending the cultural forces that molded them, often eludes casual inspection. Often the order and pattern of the research process greatly change from production to production. Only experience can speed up the process or give assurance to the scenographer that correct choices have been made. Still, most scenographers who constantly work in the theater become intuitive researchers

developing an understanding for the substrata of an historical period or of a geographical location. Thus they can imbue their productions with the spirit of a past age or a sense of locale without blindly copying exterior trappings of a distant time or an unfamiliar place.

The following outline of research principles is necessarily incomplete; nevertheless, it may prove useful as a general guideline or as a checklist of possible leads to follow when seeking out that illusive spirit of a past age or unfamiliar location. Following this section a suggested method for creating an inventory of needs for specific productions will be given. For now, keep in mind this observation made by the painter Jean Helion: "The artist is born with a definite feeling that Unity exists throughout the incongruous, and that we do not see it only because links are hidden, or missing, or misunderstood."

External Research

1. *Date of the Text*

   a. Date of the text's composition. No matter what the date of the play's action, it is always a sound idea to examine the time *when the play was actually written.* In some cases, as with some of Shakespeare's plays, this date may be unknown or disputed. Still, no matter when an author sets the action of his play, some of his own time will undoubtedly creep into the fabric of the text; it is well to pinpoint that time as exactly as possible.

   b. Date of the text's action. This date, along with the above, gives the scenographer a specific period of time around which all his research will center. In many instances, an author, wanting to treat a contemporary problem, will choose a time with similarities to his own so that he may call attention to some topical point or thesis. Shakespeare—in his defense of, and allegiance to, the monarchy of his own age—used examples of corrupt governments and rulers from the past, both foreign and domestic, to demonstrate how fortunate his contemporary countrymen were to have the rule they had. (To prove a point, he is not above unfairly maligning men or groups who differed with him in opinion. Witness the unfair treatment he gives the characters Richard III and Joan of Arc.) A careful study of both dates, while these alone will not provide the only dates he will need, will give the scenographer an excellent starting clue for his further research.

2. Period of the Text

The *period* is a deceptive concept; such divisions in time do not exist except in retrospect and after sufficient time has passed. Only then are we able to see the large outline of what has passed. But to assign a name and inclusive dates to a period of time is dangerous in that it leads to thinking that the past automatically divides itself into convenient compartments of time. It is dangerous also in that the inhabitants of any particular period become stereotyped images rather than living people. Invariably, more is omitted from this stereotype than is included; at times important things are left out simply because they don't neatly "fit" the simplicity of form that stereotypes demand. Still, many books and articles are written, and visual materials compiled, on the assumption that a span of time can be separated from others and given an appropriate name and character. The conscientious researcher should not be misled, however, into believing that a single book on any one period, no matter how extensive the coverage of that source, is sufficient. To understand the romantic era, for instance, it is imperative to examine works about the eighteenth century and also those of earlier periods and cultures against which that period revolted. Certainly all periods have their roots in those that preceded them. The astute researcher is prepared to trace these roots carefully as far back as they extend; quite often finding the meaning of an object or a practice, incomprehensible in itself, easily understood when traced to an earlier time. The understanding of words and especially their meanings can only be fully understood by going back to root uses and meanings. Shakespeare may have used many terms we recognize today, but often the entire meaning of what he said has shifted to concepts and usages that can be diametrically opposed to present-day understanding.

3. Geographical Factors in Scenography

It is self-evident that the geographical location of a play will dictate much of the detail of its setting. Even when a play is produced in a style other than realistic, there is usually some attempt to manifest the geographical spirit of the actual place. This might show only in the basic colors of the production—golden yellow and brown for the desert, cold blues and greens for northern climates. (This is especially true in the cinema version of *Othello* with Laurence Olivier; texture and colors, with a minimum of historical detail, allowed the scenographer to give the viewer an accurate sense of place and time without making imitative pictures of Venice and Cyprus "as it really was.") Geographical location, moreover, has an altering influence on similar styles of decoration and fashion, even though the differences may go unnoticed to the casual eye. Recent large-scale studies and publications such as *The Age of Expansion*, edited by Hugh Trevor-Roper, deal with particularly limited spans of time, in this case 1559 to 1660, and are able to clearly show the difference in developments in the arts, sciences, politics, and religious activities of various countries during this period. It is possible to see in Trevor-Roper's study deviations both great and small as each individual country is examined, and this can be of immense value to both scenographer and director. While material can sometimes be found altogether—as in the case of the English historian's book—more often than not, the scenographer must compile such information from various sources. Temperaments and points of view that emerge from a climate and geographical location—or from a play's characters or author—are so enmeshed in the work that ignorance of these qualities and the underlying reasons for them could lead to serious dislocations of visual ideas. While the sense of environment is important to a play, it is not always easy to distill from visual material alone.

It is not often possible for a working artist to go directly to a place and study firsthand the country from which material is needed. Travel books are helpful, especially pictorial ones, and most scenographers maintain files and personal materials on various countries in their permanent collection of sources, a practice that should also be emulated by the director. Still, one can sometimes miss important points without firsthand knowledge. All theater artists, regardless of area, should be constantly on the lookout for writers who have been places and have written about their travels. Often, this reportage, along with pictorial materials, can be invaluable to the scenographer who has not had the opportunity to travel extensively. A good example in support of this recommendation is Henry Miller's entertaining and informative account of his first visit to Greece in the late 1930s. When Miller describes Greece in *The Colossus of Maroussi*, it is a Greece he saw in more than one time dimension. While he looked carefully at the country as it existed then, he was also able to see what it had been—an ancient Greece with its history and myths evident in every vista. His book is a record of his feelings and perceptions as he experiences a world where time present and time past coexist. Although there is not a single illustration or one reference to the Greek theater, any scenographer reading Miller's book would have his visual imagination stimulated and influenced by the power of Miller's words. Similarly, Mary McCarthy's *Stones of Florence*—although it does have visual materials—is filled with perceptive observations. Nor should any cultivated researcher remain unacquainted with the writings of Jan Morris whose many works span all continents and many ages. Travel accounts are no substitute for travel itself, but the perceptive writer can often inform and inspire us when we are unable to go ourselves.

4. The Artistic Climate of the Time

In any period of history, the various artistic endeavors will reflect, better than any other form of record we have, the form and texture of the time. During the austerely religious period that followed the fall of decadent Rome, one might expect the simple but powerful Gregorian chant, massive cathedrals, and the sculpture of saints and martyrs. By the same token, it is reasonable to expect to find the spiritual lightness of the eighteenth century mirrored in the music of Mozart, the paintings of Watteau and Fragonard, and the excessively mannered busts of Bernini. Perhaps the arts are the most faithful lens we have to see into the past. Many times history, recorded only in words, can barely hint at what the arts can make very plain. Still, some arts are more useful to the scenographer than others. Architecture and sculpture very often show how humans would like to be, what they aspire to rather than what they are. Painting, on the other hand, while it too has often been used to glorify both men and gods, tends to capture our more

human attributes. Painters, even when they are thinking least about the present moment, cannot keep it out of their work. For this reason, the painter-draftsman, with his more quickly accomplished works, is probably of more value to the scenographer than any other group of artists, even though a scenographer cannot exclude thorough study of them as well.

5. The Religious Climate of the Time

The religious philosophy of some periods has been their guiding force, and all other activities have stemmed from it or have been affected by it. The ceiling of the Sistine Chapel, one of the great monuments of Western art, was a commission of the church. Even the placement of each individual panel was dictated and supervised, along with the particular subject matter for each, by church officials, not by Michelangelo. When religion has been a prime factor in the structure of a period, it usually is so strong that not to consider it as a molding force of the visual elements of the time, both spiritual and secular, is to miss the point entirely. A play such as Arthur Miller's *Crucible* (although he was also dealing with the state of America in the twentieth century) or John Whiting's *Devils* requires a thorough study of church doctrines during the seventeenth century as they relate to witchcraft and Satanism. The Whiting play is difficult to produce without an intense examination of Aldous Huxley's book *The Devils of Loudun* on which the play is based. Even when religion does not play a prominent part in the structure of a work, it is sometimes much easier to understand the characters of a play if their beliefs are given attention; a scenographer's job is not so much to reproduce the minutiae of the past as to capture the spirit of it.

6. The Political Climate of the Time

Since a great many plays concern or have political happenings current at the time of the play's composition, it is sometimes necessary to delve into the political history of the period to make any sense of the play itself. *Danton's Death* by Georg Büchner, written in the early part of the last century, and the *Marat/Sade* of Peter Weiss, in our own day, both deal with the French Revolution and the forces that motivated it. While both plays have different motivations and purposes (the Weiss play deals more with the present day than it does with the past), it is not possible to produce intelligently either play without a comprehensive understanding of the political events that brought about that revolution. Although this area of research may be more useable to the director and actor, the scenographer cannot completely ignore or remain ignorant of what those events were or how they came about.

7. *The Author's Commentary on His Own Time*

Most works of art are, either consciously or unconsciously, evaluations made by their creators on the institutions and concepts they come in contact with during their everyday life. The stage has often been used as a platform for the expounding—sometimes subtly, sometimes not—of ideas and philosophies. Sheridan, Shaw, and Brecht, to name but a few, have strong opinions concerning contemporary figures and their behavior. If the scenographer is not aware of the author's state of mind, he might very well misunderstand the author's intention and create settings that defeat rather than aid the playwright's purpose. Usually the author is explicit in exposing his ideas through the medium of the play; in *School for Scandal*—a play whose subject is the often gratuitous, always malicious, fabrication and perpetuation of scandalous stories—Sheridan attacks not only individual characters but often entire levels of society whose behavior he found offensive, unthinking, or simply not in agreement with him. And, on at least one occasion Shaw's thoughts concerning a play (*Androcles and the Lion*) exceed in length the play itself. Sometimes, however, the scenographer must turn to other writings by the same author or about the author to answer questions concerning the play.

8. *Style of Production of the Play as Originally Produced*

The theater of any period had some singular style of production that employed the accepted conventions of the day. Today, in many instances, in order to recapture some of the original force of a work, it is produced with what are now outmoded conventions. But, even when the play is presented with modifications of those original conventions, a thorough knowledge of

those conventions is essential. Much research has been done on all the important plays of the past still being produced today, and much information has been unearthed concerning theaters in which the plays were performed—details of setting, lighting practices (if any), and mode of costume. It is sometimes almost a necessity to understand fully, if not reproduce exactly, the basic format of the original production in order to secure the results the author desired. During the last part of the nineteenth century, Shakespeare was given such extravagantly designed productions that the plays scarcely survived the scenic devices superimposed on their dramatic structures. To facilitate scene changes in these plays, scenes were altered or transposed to such an extent (in many cases important ones simply cut) that little or no regard was paid to the integrity of the play's internal structure. Research since that time has shown (oddly enough) that the simple, often crude Elizabethan theater was, from what little we do know of it, an almost ideal form in which to produce the plays of the period and to a great extent actually determined the writing of them.

These, then, are some of the basic investigations a scenographer must make in seeking material about a production. Just when the external research must be done may change with different projects (as well as how much). In one production he may find one category important to explore, another useless; in another production, just the reverse might be true. Keep in mind, therefore, that any sort of research is rarely—if ever—a straight-line activity; jumping from group to group and from fact to fact, sometimes working forward, sometimes backtracking, are all part of the technique.

Examine the engraving on page 189 (fig. 135). It shows a London street in the middle 1880s. This engraving contains a great amount of visual material observed firsthand and recorded meticulously. If we look closely at this drawing it is almost impossible not to be puzzled about some of the things it contains, curious about the smaller details of the buildings, the street, and the activities of the people in those buildings and on the street. Fortunately we see more from the high angle the artist has chosen than if the picture had been drawn at ground level; this high viewing angle allows us to determine not only

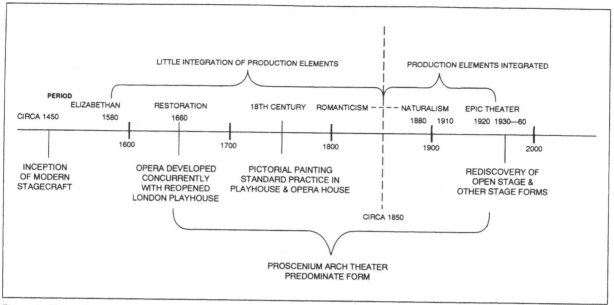

Fig. 136. Chart of nineteenth-century production philosophy

how the place *looked* but how it was *used* as well. Such images that show the activity of human beings in everyday surroundings are often more valuable to the scenographer than pictures of isolated buildings, empty rooms. Details devoid of human context are less valuable to the theater artist than images showing human activity. It is important at any stage of research to keep in mind that the actor, not the scenographer, is the primary teller of the playwright's story. Every image in a production should play a subsidiary role to the human actor. Even on working drawings, many scenographers place a simple line drawing of the human figure to remind him and all who work on his drawings of the human scale.

A singularly beneficial thing that can happen to a scenographer when in the initial stages of research is to become sidetracked, that is, to find materials, ideas, and images unexpectedly. Good reasons exist for allowing—even encouraging—diversions from the straight and narrow path of research. When this happens, the researcher is exposed to the possibility of an idea—a "happy accident"—that does not fall within the scope of logical research patterns (see previous discussion of this subject in "The Role of Chance in the Creative Process" above). By allowing chance to operate, new and inventive solutions may occur. Chance discovery should be encouraged in all art forms, not least in the theater. Another possible reward is that discoveries not presently employed may be useful at another time. Most professional scenographers will admit that in many instances what they needed to complete a design they found accidentally. It is not unreasonable to compare artwork to night vision: during the daylight hours we can see an object directly in front of us without difficulty, whereas in the dark, our eyes are so constructed that one is able to see the object in front of him *only by looking to the side of it.* As a matter of fact, as Jean Dubuffet noted, it is possible to look too hard for something and in that way miss it altogether.

Quite often, too, the necessary information the scenographer is seeking comes in an aggregate form, that is, hidden among things not important, much in the manner in which we looked at the engraving of the London street. Keep in mind, therefore, that the best historical research materials are often the richest in detail. This means that the scenographer's task is not only to find such a source (that is scarcely half the job), but to be able to interpret and understand emotionally as well as intellectually what he needs from it. Scenography is much like refining gold; there is always more dross than anything else and the process of refining is tedious.

Internal Research

1. *Explicit Directions Written by the Author*

These directions are usually the minimum amount of information to denote entrances and exits or necessary physical actions to clarify dialogue references. But stage directions are not all the same type, nor do all convey the same kind of information. In most past periods of theater, stage directions actually written as part of the scripts have been scanty or nonexistent. On the other hand, it is a practice of today's playwrights to give elaborate and lengthy directions to supplement the dialogue. Some producers of plays, both directors and scenographers, make it a practice to remove or ignore all written directions when they study the playscript; they do not wish to be too influenced by the author's instructions because they feel that he, the playwright, is not necessarily the final arbiter in actually bringing the work to the stage. (While most playwrights do not like this practice on the part of their co-workers, some have seen the wisdom of it and have said so in print.) Most directors and scenographers, in defense of this attitude, think that the better the playwright has done his work in the text, the less he will need to explain it in a stage direction. Here is a brief outline of the various types of stage directions a scenographer might encounter in a script. While it is not, perhaps, necessary to try blindly to follow their advice, it is imperative for the scenographer to know precisely what these directions attempt to say and then to make an evaluation as to how far they should be observed or disregarded.

a. Factual descriptions. Shakespeare wrote very few directions; most of the directions that are found in his work have been supplied by later editors of his plays. Most plays, in fact, until about the last one hundred sixty-odd years, have little more than act and scene divisions and one- or two-word locale references. Since that time, however, the pendulum has swung the other way. It is now a common practice to write lengthy stage directions. George Bernard Shaw's directions were, for instance, often long and carefully worded essays to give background material primarily concerning the characters of his plays. Often he would also discuss the setting where these characters lived, since he felt that that, too, revealed a great deal about what they

were or had become because of this environmental influence. Most playwrights working today, while not writing as voluminously as Shaw, present their directions more or less in this manner.

b. Poetic descriptions. Some authors, not many though, attempt to give the reader hints concerning the mood of the play by evocative and poetic descriptions (although not in verse form) of locales and characters. Perhaps Tennessee Williams is one of the best examples of a writer who uses this device. Take the beginning of *The Glass Menagerie* for instance:

The Wingfield apartment is in the rear of the building, one of those vast hive-like conglomerations of cellular living-units that flower as warty growths in overcrowded urban centers of lower middle-class population and are symptomatic of the impulse of this largest and fundamentally enslaved section of American society to avoid fluidity and differentiation and to exist and function as one interfused mass of automatism. The apartment faces an alley and is entered by a fire escape, a structure whose name is a touch of accidental truth, for all of these huge buildings are always burning with the slow and implacable fires of human desperation.

While this is not poetry, its intention is poetic. Eugene O'Neill did much the same thing in his earlier plays, but in a colder prose form. Both try to give more than just a factual account of the places where the action of the play takes place and a keener insight into the people who inhabit these places. Jo Mielziner, in speaking of Williams's practice of writing directions in this manner, has said: "If I were teaching an advanced course in scene design, I think I might ask the students to read the production notes that Tennessee Williams writes for almost all his plays. After reading his notes in the early script for *Summer and Smoke*, I felt that it would be truly difficult to design a setting for this play that was poor in concept. It might be inadequate in execution, but the extraordinarily knowledgeable and sensitive eye of the dramatist created a picture that even a mediocre designer could not spoil."

c. Stage directions in acting editions of plays. Most young students in the theater are surprised to learn that many of the directions in a published version of a Broadway success were not written down by the author but by the production's stage manager. He usually does this on the instructions of the director, since it is the function of the stage manager to compile and record the official promptscript. This promptscript, later used as the basis for the published version of the play, usually gives detailed information about all entrances, exits, directions of movements, and quite often, key words that indicate interpretations and vocal timings. The author's original directions and admonitions often get cut, inverted, or swallowed up in the general process of rehearsal and tryouts in front of test audiences. These scripts also contain detailed lists of properties, sound and light cues, costume plots, and floor plans for a particular production. In most cases, although there is a tendency especially among amateurs to regard this information as somehow sacrosanct, it can be and should be completely disregarded or at least carefully scrutinized.

2. Deductive Evidence Gained from Direct and Indirect References by Characters in the Play

It is often possible to glean information about a play's setting by careful study of oblique remarks made by the characters in their dialogue. It seems to be characteristic of well-written plays that the deductive evidence is of greater value to the scenographer in his research than explicit directions or descriptions. One of the drawbacks of seeking information by deduction is that unless the contributing factors that lead to the deduction are fairly specific and easy to interpret, the resulting information may be subject to wide interpretation. (The design and use of the Elizabethan stage are some of the best examples of the confusion that can result from interpretative study of internal evidence.) Nevertheless, the deductive process is one most followed by almost all artists and is the area in which the scenographer can make his greatest contribution to the production. It is this deductive process that is the primary focus of most of this book.

The Dramatic Inventory

Texts contain many kinds of information. Analyzing that information into a logical pattern is an important step in the research process, since information is useless if not organized. How best to accomplish this requirement concerns us here. The time-honored guidelines employed by journalists and reporters provide good models for categorizing information. Emulation of these procedures is useful in scenographic research. But what are those procedures; how are they implemented?

The basic method used by all news reporters incorporates these five questions: Who? What? When? Where? and Why? For scenographers, the first four of these categories are necessary to all forms of research. The last question—Why?—addresses motivation, an area of research usually left to directors. Scenographers cannot, however, avoid this question, since much of the information they gather is explained when this last question is considered. The basic information needed for all scenographic inventories includes the following:

Who: (1) *Succinct descriptions of both the physical qualities as well as the psychological makeup of each character in the text* and (2) *brief descriptions of the relationships that exist between and among characters.* In many works written in the twentieth century the playwright provides this information in stage directions before and during the text. For plays previous to this century, few prefatory descriptions of characters exist; such information—as well as relationship between and among characters—is disclosed through internal reference.

What: *The action of the play described by notes before or during action of the text.* While it is a sound practice to make such chronologies for oneself, help from outside sources should not be disregarded. A number of commercial printing houses specialize in publishing critical notes in inexpensive formats that are useful when studying the classic or representative modern plays widely adopted in academic play anthologies. The increasing availability of well-written dramatic criticism—such as that contained in Thomas Cousineau's reader's companion to *Waiting for Godot* or Michael Hinden's study of *Long Day's Journey into Night*, both from Twayne Publishers of Boston—represents a growing response to the need for useful information about recently produced dramatic works. These sources represent the exception; most notes available are too rudimentary to be comprehensively helpful. For most plays, however, useful commentary is difficult to find or nonexistent.

When: *The inclusive time units of the play as presented by the playwright.* Time factors are important to consider in the overall scheme of the text's action (see "Time Frames in Dramatic Works" below). Frequently such studies are given inadequate attention. Often significant features of a text are revealed when precise knowledge of its time frames are determined.

Where: *The physical location(s) of the play's action as presented (or assumed) by the playwright.* Most dramatic texts—unlike those of the Greek theater—do not obey the unity of time, place, and action. *Where* a scene takes place is often important to the understanding of *what* is happening.

Why: *The psychological substructure of the text's elements.* Motivation in dramatic works divides into several parts: (1) why do characters say what they say; or (2) why do characters do what they do; and (3) why does a playwright set the action of the text in a certain place—an aspect of the subject discussed in Where; or (4) why does a playwright begin the action at a precise time or end the action at another precise time; this is also an aspect of the subject discussed in When.

Although the information needed to complete an inventory varies from project to project, many of the following categories remain constant. While the relative value of the kinds of information also change from production to production, most inventories follow the outline given below. The scenographer usually begins this inventory, however, *after* the first reading of the text, not before.

Dramatic Inventory

I. Inventory of basic information
   1. Date of play's action (inclusive dates)
   2. Chronology of play's action
      a) Times of day for each scene
      b) Time lapses between scenes
      c) Times of year (seasons and activities associated with seasons)
      d) Climate of locale and weathers conditions of each scene.
   3. Date of play's composition (Estimate if unknown.)
   4. Period of play's action (salient features of so-

cial behavior: art, government, religion, rituals and superstitions)
   5. Period of play's composition (similar or dissimilar to above)
   6. Geographical description of each scene (Note differences between actual geographical features found by external research and geographical features created by the playwright.)
   7. List of scenes in order (Name locale and briefly describe immediate adjacent areas.)
   8. Purpose of each scene in the fewest possible words
   9. List of characters in play (Give title, relationship, or function of each character in the play's action.)
   10. List number of characters in each scene (not names of characters)

II. Production requirements (Do not orient any information to any actual stage facilities: describe all information as if it existed in the world outside the theater.)
   1. Note brief description of place of action
      a) Entrances, exits, windows, other architectural or geographical features of place (Give period or style of architectural features.)
      b) List of furniture, set properties, absolutely necessary to action of scene
      c) Levels, etc., absolutely necessary to action of scene
      d) List of of properties absolutely necessary to action of scene (Give period or style of properties.)
      e) Examples of above selected from magazines, books, etc., photocopied from library material
      f) Shape of playing area drawn in simple diagram with appropriate notes (Determine this shape in same way as demonstrated in "Research into Action: *Romeo and Juliet*" in part 5.)

III. Tonalities perceived in play (Cite period, climate, geography, social history to support choices.)
   1. Major tonalities with brief explanation for choice
   2. Minor tonalities with brief explanation for choice

IV. List symbols perceived in text. Metaphors perceived inherent in the text. Many visual theater artists find it productive to put their thoughts into short statements that detail in words visually important features found in study of a text.

It is evident from study of the above that the dramatic inventory is reductionist in nature; that is, it gives information required for the production but does not show the interrelationship of the various elements. Although inventories provide a way to determine basic needs of a text, much thought is needed to find the internal relationships between its many parts. Understanding how these parts relate to the whole is the major step in understanding what the text means. Determining how the parts relate to the whole is the primary focus of part 5 of this book.

The Chronological and Psychological Order of the Creative Research Process

The young scenographer might well ask, "When do I do the exterior research, when the interior?" The answer is, there is no good way to determine a definite priority. Student scenographers learn quickly that research is a time-consuming, often tedious process. The myriad paths that lead to materials have many unproductive sidetracks. Steps in the process are rarely marked; directions as to how to obtain information are often vague, even contradictory at times. Perhaps the only useful advice concerning research processes is that one thing found almost invariably gives meaning to what follows.

Visual research lies not so much in the skill to assemble unrelated watch-part "facts" as it does in the ability to track *feelings*—for want of a better word—through uncharted labyrinths of information. Frequently information found is visually exciting but is not appropriate to underlying concepts of the production. Other research materials, although deceptively simple, ultimately prove useful—even critical—to a production's meaning. Veteran scenographers often admit that they are unsure as to how the process works speculating only that time and careful thought is necessary to determine meaning or importance to the vague feelings they experience when looking for "the answer." It is often difficult for students of scenography to comprehend that an important part of an artist's working technique is to recognize the useful or correct detail when accidently encountered, to accept that solutions to research problems often rest on deci-

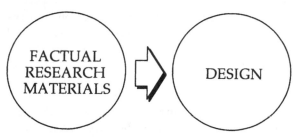

Fig. 137. Design process diagram

sions for which artists have no *conscious* reason for feeling as they do. On the other hand, rational selection is a fundamental part of an artist's working procedure. Taken together, one is left with the realization that an openly inquisitive nature is as important an ability to foster as is skill in drawing and painting or knowledge of stagecraft technique. An active curiosity is in itself a highly important and integral part of the scenographer's artistic apparatus.

In most instances scenographers work from opposite points in the spectrum of factual possibilities. On the one hand concern for discovering "facts"—gathering information from study of historical or documented materials—is critically important to scenographic design. Such information influences the design of a production no matter how abstractly or theatrically that information is used (fig. 137). On the other hand, the scenographer works to satisfy all interior demands—both factual and symbolic—of the production. Specific needs of the performers—both physical and psychological—must also be met (fig. 138).

Before proceeding to the next section, let us attempt to understand what is happening in the scenographer's mind—both on the conscious and subconscious levels—during this period of gestation. Figure 139A–D is a diagram that demonstrates how the process operates. It also shows the uniqueness of the scenographer's

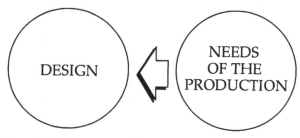

Fig. 138. Design process diagram

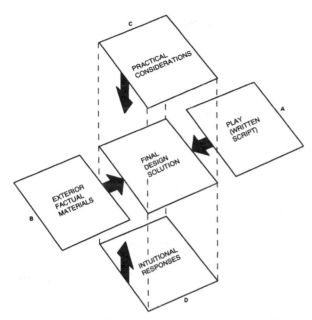

Fig. 139. Forces and influences that affect scenographic
design

purpose. The forces and influences that affect the scenographic design include:

The written script (A)—the needs of the production (the actor's, director's, and technician's needs): this is determined primarily as demonstrated in "Internal Research.

Factual material (B) concerning period, etc: this is determined from investigation as outlined in "External Research."

Internal and external research approaches were discussed during an earlier section. These play a significant role in the scenographer's conscious work pattern. But—as all working scenographers know—these are *not* the only materials that condition how they work or what they must eventually accomplish. They must also realize that there are:

Practical considerations (C)—limitations of budget, inadequacies of stage facilities, time deadlines, and—not least in every producing organization—oppositions from others concerned with the production: these are all present-oriented problems but tend to be limiting in nature.

Although these three categories constitute the rational part of a scenographer's task, there is one last area to be considered. This area determines the artistic value of a scenographer's accomplishment:

Intuitional responses and decisions (D): this

area is primarily past-oriented. It is composed of personal preferences, backlogs of assimilated information, previous solutions to design problems, and—not least of these influences—prejudices. Depending upon the bent of the individual artist, this area tips toward conservative solutions to design problems or to those more radical and revolutionary. Since the subconscious is the more difficult area of the mind to control, it is also the area most difficult for the scenographer to use directly. It is understandable, therefore, that a scenographic design can never be a simple straight-line accomplishment. One should expect, moreover, different areas of research to assume different directions with different projects; the research needed for a production of *The Odd Couple*, for instance, has little in common with the research needed for a production of *Macbeth*.

Creative research is, finally, too personal or subjective to be captured in a series of specific admonitions. Since the research process is only useful to the extent that it is individually internalized, one must expect that the evolution of a successful technique will take many years to accomplish. As James H. Austen astutely comments: "Experience tells me that research is a series of contingencies, of zigzags, joined by one fragile link after another. You would never realize this from reading the tidy, aseptic research accounts that fill our libraries. For balance, someone should present a different side of the picture—show some contemporary research in all its haphazard, unpredictable complexity." A useful explanation how the artist's mind works is contained in Anton Ehrensweig's *The Hidden Order of Art*. This difficult book presents a persuasive view of how the unconscious mind of the artist processes information gained from past experience. It is recommended to all students concerned with understanding how conscious and unconscious processes of artists work.

The Diagrammatic Map

The designer said that this *Macbeth* takes place on various levels in Hell. Now, I have always been under the impression that *Macbeth* took place in Scotland.
—Jane Greenwood (design portfolio review)
March 1986, Charlotte, North Carolina

Dramatic texts are complex language structures: metaphors, similes, allusions, analogies, all guide interpreters when it is necessary to change these words into actions and images on the stage. The scenographer's job is to translate words of the text into the things they suggest. In his book, *The Twin Dimensions*, a text that deals with the nature and perception of time and space, Géza Szamosi, writes: "One of the few things on which cultural historians of Western civilization all seem to agree is that three important developments occurred, took root, and flourished in Western civilization only. In many ways they characterize our civilization: polyphonic music, perspective painting, and experimental science. *It is remarkable, though seldom noticed, that all three came into existence as people struggled with basically the same problem: how to use the senses to find reliable measures of time intervals, spatial distances, and their various relationships. How to impose, in other words, mathematical order on the perceivable world. It is also remarkable—and equally seldom noticed—that in this crucial enterprise, the arts preceded experimental science*" (italics mine).

The underlying thought here is that human beings are curious creatures by nature; they must always know exactly where they are and what their situation is. This basic need motivates the construction of diagrammatic maps, a productive way to assemble and display information gathered from internal and external research sources.

Research of any sort is time travel in the imagination. For any kind of travel—actual or imaginary—maps provide tools to find places we want to go. Real travel—that we do on planes, on trains, or in cars—requires maps that show routes to our destination. Although some maps for the real world are difficult to find, with effort we can obtain them. Maps to imaginary places, on the other hand, are more difficult to discover. In certain instances, however, they can be found: J. R. R. Tolkien's maps for his *Lord of the Rings* trilogy, maps he drew himself, give his readers ways to find their way around the imaginary world depicted in Tolkien's story. Maps for most fictional places—for the island of *The Tempest*, the Greece of *A Midsummer Night's Dream*, or the Elsinore of *Hamlet*—must be individually constructed.

How, then, do we begin a visual reconstruction of a playwright's imagined world? What atlas shows—for instance—the crossroads of Beckett's *Waiting for Godot* or the Illyrian seacoast of *Twelfth Night*? How do the "mountains of the moon" look in Arthur Miller's *After the Fall*? Or—for that matter—what is the topography of Jane Greenwood's *Macbeth*?

In virtually every dramatic work there is a geographical substructure that allows a reader or an audience to follow the wanderings of the play's characters. Often the information that relates the lay of the land is introduced early (the first scene of any Shakespeare play contains many clues as to where the action takes place as well as the nature of the actions that transpire there); frequently this necessary information is buried within the dialogue. There are many instances when what is disclosed is not factually accurate or does not make sense historically. For instance, in the second scene of *Twelfth Night*, Viola, is shipwrecked on the coast of Illyria, the ancient name of an actual region bordering the Adriatic Sea. External research gives us information of its history; quite possibly we may find how Shakespeare came to know of it, even why he used this setting for his story. (We are reasonably certain that he had a profound interest in the writings of those who made adventurous voyages to unexplored regions of the world, and more than once he set his plays in these exotic locations.) Such information is necessary to interpreters of the play. But *Twelfth Night* is a romantic comedy in which Shakespeare creates a world that only superficially borrows from the historical record. As the noted English director Jonathan Miller points out, Shakespeare's archeology is often wildly inaccurate, his history frequently slanted, and his chronologies often border on the unbelievable. We as visual interpreters of the play must, however, find a means to survey the territory where the characters of *Twelfth Night* live as Shakespeare conceives of them. The diagrammatic map is a map drawn more from the parameters of the play's internal directions than from the pages of history. Many playwrights freely fabricate geographical locations. Ambiguous locales can and often are used for dramatic purpose; the plays of Beckett are prime examples of worlds that could only exist on the stage.

The chief difference between real world travelers and interpreters of dramatic texts is that those who decide to visit present-day London today easily obtain helpful maps. Visiting Falstaff's London, however, can only be done through imagination; maps for that London must be assembled from many visual and verbal sources. While external research gives us some visual clues to these imagined worlds, it is our responsibility to decide their borders and to define their features.

In the real world of travel, seldom do we start our journey without seeking out helpful maps. But if one desires to obtain maps of an imaginary place, two possibilities exist: (1) we can seek out ready-made maps—such as Tolkien's, or (2) we can ourselves draw the maps we need. I recommend the second of these possibilities. The advice is not as whimsical as might first appear. Moreover, good reasons exist why scenographers should seriously consider creating these maps to imaginary worlds as an adjunct activity to other research tasks.

What is the nature of the map proposed here? More important to the interpreter, what function does the diagrammatic map serve when analyzing dramatic texts? Most important of all, how do these maps aid the conceptual process preceding stage productions? How, for that matter, do the two concepts—map and diagram—relate? A dictionary definition of diagram says this: *A graphic design that explains rather than represents: A drawing that shows arrangement and relationships (as of parts to the whole, relative values, origins and development, chronological fluctuations, distribution).* About maps John Noble Wilford tells us: "The map you spread out on the table and ask to transport your mind to faraway places or point the way to the next town is one of the oldest and most basic forms of human communication. The idea of drawing a map to communicate a sense of *here* in relation to *there* evolved long ago and independently among many peoples in many parts of the world. *People were making rude maps long before they developed written language*" (italics mine).

Maps and diagrams, then—although similar in function—*are related ways of processing information into more accessible concepts and images.* The diagrammatic map is an amalgamation of the ways of presenting information individually fashioned by the interpreter—in this case the scenographer—to make the playwright's verbal

descriptions visibly manifest; it is a means by which a clear picture of the playwright's imagined world is gained (see "Research into Action: *Romeo and Juliet*" and "The Overview: *Madame Butterfly*" in part 5 for other discussions of this subject).

The diagrammatic map permits us to locate scenes of action in time as well as in space; it clarifies the relationship of scene to scene; it further permits us to record in visual form the nature and sequence of the actions required. We also have opportunity to include on these maps verbal comments that relate information affecting peripheral aspects of the play.

Diagrammatic maps are especially helpful in working with intricately plotted multi-scene plays, since they clearly demonstrate how a world imagined for one play cannot serve for another. For example, the diagrammatic map for *Hamlet* might result in a drawing like that shown in figure 140, whereas a diagrammatic map for *A Midsummer Night's Dream* would appear as that shown in figure 141. A diagrammatic map for *The Tempest* (fig. 142) clearly has little in common with the worlds of the other two. Similar differences to those that exist in the maps just seen can be demonstrated for other playwrights as well.

The diagrammatic map is never a literal representation of actual terrain; it does not show how a particular place appears. It is, rather, a graphic representation of spatial relationships that arise directly from the context of the story's internal structure. The diagrammatic map's primary purpose is to tie spatial relationships to the playwright's web of events. It is possible, moreover, to inspect events *before* the beginning of the play's action and in so doing clarify situations that are not explained in the main body of the play. These maps are most useful when the information revealed suggests visual ideas that later become incorporated in the design of specific scenes (see fig. 145). These drawings also suggest metaphorical relationships to the scenographer. For example, the central feature of the *Hamlet* diagrammatic map—the castle at Elsinore—suggests a construction known as the classical seven-ring labyrinth (fig. 143), an archaic form of architecture. The labyrinth—and its counterpart, the maze—are nothing more than large physical puzzles that the individual

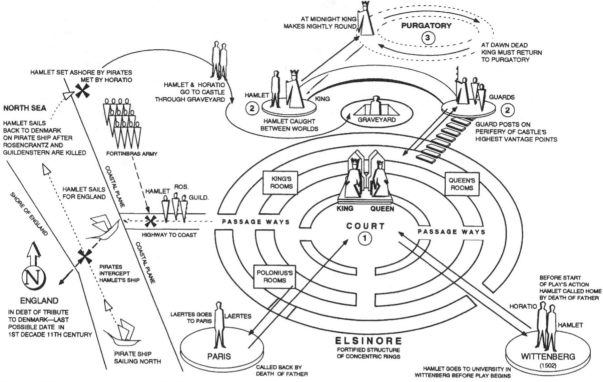

Fig. 140. Diagrammatic map for *Hamlet*

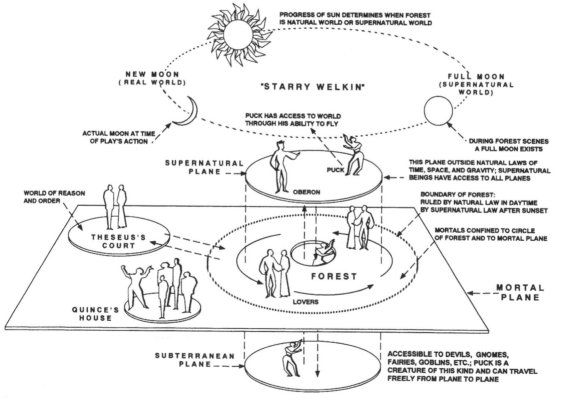

Fig. 141. Diagrammatic map for *A Midsummer Night's Dream*

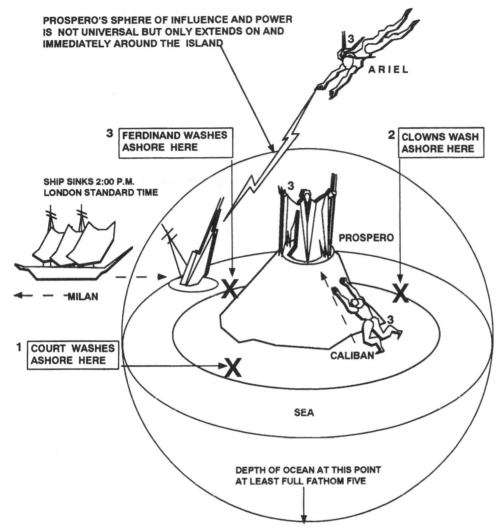

PROSPERO'S SPHERE OF INFLUENCE AND POWER
IS NOT UNIVERSAL BUT ONLY EXTENDS ON AND
IMMEDIATELY AROUND THE ISLAND

ARIEL

3 FERDINAND WASHES
ASHORE HERE

2 CLOWNS WASH
ASHORE HERE

SHIP SINKS 2:00 P.M.
LONDON STANDARD TIME

PROSPERO

MILAN

1 COURT WASHES
ASHORE HERE

CALIBAN

SEA

DEPTH OF OCEAN AT THIS POINT
AT LEAST FULL FATHOM FIVE

GROUP NO. 1: COURT; GROUP NO. 2: CLOWNS; FERDINAND IS CAST ASHORE ALONE; PROSPERO,
MIRANDA, ARIEL, AND CALIBAN ARE GROUP NO. 3, BUT ALL ACT MORE INDEPENDENTLY THAN THE
COURT AND THE CLOWNS; THE SHIP'S INHABITANTS COME ASHORE AT DIFFERENT POINTS AND ARE
KEPT APART UNTIL THE PLAY ENDS AT 5:00 P.M. LONDON STANDARD TIME

THIS IS SHAKESPEARE'S ONLY PLAY THAT TAKES PLACE IN REAL TIME AND EXACTLY MATCHES THE
TIME THE PLAY STARTED IN THE THEATER AND ENDED WHEN PLAYS GENERALLY ENDED

Fig. 142. Diagrammatic map for *The Tempest*

must solve by physically entering them. (It takes little imagination to see that the concept of the labyrinth or the maze has particular resonance to the plot of *Hamlet* as well as to the actions of Hamlet; *Hamlet* is, if nothing else, a monstrous puzzle of which the castle itself is the physical counterpart. Nor should we forget that the Elizabethan meaning of the word *amazing* is literally *to find oneself in an actual full-scale maze*.) Other suggestive features of the map, shown in figure 140, are the parapet guard stations that ring the castle core. These features—which are confirmed by external research of historical castles (fig. 144)—are further incorporated into a view showing the exact place the play begins (fig. 145).

As we work with these maps, relating what we find in our external research to what we interpret from the text itself, it becomes apparent how the links between spatial-geographic location of specific scenes builds support for the dramatic-

Fig. 143. Diagram of seven-ring labyrinth

The act of drawing sharpens the perceptions of the draughtsman; an idea passionately advanced by Ruskin, who believed that it was *only by trying to capture the external world in form and colour that the artist learns to apprehend it.* . . . If naming things is the first creative act, as Bazin alleges, perhaps drawing is the second. *Drawing is comparable with forming concepts. It enables the draughtsman to experiment with images separate from the object which originally engaged his interest, and thus gives him a sense of mastery over that object.* (Italics mine)

Constructing diagrammatic maps is an important form of communication that allows interpreters of dramatic texts to—as the telephone directory Yellow Pages advertisement promises—*"let your fingers do the walking."*

philosophic base of the production. Making diagrammatic maps is, admittedly, time-consuming. For the conscientious scenographer it is time well spent. As Anthony Storr reminds us in his study of the creative mind, *Solitude:*

Time Frames in Dramatic Works

Early in the fifth century c.e., Saint Augustine wrote: If you ask me what time is, I do not know. But if you do not ask me what time is—I know.

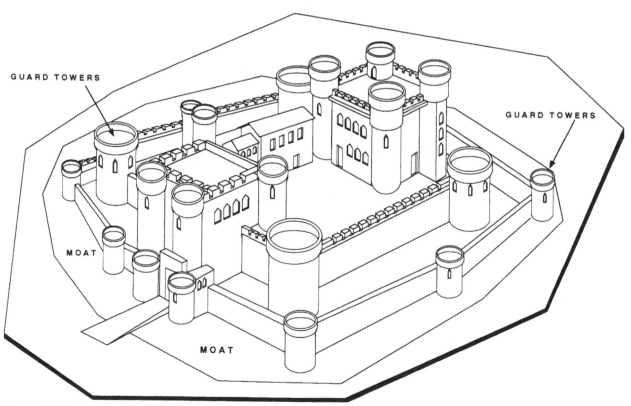

Fig. 144. Medieval castle showing guard towers

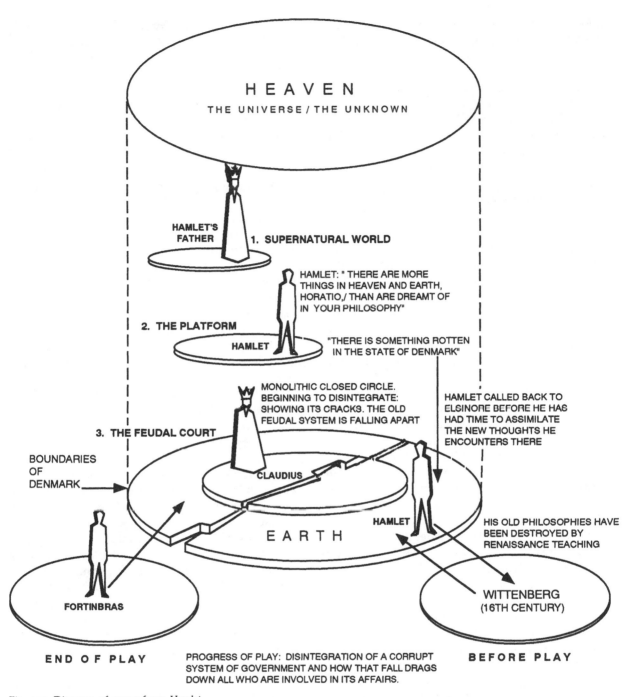

Fig. 145. Diagram of scene from *Hamlet*

Some fifteen centuries later his dilemma is still ours.

A playtext has an infinite number of possibilities for subject matter; under all, however, lies a common factor: *the passage of time and its effects*

on the characters the playwright chooses to follow. Shakespeare several times writes prologues reminding his audience that although he might *tell them in words* the outline or meaning of a story, unless they invest time to view it—"the two-hours' traffic of our stage"—understanding of the tale will remain incomplete. The nature of a text's internal time structures is often difficult to determine, frequently difficult to understand. Time in dramatic works occasionally defies an effort to cast it into logical sequences. Long before Einstein's theory of relativity, playwrights wrote works that distort commonsense notions of how time runs. How playwrights incorporate time in their work is a subject that demands conscious examination by all theater interpreters, since on the stage time assumes aspects contrary to reason. The interpreter is a *fashioner of time*.

What does this term—*fashioner of time*—mean? This subject we examine in the following pages. There we examine time (1) as it is determined by the playwright, and (2) as it is manipulated on the stage. An important skill for both director and scenographer to develop is to understand that time witnessed in the theater is different than time experienced in daily life. Three terms are essential to the understanding of our subject. These are *event, time line*, and, *time frame:*

1. An *event* is an abstract concept that includes under one heading a number of disparate things. World War I had innumerable aspects to it; when discussed, however, common relationships spring to mind; the same holds true for World War II or the Viet Nam War or the War of 1812. Although it does not have the complexity of a war, works for the theater are events. To study any event, large or small, we need conceptual tools with which to work. For our purpose, the two most important are the concepts of *time lines* and *time frames*.

2. A *time line* is a way to chart elements that form *events*. While an *event* is difficult to comprehend as a whole, a *time line* is relatively easy to discern. Works such as *The Timetables of History: A Horizontal Linkage of People and Events*, by Bernard Grun, makes the task of finding *time lines* easier for interpreters to seek out not only *time lines* but the ways they are used by playwrights. As historian Daniel J. Boorstin tells us: "At a glance, *The Timetables of History* can give us a feel for the fluidity and many-sidedness of past experience. Here we plainly see that the historian's neat categories parse experience in ways

never found among living people. While, even in this volume, the authors have found it necessary to separate events into political, cultural, artistic, and scientific categories, *when we cast our eye across any page we see how overlapping, interfusing, inseparable, and arbitrary are such separations.* Often the most interesting—and most surprising—are the miscellaneous items which the authors list in the last right-hand column under 'Daily Life.' Precisely because these items are commonplace in their time, precisely because they were so obviously in the foreground of the experience of non-historians, historians have been reluctant to give them the dignity of 'history'" (italics mine).

Although *The Timetables of History* was among the first books that show time lines, others have followed in its wake: *The Macmillan World History Factfinder*, 1984, and *The Harper Atlas of World History*, 1987—two works in a growing list—give nonhistorians accessibility to the various strands—the *time lines*—that compose the web of history.

3. *Time frames* are the combination of *events* and *time lines*. In common experience, *events* begin at a certain point and end at some later time. It is often difficult to conceive of a situation where the arrow of time does not flow in one direction only or of places that have no location. But in the imagination these conditions are possible. In the Greek theater of the fifth century B.C. such was not the case; strict rules for time shown in dramatic works existed. These rules specifically demanded that all plays observe a unity of time, of place, and of action. This meant that once a play began, the action of the play had to be continuous; that the location where the play started had to remain the same until the play ended and that no gaps in time could exist. It was a further practice for playwrights to make the time of a play's action coincide with the starting time of the performance. Plays such as *Oedipus* and *Antigone*—both set at dawn—actually began shortly before sunrise. From the Elizabethan period onward, however, rarely has the playwright observed the unities demanded of the Greek playwrights. It was during the Elizabethan age, moreover, that playwrights began to incorporate into their plays a concept that time has *no fixed nature, that it can flow at varying speed*

in any direction, that it can be freely manipulated to serve the needs of plot and action. Modifying *time frames* has become an important element in the playwright's "bag of tricks." (See "The Language of Space," in part 2, and "The Nature of the Scenographic Concept," in part 5, for examples of *time frames* used.)

Here is an example—the final speech from *Dr. Faustus* by Christopher Marlowe—how time was consciously manipulated by Elizabethan playwrights:

[The clock strikes eleven]
FAUST: Ah, Faustus,
    Now has thou but one bare hour to live
    And then thou must be damned
      perpetually!
    Stand still, you ever-moving spheres of
      heaven,
    That time may cease and midnight never
      come;
    Fair Nature's eye, rise, rise again, and make
    Perpetual day; or let this hour be but
    A year, a month, a week, a natural day,
    That Faustus may repent and same his soul!
    O lente lente currite noctis equi.
    The stars move still, time runs, the clock
      will strike,
    The devil will come, and Faustus must be
      damned.
    O, I'll leap up to my God! Who pulls me
      down?
    See, see, where Christ's blood streams in
      the firmament!
    One drop would save my soul—half a drop
      ah, my Christ!
    Rend not my heart for naming of my Christ;
    Yet will I call on him—O, spare me, Lucifer!
    Where is it now? 'Tis gone; and see where
      God
    Stretcheth out his arm and bends his ireful
      brows.
    Mountains and hills, come, come and fall
      on me
    And hide me from the heavy wrath of God,
    No, no—
    Then will I headlong run into the earth:
    Earth, gape! O no, it will not harbor me.
    You stars that reigned at my nativity,
    Whose influence hath allotted death and
      hell,
    Now draw up Faustus like a fogy mist
    Into the entrails of yon laboring clouds

    That when they mount forth into the air,
    My limbs may issue from their smoky
      mouths,
    So that my soul may but ascend to heaven.
      [The watch strikes.]
    Ah, half the hour is past; 'twill all be past
      anon.
    Oh, God,
    If thou wilt not have mercy on my soul,
    Yet for Christ's sake whose blood hath
      ransomed me
    Impose some end to my incessant pain:
    Let Faustus live in hell a thousand years,
    A hundred thousand, and at last be saved!
    O, no end is limited to damned souls!
    Why wert thou not a creature wanting soul?
    Or why is this immortal that thou has?
    Ah, Pythagoras' metempsychosis—were
      that true,
    This soul should fly from me, and I be
      changed
    Unto some brutish beast. All beasts are
      happy,
    For when they die
    Their souls are soon dissolved in elements,
    But mine must live still to be plagued in
      hell.
    Cursed be the parents that engendered me!
    No, Faustus, curse thyself, curse Lucifer
    That hath deprived thee of the joys of
      heaven.
      [The clock strikes twelve.]
    It strikes, it strikes! Now, body, turn to air
    Or Lucifer will bear thee quick to hell!
    [Thunder and lightning.]
    O soul, be changed to little water drops
    And fall into the ocean, ne'er to be found.
    My God, my God, look not so fierce on me!
      [Enter DEVILS.]
    Adders and serpents, let me breath awhile!
    Ugly hell, gape not—come not, Lucifer—
    I'll burn my books—ah, Mephistophilis!
      [Exeunt DEVILS with FAUSTUS.]

This is a long speech, but it certainly would not require a whole hour—the time period it purports to follow—to give. There are, it is clear, no time lapses during the speech. The beginning (11:00 P.M.) is specifically indicated in the text. The passage of time, moreover is commented upon by Faustus himself. And yet although Marlowe chronicles the passage of the entire hour before Faustus dies, the scene only takes a quarter of an hour as measured by the clock; clock time in the theater becomes *symbolic time*. The rise and maturation of the Elizabethan theater marks the beginning of our present-day theatrical concepts of time. It was during this period that experimentation with time became part of a playwright's modus operandi, that bending the ordinary concepts of time to the purposes of narrative became an accepted practice. Gezá Szamosí tells us how time can be fashioned to suit particular purposes:

A new and uniquely human world of time and space started with the evolution of language. But this world is not perceivable. *It is purely symbolic.* When I describe where I was an hour or a year ago, when Homer wrote about *The Trojan War*, or when Einstein calculated the motion of the perihelion of the planet Mercury, it was all done by using symbols: words, number, and the like. When we measure the length of an object or estimate some time span, the results are expressed in units and numbers which are, again, human symbols. *Thus can we speak of symbolic time and space accessible to the human mind only.* . . . Rhythms, melodies, stories, *plays in a theater*, poetic meters, holy days, and eternity, all signify symbolic times. There are all different from each other, and all are different from the, say, symbolic time a digital clock describes with digits. . . . when humans refer to "space and time," they usually mean *symbolic space and time in one of its many forms. A symbol is just a symbol and never the real thing.* (Italics mine)

The passage of time in the theater is a flexible commodity. But how do the ideas listed above affect those who work in the "practical" world of theater? Do such considerations have any real application for a director's work or for a scenographer's design? Theater interpreters—scenographers among them—soon discover that they do. Understanding the precise time frames of a play is an important step in understanding the way to produce it on the stage. Is it simply the great plays of the past that demand a different relationship to the perception of time in the theater? Tennessee Williams, particularly sensitive to the quality of time as it relates to theater, says this concerning time as used by modern-day playwrights:

Carson McCullers concludes one of her lyric poems with the line: "Time, the endless idiot, runs screaming 'round the world." It is this continual rush of time, so violent that it appears to be screaming, that deprives our actual lives of so much dignity and meaning, and it is, perhaps more than anything else, the arrest of time which has taken place in a completed work of art that gives to certain plays their feeling of depth and significance. In the London notices of *Death of a Salesman* a certain notoriously skeptical critic made the remark that Willy Loman was the sort of man that almost any member of the audience would have kicked out of an office had he applied for a job or detained one for conversation about his troubles. . . . Facing Willy Loman across an office desk, meeting his nervous glance and hearing his querulous voice, we would be very likely to glance at our wrist watch and our schedule of other appointments. . . . But suppose there had been no wrist watch or office clock and suppose there had not been the schedule of pressing appointments. . . . suppose, in other words, that the meeting with Willy Loman had somehow occurred in a world outside of time. Then I think we would receive him with concern and kindness and even with respect. If the world of a play did not offer us this occasion to view its characters under that special condition of a world without time, then, indeed, the characters and occurrences of drama would become equally pointless. (*The Timeless World of a Play*)

In Williams's own plays, time frames form the skeletal structure of plots. Each scene unit—vital links in the plot chain—has both a specifically fabricated time frame that renders the narrative understandable while at the same time propelling the story to its necessary conclusion. These time frames almost invariably pass without calling attention to their artificiality. Good playwrights—like Shakespeare and Williams—bend time to their purpose and get away with it. Bad playwrights more often than not call attention to this manipulation to an audience as simply unbelievable. In *Hamlet* Shakespeare piles coincidence upon coincidence to the point of absurdity; careful analyzation reveals that the plot is nothing more than a series of improbabilities where time has been made to serve the playwright's narration. The first chore of any interpreter of a play, therefore, is to analyze the entire text into easily comprehended outlines that show the time lines that the playwright has imposed on narration. Here is such an analysis for *A Streetcar Named Desire*:

Place: New Orleans French Quarter
Time: 1947 (Approximately)
Time span: Early May to Mid-September
Location: Kowalskis' First-Floor Apartment

Act I	Sc. 1	Early evening (late Spring)	Blanche arrives on "Streetcar named Desire"—shocked at surroundings—"end of the line" for her in several ways.
	Sc. 2	6:00 next night	Preparation for night out—Stanley challenges Blanche over loss of Belle Reve. Seeks explanations.
	Sc. 3	2:30 A.M.	End of poker night—Blanche meets Mitch—first violent scene with Stanley. Blanche shaken and threatened.
	Sc. 4	Next morning	Blanche talks to Stella about old life at Belle Reve, asks Stella to choose between her present life with Stanley and past life. Stanley in next room overhears all.

End of act 1 (time lapse between acts approximately three months)

Act 2	Sc. 5	Late summer (sunset)	Blanche plans (plots?) for her future. Young man (newspaper boy) appears—Blanche recalls past. Mitch arrives. They go.
	Sc. 6	2:00 A.M.	Blanche and Mitch return from date. They exchange hopes and aspirations. Mitch proposes marriage. Blanche accepts.
	Sc. 7	6:00 P.M. (mid-September)	Blanche's birthday party—Stanley now knows of Blanche's reason for leaving Laurel, reveals he has also told Mitch.
	Sc. 8	7:00 P.M.	Mitch did not come to party. Stanley gives Blanche bus ticket back to Laurel. Confrontation causes Stella to go into labor. Stanley takes her to hospital.
	Sc. 9	11:00 (?) (same night)	Blanche now drunk. Mitch appears. Has also been drinking. Confrontation. Mitch sees real age of Blanche. Flower lady appears. (Death symbol?) Blanche drives Mitch away.
	Sc. 10	Midnight (approximately)	Stanley returns from hospital. Confronts Blanche with her lies, deceits. Struggle follows. Rape of Blanche at end of scene.
	Sc. 11	Early evening (a few days later)	Blanche has suffered nervous breakdown. Doctor and nurse arrive to take her to mental hospital. They leave taking Blanche with them. All is as it was at the beginning of the play.

From study of this outline several things become apparent: (1) the cycle of time created *matches emotional events in the play*, (2) the dark tone of the play is *underscored by the times of day the playwright sets his action*. This play consists of four time units. Whereas act I transpires within one forty-eight-hour period, act 2 shows three separate time periods: scenes 5 and 6, a single day from sunset until early morning; scenes 7 through 10, a later day from 6:00 P.M. until around midnight. Scene 11—a few days after scene 10—is really an epilogue or a coda to the main action of the play. Its primary function is bring the story back to the point where the action of the play began. In other words, *this scene completes the playwright's time frame.*

By analyzing plays in this manner we can discern not only factual time structures but also the shape of a playwright's intention. Blanche emerges in this play as a "fly in the ointment" of Stanley's slovenly comfortable life (one reviewer of the play also called her "a moth that, attracted to the strong flame of Stanley, is destroyed by it"); at any cost she must be removed from it. The time structure of any Tennessee Williams play needs careful attention; often it is the passage of time—as well as what happens to people and relationships—that underlies his concern. Of the many plays Williams wrote, this play along with *Summer and Smoke* and *The Glass Menagerie* are in particular *time obsessed*.

Williams is not, of course, the only playwright who was *time obsessed*. Let us briefly examine two other plays in which the playwright uses time frames for dramatic purposes: *The Cherry Orchard* and *Long Day's Journey into Night*.

The Cherry Orchard, is customarily considered typically naturalistic in that it purports to show how Russians lived during the last years of the nineteenth century and the first years of the twentieth. (This approach to Chekhov is primarily due to Constantin Stanislavski. We know that Chekhov himself dissented from Stanislaviski's insistence that the theater should reflect directly life as perceived outside the theater.) It is now clear to us that the plays of Chekhov—while set in certain places at certain times—are not literal pictures of Russia—dramatic snapshots made to *remind* us of what some people looked like a century ago. When we examine the way in which Stanislavsky produced these plays, we find indelible marks of a strong director that demonstrate how lasting a particular interpreter's point of view can be. Subsequent perceptions of a play's text often are distorted by such directors. By approaching Chekhov's plays *only* through the eyes of Stanislavsky, however, we could easily miss important elements of the playwright's own intention as to how the text should be put on the stage. In the case of *The Cherry Orchard* we would certainly miss the true nature of the time frame that Chekhov gave the play. Ostensibly, the play is nothing more than four scenes placed in a rough chronological order all of which transpire during a brief summer stay at a Russian country house. In the text these times are listed thus:

Act 1—Spring: nursery; early morning
Act 2—Early summer: sunset to evening
Act 3—Late summer: evening to late night
Act 4—Fall: early morning

The selection of time periods appears casual; they follow a simple chronological order: the characters arrive in the spring, they live quiet uneventful lives for a few months, and then, in the fall, they leave their summer home to return to their city homes. Two things make this visit memorable, however: (1) this is the *last* time they will come to this particular place, and (2) the unproductive cherry orchard—the playwright's symbol for the privileged Russian gentry—will be cut down to allow for twentieth-century progress. This is the outward pattern of the play. Chekhov's hidden plan, however, shows an entire period of time—a span of many months—cast in the time frame *of a single day*. Moreover, he takes great care that each of the four acts is placed squarely within its proper quarter of the day. What he does in this play is impose on the larger seasonal cycle the diurnal pattern of a day. In adopting this hidden time frame, Chekhov gives us both a precise picture showing how these people spent the time during the period of residency and a symbolic set of images showing how an old way of life is passing. The time structure of this play provides ample opportunity for an audience—during the span of an evening's performance—to examine in minute detail the lives of a doomed class of people. Although audiences sitting in the theater are not consciously aware how their attention is manipulated, the sense of an age and a class of people passing into oblivion is communicated. Whether or not Chekhov's method is calculated or intuitive—it probably includes elements of both—is of little importance to an interpreter. Manipulation of time—stretching or collapsing it—is integral to the playwright's purpose, an important part of the playwright's method. In *Long Day's Journey into Night*, by Eugene O'Neill, the reverse of what we see in Chekhov's play takes place.

We do not know if the title for this play came quickly to O'Neill, or if he selected it after long deliberation. What we do know is that it possesses a dual meaning for O'Neill. Unlike Chekhov's *Cherry Orchard*, the time period of this play is limited to one particular day in O'Neill's life; the action begins shortly after sunrise, progresses from afternoon into evening, ending at the threshold of a new day. The hidden time frame for this play is not one day but several months, roughly comparable, perhaps, to the season in Chekhov's play. Although we must give careful attention to the implications of the title, we should not accept the title at face value. Although the action of the play ostensibly transpires in a single day, the substance of the play is a distillation of as much as half a year in "real" time.

The title—*Long Day's Journey into Night*—is at once ironic and chillingly appropriate. O'Neill wrote this play many years after he lived the events it portrays. The episodes of many months—his mother's return to drug dependency, his father's parsimonious refusal to provide adequate medical aid for him or his mother, his brother's increasing inability to extend support or guidance, his own increasingly serious tubercular condition, events that in actuality took months to experience—precipitate into one torturously long day.

The play begins in a bright early morning light, but as the play progresses from act to act, Edmund's world begins to darken both figuratively as well as literally. At the end of the play, his mother lapses back into a world of the past, his brother retreats from his own unsatisfactory world into an alcoholic stupor, while their penurious father's only real concern is to save money on the electric bill by turning off all but the smallest of lights in the room. All sit alone in the dark room, the same room that had been filled with light at the beginning of the play. To strengthen his time frame, O'Neill ties specific features of day and night to the conceptual background of the play: light as it progresses from morning into night—to the inexorable spiritual darkening of his own life.

We do not know exactly what goes through the mind of Edmund in the final moments of the play; O'Neill gives him no words to tell us directly. We can surmise that this is the lowest point in his life, the moment when he realizes that no guidance—no light—will come from those closest to him; that if there is to be any light by which to find a way, it must come from within himself. Those who knew O'Neill in later years spoke of his eye's unusual brilliance. "It was as if," as one friend said, "he had within him a fire that he only allowed to show through his eyes."

Understanding the ordinary nature of time is at best perplexing; when we encounter a playwright's personally constructed version of it, the confusion can be confounded. An important part of the scenographer's task is to understand (1) the nature of the time frame required and (2) how the a scenographic design can reflect that scheme on stage.

Here are three general principles I find useful in discussion of a text with others while working on a common project:

1. On the stage *time* is both a *temporal framework* and a *dramatic blueprint* for the action of the play. Always discuss this framework with others.

2. A play begins at the *latest possible moment* and ends at the *earliest possible point*. Determine what these moments are and why they are chosen.

3. *Diurnal rhythms* and *seasonal patterns* are clearly linked to dramatic purpose: the key to a play lies in the *time frame* established. Make an exact calendar of the play's specific chronology and annotate specific time frames that compose it.

Just as the passage of time is reflected in the change we see around us, the nature of time for a particular production must be reflected in the scenographic design. Time—although invisible in most ways—can, when necessary, be seen on the stage. A significant part of a scenographer's job is to understand fully how the playwright regards time and to visually aid an audience's perception of it on the stage. The key to a play's meaning often lies in understanding precisely the various ways time is treated in it.

Historical Accuracy and Conscious Anachronism

In the late nineteenth century there was an intense desire in the theater to dress the stage and actor with settings and costumes as correct in period detail as was possible to determine from research. To our eye, the results of this activity, if we accept the visual materials that have come down to us as representative, have a certain quaint but essentially moribund charm. Part of this feeling can be explained by the time lapse between then and now; styles and customs of the past have always seemed slightly humorous. Yet much of the strangeness associated with these settings and costumes stems from a lack of understanding on the part of the scenographers of the period that accuracy of detail alone does not, cannot in fact, ensure that the intangible spirit of the original will automatically be recreated in the reproduction. All too often, when we study a costumed actor (and we have had photographs of actors for over a hundred years) what we see is a real person in a mode of dress he did not ordinarily affect, not a believable character wearing appropriate clothes; what he was *not* is more evident than what he was supposed to be. The same relationship (or lack of it) doubtlessly held true for the actor's involvement with his scenic environment. Even though the theater has developed in many directions since then, the desire to be *real* and accurate is still a dominant attitude in production today. It is unfortunate that we unquestioningly accept accuracy as a true test of theatrical accomplishment; this attitude is slowly changing, but it is apparently too deeply embedded in both producers and audience to disappear quickly or altogether.

Many student scenographers follow a fairly consistent pattern of development in regard to the problem of historical accuracy in design. There is at first an almost total disregard of any research at all. This cavalier approach is often replaced (after is is discovered that research need not be an unavoidable chore when inspiration fails) by an intense insistence on complete accuracy. There is a third period—which engenders an attitude that comes only with maturity and experience—that can only be described as one where the scenographer allows himself to be *consciously anachronistic*: to combine periods or use a detail from one period out of its time. The reasons for doing this cannot be completely or logically explained; it is a practice, however, that many scenographers follow. Peter Brook, the eminent English director who often either works very closely with a scenographer or designs his productions himself, has said this on the subject in his book, *The Empty Space*:

One of the pioneer figures in the movement towards a renewed Shakespeare was William Poel. An actress once told me that she had worked with Poel in a production of *Much Ado about Nothing* that was presented some fifty years ago for one night in some gloomy London Hall. She said that at the first rehearsal Poel arrived with a case full of scraps out of which he brought odd photographs, drawings, pictures torn out of magazines. "That's you," he said, giving her a picture of a debutante at the Royal Garden Party. To someone else it was a knight in armour, a Gainsborough portrait or else just a hat. In all simplic-

ity, he was expressing the way he saw the play when he read it—directly, as a child does—not as a grown-up monitoring himself with notions of history and period. My friend told me that the total pre-pop-art mixture had an extraordinary homogeneity. I am sure of it. Poel was a great innovator and he clearly saw that consistency had no relation to real Shakespearian style. I once did a production of *Love's Labour's Lost* where I dressed the character called Constable Dull as a Victorian policeman because his name at once conjured up the typical figure of the London bobby. For other reasons the rest of the characters were dressed in Watteau-eighteenth-century clothes but no one was conscious of an anachronism. A long time ago I saw a production of *The Taming of the Shrew* where all the actors dressed themselves exactly the way they saw the characters—I still remember a cowboy, and a fat character busting the buttons of a pageboy's uniform—and that it was far and away the most satisfying rendering of this play I have seen.

This third period can only be reached by going through the second (and few scenographers ever completely fall out of love with the past and the desire to render it faithfully on a stage). Let us assume, then, that the student scenographer is currently approaching, or is in the second phase of, this development, that he has learned research can be an engrossing activity as well as a necessary part of his work. He will, almost certainly, find that many plays that demand extensive research quite frequently contain puzzling questions seemingly with no logical solutions. For a moment, therefore, let us examine one such question that quite possibly might arise from a study of the play *Hamlet*.

Suppose that a director and scenographer agreed to produce *Hamlet* as much in period as possible; that is, as close as possible to the time when the story was intended to occur. If the play were *Julius Caesar*, the problem would not be too difficult; the facts and dates for the original story are well documented. *Hamlet*, however, is a very different case; we know a great deal less about who Hamlet really was (if he existed at all) and about the period in which he was supposed to have lived. Shakespeare probably was not too certain about these facts himself. Still, if we desire to be "historically correct," we must at least attempt to obtain as much information as possible from examination of the internal evidence of the play before starting our search for external material. In other words, what did Shakespeare himself know and how much has he told us in the play?

In 1874, E. W. Godwin (the father of Gordon Craig) published an article in the British journal the *Architect*, called "The Architecture and Costume of Shakespeare's Plays." In this essay he attempts to determine the historically correct period in which this play, *Hamlet*, should be set; the date around which he centers his research is about 1012. How did he arrive at this explicit time? He uses as his prime clue a reference made by Claudius in act 3, scene 1, to the "neglected tribute" that England owes the then more powerful Denmark. Following his research, Godwin notes that the last time England was under such an obligation to Denmark was about the first decade of the eleventh century. He believes, therefore, *that this is the right and proper time to set the action of the play*, the scenery and costumes to be designed accordingly. Having once made this decision, he then proceeds to provide a highly detailed analysis of the locales needed, descriptions of the architectural features of the period (along with information concerning building materials and finishing techniques), and most specific of all, a minutely detailed account of the dress of the time. The primary source for his findings was, according to him, a manuscript now in the Bodleian Library, that contained many illuminations showing contemporary scenes. It is difficult to quarrel with the facts as Godwin presents them; his research is thorough and carefully documented. But does this settle the question of when and how the play would be set if one wants to be completely "accurate"? For a number of reasons the answer must be no.

If one assumes that Shakespeare must have known something of the past history of England and Denmark in order to include such a fact as "neglected tribute," why not then accept the contention that what he said is what he meant, that he wanted the play to be considered as taking place in the time period to which the reference alludes? And if we do give Shakespeare the benefit of the doubt for knowing what he is writing about, there seems to be no reason for not accepting Godwin's research as not only historically correct but also right and, consequently, the way the play should be set. Yet in the same

play that gave this information there are other remarks that shed doubt on the correctness of this decision. In the second scene of the first act, this passage occurs:

KING: For your intent
      In going back to school in Wittenberg,
      It is most retrograde to our desire:
      And we beseech you, bend you to remain
      Here, in the cheer and comfort of our eye,
      Our chiefest courtier, cousin, and our son.
QUEEN: Let not they mother lose her prayers,
      Hamlet;
      I pray thee, stay with us; go not to
      Wittenberg.

Surely Godwin read this passage. And it could also be assumed that he must have been aware of the fact—since his reasoning for the chosen time of the play's action was based on a much more obscure piece of knowledge—that the action could also be dated, using this reference as proof, no earlier than 1502, the year Wittenberg University was founded. Nor would it be reasonable to assume that Shakespeare thought that that university had been in existence for five hundred years.

What do these contradictory "facts" tell us? Karl Elze, the nineteenth-century German critic thinks that Shakespeare's reason for using Wittenberg as Hamlet's school was that "Shakespeare had to send the *Dane* Hamlet to some northern university, and probably none other was so well known to him or to his audience as Wittenberg." In other words, the decision to use this particular school was more an expedient measure than anything else, not a deeply considered point of reference; certainly it does, however, indicate to us that Shakespeare considered Hamlet a Renaissance figure rather than a medieval one. The play fits much more the sixteenth century than it does the eleventh in spite of the fact that the legend has its roots in the latter. Godwin probably was aware of the possibilities but chose to ignore them in order to satisfy his desire to be "historically accurate." This same problem will face the scenographer of today many times during his career.

In the cinema version of *Camelot*, all those involved in the production knew that they were working with a legend that supposedly took place before the sixth century C.E. Nevertheless, *they consciously used design elements that spanned a time period of more than nine hundred years.* One complete scene, for instance (the "Lusty Month of May" song and dance sequence), took its entire visual motivation—setting, costume, atmosphere—from Botticelli's *Primavera*, a painting created in or around 1477. The scenographer often uses an anachronistic detail (or as in this case, a whole series of details) not through ignorance but from the need to reinforce a theme or bridge a gap in understanding that may be caused by differences in time.

Interpretation of a play is rarely in the hands of the scenographer alone, nor are even all the visual aspects of the production. While he has the prime responsibility for the way it appears to an audience, his decisions are almost always the product of more than one mind, more than the reflection of a single artistic sensibility. Jan Kott sums up the problem that interpretation precipitates when the members of a production ask themselves the question, "How are we going to set this play, in what style and period?"

Hamlet cannot be played simply. This may be the reason why it is so tempting to producers and actors. Many generations have seen their own reflections in the play. The genius of *Hamlet* consists, perhaps, in the fact that the play can serve as a mirror. An ideal *Hamlet* would be one most true to Shakespeare and most modern at the same time. Is this possible? I do not know. But we can only appraise any Shakespearean production by asking how much there is of Shakespeare in it, and how much of us.

What I have in mind is not a forced topicality, a *Hamlet* that would be set in a cellar of young existentialists. *Hamlet* has been performed, for that matter, in evening dress and in circus tights; in medieval armour and in Renaissance costume. Costumes do not matter. What matters is that through Shakespeare's text we ought to get at our modern experience, anxiety and sensibility.

There are many subjects in Hamlet. There is politics, force opposed to morality; there is discussion of the divergence between theory and practice, of the ultimate purpose of life; there is tragedy of love, as well as family drama; political, eschatological and metaphysical problems are considered. There is everything you want, including deep psychological analysis, a bloody story, a duel, and general slaughter. One

can select at will. But one must know what one selects, and why. (*Shakespeare Our Contemporary*)

But one must know what one selects, and why. This could very well become the touchstone of the scenographer's philosophy of interpretation.

The past cannot be re-created, only evoked. If there is one thing to be learned from the Belasco experiments that finally made visual authenticity the only standard in scenography, it is that following this practice—although few do today—almost always produces the opposite effect desired; the minuteness of detail, out of context as it must always be in the theater, puts the attention of the audience in the wrong place—on the setting, not the performer seen within it. What is more, it provokes the audience into a situation detrimental to the total production: the more "real" the setting, the more intense the desire on the part of this audience to discover its secret, that is, seek out the unreality they know is there. Given time they will; this cannot be done, however, except at the expense of the actor and the play.

It is important in our definition of research that we do not make the limits too narrow; it is possible that not everything needed for a design will be found in a library (or at least not always where one would think to look). Attitudes toward interpretation are constantly changing and with those changes come changing production demands. The ability to conduct patterns of research that will reveal significant features of other cultures or other ages is an important skill for the scenographer to perfect; but it is not the only kind of research that will be expected in the modern theater. Many scenographers, often at the request of a director, find themselves exploring images, objects, and materials for plays that cannot be located in a precise culture, assigned to an exact historical period, or, for that matter, be found in any place except on the stage of a theater. All of Samuel Beckett's plays, for instance, evade traditional approaches to research; and it is an integral part of most of his plays that they exist in a time frame that has no relationship to that which exists outside the theater. Just where does one begin to research *Endgame* or *Krapp's Last Tape* or *Waiting for Godot*? This is clearly one of the thorniest problems any scenographer ever has to face, since plays like Beckett's are not the only ones to raise this question.

One of the most significant reforms in theater production during the last century was the abolishment of the unauthenticated approach to design of setting and costume; with the advent of the Duke of Saxe-Meiningen company and the establishment of Wagner's Bayreuth Festival Playhouse, theater artists were enjoined to become more accurate in their presentation of historical detail on the stage. And while the results of their work look quaintly unnatural to our eyes today, there was a noticeable improvement when a more unified approach to production was adopted. Star performers no longer went unchallenged when they wore selections that they fancied from their own wardrobes, but which were often inappropriate to the style or atmosphere of the text or the conceptions of the producers; current modes of dress, often mixed with inaccurately crude approximations of authentic costume styles, were no longer the standard practice as it had been in the earlier part of the nineteenth century and during the whole of the eighteenth. This was also true for settings and properties; and while the traditional painted wing-and-drop setting remained the standard mode of practice in some forms of theater—opera and ballet in particular—until well into the present century, there was a steady movement from the middle of the nineteenth century on toward three-dimensional form rather than painted simulation.

The insistence on historical accuracy became, in time, as deadly as its disregard had been earlier; the cavalierly romantic attitudes toward exactitude of historical detail became by 1900 an equally moribund philosophy. But the reason is easier to see in retrospect than at the time; the primary mistake the scenographers of the late nineteenth century made was to omit from their thinking two very important qualifying elements. First, they copied exact detail with little regard for understanding the period from which these details were taken (their only objective being to copy the detail without attempting to understand the culture from which they were extracted). And second, there was no real link between the desire to be historically exact and the individual qualities of a particular text; if, for

instance, the period of *Macbeth* was difficult to determine (as it still is), merely find some approximately plausible period in which it can be set and then duplicate the details from that time. Any other text whose action was set in roughly the same time frame, it was accepted, could use the same costumes and scenery. There was little thought given to unique atmospheric qualities that each text possessed *independent* of its historical period.

The vision of those who would be historically correct and *only* historically correct was, in a word, too *narrow*. No matter how exact a copy is placed on the stage, not to have an understanding of its particular place in the context of the singular text is to preclude its assimilation into a unique total work.

Historical accuracy still has a usefulness in the modern theater; there are many instances when a strictly historical approach to a production is essentially the correct one. But there has been a growing understanding during the past fifty years that a text of a theatrical work has subjective requirements that cannot be satisfied by simple reproduction of period detail; verisimilitude is not dependent on literal copying of source materials alone. The evocation of the past depends more on the sensitive use of the selective eye than on simple photographic copying of details from the past. Conscious anachronism is most often employed in a production to give a sharper edge to a director's or scenographer's vision as to what is presently important in a text whose past meanings have been blunted through time. Further, it often helps a modern-day audience form a more understandable link with the past than do slavishly accurate copies of it. This is the crux of creative research. As Lawrence Kubie points out: "By the creative process we mean the capacity to find new and unexpected connections, to voyage freely over the seas, to happen on America as we seek new routes to India, to find new relationships in time and space, and thus new meanings."

The theater, while it can bring to us an accurate vision of past times, is not simply an institution that seeks to give animation to museum exhibitions. Although it is not possible to predict attitudes of the future or to state just how materials of the past will be used in future productions, what undoubtedly will be part of any attitude is the scenographer's increasing use of hybrid forms of research. This is not as difficult to understand as it might first appear. Let me explain by way of a few striking examples I have seen during the past three decades (although these are by far not the only examples which could be cited).

During the 1964–65 Tyrone Guthrie Theater season, two of the plays presented were Congreve's *Way of the World* and Shakespeare's *Richard the Third*. The scenographer of the Congreve play designed the production strictly in period: not only were the costumes faultlessly correct in cut, material, color, and detail, they were also constructed in the same manner as they would had they been sewn in the time of the play's writing. No convenience was allowed the actor who had to make a speedy costume change; every button had to be undone—no Velcro, not a zipper on any costume. *Richard the Third*, on the other hand, gave the impression of historical accuracy but was conceived with a totally different concept in mind. Asked what this concept was, the scenographer replied, "Bugs. Bugs, beetles, scurrying, iridescent, shiney, hardshelled insects." As a concomitant feature of this concept, the director had seen the particular atmosphere of this play as that which one might find in a highly volatile police state: where power shifted from moment to moment, and where no one was untainted by the poisonous politics of the time. The two concepts worked well together: the world of this *Richard the Third* was a dangerous place, and its inhabitants had the worst features of the insect world. In order to best create this world it was decided to use materials from our own modern world: vinyls, materials that changed color as they shifted in the light, iridescent taffetas, plastics, metallic finishes— none of which existed during Richard the Third's period.

Much of the scenographer's work, as even the most cursory glance will reveal, depends upon using existing images or elements from existing images; many scenographic designs are "lifted" in part or totally from sources complete in themselves. (Figure 119 provides a good example of this practice.) But even when the source material is rich in suggestion, the scenographer often experiences an inability to choose what

seems to be the right image or element to use. In most instances this impasse (or block, to use a more current word) is broken by the need to make a decision, and the result of this selection is that it is often arbitrary. In my own experience, I have found that decisions are easier to make when confronted with myriad possibilities, if I have formed in my mind a clear view of how the characters of the text look. That is, I cannot easily visualize an environment empty of people, and I cannot visualize people simply as store-window mannequins. They must have an actuality to their appearance and actions. (I have discussed this problem with many directors who also voice something of the same concern: they tell me that it is not possible to *see* an action or series of actions without having a particular person with specific characteristics in their mind's eye; not a few directors have confessed that in the earliest stages of studying a text they "cast" the play with strong well-known personalities—and not always from the performing arts. I find this practice helpful to my own work and often make the "casting" of the text part of the research problem.)

Now, this may seem, on the face of it, a needless chore for the scenographer to undertake; after all, he is not concerned with the selection of the performers who will enact the roles, nor in most instances, will he be given the task of designing the costumes those performers will wear. But the practice I am suggesting here is primarily concerned not with individual actors, makeup, or costume but with a better understanding of the total production and, perhaps more important than that, a more complete, exact image—albeit an imaginary one—of the playwright's world, and that *is* the work of the scenographer. How those characters appear, and more importantly, how they use what he creates are very much germain to his function. The ability to see the characters who will inhabit that yet-to-be production often aids in the determination of that world; when visual possibilities are numerous it makes the selection process less arbitrary. In some instances, I have found it necessary to go a step further than just imagining how a character looks; there have been occasions when it became necessary to make this information visible. Let me cite an example as to how this principle works.

While working on a production of *Krapp's Last Tape*, I found myself unable to "see" the place where he lived. (Beckett does not, after all, give much help; clues as to the physical appearance of Krapp's room are few; and the usual pattern of external research just does not work for his plays. Simple though the requirements of this play are, it is precisely this kind of simplicity that often gives the scenographer the most difficulty: there is no leeway for error.) It seemed to me that the best way to address my problem was to become better acquainted with the single character living in the place I needed to design. To this end, I began a series of small, quickly drawn character sketches—in much the same way a novelist might seek out a fuller knowledge of a character by seeking to understand his physical background. Part of the purpose of this activity was to let the pen "have its own way," as Toulouse-Lautrec once described his own style of drawing, and in so doing bring into my search the blocked levels of my mind. Out of many attempts, the figure of Krapp began to emerge (figs. 146–148). Finally, I had before me an image of the person I was seeking (fig. 149). Having this physical image directly before me provided a sharper focus. I now found it easier not only to imagine the person of Krapp but to visualize

Fig. 147. Sketch of Beckett character

Fig. 146. Sketch of Beckett character

the actions he performed as required by the text. As I watched his actions I also began to find it less difficult to visualize the space he moved through and the objects he touched as he spoke the random words and snatches of thought that Beckett sparingly supplied him. What had formerly been a hazy and formless impression began to take on the sharpness of an actual objective image. The physical qualities of Krapp himself began to inform those things he lived with and used. And I began to "know" what colors, forms, and textures were necessary to Beckett's vision. Most important of all, I found that it became easier to discuss my views of Krapp's world with a sharpness and clarity that had been totally missing from my earlier conferences. But, this did not greatly surprise me because I now *knew* Krapp, the man, better, and not merely knew *about* him. He was a recognizable figure to me; I was able to say to myself, "Knowing this person has also told me something about the place where he would live."

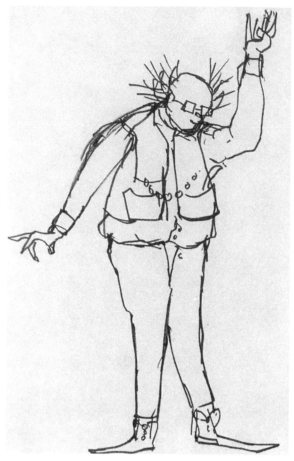

Fig. 148. Sketch of Beckett character

Fig. 149. Final sketch of Beckett character

The process I have been describing may seem to be the singularly idiosyncratic method of an individual scenographer. But I believe it to be a more widespread means of approaching early stages of research than might at first appear. To cite another example that indicates that this practice forms at least part of other scenographer's working methods, let me quote the answer of the cinema designer Harry Horner to this question:

Question: What are your first steps as a production designer on a film?
Horner: I find that the first things that I become interested in are the characters and the relationship of the characters. Now the characters, naturally, are tied to a period—a Victorian group of people will act differently toward each other than a group of people who live in our own century. I study the script, and sometimes it takes a terribly long time, with frequent read- ings, because nothing happens—one has *no* vision. . . . It is interesting that when you familiarize yourself with a world very thoroughly, you find yourself ultimately not copying the research, but inventing, becoming a person of that period. Many designers fall into a trap of going to the research department and asking, "What might a Gothic window in a restaurant look like?" They take the window from one book and the door from another book, put them together, and they think it looks Victorian. But when you are really familiar with a world, you suddenly find that you don't need any more to copy because you become a period person. (*Dialogue on Film*, American Film Institute)

Some scenographers take this approach to even greater lengths; Andre Acquart, the noted French scenographer, says this concerning those crucial first encounters with a text: "In my work, I let myself be guided above all by intuition. *I try to imagine the acting of all the players, all their movements.* I create a setting which is intended to be an ideal acting machine, a sculpture of the scenic space, and I try to bring the setting to life" (italics mine).

I would not suggest that the process I have been discussing—and have demonstrated in the specific case of *Krapp's Last Tape*—is one which could always be followed to the extent given here; there is simply not enough time to undertake such a detailed portrait study of every character in every text. (Nor does every character or every text deserve such treatment.) But the kind of thinking underlying this demonstration is important to grasp. This is especially true during the formative stages of a scenographer's education. Even when actual sketches of characters are not attempted, there should be a strong endeavor to visualize their physical characteristics along with their actions. The process is not unlike the development of directorial skills: it is imperative that students of directing master the techniques of preblocking action on paper, making their movement intentions clear by diagrams charting that movement. This is a necessary discipline that makes the young director aware of the uses and patterns of movement required by the interpretation of a text; it is entirely beside the point that many directors subsequently arrive at a time in their careers when they no longer preblock productions on paper but approach their work directly in the rehearsal period without first writing out their thoughts. The jettisoning of previous activities is natural in the growth of the professional artist; this same kind of growth could be discovered in that of the scenographer: he too might very well cease to make actual drawings of images that occur to him in the manner that we have been discussing. But it is very important to understand that this advanced stage cannot be reached *without having done the physical work* during an earlier period. The point that must be understood is that only by a thoughtful recording of actions can the director come to the point where he need not preblock,

and only through a similar period of time can the scenographer abandon the laborious activity suggested here. The apprenticeship of all artists requires disciplines and practices that, when the art is mastered can be altered or discontinued. A pianist spends untold hours practicing scales; but no one would attend a performance that only included the playing of scales, no matter how expertly played. Preblocking action on paper is, as it were, a form of playing scales for the director; visualization of a text's characters in sketches, I would also suggest, is also a form of playing scales for the scenographer—and a valuable one at that. Practically all artistic education consists of mastering exercises which, when mastery is attained, are no longer necessary except in the imagination.

One last point concerning the visualization of the characters in a text: it would be a grave mistake to limit ourselves to those images that are obtained only from our own imaginations, which are products of our own drawing skills. Our searches should also include the work of other artists. There have been many instances in the past when my own imagined vision of a character was both sharpened and extended by what I found, not by what I drew. One last brief example should illustrate this point.

In Peter Weiss's *Persecution and Assassination of Marat under the Direction of the Marquis de Sade*, there is a demented abbot who at one point in the play must act out the passion of Christ. The character in the play is not a major role; his "scene"—like that of the apothecary's in *Romeo and Juliet*—is a short one. Nevertheless, brief though his appearance is, the impact of that appearance must be strong and immediate. This character is not explained so much as he is allowed to be seen; his physical appearance must carry with it the information the audience needs to know about him. Moreover, this information must be instantaneously projected to an audience. As the scenographer in charge of all elements of this production—setting, costume, lighting, makeup—my main problem was to make each of the characters in this production a self-contained piece of information. (While this might be true for most productions, in works such as *Marat/Sade*, the problem is more critical: in most texts characters are either explained or prepared for by other characters, or the character has the opportunity to reveal himself more slowly to an audience; for example, by the time a reading of *Hamlet* is finished, an extremely clear picture of Hamlet emerges.) The problem presented itself in this way: *How can I show a man suffering from a particular form of insanity, in this case a messianic delusion, without resorting to the stereotyped images of insanity so often seen on the stage?* The power of this play greatly depends on performers who do not "act crazy"; and the particular requirements of this text demanded that almost all of the characters in it are disturbed by recognizable forms of insanity. During the rehearsal period of the Royal Shakespeare Company's production of *Marat/Sade*, Peter Brook—the director—took members of the play's cast to English asylums for the insane to observe the effects of specific mental illnesses on those who suffered from them. While this form of research is necessary, it may not provide all the information needed to produce the play. Let me give an example from my own experience with this play to illustrate my point.

Figure 150 is an action photograph taken during the first act of *Marat/Sade*. In this image we see the moment when the torment of the bishop is greatest; his face is not, however, the beneficent one we are accustomed to seeing in romantic representations of Christ's suffering. What we see here is a vision of a man driven to desperation by his madness. While the creation of this face may seem a task for the performer alone, in this instance his work was aided by the research of the scenographer. Examine figure 151; observe how remarkably similar the face is to that of the performer shown in figure 150. This painting of Christ by James Ensor was used, in fact, both for the makeup design of the performer and as a guide for his study. Figure 152, which shows the massing and the makeup design of a group of inmates, was suggested by a similar image of masks taken from another painting of Ensor (fig. 153).

This is, of course, a singular example which cuts across many lines—makeup, costume, acting, direction, not to mention art history. What this instance clearly points out to us, however, is that scenographic research rarely stops at some arbitrary point or is bounded by strict categorical lines; the research we must do in the theater often pervades a whole spectrum of needs and possibilities.

Fig. 150. Scene from Peter Weiss's *Marat/Sade*. Photograph by Don Drinkwater

Fig. 151. *Man of Sorrows* by James Ensor

Fig. 152. Scene from Peter Weiss's *Marat/Sade*. Photograph by Don Drinkwater

These examples, admittedly, may seem far afield of the usual methods and materials of scenographic research. But there must always be in our investigations the allowance for pursuit of information that does not conform to strict lines of inquiry; creative research must be an activity that is sufficiently open enough to explore the unusual, to capitalize on the unforeseen. Nor should we ever be ashamed to give full credit to the accidental insight that changes (and also charges) our conscious mind and stimulates our imagination. New directions are very often begun when the prepared mind of the artist clashes with unsought materials; the use of Ensor's work in *Marat/Sade* began with just such an accidental encounter. To progress in any aspect of theatrical art we must allow curiosity a high place in our

working procedure and chance a proper respect. Albert Einstein states the case well when he tells us that "the most beautiful experience we can have is the mysterious. It is the fundamental emotion that stands at the cradle of true art and true science." Creative research should always retain, in the bustle of the practical working theater, an element of the mysterious.

This may seem a highly speculative task for the scenographer whose workaday world depends on meeting deadlines and delivering predictable results; but he must come to realize that a significant part of his profession lies specifically in those areas that must be approached intuitively as well as understood objectively. Inanimate objects no longer used, representations of life long since vanished, people dead for perhaps

Fig. 153. Painting by James Ensor

thousands of years, must not only be sought out from the cases of museums and from pages of historical account, they must, in the mind of the scenographer, be restored to a form of life; for much of the past can only speak to us if it is seen in the context in which it existed. This is not as difficult or mystical a task as it might at first sound. There is a kind of understanding that could be best called *time vision* and that can be summoned up by the inquisitive and intuitive mind. The type of information we speak of here, and which must be part of the scenographer's working methods, is a direct result of a certain attitude toward research of the past. *Time vision* is not only a possibility that the scenographic artist must seek out but is a responsibility that he cannot evade. It is, moreover, very much a part of that practical world of production.

The world scenographers seek to find through their research must never be a dead or sterile place; as on Robinson Crusoe's island beach, of all the things found there, the greatest interest lies in the human footprint we finally detect.

Let us leave this subject with the observations of the present-day critic Donal Henahan whose firm grasp on the issues just studied are evident.

During the reign of Louis XIV, about two centuries before Wagner proclaimed his doctrine of Gesamt-kunstwerk, the blending of the arts into a united experience was already an esthetic ideal, honored in daily practice. It was not only an attractive theory but a way of life for composers, choreographers and designers. What is less commonly appreciated is that even playwrights followed the gleam, none more successfully than Molière.

In Paris last month I attended the premiere of An Arts Florissants production of Molière's last play, "Le Malade Imaginaire," that was a revelation in many ways. For one thing, it was strange to attend a Molière comedy in the company of a Parisian audience that seemed intent on muffling its laughter. Possibly no one wished to have anyone else think they were hearing the classic lines for the first time.

Still, I came away not only delighted but impressed by as ambitious and successful a staging of an old work as I have ever experienced. Although it is generally understood nowadays that French Baroque operas were mounted as grand spectacles in which music, words, dance, costumes, scenery and lighting were meant to function in close partnership, until recent years only a few university or dilettante groups have attempted to produce Molière's plays in a historically proper style. But William Christie, the American scholar who directs Les Arts Florissants, staged "Le Malade Imaginaire" at the elegant Châtelet theater as the lavish comédie-ballet that is was intended to be, in the original version of 1673. . . .

The play, by contrast, made do with the few props suggested by Molière. The actors, led by Jean Dautremay as the miserable hypochondriac Argan, needed little help to make the play's sharply witty points, but there prose was occasionally augmented—by a raucous commedia dell'arte interlude. . . .

Perhaps the most remarkable thing about the evening was the air of vitality it radiated. *Missing, though not at all missed, was the faint odor of formaldehyde that arises from many supposedly authentic but in fact merely dead quaint productions of old works. Here, one had the feeling of encountering a living work, not a well-preserved corpse.* There was, too, the appeal of a poignant subtext, impossible to ignore in any performance of "Le Malade Imaginaire": Molière, who was himself snidely rumored to be a hypochondriac by his enemies, died shortly after the first performance, in which he took the role of Argan. (Italics mine [*New York Times*, 8 April 1990, *Music View* Section])

The Scenographer's Personal Research Sources

Most scenographers are—or soon become—avid collectors of books, images, and printed materials. This is understandable since the mature scenographer uses these materials daily as factual verification as well as sources of inspiration. Imagination—an indisputable part of any art—has a voracious appetite. It needs constant feeding. As a result, many scenographers develop early a craving to collect visual materials, building over time large personal collections.

An argument can be made for using large public collections of visual materials. Many larger cities have libraries that house these collections. In many instances such a resource proves necessary to the scenographer, since few can compete with the scope or size of collections found there. The personal library, however, is more than privately owned works. Items personally collected over time—images, lists of materials, photographic slides, technical specifications, etc., in addition to books—become an extension of the individual artist's personal vision. In many ways a personal collection determines the direction of a career. Such collections invariably reveal clues to ingrained thoughts and emotions of the artist; they function as a sort of exterior manifestation of the individual artist's subconscious mind. The propensity to collect certain kinds of works is a specific way by which the artist can chart inner directions. One of the twentieth century's most practical politicians—Winston Chur-

chill—gives us a practical reason for a personal library:

"What shall I do with all my books?" was the question; and the answer, "Read them. . . ." But if you cannot read them, at any rate handle them and, as it were, fondle them. Peer into them. Let them fall open where they will. Read on from the first sentence that arrests the eye. Then turn to another. Make a voyage of discovery, taking soundings of uncharted seas. Set them back on their shelves with your own hands. Arrange them on your own plan, so that if you do not know what is in them you at least know where they are. If they cannot be your friends, let them at any rate be your acquaintances. If they cannot enter the circle of your life, do not deny them at least a nod of recognition.

Make a voyage of discovery, taking soundings of uncharted seas. No better advice, no better reason exists for the active making of a personal library. Moreover, the scenographer today is more fortunate than those who started even twenty years ago. The printing of low and medium-priced paperback art books has grown tremendously during this time. Concurrently, a phenomenal interest in printing high-quality visual materials has taken place. Pictorial records of private and public buildings, detailed studies of architecture, furniture, and the like, are being brought to a wider public in a diversity unparalled in printing history. A helpful development—especially to the scenographer—is the inclusion of images that elucidate the social and economic reasons underlying the time frames of a certain historical period or style. Books such as *Private Life in the Fifteenth Century* (a collection of letters and documents of a specific family living during the period) has numerous illustrations interwoven with verbal commentary of the text. These books *show* history as well as explain it words. Such works demonstrate clearly how different countries in different ages reacted to, or produced variations on, prevalent styles of art and architecture. Many of these books are expensive. Still, the scenographer should consider them wise investments. While the acquisition of books—even the reasonably priced ones—is always expensive, the practice of buying books on a regular basis is ultimately the least costly way to acquire a working library. (If the scenographer buys a resource work to use in a specific project, that expense, as with other art supplies, is tax deductible.) Personal libraries are positive means by which artists continue to grow in imagination and productivity.

At the end of this book an extensive bibliography is given. Three purposes underlie the selections included: (1) to give sources that informed or influenced the writing of this book, (2) to suggest works useful to the scenographer in daily work, and (3) to recommend books for a personal library; these are accompanied with an asterisk and are at the present time available for purchase. A small number of books in the bibliography are not directly related to theater; many lie in adjunct areas of art; some have little or no direct connection to the everyday problems of the producing theater but are still useful in gaining a wider view of the world that theater serves. The bibliography attempts to guide students both to helpful craft-oriented technical information and to more wide-ranging resources necessary to practice scenography.

(Note: While no single press has on its lists every visual research source the scenographer needs to practice, one publisher comes very close: Dover Publications. This company is unique in the scope and the number of its offerings. The materials published by Dover are almost entirely presented in economical paperback editions [a few books are hardback editions]. Each year Dover publishes over two hundred books on fine art, music, crafts and needlework, antiques, languages, literature, children's books, chess, cookery, nature, anthropology, science, mathematics, and other areas. While some of Dover's offerings are included in the bibliography at the end of this book, that selection by no means indicates this publisher's extensive range of books. It is recommended that student scenographers order all the catalogues available as well as begin a systematic acquisition of Dover's books. The current address for this publisher is Dover Publications, Inc.; 180 Varick Street; New York, NY 10014. Please indicate field of interest.)

An important part of a scenographer's personal research materials is photographic images. These materials provide several functions for the artist/researcher: not only do they provide verification of facts, they often serve as inspirational points of departure for the imagination

Since Jacques Mandé Daguerre in 1839, the principal inventor of photography, gave us the ability to capture exact likeness by mechanical means, access to a wide variety of visual material has expanded. As Naomi Rosenblum remarks: "By the time it was announced in 1839, Western industrialized society was ready for photography. The camera's images appeared and remained viable because they filled cultural and sociological needs that were not being met by pictures created by hand. The photograph was the ultimate response to a social and cultural appetite for a more accurate and real-looking representation of reality, a need that had its origins in the Renaissance. When the idealized representation of the spiritual universe that inspired the medieval mind no longer served the purposes of increasing secular societies, their places were taken by paintings and graphic works that portrayed actuality with greater verisimilitude."

While the photograph is now the principal means by which we record productions, it is also among the most valuable resources we have in assembling visual materials during preliminary stages of our research. With the advent of an increasingly sophisticated computer technology, scenographers are now able to scan into computer graphics photographic research images that can be modified into working drawings. Use of computer programs also means that the gap between photographic technique and freehand drawing skill is rapidly diminishing.

The photograph is also of value in training scenographic artists; photographers teach us much even though their work is static, while ours deals primarily with images seen in time (a similarity that we share with the cinema, which Peter Brook pointed out previously). Behind these different basic approaches to seeing the world, there exists profound similarities, concerns and attitudes that the scenographer should attempt to understand and take advantage of.

Shortly before her death in 1971, Diane Arbus said this about her work: "I do feel I have some slight corner on something about the quality of things. I mean it's very subtle and a little embarrassing to me, but I really believe there are things which nobody would see unless I photographed them."

The photographer is frequently able to reveal things that would remain virtually hidden from us despite our visual training and sensitivity to imagery. The role of photography is an important one for the scenographer. Sadly, many students do not take advantage of important photographic documents their university or city libraries hold. Most professional scenographers realize that the photographer's work is an invaluable aid to their own. As Samuel Wagstaff, the noted collector of photography points out, "the most interesting thing in looking at photographs is not their art qualities but the ways they open us to all other aspects of life. . . . Photography whets one's eye enormously." Let us direct our attention to a few examples that demonstrate how photographic materials can be useful in the theater research process.

Dickens's *Oliver Twist* has had a long life in both the cinema and on the stage; there have been a number of versions done in both mediums. Dickens himself gives many evocative descriptions of the London where much of the action takes place, a city with which he was intimately familiar. Peter Ackroyd calls especial attention to that relationship when he reflects that "London created Dickens, just as Dickens created London. . . . London entered his soul; it terrified him and it entranced him. It became the material for his fantasy and the arena for his polemic. And in the end, it was truly Dickens' London."

But what was the London Dickens actually saw? Little is left of that city to which he came as a small boy. Nor is there much left of the London he knew as the mature reigning novelist of his age; many of the buildings he knew have since been demolished; many of the buildings that now form London were not yet built. But many visual records still exist of that world, and many of them are in photographic form. These have played a significant part in the research done for those many versions of *Oliver Twist*. This is not to say that drawing has not also played its part in that research process; there have been some extremely valuable documents left to us from artists of the time, and they too have aided in understanding the visual aspects of Dickens's world. In point of fact, the drawings have actually helped us to better access the photographic records we have. One of the most helpful of those documents is large book printed in 1874 by Gustave Doré and Blanchard Jerrold, *London: A Pilgrimage*. This one book has probably

been used as the visual record of Dickens's London by more directors and scenographers than any other single source. Although actually drawn some thirty to forty years after the time Dickens set his novels, we have come to regard the Doré-Blanchard view of London as the last word as to what the city looked like during that earlier period. Not only did David Lean base his 1949 cinematic version of *Oliver Twist* on the materials of this book, but so have many filmmakers since: the production designer John Box of the more recent musical version, *Oliver!* made extensive use of these same drawings. And what is even more surprising to find is that the settings for the 1931 German film *The Threepenny Opera* are veritable three-dimensional replicas of some of the plates from the book. Nor is it doubtful that directors and scenographers in the future will soon abandon this unique source of visual information. Figure 154 shows a plate from this book. Figure 155 shows an almost identical photographic view of the same locale. Having two views of the same subject in different mediums raises provocative questions. These different images not only cause us to consider carefully the

Fig. 154. Doré drawing of Ludgate Hill. Courtesy of Dover Publications

Fig. 155. Photograph of Ludgate Hill

Fig. 156. Map showing London area

distinct elements of each image but force us to consider any differences. It is obvious that the viewpoint is roughly similar in both images. It is equally obvious that Doré made changes in what he saw. What is valuable to notice here are the common features of both views. It is clear in both pictures that this area of London—just below St. Paul's Cathedral—is a busy place; Ludgate Hill was at this time (and still is) a great intersections of London's various kinds of traffic. Although maps of the area, such as figure 156, provide us with an accurate location of the place, if we want to *see* what the place was like—to better understand how it *felt* to be on that particular London street during the middle of the nineteenth century—we need information that only figures 154 and 155 can show. More important still, by having the two images, we find that although differences exist, one image helps verify the other.

It might be well to mention at this point the curious relationship that has grown up between the photograph and graphic work in general since the inception of photography and to show briefly how the subject matter of graphic art has developed during that period of time. Even as long ago as 1855 artists were sometimes using photographs rather than firsthand observations as a basis for drawings and paintings. Eugène Durieu took a number of photographs in 1854, which Eugène Delacroix then used the following year. Some years later Toulouse-Lautrec made

numerous on-the-spot visual observations of the night haunts of *fin-de-siècle* Paris, recording the people he saw there as well as their actions. Many of these drawings were used as inspirations for later paintings. Doubtless many of his works were based on these sketches; but what few have realized is the extent to which he also used photographs in his work. Figure 157 is a photograph—quite possibly posed—of a couple seated in some local restaurant or bar. In figure 158 we see Toulouse-Lautrec's rendition of this image; and we can also see how he changed the original image to more clearly suit his own purpose. It is a curious irony, therefore, to find that images of Toulouse-Lautrec have been used by directors to re-create the original things he saw: in *An American in Paris*, director and choreographer Gene Kelly used Lautrec's drawings and paintings—as well as the images of other painters of the period—as the basis for a series of dances. But directors on the stage also find that they can use these drawings as clues to explaining actions to performers. (See figure 58, which shows an action photograph taken of a particular moment in *Oh, Dad, Poor Dad, Momma's Hung You in the Closet and I'm Feeling So Sad*, by Arthur Koppit. In this scene the director wanted to show that the passion Madame Rosepettle and the Commodore display is a theatrically extravagant one, a passion similar to

Fig. 157. Photograph of couple in Paris café

that projected by Toulouse-Lautrec's image shown in figure 59. By allowing his actors to see this image, the director could better show what he wanted; he could say to them: *Look at this drawing. Study these people dancing. Think carefully about what you believe to be their state of mind. Are they really feeling what the image suggests? Or is there*

Fig. 158. Painting by Toulouse Lautrec

something "phony" about their physical attitudes? In your dance what I want is a swoon such as that called for in the tango you have to perform. But I also want your physical attitude to project the same mocking character as I perceive in this Toulouse-Lautrec drawing. It is a further curious result of showing this image to performers that the actual results on the stage reproduced a natural effect that the director did not consciously plan: while the performer playing Madame Rosepettle did not consciously hold her hands in a set position, the natural result is similar to the observation Toulouse-Lautrec recorded, which to some extent validates the precision of his vision.)

The use of the photographic image can be of great value to those who work for the stage. While it will always aid us in verifying details of places and things we cannot easily reach or see, it can also—as in the example just cited—serve as a triggering device for our imaginations. As Van Deren Coke points out in his study *The Painter and the Photograph*: "In the nineteenth century the photograph was most frequently used as a crutch. Only a few artists expanded the potential of their work by using camera vision. In the twentieth century, due to the veritable tidal wave of photographs that appeared in magazines and family albums, the vision of the camera became unavoidable and was absorbed by the artist and the public. *This potent force became more and more recognized as a conceptual agency*" (italics mine).

It is not only to the painter or graphic artist to which these last words apply. Photography can act as a potent conceptual agency that triggers ideas in other artists as well: the writer being a prime example. Although there have been numerous instances where writers have indicated that their original inspirations came from graphic images—Michel de Ghelderode's use of a Bruegel painting for his play *Three Blind Men* is a good example—some writers during the last hundred years have had their work directly influenced by subject matter that they encountered through the photographic work of their contemporaries. It can be demonstrated that the photographers and writers living at the same time and in the same place often shared, as it were, identical subject matter. (The playwright Jean Giraudoux and the photographer Brassaï had similar encounters that resulted in different outcomes. Both lived in Paris during the first half of

Fig. 159. Setting for *Le Bourgeois Gentilhomme* by Susanne Lalique

this century, and both shared many of the same personal relationships and observed many of the same sights. Figure 103 is a photograph Brassaï made of the woman known as Miss Diamonds, the reputed model on which Giraudoux's leading character—Aurelia—is based.)

A good principle to follow when researching the visual background of the works of twentieth-century playwrights who have written plays set in their own time is to seek out those photographers who also lived in or documented these same places during that same period of time.

Students of scenography should keep in mind from the very beginning of their training that their relationship to photographic images is not only a valuable part of their education but an important factor in their professional practice. Furthermore, their investigations of photo-

graphic images should remain a constant activity throughout their lives and not merely applied intermittently to isolated projects. As Robert Hughes said of the painter Wilhem de Kooning, "He is a fierce looker." So should all scenographers aspire to be: *fierce lookers.*

Along with photographs, other collections of loose material—clippings from magazine, brochures, and the like—are used in the research process. Most scenographers, in addition to their libraries, also maintain extensive file collections. These files are as important to their efficient operation and production as is the dictionary or encyclopedia to research scholars. Since scenographers cannot purchase these collections ready-assembled, as they might a set of books, these must be assembled item by item over time. Most scenographers have extensive collections of ma-

Fig. 160. German room, from *Duetsch Wohn-Und Festraume Aus 6 Jarhunderten*. Courtesy of Verlag Von Julius Hoffman, Stuttgart

terials accumulated over many years. An additional problem to building a good system of files is that much of the materials needed has a short-lived general exposure. Magazine articles and newspaper items are here today and gone today. The explosion of transitory visual materials means that the working scenographer must possess a quick eye as well as a pair of scissors always near to hand.

A file system is the best method of keeping track of the vast amount of information that constantly presents itself. (Scenographers living near large cities such as New York are fortunate, since extensive image files are frequently kept in public libraries collections. The New York City Public Library has a large and well-maintained collection of images and clippings of which many

professional scenographers living there make extensive use.)

How directly these transitory visual materials are used changes greatly from production to production, from scenographer to scenographer. Individual scenographers vary widely as to how much or how little original sources are used; some are eclectic incorporating into their designs many "quotes," while others rely on a single found image. An example of a design derived from a single-source image is Susanne Lalique's setting for *Le Bourgeois Gentilhomme* (fig. 159). Although the structure of the room is simplified and the feeling of the room has been lightened, the resulting design owes much to an actual room in Danzig, Germany, built in the middle of the seventeenth century (fig. 160). Another example of a scenographic design that owes much to a particular historical resource image is the setting for the premier production of Peter Weiss's *Marat/Sade*. Figure 161 shows the original sketch by Jacques-Louis David of a proposed painting—never completed—called *The Oath of the Tennis Court*. Figure 162 shows how a twentieth-century scenographer made use of the 1790 David drawing.

Given below is a suggested list of file folder headings. The categories should be sufficient for the beginning scenographer, although it should be expected that these categories over time will be subdivided as well as refined. Do not forget that a good file system—like a good personal library—conscientiously kept and periodically revamped, will save the scenographer many hours of research away from the studio. Even the fact that the scenographer has a file system causes an increased alertness to new visual materials.

Many scenographers, in addition to general files, also begin a separate file for each new production. If a file is created at the start of a project, all the information collected during the designing of the production can be kept in one place. This becomes a valuable resource for later productions of the same shows. In this file, one might expect to keep not only initial ideas, sources, and working drawing, but photos of the finished production, notes and communications with the director, reviews, and so on.

File Folder Headings

Source 1—Interiors (broken into periods and styles)
Source 2—Architecture (broken into period and styles)
Source 3— Architectural Detail
Source 4—Architectural Exteriors
Source 5—Windows and Doors (broken into periods and styles)
Source 6—Furniture (broken into periods and styles)
Source 7—Ornament and Decoration
Source 8—Machines, Factories, etc.
Source 9—Vistas (also trees and plants)

Fig. 161. Drawing by David for *The Oath of the Tennis Court*

Fig. 162. Setting for *Marat/Sade*

Source 10—Set Ideas (photos and drawings with
    striking images)
Sculpture—(broken into periods and styles)
Paintings—(broken into periods and styles)
Costume 1—(broken into periods and styles)
Costume 2—Sources (catalogues, companies, etc.)
Costume 3—Materials
Costume 4—Accessories
Costume 5—Construction
Properties 1—Historical Visual Materials
Properties 2—Construction and Materials
Properties 3—Property Plots
Properties 4—Sources (catalogues, companies, etc.)
Photo 1—Set
Photo 2— Models
Photo 3—Costume
Photo 4—Miscellaneous
Working Drawings 1—Floor Plans
Working Drawings 2—Elevations
Working Drawings 3—Detail Drawings
Working Drawings 4—Paint Schedules
Working Drawings 5—Properties and Furniture
Working Drawings 6—Special Effects
Stage Equipment and Hardware
Material 1—Paint
Material 2—Fabric
Material 3—Wood
Material 4—Plastics
Material 5—Metal

Lighting 1—Instruments, Control, Support, etc.
Lighting 2—Color Mediums
Lighting 3—Projection Data
Lighting 4—Light Plots
Stages and Auditoriums
Designs by Other Scenographers
Articles on Scenography and Related Fields
Articles on Production and Stagecraft
Scene-painting Techniques

"A Setting for Ibsen's *Ghosts* from a Director's Diary, 1905"
By Konstantin Stanislavsky

[The following article is drawn from the director's diary of one of the twentieth century's most
important theater figures: Konstantin Stanislavsky. The time period include here—nine
days in 1905 during which *Ghosts* was being
planned for production—concerns the numerous dramatic problems in the play, which had to
be solved in visual terms. (The play was not
only the first production in Russia but was still a
controversial new work in the world at large.
There were, therefore, few previous productions
from which to draw information.) While a direc-

tor by profession, Stanislavsky reveals that he is highly sensitive to the intricate relationships that exist between all who fashion the physical environments for performers from written texts. These excerpts clearly demonstrate a certain timelessness in methods of research, in creative approaches to dramatic problems inherent in the conceptual processes of scenography. They also give a good picture of how a director's mind works and an insight into the way a director's eye looks at visual aspects of interpretation—D.R.P.]

January 30, 1905

When Nemirovich-Danchenko first read *Ghosts* aloud to me, Simov and Kolupayev (the Moscow Art Theatre's scene designers) suggested the following mental images: a dark house (a sort of Norwegian *Uncle Vanya*), with a view of mountains and plenty of air. A rainy day. Many rooms. Portraits of ancestors. A lighted fireplace in the dining room. Then there is the burning down of the orphanage, a most interesting scenic effect. Several scenes and visual impressions stuck in our minds: the pastor, the open fireplace (a welcome, unexpected detail). Mrs. Alving's love for the pastor. The traces of this and of her past make her interesting. A comic scene over the insurance. Note: the pastor and the woman who once was in love with him. The picture at the end of the first act: the first attacks of the boy's illness, the conflagration, the contrast between the doomed boy and his mother, who now loses everything. The fading out of a young life which cannot go on functioning. . . .

January 31, 1905. Stage Set Models.

We went to the scene shop: I, Simov, Kolupayev, Nemirovich-Danchenko, Savistakaya, Moskvin, and Andreyev (an electrician and apprentice designer). Kacholov [Pastor Manders] and Sulerzhitski joined us briefly.

We set up the requirements for the designer. (1) The conflagration, the orphanage, a fjord, and a glacier must be visible to the audience from all parts of the theatre. The sets therefore should not be too low, although that would be conducive to creating the right mood. (2) One must feel that it is a gray, rainy day, with low-lying clouds, and hear the monotonous drip of the rain. (3) It is necessary to show the whole dining room to the audience and it would be desirable to suggest a series of rooms in an old house. (4) The house is very old (Norwegianize the manor house in *Uncle Vanya*); but the gloom of the house and its age should be conveyed through bright rather than dark colours (which would be too banal and medieval). Every corner reeks with the atmosphere of vice. (5) There must be a staircase leading to an upper floor. (6) Portraits of ancestors are recommended. The walls should be crowded with them to suggest age. (7) The furniture should be upholstered in worn red velvet. (8) The sunrise must be clearly visible. (9) The principle moments for stage pictures (the acting areas for these must be prepared) are: the pastor conversing with the woman who once was in love with him (this in a cozy corner); the death of Oswald; the sunrise (finale); the drinking scene before he dies. (10) There must be a fireplace (a typical one). The conflagration effects must be experimented with—a magic lantern, etc. The same is true of the rain and the sunrise.

We examined and compared similarities and repetitions among favourite Norwegian motifs. We pick out: (1) a rising staircase with an alcove under it, and a fireplace; (2) panelled windows; (3) low alcoves with divans; (4) Norwegian rugs, mats, and tables; (5) the walls and windows painted yellow, green, red (red doors); (6) a special design for the ceiling; (7) upper passageways with arches and balustrades (it is obvious that the rooms are low upstairs). Also a special semicircular landing at the foot of the stairs (this will suggest that naïve fancies of olden times and that is what we most of all want).

I went over each picture and everything I found that seemed original I copied architecturally in my notebook. Simov did the same. Tomorrow we shall compare all the designs. Perhaps we shall find something of interest. We shall assemble the models. So far we have found only a few individual angles, but the total picture of the room is still lacking, especially the arrangement of the furniture and blocking scheme. So far, I visualize only several scenes on the stairs (conversation with someone above), and I see the alcove under the staircase and the fireplace.

Things haven't warmed up enough for our work to reach the boiling point. As I was leaving the theatre a few things occurred to me. (1) When the fire takes place in the orphanage, is the alarm given by a bell or by the distress whistle of a steamer in the fjord? (2) A steamer should be by and leave a trail of smoke as it would on a rainy day. (3) The firemen are volunteers. Perhaps Oswald, or one of the men-servants, may dash out hurriedly putting on his coat as he runs. (4) In the distance, sounds of building the orphanage, which is almost finished, are heard. (5) There must be a portrait of Oswald's father resembling Moskvin. (6) The carpenter plays the first scene at work. He has been sent for to repair a door.

February 1, 1905

I, Simov, Kolupayev, and Andreyev. We assembled our models—none of them proved satisfactory.

Simov's first model has on the right an alcove with the staircase. Under this is an archway leading into the dining room, where there is a bay window through which we see the orphanage burning down. But it is not a success. The staircase, on which we counted so heavily, suggests more an entryway or vestibule. The alcove on the right certainly suggests a good mood. However there is no room there to stage a scene. There are no angles for the death scene or other intimate scenes. Nor is there any feeling of an old house which had belonged to a libertine.

Simov's second model, with long vaulted arches for half the length of the front of the stage, suggests an old boyar palace but not Norway. The fire next door cannot be seen. Still, the set does contain two or three comfortable corners in which scenes could be staged.

Kolupayev's model is overcrowded, and has no view of the fire. The overall impression is that of an entryway.

My model is a variation on Simov's. There are comfortable corners and other places for staging, a good view of the conflagration, but it has little general atmosphere.

Kolupayev's model is better adapted to playing but lacks interest. Andreyev fiddled around but did not turn up anything. . . .

February 2, 1905

Simov, Kolupayev, and Andreyev worked on the designs. I was detained by a rehearsal and came later. Again no inspiration, not even a hint. In accordance with my plan, they made a very shallow model, the stage scaled less than twelve feet in depth. We have never had a set in this shape. Very convenient for *mise-en-scene* (this suggest we are near a solution). Yet we still cannot capture any mood. We are beginning to get nervous and fear that we have exhausted all our resources, have tried out every line and shape. This gives us a chill. We keep making combinations of a staircase, a dining room and a conflagration—all of which must be visible from every angle of the auditorium. Perhaps this is an insoluble problem. Nevertheless we are obliged to find the right model for the first act, that is to say: Norway, an ancient building, a sense of a sinful life led there.

All these torments and searchings, and tomorrow is the deadline, the last day to get the models into rough form, if the production is to be ready by the second week in Lent.

We decided to work from my latest model.

A torturing stage to be in—to see various components in the mind's eye, to sense the atmosphere of this old-fashioned room, filled with ancestral relics, and yet not be able to translate it all into material form. I remember similar tortures while preparing the first and third acts of *The Cherry Orchard*. We had to create something never seen, never heard of, and I had to make a visual image of it. In the first act it was necessary that the whole audience should see the cherry orchard. Until you have the right design, you cannot begin to plot the action. The set is half the job. I gave up and went away because I felt my brain was tired and my imagination was going around in vicious circles.

February 3, 1905

I, Simov, Kolupayev, and Andreyev worked from 1.00 to 5.30 in the scene shop.

Simov arrived to put the finishing touches on the model I had proposed. He made several changes of his own. For instance, I had thought the model original because it was all done in straight lines (we have used curves too often). But Simov again broke the straight lines by introducing curves. He was carried away with the view of the landscape and wanted the audience to be able to see it. The house now assumed the shape of a Russian letter "L" upside down. In order to open a vista of the landscape he found it necessary to angle the perpendicular line to the right, and that slanted the rear wall. The patriarchal and archaic quality of the room vanished. It was neither one thing nor the other. I was in that same state myself. I could not visualize and sense what this room looked like—a foreign manor house (not a castle), filled with portraits of ancestors and their relics—but I was incapable of converting its characteristic essence in practical terms.

It is a painful situation when you cannot express yourself and cannot guess the thoughts of another person. But neither Simov nor Kolupayev had anything to suggest. They argued this way and that, but found no firm ground under their feet. They finished the model, shook their heads, and realized it was not right. Nemirovich-Danchenko came in. He had missed our earlier searchings so he could not, of course, grasp very readily all we had been through. First he began to criticize what we had done, repeated his advice, and urged us to make the very mistakes we had eliminated. "Why did you throw out the fireplace and staircase?" We answered, "Because to show them in profile wouldn't leave any comfortable acting areas, and we couldn't show them full front because they take too much from the view of the landscape," etc, etc. Andreyev was even more irritating. He kept offering naïve and banal proposals. We simply had to inform him that two times two equals four. My nerves gave way. I was harsh and began to say unpleasant things. Apparently this outburst of temperament worked on my imagination. My nerves reached such a pitch that there and then I managed, though with great difficulty, to sketch out the whole room. Of course, all I could do was to indicate the position of the windows, doors, furniture; nor could I catch the spirit of the setting. In the vacant corners I put new furniture,

pictures, a clock. Gradually the room was filled with my grotesque and incorrect drawing of objects and a faint suggestion of a mood. The others felt this but were unanimous in saying that it was too Russian. I felt the same way, but nevertheless it did fit the needs of the *mise-en-scene*, which was no mean accomplishment. We began to consider how to inject a Norwegian flavour into it. The furniture would be arranged as in my plan but would be replaced by things that were typically Norwegian. There would be panels of worn red velvet or silk. The windows would be foreign in style, the stove and the bay window Norwegian. Simov waxed enthusiastic after he was given detailed explanations of the drawing, and he was all the more pleased with it because it offered a sense of space for air and a view of the outside landscape. He drew a pencil sketch which included all the details.

On my way home I began to get the feel of various scenes in my set and visualize them. Everything fell beautifully into place, but in the evening, when I read over the long stretches of dialogue which did not suggest any basis for crosses or even of any real movement, I realized that my plan was probably inadequate. So I began to draw and added areas so the furniture could be rearranged. All in all, everything seemed workable for the first act. I began to plot the first scene and immediately stumbled on a vexing obstacle. In Ibsen's text the carpenter (Regina's father) enters the living room without motivation and stands there doing nothing while engaged in a lengthy conversation. But this is the theatre. There must be changes! So I invented this: From the start of the act he is busy fixing the lock on the door leading into the garden. Then a steamer passes. The carpenter begins to hammer. At the noise, Regina hurries in. The scene continues with him doing his job while she tidies up the room. However, to do this it will be necessary to change some of the words in the very beginning and to transpose some phrases. What else can one do? I think it would be pedantic not to make such modifications.

February 4, 1905

I arrived late at the theatre, almost two o'clock. Simov and Kolupayev were upstairs working on a model based on yesterday's drawing. Kolupayev was glueing, Simov was making sketches. We went all over it again and criticized it. The originality of the design lies in the shallowness of the downstage acting area (near the footlights). There was too little space for movement, so they decided to shift the furniture more centre. Near the fireplace they decided to put a glazed tile bench with cushions and to angle it parallel with the footlights. The bay window is good and serves to give both a dark and multi-coloured effect since the panes will be various tones of bottle glass. The cornices and the ceiling will be decorated in Norwegian style, with reindeer, primitive figures, etc. The ordinary wooden panels on the walls will be replaced by panels covered with velvet or silk (old materials, beautiful, faded). They maybe bordered or plain. I recall that the floors in Norway or Sweden are painted white (we decided to do that too.) A balcony with a door leading out on to it proved to be necessary for the *mise-en-scene*.

In discussing this we discovered an effect. We will put a trap below the balcony, cover the balcony with a painted tarpaulin and let rain drip down onto it. The water will flow over the tarpaulin into the trap; and the balcony floor, as well as the balustrade, will gleam with the moisture. We decided to omit the steamer. . . .

February 5, 1905

Judging from Simov's sketch he is using modern Norwegian art. That's what it looks like. In an old family house, filled with the sins of generations, suddenly we are confronted with *art nouveau*! This is dreadful. I must find some way of aging it. There is something in the back of my head but I can't quite pin it down. . . .

February 6, 1905

Simov did not appear. Luzhski brought some things in from Madame Take, who lived for a long time in Norway—nothing of interest or adaptable for stage use; also some books. They suggested something about life in Norway and the play's background. But the day was wasted.

In the evening I did some writing and found myself caught up in the early scenes. I sensed the stillness in the house, the wet weather, the time of day. Various details became clear and sharp. I have written as far as Oswald's entrance. That is a great deal.

February 7, 1905

We sent for those lazybones, Simov and Kolupayev. During the morning they finished the sketch (it's not bad but it's still too much on the *art nouveau* side) and they built the first rough model without any colour at all. We set the stage according to the model. It turned out they had made a mistake in their measurements. We had to remove the fireplace because it blocked the bay window. The bay window will have to be enlarged. The other windows are so wide they look like gates. The space for the writing table is too small. The staircase is too high and it resembles the one in *Pillars of Society*. Anyhow there was a general resemblance to *Pillars of Society* so we decided to reverse everything (strangely enough we always tend to overload the left side of the stage).

The arrangement of furniture proposed was not good. We had to change it because it left two tables standing right beside each other. This was not the case on my drawing, but I had not made it to scale so this is how it turned out on stage. It originally looked as though, by placing the pieces parallel, there was an effect of style. This must be tried out.

Now I see that the bay is a place where one can stage a scene, and even the terrace can be used; the main acting focus is by the staircase, which runs parallel with the footlights. I made a note of a place that calls for Oswald to have his moments of deep thought: on the bench next to the fireplace—he can stand on it beside a pillar (at the foot of it he looks like a condemned man, bound to a pillory).

In general the long shallow room is turning out to be original, and four to five characters playing near the footlights are thrown into high relief. It is all very easy to play in. But now we have to add some archaic flavour.

5

The Scenographic Vision Employed

There is nothing more difficult than to become critically aware of the pre-suppositions of one's thought. Everything can be seen directly except the eye through which we see. Every thought can be scrutinized directly except the thought by which we scrutinize. A special effort an effort of self-awareness is needed: that almost impossible feat of thought recoiling upon itself almost impossible but not quite.

—E. F. Schumacher

In the last analysis the designing of stage scenery is not the problem of an architect or a painter or a sculptor or even a musician but of a poet.

—Robert Edmond Jones

You can't invent a design. You recognize it, in the fourth dimension. That is, with your blood and with your bones, as well as with your eyes.

—D. H. Lawrence

The following sections contain a number of written explanations whose purpose is to expose the reasoning behind sceno-graphic designs as they were realized on the stage. They were recorded here in order not only to reveal the thinking process that informed those designs but to demonstrate that there can be a logical approach to the art of scenography, as well as an intuitive one.

It might be wise to draw the attention of the student scenographer to the fact that it will be a rare instance when, at some point during the production of a play, he does not have to defend in some manner, usually verbally, his decisions, explaining how and why he has created a partic-ular design. Such explanations are a customary as well as a necessary part of the planning of any production (although they would not be pre-sented, as here, in written form). Naturally it should be expected that the scenographer will most likely present his ideas in visual terms; but he must also be prepared to communicate in words, when called upon, the reasons behind those ideas. How well the scenographer uses words varies from person to person; many com-petent artists find it difficult to "talk" a design without extensive use of pen and pencil. Quite possibly, the real test of a design (apart from its final realization on the stage) lies more in this form of communication than in words or theo-ries. Nevertheless, discussion of the sceno-graphic concept—what it means and how it fur-thers the aims of the production as a whole—is usually the only sure way the director can determine if he is understanding the scenogra-pher or, equally important, if the scenographer is understanding the director's point of view. The danger in talk, however, is that it can all too easily become an end in itself, degenerating into vague rationalization that serves no real purpose in the creative process. Be that as it may, most scenographers will admit, discussion of ideas is a positive activity that can, when both parties strive for honest exchange of points of view, produce results in production more satisfactory (and no less personal) than the efforts of either the scenographer or director alone.

The ability to explain underlying motives in a design is an important part of the student scenographer's development, not only to inform others of what he is trying to achieve but to make himself aware of these motives as well. Often he will not have a clear understanding of what these are until he has faced the challenge of explaining or defending them to another. It is during this formative stage, moreover, that he should be encouraged both to improve his techniques of verbal communication and to learn the all-important difference between positive defense of an idea and self-protective rationalization. Most important of all, he must learn not to hide behind superficial theories. ("Truth is concrete," according to Bertolt Brecht and so is good theory.) Scenographers, like almost all other artists generally withdraw from discussions when their ideas or schemes are attacked or refuted; but by carefully thinking out what he will say and why he believes as he does, the scenographer will have a much better base from which he may present or defend a considered position or design.

From here on, what follows is more or less a matter of individual critical and artistic judgment. What is presented does not purport to define any universal principles or to suggest that any such principles can be formulated out of these examples. Most of these judgments, although not all, were made by a single person, the author of this study; to that extent they represent a singular and limited point of view. (I prefer the open stage or variations of it even in the proscenium theater, rather than strict proscenium theater productions, and this predilection will be fairly obvious.) No apology is made for this situation, since a universal point of view is not possible even if it were desired. It will be noticed too that while these examples are not given as the final word on, or the solution to,

the design problems in them, what is shown by way of illustration is presented from a predominantly realistic point of view, although not necessarily a naturalistic one. The style of the designs is based less on personal expression (as the designs of Salvador Dali always have been) and more on actual observation of the world as it appears to the outer eye. In other words, the designs presented and discussed will be more likely to resemble figure 163 than figure 164.

While the first design is not an attempt to reconstruct in the theater a replica of an actual room as it might have existed in the O'Neill family home in Connecticut at the turn of the century—the locale and time of O'Neill's biographical drama—it is certainly a more realistic representation than is the setting for the de Ghelderode play, which in no way tries to show how the countryside in the province of Brabant looked during the sixteenth century. The reason for this particular emphasis here is not a prejudice against imaginative designs; it is that as interesting as they might be in themselves, they are too subjective, too personal to have much value in demonstrating the process of scenography, which is our real focus. (Besides, there are many designs that simply cannot be "explained" but still may be artistically right for the productions they serve. The examples that were selected are those that allow discussion—if not final justification—of this scenographic process rather than of the artistic merit of the individual scenographer or his results.) This process is, it is hoped, a fairly logical one (although it never can be that completely), at least to the degree that it might aid the student new to the study of scenography to gain some insight into the conceptual considerations that all scenographers—no matter how intellectual or intuitive—must face. The prime reason for this book is to show that it is possible—perhaps even unavoidable—to study and build on this process.

From Text to Stage

We now begin to consider the process by which the written words of the text engender visual ideas for the scenographer; the subjective limitless world of the imagination must begin to come to terms with the objective limits of the

Fig. 163. Design for *Long Day's Journey into Night*

stage. This is a critical juncture in the design process; it is the time when the scenographer directs attention to the range of possibilities open and—more important—begin making selections from those possibilities. Yet the problem is never the same from production to production; some scripts tell more than others, some tell little at all, some give misleading or false information (written stage directions in play text from companies that licence performance often are taken from the original production's prompt script and will frequently contain information that relates to that production alone). Formal research into period or decorative style, important as it will be at a later time, is not a primary focus at this point.

If, as suggested in the next few pages, the first reading of the play is possibly the single most influential creative act in scenography (not all would agree with this contention however), then the steps discussed in this section are cer-

Fig. 164. Design for *Three Blind Men*

tainly next in importance. These define—although only crudely and tentatively—the limiting boundaries of the design; they also represent the scenographer's personal concepts—intuitions as well as rational decisions—in fundamental forms. Quite possibly this is the period when the scenographer's intuitive powers operate most strongly. It is a also dangerous period since in almost every instance—that is, at the beginning of every production—many more concepts and possible solutions present themselves than the scenographer can ever use or fully investigate. Knowing what to reject, as well as what to pursue and refine, is as important as getting an idea in the first place. Most scenographers—although they find this period to be an exciting one—suffer doubt and anxiety as they explore the various possibilities open to them. It is rare, most scenographers will assure you, when the initial ideas or drawings prove to be usable without development and modification. That young scenographers may quickly stumble onto successful solutions is—and must be seen for what it is—an occasionally stroke of good fortune, not a method of work by which one can build a career.

Initial visual thoughts do possess merit; often they may contain in unrefined form the seeds of ideas that eventually prove useful in the final design. During this period, a scenographer should trust least painting and drawing skills; that is, one should not too quickly make detailed or finished sketches until the dramatic structure of a scene is clearly understood. The necessary framework of a scene—or the place of a scene in relation to others—can only be derived from a thorough analysis and an understanding of not only what the text does say but what it leaves unsaid. It is well to recall the words of Peter Brook: "What is necessary . . . is an incomplete design; a design that has clarity without rigidity; one that could be called 'open' as against 'shut.' This is the essence of theatrical thinking."

The Spectacular versus the Pictorial Image

Before proceeding further, let us address ourselves to a troublesome point that needs clarifi-cation: the difference between *pictorial* images and *spectacular* images. In much that follows, these terms *pictorial*, *spectacular*, and, later, *diagrammatic* are used. For now let us examine the first two of these terms.

The first thing we must do is to divest ourselves of the popular connotation of the term *spectacular*. Few do not know what is meant when the term is used; what is less known is the role spectacle plays in the theater, and the role it played in the past. Currently spectacle is frequently used as a pejorative term; it implies an antagonistic role to "serious theater." It is not an uncommon attitude that the two—drama and spectacle—are pitted one against the other, or at best, that they represent mutually exclusive poles of intent. A common perception persists that they are, in fact, absolute enemies on the stage: that is, when spectacle is present, the drama automatically takes a back seat; when the drama is to be emphasized, spectacle must, perforce, be limited.

There is little contention, however, that an important part of any theatrical event, of "going to the theater," is the enjoyment of this thing called *spectacle*. Especially in our present age, spectacle has become increasingly important to that enjoyment. What is important to understand, however, is that spectacle is not necessarily an unessential frill unthinkingly added to a production simply to excite less critical faculties of an audience. It is in many instances a necessary part of a drama's presentation. Even in the relatively simple, often sparse, surroundings of theatrical history's greatest periods—the Greek theater or the Elizabethan for instance—spectacle played an important part of the dramas being presented. Moreover, there is indication that the world's greatest playwrights always considered spectacle as an integral part of the theater performance, not just added adornment to it. Spectacle has its own special place in theater; it is ingrained in the basic nature of it. Only when spectacle thoughtlessly usurps the human scale that we need question its use. We should realize too that as one moves through time, or from geographical culture to culture, differences in emphasis do appear: English scenography of the 1950s is different from that of the 1970s; but English scenography of the 1950s was vastly different from Italian scenography for the same period of time.

The same holds true as one moves from country to country or from period to period.

Actually, throughout most of theatrical history, there has been no intense division of purpose between *drama* and *spectacle*. These two elements have, in point of fact, not only been allies on many occasions but have often been necessary to one another. But not always. Scenic production has been used during various periods of theatrical history to draw an audience into the theater simply for the sake of visual excitement. This was especially true of the English theater directly after the Restoration of the English crown in the early 1660s. Those who remembered the playhouses before the closing of the theaters during the period of the Commonwealth were amazed and delighted to see not only new plays being done in "scenes" but familiar ones—such as Shakespeare's—being given explicit locales painted on canvas instead of using the actor's words to set the scene, as Shakespeare had done. As the noted present-day Shakespearian scholar Gary Taylor tells us: "Shakespeare's plays had been performed [in Shakespeare's time] in ornate theatres by actors lavishly costumed, but upon stages that gave no pictorial representation of place or time. The action in every play happened on a flat, dusty promontory between 'the heavens' above (an overhang painted with astronomical symbols) and 'hell' below (an invisible hollow, reachable by trapdoors). Location was signaled, if at all, by three-dimensional functional props like thrones, not by two-dimensional inert painted scenery. This definition of space is cosmic and human: 'where we are' is determined by theological architecture and portable accessories. The post-Restoration definition of space was, in contrast, Cartesian and Newtonian: there was no theological frame, only a succession of spatial categories—unindividuated 'stock' scenes, generic woods or gardens, city squares or interiors—neoclassical generalities of locale that framed recurring situations in many different plays. . . . changeable scenery fundamentally altered the history of Shakespearian performance, criticism, and editing."

Even from the beginning of this new approach to theater, there were critics who drew attention to the danger of making the scenic machine more important than the playwright's text.

During 1675, only some fifteen years after the introduction of scenery as a regular feature of drama, complaints that scenic production was causing a general debasement of the theater began to surface. *In Love in the Dark*, a play from that year, contains in its epilogue this passage:

For Songs and Scenes, a double Audience bring,
And Doggrel take, which Smiths in Sattin sing.
Now to Machines, and a dull Mask you run. . . .
....
  Players turn Puppets now at your desire,
In their Mouth's Nonsense, in their Tails a Wire,
They fly through Clouds of Clouts, and showers of
  fire.

Nor have we, some three hundred years later, outgrown the taste for such spectacles; both the London and Broadway productions of *Phantom of the Opera* required that the theater be extensively altered in order to accommodate the scenery (nor would *Starlight Express* have caused much stir at the box office if mounted on an Elizabethan stage).

The problem lies not in the use of spectacle in the drama but in the intent behind its use. Spectacle can be—and should remain—a vital part of theater. It is entirely possible, moreover, that the drama attains added importance when spectacle plays its proper role. The key to this successful collaboration lies in the phrase "its proper role."

The early part of the twentieth century fostered an unceasing war not on spectacle but on the abuse of spectacle. (Although some philosophies have ruled spectacle out as an evil in and of itself; Jerzy Grotowski's *Towards a Poor Theater* is an eloquent but devastating attack on every element of the present-day theater with the exception of the performer.) There is no doubt that much of the drama of the past three hundred years has relied too heavily on scenic production; during the nineteenth century the plays of Shakespeare, in particular, were given productions that caused the text to suffer if not expire entirely under the weight of heavy scenic mountings. It has only been during the past twenty or thirty odd years that the inherent spectacular elements in his plays (and it is these elements that we should always search out) have once again been restored to a proper balance with his text. The Royal Shakespeare Company in England has, perhaps, become the single most important company in the world to seek out these inherent elements, to redress this balance; in their productions there has been a steady progress toward a form of spectacle whose function is not to "improve" the text with pictures but to legitimately augment it with the form of spectacle that Shakespeare himself envisioned as he wrote.

To deny categorically the element of spectacle as a totally unthinking and devastating influence is an austerity that robs the theater of one of its greatest joys: the visionary aspect of a theatrical performance. The works of many contemporary playwrights do, it must be admitted, demand a restrained mode of production. We must be equally careful to consider the positive aspects and virtues of spectacle in its relationship to the drama. Consider this observation by Aldous Huxley: "'Carpentry,' said Ben Jonson sarcastically, 'is the soul of masque.' His contempt was motivated by resentment. Inigo Jones was paid as much for designing the scenery as was Ben for writing the libretto. The outraged laureate had evidently failed to grasp the fact that masque is a visionary art, and that visionary experience is beyond words (at any rate beyond all but the most Shakespearean words) and is to be evoked by direct, unmeditated perceptions of things that remind the beholder of what is going on at the unexplored antipodes of his own personal consciousness. The soul of masque could never, in the very nature of things, be a Jonsonian libretto; it *had* to be carpentry. But even carpentry could not be the masque's soul. When it comes to us from within, visionary experience is always preternaturally brilliant."

Huxley is, of course, speaking of one form of theater that did emphasize spectacle at the expense of the drama. But he touches on a point that has validity if applied to a larger aspect of theater. And while no theater artist should remain unaware that different forms of theater must be considered separately in respect to their scenographic needs, we should be sensitive to what those differences are, not foster a false division between spectacle and drama. Even from the few words quoted above it should be deduced that spectacle and pictorial extravagance are not necessarily the same things; while pictorial extravagance is almost invariably spectacular, an image can be spectacular without being pictorially extravagant. And while these two have often been thought to be inextricably linked, the attainment of spectacle does not automatically assume the attendance of the pictorially extravagant. When, for instance, the actor playing the title part in a recent Royal Shakespeare Company production of *Coriolanus* was instantly thrust high into the air on two staffs held by his followers (fig. 165), the effect was extremely spectacular even though the ingredients of this stunning image were simple enough. Here the human actor was made the focus (as well as the cause) of the spectacle, and the resulting image had a purpose. While the audience's attention was immediately engaged and excited by this bold acrobatic vaunt into space, a distinct "message" was sent to them concerning the innermost nature of Coriolanus himself: here, we were shown, is a fearless warrior, not only one who is idolized by his men, but one who will allow himself to be put into extreme physical danger by them at the very moment they are seeking to glorify him. The act of suddenly being placed high above the heads of other men in this manner both shows exultation at being a victor and demonstrates a foolhardy disregard for personal safety. Spectacle in the theater, then, is most exciting and satisfying to an audience when the human performer is the center and cause of it. Pictorial extravagance, on the other hand, almost always occurs at the expense of the performer and creates a chasm between the action of the performer and the environment of the drama; the character gets lost somewhere between. In many instances, there is no possible way in which the human performer can compete with an image that is so outside his own scale or so immune to his own capability of affecting (fig. 166).

Indeed, spectacle is a requisite element to our enjoyment of theater; but we must always keep in mind that it is a primary responsibility of the scenographer to integrate this element with other needs of the production. Nor does sincerity of purpose always protect the scenographer from erring on the part of the spectacular at the expense of those other elements. Even so great a theater artist as Robert Edmond Jones occasionally made grave errors in artistic judgment, and the total production suffered for it.

Fig. 165. Scene from *Coriolanus*. Courtesy of the Governors of the Royal Shakespeare
Theatre, Stratford-upon-Avon. Photograph by Reg Wilson

In the bad old days of changeable scenery the most that Shakespeare had to contend with was a stuffy excess of prettiness and fussiness, so insignificant that one blast upon his bugle sent it to heel.

But now another poet challenges him to take the stage if he can, a poet vividly and most authoritatively intent upon quite a separate drama of his own—the drama of light and shadow, of line and mass, and all the romance and splendor and significance which he so intensely, so devotedly feels in these things that he is willing to put them over by whatever means comes to his hand, through even a play of Shakespeare, or

Fig. 166. Scene from *Aïda*

any other medium having in it something that, by a little dexterity, he can wrench into their service. But alas! he cannot entirely stifle the writhings and mutterings of the drugged giant, bound hand and foot to be shaped, colored, clothed and nailed flat to the design of an artist believing in a world created out of repose, order, pure color, the most absolute simplicity, the absolute banishment of the detailed or the colloquial, a world above all statical, like the Arch of Trajan seen against a consistently night-sky. But does anyone really think that this is Shakespeare's world? (Virginia Tracey, letter to the *New York Times*)

Here spectacle did get out of hand; even though Jones made an effort to avoid the pictorially extravagant, that effort failed. Now consider this description of *Macbeth* that David Addenbrooke records in his book, *The Royal Shakespeare Company*:

John Bury's setting and many of the production effects used in *Macbeth* were theatrically exciting. The stage floor was entirely composed of great lengths of blood red carpet; this carpet was laid in sections and as the play proceeded, various sections were removed from the stage to reveal "bone-bleached white" areas which grew and diminished as the action demanded. The carpet was said to look "like heather," or "like the hide of some great beast," or—most obviously—an ever-present symbol of blood. The action moved against rugged backing; ". . . a geological set, red granite cliffs like blood-rinsed Old Men of Hoy." The opening sequence of the play was a scene of brilliant inventiveness and effect: ". . . quite electrifying. There was a 'white sheet' across the stage. Suddenly there was a great crash of thunder, a flash of lightening and silhouetted against this sheet you saw Witches—with a crucifix held upside down. The thunder crash was followed by a quick blackout—the 'sheet' was flown away—and the Witches were discovered standing on hummocks of this red carpet, pouring blood down the inverted crucifix and chanting, 'When shall we three . . .'. While this scene was going on the carpet started heaving and moving, and there was a sense of earthquake—of everything unstable—almost as though the stage itself was boiling! . . . when the Witches disappear, soldiers—who had been hiding underneath the carpet—stand up through it, ready for Duncan's entrance."

The good versus evil and "blood will have blood" theme was carried through the production, and the symbol of the Cross was prominent throughout.

Even from this brief description it is evident that spectacle played an important part in the scene. What is different, however, is that the spectacle employed here it is more supportive of the performer's performance, that it has become an integral part of the actor's world, not just a superficial element of it.

Unfortunately during the past ten years— from 1980 until 1990—the trend toward creating spectacular productions that dwarf performers by size and complexity of detail has resurfaced particularly in the musical world. The trend has not gone unnoticed by more thoughtful critics. Here is what Donal Henahan says in a *New York Times* article, "An Opera? No, It's a (Gasp!) Set," dated 29 March 1987:

The "Bayreuth hush," the reverential, all but papable silence that prevails during performances in the Wagnerian shrine known as the Festspielhaus, is part of operatic legend. Well, don't be jealous, New York. You are developing your own legend: the "Metropolitan gasp." The latest manifestation of the phenomenon—the sudden, communal drawing-in of breath, followed by fervent hand clapping—comes during Franco Zeffirelli's (sometimes known as Puccini's) "Turandot." The Act I, Scene 2 curtain rises on a dazzlingly bright throne room so grandiosely proportioned that the poor old Emperor of China becomes a fly on a distant wall. Does it matter that the set is so deep that people in balcony and family circle seats complain that they cannot see the Emperor or, in fact, much of what it is that goads the main floor to stunned applause? Apparently not to those who control the destinies of the Metropolitan, where every new production evidently must now offer at least one show-stopping visual coup rivaling Broadway's "Starlight Express." What does all this current fascination with empty spectacle mean, and where can it lead? A Spenglerian pessimist might point out, for a start, that Rome in decline specialized in circuses.

Of late, the Metropolitan has been building up quite a repertory of such gasp-worthy, essentially anti-musical moments, including scenery designed and directed by Mr. Zeffirelli. The Met should consider putting on an entire evening of these big scenes, without music. Money would be saved and no real opera lover would be offended. . . . the director and/or designer, whether avowedly traditional or avowedly avant-garde, has indulged his fantasies and for a moment taken the spotlight away from the composer. Audiences, trained to savor that spectacle, now actually pay for the privilege of seeing Mozart or Handel upstaged. It pains one to say so, but despite superficial differences of age, nationality, politics or artistic ideology, our era's most celebrated opera producers must be considered brothers under the skin: they live for the thrill of impersonating their creative betters.

Spectacle in the theater must be, therefore, not a garnish to the play but an integral part of it; the prime purpose of spectacle is to render the words of the text back into the original images and actions that caused these words to be written in the first place; more than that, it is the responsibility of every new production of that text to seek out not just the unique solution but the solution that best serves the time in which the production is being done. No doubt, many twentieth-century scenographers feel themselves walking a tightrope between self-serving image making and self-denying service to the playwright's text. Robert Edmond Jones did not set out to pervert the playwright's intention; still the introduction of spectacle into a production brings the scenographer to a line that must be approached with consideration and humility; crossing that line can subvert the efforts of many as we frequently note in many of today's productions. The development of a professional scenographic vision demands that we find the best way possible to serve two demanding masters: self and the text. It is not the kind of image used on the stage that makes it an appropriately spectacular one or an inappropriately pictorial one, but the usefulness of that image in the context of the production. The responsible scenographer seeks to create on stage an imagery that augments a playwright's or a composer's original vision.

Environment in the Scenographic Process

If it is true that the scenographer is, as Robert Edmond Jones has written, an "artist of occasions," it is equally true that he is an artist of environments. Although not quite the same, these two designations do work hand in hand; what is done is somehow caused by, or reflected in, where it is being done.

First, let us be clear how we do use the term *environment* in the theater. Most dictionaries include the following information in their definitions:

1. Surroundings, milieu, conditions, influences, circumstances, Fr. *mise en scène*; habitat, medium, element; entourage, ambience, atmosphere, mood, aura; setting, background

2. Encirclement, surroundings, encompassment

As one can see, the word has many shadings to its meaning. In the theater we also use the term in several ways:

1. To indicate physical theater form: *arena stage* (performance area completely surrounded by audience); *open stage* (performance area surrounded by audience on approximately three sides); *proscenium arch stage* (performance area in separate space directly opposite auditorium space)

2. To describe ways a playwright incorporates physical descriptions both in stage direction and in character dialogue references

3. To describe the process by which scenographers gather documentation materials for use in the physical setting

Of the various ways environment is used in the theater, two stand out: (1) the physical environment's effect on characters of the story, that is, their reaction to it as characters, and (2) its effect on an audience. Environment often aids in delineating characters or plot lines; the effectiveness of plays such as *The Lower Depths* depends largely on an atmospheric background that shows visually the conditions that physically affect characters of the story. Playwrights usually are careful in the selection of an environment for their story. It has become standard practice for twentieth-century playwrights to give this information as stage directions although they cannot, as novelists do, completely "spell it out." Eugene O'Neill's careful description of the environment for *Desire under the Elms* is an excellent example that demonstrates the usefulness of such information. Tennessee Williams's notes delineating the atmospheres of particular plays also prove useful to those producing them. Some playwrights, however, have admitted that specifying the atmosphere to be created on stage is not only out of their hands but outside their understanding (See Michel de Ghelderode's letter in "The Scenographer's Relationship to the Playwright" in part 3).

In the theater, the function of environment does not have a single purpose. Although an important purpose is to provide appropriate places for the actions of plays to transpire, an auxiliary function is to underscore moods and atmospheres attendant to those actions. Environment should rarely, however, attempt this in an overt fashion. That is, the setting of a production should not *tell* the story or usurp attention that is rightfully the performer's. (Any theatergoer can cite numerous productions where the setting was so explicit, so overpoweringly atmospheric that the individuality of the performer got lost in the visual complexity of the setting. Andrew Lloyd Webber's musicals often leave audiences with vivid memories of the setting, whereas little recall of what happened in them remains. Critics who reported audiences leaving the theater "humming the scenery" had frequent opportunity to complain in the 1980s. There is little evidence that visual reticence is becoming fashionable as we approach the year 2000.

What is environment in the theater? How is it brought into the design of a setting? For what purposes is it desired other than as visual background or to create what we call a mood? Environment in life outside the theater is often subtle, its effects not easily seen from day to day; how does the consideration of environment change when we work on the stage?

Two basic questions emerge when scenographers begin to consider the environment in the theater. These are:

1. How will this environment help the actor to display more of his character's possibilities in terms of action than he could display without it?

2. How will this environment increase the depth of visual understanding of an audience and thus deepen their total appreciation of the production?

Suppose that a playtext calls for an alley in a large city. We might find research sources images like that shown in figure 167. In this image the environment can be divided into two basic

Fig. 167. Environment diagram with background and
physical properties

Fig. 169. Environment diagram with physical properties
only

categories: things primarily visual (background) and things primarily usable (properties). Figure 168 shows the background portion of the alley: the brick walls. Everything that a performer could use directly has been removed.

Figure 169 shows an opposite situation. Here the walls are removed; only those things that affect a performer directly—that can be used or that channel movement—remain. The *sense* of the environment still persists however, perhaps more so than in figure 168. There is no doubt, either, that figure 169 is more important to the performer and that he will relate to it, quite possibly make use of it, much more than he would figure 168. Even visually figure 169 is more im-

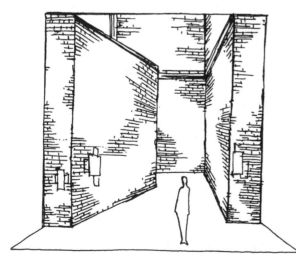

Fig. 168. Environment diagram with background only

portant than figure 168. If a choice had to be made between the two, as it would be necessary if this alley were to be put into an open stage form such as figure 170, there is little doubt which would be cut out and which would be retained. In any form of staging—arena, three-quarter, or proscenium arch theater—the principle exposed here would remain basically true; environment is not only visual but physical as well. There are good reasons for considering the physical aspects of environment more closely today than even twenty years ago. Until recently an actor's performance requirement had become almost entirely psychological and was structured along these lines:

1. Thought—analysis of text and script directions to determine "inner motivation." The great emphasis put on this step was in reaction to the virtual thoughtlessness of the philosophy of acting during the nineteenth century, which put its emphasis on individual bravura performance, beauty of voice, and grandiloquent styles of delivery.

2. Verbal reaction—rehearsed and set in rehearsal to produce as little variation in performance as possible.

3. And, only after these two steps were assured, action.

In "real" life words arise from actions as well as actions resulting from words; in theater, all too often, actions become secondary to the words. This philosophy results frequently in

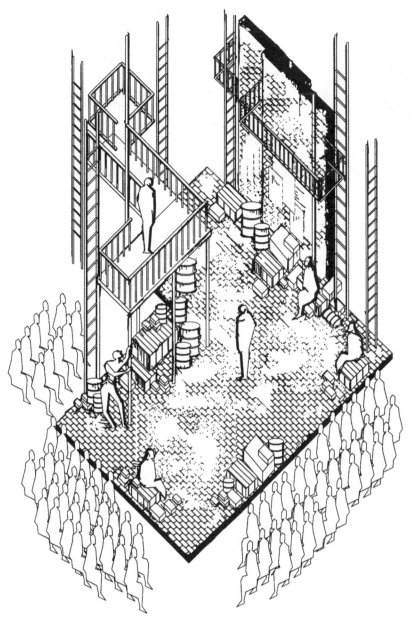

Fig. 170. Environment diagram developed for open stage

thinking that the actor's primary function is to make the playwright's intentions plain through verbal communication; action becomes an auxiliary adjunct to this performance. Now the prevalent trend is to make movement and physical involvement with the scenic environment at least coequal in importance (if not more) with verbal utterance. While this reversal of priorities is by no means universal, it has had a marked effect on actor's training programs throughout

the whole world of theater. It is quite possible that the most significant companies of our period have created new priorities unique in the theater history of Western civilization.

The 1970 Peter Brook production of *A Midsummer Night's Dream*, for example, used circus equipment—notably trapezes—that the actors were required to use in the performance of their roles (fig. 171). While this might seem to be a "stunt" device imposed on the play, it had a

Fig. 171. Scene from Peter Brook's *A Midsummer Night's Dream*

curiously appropriate application to this production; the circus elements used by Brook's performers helped to reveal a whole new aspect of this particular play. What this trend plainly indicates is that the actor is being forced—and is forcing himself—into a much more active relationship with the physical aspects of the stage. By contrast, compare Brook's approach to that of Max Reinhardt as shown in figure 172.

The basic problem for the scenographer, therefore, is to bring two desires of the present-day theater together, that is, to create a scenic environment that not only shows abstract qualities of the production more directly but also makes these qualities physically accessible to the actor.

While the creation of an environment, as we have noted, is not restricted to naturalistic settings alone, for our purposes it is easiest to see and understand in that context; it is hard to conceive of *The Lower Depths*, for instance, in a set-

ting that did not present graphically and explicitly to an audience the abject conditions of the people who must live there. Still, the fashioning of an environment on the stage is not limited to reproduction of accurate detail or completely factual documentation. Very often the scenographer must abstract the qualities of an environment for a design rather than create a locale that might plausibly exist or pass for the actual place. The result might very well be, in fact, a creation that could exist nowhere but on a stage in a theater and still serve as an authentic environment for the play and the characters in it. As a matter of fact, it is impossible to lift a real locale, such as a room, from its natural context and put it on the stage without sacrificing some of its original form to the demands of the stage. For example, the house where Stanley and Stella live in *A Streetcar Named Desire* may very well be in or near the older part of New Orleans, the French Quarter; and while this area still retains much of its original charm, the actual type of house where the play takes place is, in all probability, of the "shotgun" variety. These houses were built in the late nineteenth century and are structured in the most economical manner—living room in the front, bedroom in the middle, kitchen and bathroom in the rear. They have little in common with much of the older architecture that often exists alongside these newer structures. Actually, there is no strictly residential section in the Quarter; warehouses and private houses coexist side by side (fig. 173).

Too often, though, the scenographer working on this play ignores this less romantic style of architecture because he becomes intrigued with the more interesting possibilities of the older buildings that exist in the Quarter. He selects the graceful wrought iron and interestingly weathered stone of these buildings in favor of the ill-kept rotting wood and mildewed wallpaper of the later structures. But it is precisely this second type of building that creates a more accurate environment for this play; the cramped rooms and cheapness of these houses figure greatly in Blanche's final downfall. She is extremely sensitive to her surroundings, and this place where she now finds herself is an active force that helps to drive her mad.

Still, one cannot simply reproduce a facsimile of this house on the stage; there the features of

Fig. 172. Scene from Max Reinhardt's *A Midsummer Night's Dream*

the actual location (which quite possibly might also include elements of the older more romantic buildings surrounding this one house) must be taken apart, studied, and then reassembled to fit both the performer's needs in acting the play and the audience's view. Again, as we have said before, the resulting setting may be both a fitting and "real" environment for the play, as well as a creation that belongs nowhere except in the theater (fig. 174). These configurations assume many forms, however: figure 175 shows another setting derived from the materials shown in figure 173.

If a scenographer does nothing more than reproduce without question or thought the findings of his research and documentation, then his designs will offer nothing more than the antiquarian atmosphere of a museum instead of providing a living and developing place where the characters of the play can live and move. If, on the other hand, he uses documentation in its proper role, which is to reinforce the intuitive solutions that he has distilled from study of the text, he will find that the specific needs of the play often will dictate much of what can be used and what may be disregarded. This ability to select, reject, and simplify is, if you study the body of work of a mature scenographer, something that grows over the years and is the hallmark of the disciplined artist. In *Designing for the Theatre*, Jo Mielziner takes himself to task for failure to select, reject, and simplify.

As late as 1931, when I should have known better, I committed an equal offense against honest theatre with my settings for Schnitzler's *Anatol*. I looked upon this lush and lavish production of love and high life in old Vienna as a banquet table arrayed with tempting delicacies exclusively for me. Scene after scene offered an opportunity for elaborate pictorialization, and I

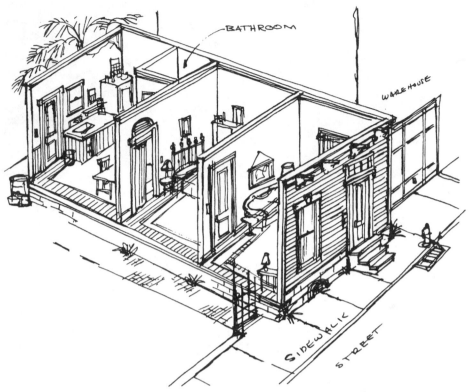

Fig. 173. New Orleans "shotgun" house

Fig. 174. Design for *A Streetcar Named Desire*

Fig. 175. Alternative design for *A Streetcar Named Desire*

seized each one greedily. It was one of the first times in my career that I received widespread praise from the critics, and there was applause from the audience every time the curtain went up on a new scene. But the fact was that my settings usurped attention that properly belonged to the script and the actors. The nine settings were nine separate and attractive pictures in which the scenes played, and played well, but there was no unity to the production. It would have been better to sacrifice the completeness or charm of an individual set in order to lighten the production, speed the changes, and bring harmony to the evening as a whole.

There has been a trend during the past two hundred years for the playwright to become increasingly more specific in his placement of action and in the description of the necessary details of the setting of his play. At one time, those in charge of creating a visual picture (scenery) for the stage merely provided the place described by the playwright, and only that place. If the play required a front parlor, or a palace, or a garden, the scenographer would feel that he had fulfilled his obligation when he had provided the features specifically set down by the playwright. (Quite often he read not much more of the play than the directions at the beginning of acts or

scenes.) During the fairly recent past, the scenographer's attention was focused on, and ended at, the boundaries set by the playwright and by those things which lay inside those boundaries; if a room was desired, the scenographer considered his task completed after he had set the line of the walls, assured the placement of necessary objects within those lines, and satisfied himself as to the correctness of the decor. Hardly any attention would be given to the world that lay outside and beyond the immediate area shown on the stage, that area that satisfied the minimum requirements of the script. (*"What world?"* the scenographer of a hundred years ago would inquire. *"The only 'world' behind the set is back-stage!"*) If any of that other world were shown, it would usually be confined to only so much as could be seen through a window or open door; little opportunity for actions outside the room proper would be given the performers.

With the development of cinema and later television, it became possible to follow actions of the story through successions of locations rather than confining the action of the story to one static locale. The mobility of the camera opened up whole worlds. Early writers for the film, even though sound was missing, first thought as stage

Fig. 176. Church scene for *Much Ado about Nothing*

playwrights; soon they discovered that stage-writing technique was not suitable for the camera, that such an approach simply did not work. Playwrights working for the stage began to create scripts as if they were writing screenplays. Flashback, montage, cross-fading, all part of the moving picture, became part of playwriting for the stage.

Even though many playwrights have gotten over the desire to write movies for the stage, the cinema's influence on scenographers designing plays written under the influence of film cannot be altogether discounted or forgotten. Required to cope with plays that use cinema technique, scenographers began to apply this same mode of thought to plays not specifically written with such treatment in mind. According to this line of thought, numerous works written before the advent of the cinema might benefit from considering the settings of these plays in larger more complex visual contexts than heretofore imagined. Many dramatic works, the reasoning goes, lend themselves to cinematic techniques better than the mode of production they have become associated with. Every Shakespeare's play, for instance, is composed of short scenes that quickly jump from one location to another, from one time period to another.

Let us consider for a moment how plays were produced just prior to the advent of the motion picture. In the last half of the last century almost all plays were given elaborate and cumbersome productions. Shakespeare, for example, was produced quite literally; every scene was realized on the Victorian stage as completely as carpenters and (especially) painters were able. Time required in shifting the scenery as well as limited stage space and expense meant that there had to be a priority applied to the settings. Large scenes and long scenes naturally received the most attention; the smaller ones were either incorporated into the larger ones, transposed, or more likely, cut out entirely. The structure of the play was determined by the needs of the scenery alone, all other considerations became secondary. In the last years of the nineteenth century into the first years of the present one, directors and scenographers began to see the error of this static approach to Shakespeare as well as to the theater in general. Figure 176 shows a setting produced in typical manner of the late 1800s.

Since that time, however, the static picture has given way to the fluid image; scenes no longer end with the lowering of the curtain, they dissolve into the next one. The curtain, in many cases, has disappeared altogether in the proscenium theater. It has been conjectured that if Shakespeare were living today, he might very well be writing for the films or television rather than for the stage. Although not a wholly valid assumption, it does point out one significant aspect of his technique of playwriting, which is that much of his effect depends upon a fluidity of action and a variation of locale that is similar to what we experience in the cinema. While the camera has caused the stage to reevaluate many of its production philosophies and modes of presentation, something more fundamental has slowly eroded the old conceptions of what a stage setting should be, and more importantly, what it should do.

As early as the first part of the nineteenth century, attitudes toward acting and directing began to change in fundamental ways; particularly performer's involvement with physical environments on the stage and the director's increasing demand that performers become more physically active within those environments. The time when performers need not concern themselves about character until an entrance is made—that is, comes into sight of the audience—has long since gone. Practically every serious actor working in the Western theater spends much time "building a character"; not only does he deeply consider what his inner motivations are while actually on the stage, he also gives as much thought to what the character has been doing before his entrance as to what that character will do once he has left the audience's immediate view. Undoubtedly some schools of acting have made too much of this practice; some actors, in reaction to the "method" philosophy (the deeply psychological approach to character development) contend that they do not to any great degree think of these characters when not on the stage or in a scene, but their performances often belie this denial (and sometimes unfortunately substantiate their claim). English actors, particularly those of older generations, are often notably antagonistic to this "inside-out" approach to theater. The late Laurence Olivier was often outspoken in his mistrust of too much intellectual analyzing of the actor's motives or his psychological states of mind. (It is curious that it was Olivier who based his interpretation of Hamlet on a number of questionable abnormal psychological quirks he perceived in the character; probably a great many more than any American actor would have thought of including.)

Is this kind of thinking that attempts to understand the past and future of the play the province of the actor or director only? Is this extended view of the play, and the speculations it engenders, of no importance to the creative processes of the scenographer? It is probably every bit as important to the scenographer as it is to the actor to consider what the script does *not* say as well as what it specifically demands. Moreover, a great number of scenographers have come to believe that one of their chief functions is to assist, in whatever way they can, the actor in continuing to "be" his character beyond the line set by the script's "enter" and "exit" directions; that in addition to creating the locale definitely needed for the play's primary actions—those stated or implied by the script—the scenographer must also consider, and sometimes provide, the surrounding environment, even though the playwright does not specifically call for it in his directions. What is being advocated here, however, is not necessarily a matter of reproducing on the stage a naturalistic copy of a piece of the world outside the theater. The theater of today asks more of scenographers (as well as the actor) than mere realism; but, like many other artists, their experimental learning processes are often based in realistic observation.

Until well into this century the task of scenographers was only to be responsible for a setting that showed a specific locale (fig. 177C). In today's theater a play may often require that they be responsible for more than this limited and limiting view; it may ask that they provide a larger more comprehensive context in which the action of the play may develop. (Most of the plays of Tennessee Williams simply cannot be played in a single location; almost all require composite settings.) Even if not directly called upon to do so, the scenographer may decide to open up the setting to include a larger view (fig. 177A and B). Undoubtedly this is due to the fact that many scenographers now design in other forms of theater like the cinema and television and have had their visions expanded by the experience. It is certainly true that many directors now wish to have the opportunities afforded by opening up the action of the text to include acting areas not envisioned or called for by the playwright.

But what is the import of this diagram? How

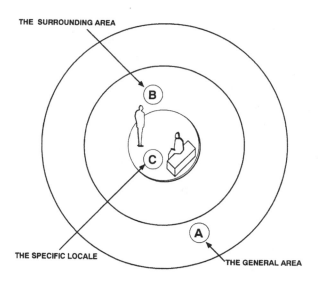

A. THE OVERALL VIEW SEEN FROM A HIGH DISTANT POINT SHOWING WHERE
   THE ACTION OF THE PLAY (OR A SCENE FROM THE PLAY) TRANSPIRES

B. THE ADJACENT LOCALE TO THE SCENE'S ACTION

C. THE EXACT LOCATION OF THE SCENE'S ACTION: THE PLACE THE AUDIENCE
   IN THE THEATER SEES ON THE STAGE — THE SETTING

Fig. 177. Specific locale and surrounding environment
    diagram

does this concept of expanded interest and vision work? Let us take a look at a drawing made
from research materials dealing with a Dublin
street during the period that Sean O'Casey wrote
Juno and the Paycock, the Dublin of the 1920s—
the time of the "troubles." It shows a street with
building that might very well contain an apartment similar to the one described in the script
(fig. 178). Another view with a wall removed
(Juno and her family live on the second floor)
can be seen in figure 179.

The purpose of this inspection is to begin to
understand better the relationship of the exteriors of the buildings (those were not difficult to
find) with interiors (those are comparatively easy
to research also). What the scenographer must
do for himself, however, is reconstruct—as it
has been done here—a view that combines both.
That is not so easy to obtain; and it is at this point
that the scenographer's peculiar function begins.

Copied from actual photographic sources
contemporary with the play's action, matters of
detail can be determined concerning the outward form of Juno's flat; it is easy to ascertain
styles and details of architecture, building materials, and the effects of age (although not as
clearly discernible here as in the photographs

from which the drawings were made). However,
what is more important is not only how this one
building looks (its literal visual description) but
how it fits into its greater context; equally important is the "feel" the scenographer develops by
understanding how the particular place the author sets his action relates to its adjoining surroundings. It is quite possible the scenographer
will find a need to employ this information in
ways not envisioned by the author or at least not
specifically noted by him in the play's specific
written directions.

O'Casey announced that he was going to
write a play about a certain Johnny Boyle (an
actual person with whom he was acquainted and
who had been a member of the Irish Republican
Army). Later, when he had finished *Juno and the
Paycock*, this character, Johnny, had few of the
lines in it and was not, apparently, a major character. But, if one examines the play closely, noting who speaks and how much, he will find that
Johnny is an important structural device; he is
not so much an active character as an important
pivotal one—one around which the other characters of the drama gravitate and relate, even
though the action of the play does not center on
him. Indeed, much of the play's meaning and
force depends upon him and cannot be understood if his function is not clearly realized or
presented; the scenographer can very much help
the actor portraying Johnny (and thus the play
as a whole) to expose what he thinks and how
he feels. While part of the scenographer's task is
to show how Juno has done the best she can to
make this tenement flat a home for her family,
it is also his obligation to show an audience what
Johnny *sees* as he sits alone, crippled and broken
in spirit, looking out of the second-story apartment window. *What does he see?* Row after of
row of dirty, stained rooftops of other tenement
buildings. Bleak structures crowding in on the
place he lives, cutting him off from the active life
he formerly led before his arm was blown off
and his usefulness to the IRA has ended. Much
of this play, even if it does not seem to deal
directly with it, reveals the influence of the atmosphere and nature of the neighborhood O'Casey
knew and set his play. To concentrate only on
the interior of the room where the main action
of the play transpires is to ignore more than half
of the world O'Casey includes in the play.

Fig. 178. Dublin street, 1922

The important part that the visual atmosphere can play is not the only reason to consider what the surrounding environment is like, nor is visual atmosphere the only advantage to be derived from exploration of the environment's possible uses. Expanding the limit of what the audience sees means that you also increase the possibilities of what the actor can use. Consider the scene where Joxer, the profligate crony of Captain Boyle, must hide to escape the wrath of Juno: not able to exit through the front door and not able to escape through a back entrance (there is none), Joxer—on the advice of the Captain— decides to risk hiding on the small roof outside the window. Usually, once he is through the window, the actor is lost to the audience's sight. But, if this area is included in the scenographer's thinking, the audience will be able to see and appreciate Joxer's precarious position and obvious discomfort more than being told about it later. In a simple box interior (all that O'Casey asked for), these possibilities are lost both to the actor and the audience.

What the scenographer finds in his or her

Fig. 179. Apartment building on Dublin street

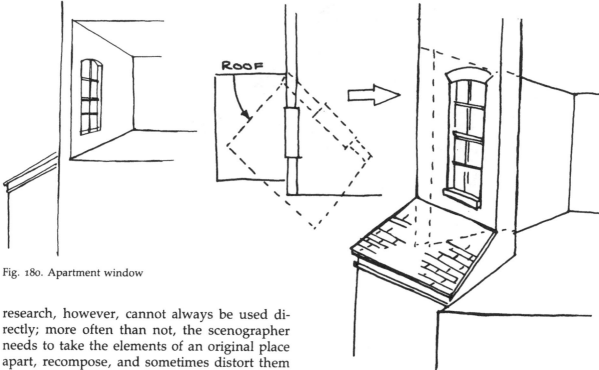

Fig. 180. Apartment window

Fig. 181. Apartment window in two parts

research, however, cannot always be used directly; more often than not, the scenographer needs to take the elements of an original place apart, recompose, and sometimes distort them in order that they may become useful in the final setting as it appears on the stage. This requires both judgment and reticence.

The window that might be used for Joxer's place of hiding may exist in an original building, although not be completely usable as it is. The scenographer quite possibly might take a window (fig. 180) and twist it to allow the audience a better view of the outside (fig. 181). Or he might take a wall (fig. 182) and cut it away, leaving the window, so that more of the outside will be exposed (fig. 183). Perhaps this is the window that Johnny sits at and looks out of; what he sees the audience sees too (fig. 184).

In this visual editing process we begin to see that the needs of the actor in part determine the scenic requirement of the play; by providing a window seat we give Johnny an opportunity to stay at the window for a longer period of time than he might if he had to stand. In a sitting position he is also better able to show the audience an attitude of quiet despondency. O'Casey did not specifically ask for this scenic structure; but it is possible the play will be a little clearer, perhaps more meaningful, by its inclusion.

These are but two isolated examples of how widening the scope of the locale—showing more than the author asks you to show—can have a

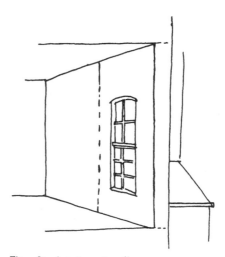

Fig. 182. Apartment wall

specific usefulness to the actor in his attempts to create his character in a greater dimension. However, there is a danger for the scenographer who provides a more comprehensive environment in which the characters of the play may live and move. With the very best intentions this practice can lead to environments so elaborate

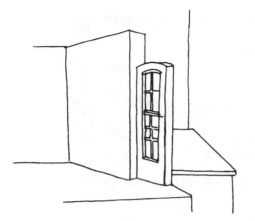

Fig. 183. Apartment wall removed

Fig. 184. Cutaway wall

and detailed that the visual impact overpowers the work of the performers. No matter how realistic the play, scenographer and director should take care that in reproducing detail for its own sake—satisfying though this activity may be—they do not forget the greater purposes of the production. Remember the warning of Robert Edmond Jones: "We may put aside once and for all the idea of a stage-setting as a glorified show-window in which actors are to be exhibited and think of it instead as a kind of symphonic accompaniment. . . . as evocative and intangible as music itself." This is a criterion that applies to all

designs regardless of style or period; the larger aims of a production should be foremost in the scenographer's thoughts and work. Perhaps it would not be unwise to remember, at this point, the old adage that *what does not help hinders*.

Figure 185 is a line drawing of a production of *Juno and the Paycock* that puts into practice some of the ideas just discussed. The scenographer and the director decided to show more than the author dictated. The method used to arrive at this result was, essentially, to find and study research sources that allowed the scenographer to see the larger area where O'Casey's specific locale might be set. In showing more than they are usually given opportunity or scope to do, the director and scenographer provided a setting that would both aid the actor and, at the same time, give the audience a better look at just how this specific flat fitted into a larger more understandable context. By showing both inside and outside, it was possible to see just how much Juno had overcome the harshness of a hostile world.

While this way of seeing is not a formalized method or system, it does bear further examination. Therefore, we will now take another example to show in more detail how the concepts exposed in the design for *Juno and the Paycock* works. And since this method of approaching the design is based on the assumption that reconstruction of the larger picture can be helpful to the scenographer in several ways, not merely as literal documentation alone, let us give this activity a name. Since it is predicated on seeing the environment from a distant perspective and then progressively moving in, let us call this activity an "overview."

The Overview: *Madame Butterfly*

Although it is not necessary in every work to know in precise detail the complete lay of the land surrounding the locale being represented, in some instances it is not time wasted to consider the larger area of which the specific place (that which shows in the setting on the stage) is a smaller part. The overview is, in operation, much like a camera panning from a great height and distance, and down into the actual spot where the action is to take place.

Fig. 185. Design for *Juno and the Paycock*

As an illustration of this process let us examine the opera *Madame Butterfly*, by Giacomo Puccini. Puccini himself had a fairly keen sense of direction and is, particularly in this opera, much more consistent and logical in designation of locations than most opera composers. Only once in the text, however, does a character (the American counsel Sharpless) refer directly to key landmarks. But since this one reference is quite specific and detailed, it makes it necessary for anyone involved in making decisions concerning the design of the setting to make clear judgments as to these locations. Not only must Butterfly's house be seen in relation to its immediate environment, but its relationship to the nearby city of Nagasaki, to the points of the compass (since times of day complete with setting and rising suns are integral parts of the opera's action and development), to the location of the harbor where important events take place (although not seen by the audience), and to the open sea (which Butterfly watches for the better part of three years) must also be considered. The overview is a means by which some of these decisions

can be realized. At this stage of planning a production, it is important that both scenographer and director work very closely. Of course, it should be understood that no amount of research would turn up the exact place Puccini had in mind, since this work was modeled not on a real occurrence but on another stage work, *Madame Butterfly* by John Luther Long and David Belasco. Therefore, in order to reconstruct this larger picture, the scenographer and director must first search the text carefully for points of reference and possible clues to physical relationships that might correspond to actual similarities in and around the actual city of Nagasaki. There are a number of references in the text that help to some degree. To list a few:

1. The house is away (how far?) from Nagasaki, but close enough to walk to or to determine a ship's flag in the Nagasaki harbor with a small telescope.

2. The city is below the level on which the house stands. The American counsel complains of the steep climb but remarks on the splendid view one gets from this vantage point. It is possi-

ble, we can deduce from his remarks, to look down into the harbor and to see out into the open ocean.

3. The house is fairly isolated inasmuch as Butterfly sees very few people during a three-year period, and it is apparently not on any main path or road.

4. The house is surrounded by a fairly extensive garden, since at one time during the course of the opera Butterfly and her maid must gather a great number of flowers quickly.

These are but a few of the clues derived from the text. This information, along with drawings and photographs of actual scenes in and around Nagasaki, serves as a start in making a simplified long-range view of the general area (fig. 186). But what value does this drawing have for the scenographer? So far, we have nothing we can put on the stage. Several things are clearer, however; these being the basic relationship of the house to town, harbor, and sea. It is also now possible to establish the very important directions of north, south, east, and west. (Times of day, as stated earlier, figure importantly in the action of the opera, and much of the action is

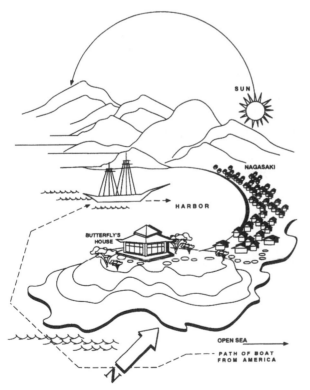

Fig. 186. Immediate area around Butterfly's house

linked to these time changes.) Even at this point we can see, knowing practically nothing about the finished design, that if Butterfly is looking toward the harbor she is looking north and that the sun will rise on her right and set on her left. We know that if she has her back to the harbor, land is to her left and the open sea lies around her. (Even now we begin to perceive certain internal relationships to the story; she is isolated from the city, that is, cut off from all past life and family, yet she can see down into the town where those who were dear to her live and where her own past life was spent.) This sort of orientation is especially helpful to the director and actor, since it gives them a "world" in which the arbitrary direction-less world of "up-stage," "off-right," and "downstage-center" becomes one in which realistic and meaningful relationships may be established. (There might even be a special case made for working in this manner on this particular opera, since, although highly romantic in conception, its basic idiom is realism.) The primary objective, however, is to increase the visual understanding of the scenographer.

The next step in this process is to "zoom in" to take a closer look at the focal point of this general view. This is, of course, Butterfly's house and its immediate surroundings. We now begin research into the actual materials that will show Japanese architecture, and more important for the moment, how it relates to its exterior setting. Figure 187 is a drawing (actually made from the period the opera is set in) that gives a closer view of the area we wish to study. Still, a set cannot be designed from this picture, although it might help to clarify a few more points and questions. At this same time, we also need to begin study of plans of domestic architecture and individual houses in more detail (fig. 188) or perhaps pictorial views of this architecture (fig. 189).

These items, considered by themselves, do not help much; they must be incorporated into a drawing that will allow the scenographer to study the possibilities of the first general overview at closer range. While figure 189 is pictorial, figure 190 is more helpful. This is not a floor plan for a setting on the stage, however. Nor do we, at this point, have an audience orientation, an angle at which the scenographer wishes to compose his setting for the view of an audience. There are still too many questions that must be

Fig. 187. Japanese landscape from *Landscape Gardening in Japan*, by Josiah Conder. Courtesy of Dover Publications, Inc.

answered, too many possibilities that must be explored before that decision can be reached and the design finalized. But, even now, it can be seen that this process—zeroing in from a distance—is more comprehensive and artistically productive than simply putting together a set composed of flats and platforms like a jigsaw puzzle. This is not the time for stagecraft. Scenographers, whenever possible, let the setting design itself, that is, evolve out of the research materials they uncover as these data come into contact with their imagination and awareness of the requirements of the script. What we are attempting to show here, then, is a technique (although not complete in itself or automatically productive) that will most effectively allow this

to happen. And while this procedure may seem arbitrary and a matter of cut-and-dried research technique, the scenographer will soon find that he or she is never relieved of the need to make subjective judgments that are, for want of a better word, artistic in nature.

As we proceed in our design, in our use of this technique, we must think progressively smaller and in a more comprehensive manner; having seen and comprehended the larger picture, we are free to let our eye become more selective and study the various elements of the total at closer hand. For instance, our plans show a porch outside the house, but it does not reveal anything about it in any great detail. Part of the problem now becomes more specific; not only

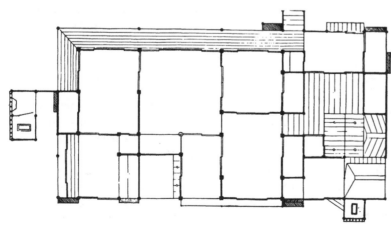

Fig. 188. Drawing of Japanese house plan from *Landscape Gardening in Japan*, by Josiah Conder. Courtesy of Dover Publications, Inc.

Fig. 189. Drawing of Japanese house from *Landscape Gardening in
Japan*, by Josiah Conder. Courtesy of Dover Publications, Inc.

do we need to find a more precise view of this porch, we want to know how it fits into the architectural scheme of the house and gain some idea of the manner in which it relates to the area surrounding the house. Figures 191 and 192 are two such drawings that answer some of these questions. From these two drawings (taken from *Landscape Gardening in Japan* by Josiah Conder, a Dover paperback book), it is possible to determine a number of useful pieces of information that will have a direct bearing on the final design:

1. Construction and design of the porch itself
2. Landscape features immediately around the house

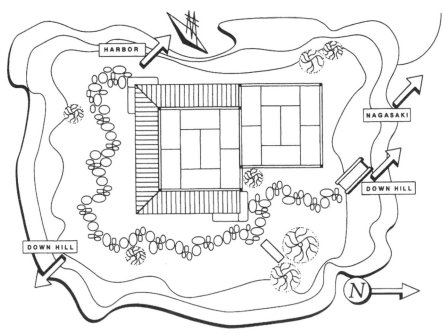

Fig. 190. Plan of Butterfly's house

Fig. 191. Detail of Japanese house from *Landscape Gardening in Japan*, by Josiah Conder. Courtesy of Dover Publications, Inc.

3. Construction and design of the house

4. An indication (although not completely clear) of materials (wood, bamboo, stone, tile) used in the house and in the landscaping

5. An indication of the native vegetation and, more important, the manner in which natural features are manipulated into an aesthetically pleasing union with the architectural structures.

While these items are by themselves helpful, the advantage we gain by working from the larger view to the smaller is obvious; our understanding of the total is more complete than if we started with these details alone and tried to incorporate them into a setting without a firm knowledge and understanding of their relationship to the total picture, the complete environment.

It should be understood, however, that this approach to the design of a setting leaves out more than half of the work the scenographer must accomplish if he is to make a significant contribution to the production as a whole; what the scenographer has not done is to consider just how this information will be used by the director and the performer. Nor is it suggested that this particular approach will be applicable or useful in all productions (plays or operas); while opera in general seems to have more inherent limiting factors in it, no one approach could every serve for all. Figure 193 is a design based on the materials and observations revealed or "explained" by implementation of the overview principle.

This is, by necessity, a quick and sketchy accounting of how the overview process works; there are many important steps—mostly subjective—that are left out. Recounting their specifics would only be useful to someone designing this particular opera. However, the usefulness of such a technique and procedure (though purposely limited here) can be seen even at this stage. It should also be pointed out that many

Fig. 192. Detail of Japanese house from *Landscape Gardening in Japan*, by Josiah Conder. Courtesy of Dover Publications, Inc.

Fig. 193. Design for *Madame Butterfly*

scenographers are able to accomplish this total understanding without going through the complete process in a formal manner as outlined here; some are able to jump directly to the last stages of design with the same depth of understanding that another could only attain by doing the whole process step by step. The reasons for this are manifold; but the greatest reason this might be true would depend on the individual scenographer's previous experience, not only in the actual design of scenery for the stage but in the exposure to information through travel and allied studies—art history, architecture. Travel gives the scenographer a firsthand understanding obtainable in no other way, although the study of photographs, books, artworks cannot be discounted.

Research into Action: *Romeo and Juliet*

"Suit the action to the word, the word to the action." Shakespeare gave this advice to the players in *Hamlet*, but he meant it for all players everywhere, and while he did not have the scenographer in mind, that advice, nevertheless, holds equally well for him. But before we can determine what these actions in *Romeo and Juliet* are and just what the scenographer's responsibility to the production is in this regard, we must find out something about where they happen.

Actually there are, at the beginning of our research, two Veronas, not one. There is the Verona that can be discovered by factual research, and there is the Verona of Shakespeare's mind. Just how alike or how different are they? A great part of our job (but not all) is to find out how much of one is in the other. At the end of our work there will be a third Verona: the one we must create on the stage. We must also ensure that that Verona will be every bit as vital and as equally a living place as the originals, no matter what style we impose on the production, no matter how much or how little our Verona owes to those other two. Above all, *it must be a place where action is possible.*

Keep in mind, however, that what will be presented in this example has, to some extent, been put into a logical sequence (although not completely), even though the import of the actual research was not as quickly or easily perceived or organized as it might appear. What is important to note, then, is the clearly exposed principle that the research process does not follow a single line of development from conception to final resolution. In fact, no final resolution will be offered here and it would not really be worth much if it were—what is demonstrated is not *how* this play should be designed but the means by which one scenographer did arrive at a solution he considered workable. And, what is even more important to note and comprehend is that the final design will always be in great part the result of many digressions, intuitional judgments, some incorrect assumptions, and numerous backtrackings; in other words, what we have is a voyage of exploration with all the attendant dangers such an expedition might entail. At any one moment in the creative process, the artist is working on more than one level and in more than one way. It can be a dangerous terrain.

Two households, both alike in dignity,
In fair Verona, where we lay our scene,
From ancient grudge break to new mutiny,
Where civil blood makes civil hands unclean.
From forth the fatal loins of these two foes
A pair of star-cross'd lovers take their life;
Whose misadventures piteous overthrows
Do with their death bury their parents strife.
The fearful passage of their death mark'd love,
And the continuance of their parent's rage,
Which, but their children's end, nought could
    remove,
Is now the two hours' traffic of our stage;
The which if you with patient ears attend,
What here shall miss, our toil shall strive to mend.

The first four lines of the prologue give us an overall view of the city—again, to use the terminology of the cinema—from a long shot. Shakespeare's purpose is not only to tell us where this play will take place but to give us a more total physical context in which to understand it: a place where, for some very particular reasons, the inhabitants are at war with each other. The second four lines call our attention to

a particular event (the story of Romeo and Juliet) that occurs within this particular context. The third four lines tie these two, the city, and its feuding troubles together, and then, with a short apology customary in the Elizabethan theater that says, "if you didn't get or understand the point of what this whole thing is all about, don't worry; we will work very hard to show you," he sets you down squarely in the middle of the situation he has just been describing—a city street of Verona. Shakespeare was an able dramatic craftsman; he did not waste words, nor did he waste time establishing what he considered to be environmental conditions necessary to the progress of the story. We would do well to heed this careful path he has led us on. We find, by following these strong clues, that the city itself is a very real and active force in the structure of the play; almost an actor in its physical presence and hostile nature. Before making any drawings or decisions, though, we must set up an order of things to do, a priority of activities:

1. We must read the play. (If for the first time, just for the pleasure of reading an unfamiliar work. For the time being, theater does not exist.)

2. Having read the play, even once, certain things are evident and understandable, much more probably not. Certain questions will immediately want to be answered: Where did the play take place? When? What was this place—Verona—like then? Where can I go to find out some answers to these questions?

These questions can only be answered by doing a little preliminary research concerning the play itself, the structure of the Italian city states of the sixteenth century, and the nature of not only the cities during that period but of Verona in particular. (Although not a large country, the cities of Italy have always been highly individual places, each with its own interests and unique features, each with its own distinct collective personality, and each with its own style of living. All cities of the world are similar in this respect; no scenographer in America would think of considering Boston as the same kind of city or having the same features as New Orleans; San Francisco would never be confused with New York. Still, when we travel into the past in our imaginations, all too often cities in other countries or in other times are thought of as being essentially alike.)

First, let us set a probable date for the play's action. Shakespeare got his plot from a story by Luigi da Porto, of Vicenze. The Italian novel that contained the story did not appear until some years after the death of da Porto and was first printed in 1535, and since da Porto died in 1529, it is probable that the story could be historically placed around 1526. There is good reason to believe that Shakespeare's play was first produced between July 1596 and April 1597, and it was in all probability costumed in contemporary English dress. This information helps us orient our research problem to a period of time and to the possibility of at least two primary approaches to the visual design of the play: England at the end of the sixteenth century or Italy during the first quarter of the sixteenth century. And our first problem is not to confuse the two.

Now let us take a brief look at the primary locale of the scenes in the play, the city of Verona. During the investigation of this play we will, time and time again, return to study the city itself and to the question of how it relates to the play in general, but now all we want is some general information.

Verona was an important Renaissance city. But before that, it was a medieval city. (Perhaps Shakespeare had visited it at one time or another; we really do not know. He certainly knew of it by report if not from firsthand.) All medieval cities were similar in some respects while being quite different in others. One of the important similarities, at least for our purpose, is that they were all *walled cities*. Why is this fact important? Most scenographers know that, given a number of facts, certain ones seem to have an importance more felt than understood; the fact that Verona is a walled city is just such an example as will be demonstrated later. So, let us start our investigation of this particular city at this point, that is, at the city wall.

In *Medieval Cities*, by Howard Saalman, the following information can be found: "The walls of medieval cities were subject to an immutable law regarding their dimensions: they invariably followed the *smallest* possible perimeter! Every extension of the town diameter—every extra foot of wall—implied greater building costs, greater maintenance expenses, and a larger garrison for adequate defense. The attitude of the medieval man on the street regarding expenditure of pub-

lic funds on enlarging the walls may be summed up with equal simplicity: as long as *his* house and *his* ship, *his* parish and *his* church were contained within the walls, then the wall was quite big enough."

The selfish attitude displayed during that period of time does not seem to have changed by the time of *Romeo and Juliet*. Not only was there an attempt to keep out those not contained with the walls, even those within the city were also constantly at war with one another; the feud between the Montagues and Capulets had its origin in the historical one (nor was it an uncommon occurrence) between the families of Montecchi and Cappelletti. A question we might begin wondering about is *why* did they fight, what was the real basis of the feud, and was the city itself to blame in any way? Already we can begin to relate a little to what we know of the city; some of its problems we ourselves face today. Again Saalman provides relevant comment: "The story of medieval cities is of people trying to get *into* town, not out of it. . . . Only in the city were there the conditions and facilities for an existence based on the production and exchange of goods and services as opposed to the life of baron, soldier, and serf on the land outside. . . .The closer you could get to the center of the city which, with its crossing roads, was the hub of the most intense urban activity, the better!"

The walls of Verona were built much earlier than the time of *Romeo and Juliet*, so it is reasonable to assume that the town was beginning to suffer the pangs of urban areas that outgrow their hard limits—the city walls—and cannot expand those limits easily. Let us listen to Saalman once more: "Space within the walls was limited. Two inherently different interests were competing for this space: private and public interests. . . . Perhaps the most essential difference between public and private space within a city is their relative penetrability. . . . Private space, whether it be enclosed or open, is impenetrable. *It cannot be used, crossed, or entered except by consent of the owner*" (italics mine).

Now we are beginning to acquire information that has some bearing on our own problems in this particular play; a number of important scenes in *Romeo and Juliet* deal with situations that require someone to gain access to or escape from a confined area. And several also deal with people in places where they should not be. Perhaps it would be well to list some of the scenes that depend on the closing up or closing off of a space in order to keep out or keep in a character in the play.

1. The balcony scene is the first scene that comes to every mind, and it deals with confinement of Juliet (one of Capulet's family—whom he thinks of as part of his goods and possessions to be disposed of as he sees fit) from the rest of the world. She even asks Romeo, fearfully, how he was able to penetrate the security of the private garden surrounding the house. His reply: "On love's light wings did I o'er perch these walls, / For stoney limits cannot hold love out." In other words, he had to climb the wall, and, discounting his poetic fervor owing to his youthful passion, it probably was not all that easy. (One production comes to mind where Romeo had some difficulty in getting on top of a wall— actually to hide from the band of friends looking for him—and then disclosed himself to Juliet from that position. When he came to the above mentioned lines, he gave them as if the scaling of the wall were an easy and insignificant accomplishment. The laughter from the audience was desired from the performer; it gave the youthful ebullience so often lacking in performances that stress only the formal poetry of the play.)

2. The second most important scene, in many respects, is the tomb scene. Its quality of confinement is especially horrible, so much so that Shakespeare carefully describes it before we actually see it; Juliet tells us directly of her fear of being too long in the locked tomb and the consequences that might result. (This speech contains many good images that might help in the visualization of the tomb):

How if, when I am laid into the tomb,
I wake before the time that Romeo
Come to redeem me? There's a fearful point!
Shall I not then be stifled in the vault,
To whose foul mouth no healthsome air breathes
    in,
And there die strangled ere my Romeo comes?
Or if I live, is it not very like,
The horrible conceit of death and night,
Together with the terror of the place—
As in a vault, an ancient receptacle,

Where for these many hundred years the bones
Of all my buried ancestors are pack'd
Where bloody Tybalt, yet but green in earth,
Lies festering in his shroud where, as they say,
At some hours in the night spirits resort—
Alack, alack, is it not like that I
So early waking—what with loathsome smells,
And shrieks like mandrakes' torn out of the earth,
That living mortals, hearing them, run mad—
Or, if I wake, shall I not be distraught,
Environed with all these hideous fears,
And madly play with my forefathers' joints,
And pluck the mangled Tybalt from his shroud,
And in this rage, with some great kinsman's bone,
As with a club, dash out my desperate brains?

3. The first time Romeo sees Juliet is at a private ball given by Juliet's father. Romeo is a gate-crasher and is almost thrown out by Tybalt when he is discovered.

4. One of the worst punishments that a dweller of a Renaissance city could receive was not death but perpetual banishment. Romeo was not alone in intense devotion to his home city and his great distress at being physically shut out of it. It may have been a small place, relatively speaking, but it was the whole world to him.

These, then, are necessary elements of the plot's construction that deal directly with enclosure; much of Shakespeare's imagery either directly or indirectly alludes to these restraining structures. If, however, one were to seek the dominating image in this play, it would be found to be, as Caroline Spurgeon has pointed out in her admirable study *Shakespeare's Imagery* (a book that should be in every scenographer's permanent library), light in various forms. It is certainly true that the scenographer must be keenly aware of this dominance and the special poetic atmosphere these images impart to the play. But the prevalence of light images—or rather light (usually faint or brief in duration) set against a vast dark void—is more symbolic in nature than accurate in descriptions of actual situations or things found in the literal world of this play. As scenographers we must also be aware of that imagery that summons up the concrete detail and helps us create the objective world where the characters of the play live and move. And the single most important element in that world is the wall. *Romeo and Juliet* gets its very special atmosphere precisely from the environment out of which the

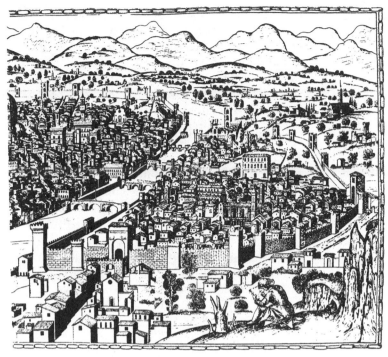

Fig. 194. Sixteenth-century Italian city

characters have evolved; so basic and integral are the functions of this one element—the wall—to the total picture that to disregard its purposes is to practically misinterpret the entire play.

Now let us begin a more detailed study of the city in relation to the space it encompasses. A contemporary view of an Italian Renaissance city (ca. 1470) gives us a fairly accurate idea of what Verona might have looked like (fig. 194). While this is not Verona, it does have many features in common with it. And when we represent this diagrammatically (fig. 195), it can be seen even in this simple diagram that within the confines of the city lie not one area but many—spaces within spaces or, rather, walls within walls, and all crowding one another.

Now let us select the two spaces that concern us most directly—the larger confined area within the city wall and the smaller independently controlled spaces—the houses of Montague and Capulet. This also can be represented diagrammatically (fig. 196). "Two households both alike in dignity" (i.e., power, wealth, position in the city). We now have a simple geometric image of the situation that exists when the play begins. However, there is more to the situation than is told by this diagram alone. The influence and

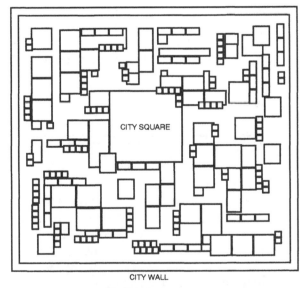

Fig. 195. Diagram of Italian city

the power of the respective houses is maintained and guarded by members of the family (families were large and had fierce loyalties to the family name) and retainers, who also tended to adopt their masters' points of view and allegiances. They carry this allegiance with them when they leave home base and enter into the areas com-

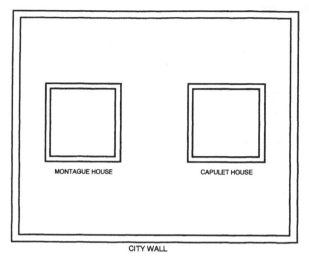

Fig. 196. Montague and Capulet households

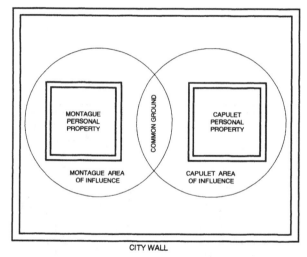

Fig. 197. Montague and Capulet influence

deadly one. In many of these encounters, the confrontation begins as a type of schoolboy daring and ends in deadly seriousness; Mercutio is finally killed in such a fray. And it is not until the very last moment before he dies that he himself sees the senselessness of the whole foolish situation. A scenographer might very well wonder just what Mercutio *sees* in those last moments of his life. Examine that scene for a moment: Tybalt is in the act of baiting Romeo, who, now in love with Juliet, does not want to fight with her cousin. Mercutio takes Romeo's remarks for cowardice and challenges Tybalt himself.

MERCUTIO: Tybalt, you rat-catcher, will you walk?
TYBALT: What wouldst thou have with me?
MERCUTIO: Good King of Cats, nothing but one of
  your nine lives; that I mean to make bold
  withal, and, as you shall use me hereafter, dry-
  beat the rest of the eight. . . .
TYBALT: I am for you. (*Drawing.*)
ROMEO: Gentle Mercutio, put thy rapier up.
MERCUTIO: Come, sir, your passado. (*They fight.*)
ROMEO: Draw, Benvolio, beat down their weapons.
  Gentlemen, for shame, forbear this outrage!
  Tybalt, Mercutio, the prince expressly hath
  Forbid this bandying in Verona streets.
  Hold, Tybalt! Good Mercutio!
  (*Exeunt Tybalt and his Partisans.*)
[Mercutio has been stabbed at this point.]
MERCUTIO: Help me into some house, Benvolio,
  Or I shall faint. A plague a' both your houses!
  I am hurt;
  They have made worms' meat of me. I have it,
  And soundly too. Your houses!

mon to the city's general population. For this reason, the influence of the Montagues extends a little farther than their own personal property and neighborhood. The same can be said for the house of Capulet. Our diagram might take on this added dimension (fig. 197).

We can see immediately that the situation lends itself to disputation through overlapping spatial claims. Indeed, the very first scene of the play is a confrontation between factions of the two rival houses in just such an instance. Although they are both on "neutral ground," the basis of the scene's action is to determine who has the preeminent right to the space at that moment. Actually it is a kind of game; but it is a

What was a moment before just a joke and a game has now turned sour and serious. For a second time, a character in the play has made an allusion to the rival houses as being equally matched; the Chorus speaking of their official recognition as important families, Mercutio now implying they are to be cursed for their equally unbending willfulness and pride.

For a moment put yourself in his place, with lifeblood flowing out and a premonition that death is near. Take a good look around the street and try to see what he is seeing for the last time: narrow dirty streets, ancient walls much used and many times repaired, yellowed and dirty from men and dogs having made water on them for hundreds of years, windows and doors

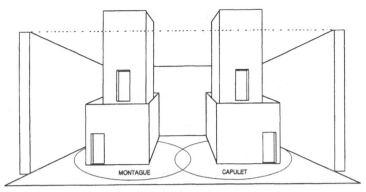

Fig. 198. Montague and Capulet environment

locked and barred; and only by looking straight up can a little of the sky be seen. This is a far cry from the romantic image of Romeo in the moonlight under Juliet's balcony. Yet it is the very same play. All too often a scenographer will concentrate only on the attractive scenes of this play and completely ignore the more brutal and repellent aspects of it. But Shakespeare meant us to know that side of the story as well, or else he would not have been so careful to provide the many details that clearly show the cruel and ugly side of life in Verona.

Let us consider this aspect of Verona. The first scene of the play is the occasion of a fight similar to the one in which Mercutio is provoked and slain. And like this scene, it also takes place in a street somewhere in the city. Two men of the house of Capulet are walking along with no real purpose or destination in mind. (Their aimlessness helps the playwright underscore the mindless way in which the various brawls in the play get started.) Very early in their discussion they allude to walls and the use of them when walking in the street. (This banter is based on the symbolic nature of walls as well as the actual physical properties of them.)

SAMPSON: I will take the wall of any man or maid of Montague's. [Keeping next to the wall on a street was the pedestrian's safest way to keep from getting soiled either by being splashed from the dirty streets or by being hit from slop jars being emptied from second story windows. To "take the wall" could also be an insult; ordinarily to yield it would be considered courteous, but, in this case, it would show cowardice.]
GREGORY: That shows thee a weak slave; for the weakest goes to the wall. [He changes the mean-

ing here somewhat—a favorite pasttime in Shakespeare's day was wordplay.]
SAMPSON: 'Tis true and therefore women, being the weaker vessels, are ever thrust to the wall [this is an allusion to a sexual assault on women]; therefore I will push Montague's men from the wall [take the best place] and thrust his maids to the wall [sexually assault them].

This gives a pretty fair idea of how each side regarded the other. At best it is not a friendly atmosphere in Verona; but what is significant is that so early in the play an important clue is given the scenographer concerning some elements of the physical environment the play will demand.

A more complete diagram of this total environment may now be attempted (fig. 198). Keep in mind that these diagrams do *not* represent settings or scenery; their purpose is to help us understand the play in relation to its simplest physical needs (although psychological elements also play a part in these considerations). Once this stage has been reached, the scenographer must begin to "test" the rightness of his ideas and plans. He must begin to think about individual scenes and their needs in greater detail. By this time some investigation of actual materials from the period would be underway— paintings, photographs of architecture, and the like. But what are we looking for? Right now we are primarily interested in buildings, walls, juxtaposition of structures that might show the overcrowded aspect of the Renaissance city. We might also begin to look for details of architecture—door and window design, treatment of building materials, techniques of building structure. But is that all we need? No, not quite.

So far we have been working from the outside in—observing the overall environment rather than noting individual events within that environment, that is, scenes from the play. (This is not entirely true, but the greater number of our observations have been basically external, not greatly concerned with specific actions.) Still, it would be safe to say at this point, that the main action of the play concerns itself with people getting into places where they are not supposed to be and getting out of places where they do not want to stay. The constant factor in both cases, then, is the wall both physical and psychological (the solid walls of the city and its buildings and the enmity that has built a wall of hate between the two families). In both cases, the function of these walls is to contain, repel, or cut off.

We are now at the point where the attention and efforts of the scenographer must be more carefully focused, more specifically detailed and channeled. We are also at the point where the focus of attention must be directed to the internal needs of the play rather than only toward the external information we have so far uncovered. Thus far we have accomplished three important steps:

1. A reading of the play

2. An attempt to see the "large picture"— the total background of the age, the locale, and nature of the people who have created this place and who in turn are influenced by it (and that, of course, cannot be understood by examining only those directly involved but those who lived before and left their mark)

3. A free and unstructured examination of several scenes that contain information and, more important, significant actions or series of actions

Until now there has been much jumping around in the play; the meanings of the text cannot be understood by examining each separately without regard to others. Cross-references are essential bits of information that help form the web by which the playwright holds his play together; the scenographer must be able to discern these threads and where they lead. Now we must begin to limit our focus and begin a more detailed study of a fewer number of scenes. (This is a natural development in the study of the play, because in examining a great number of scenes, we realize that some are more important

than others and that some need more attention; it gives us a priority by which to scale and direct our work.)

One of the key or crucial scenes (and also probably the best known) in the play is the so-called balcony scene. Not only is this the most famous scene, it is quite probably the most dangerous one, the one that has led more scenographers astray than any other.

Several years ago, a student picked this play as a subject for her term project. She labored mightily on it and performed all the exercises with diligence and care. But her work did not progress, and it seemed to lack something; she was not able to crystallize any concrete ideas for her designs. Part of the requirement for the project was that she give various oral reports on her research and on the progress of her ideas— in general, explain to the rest of the class what she was doing (or was not able to do) to forward her work. In these discussions with the other members of the class, it became apparent that she either was sidestepping certain aspects of the play, was not herself aware of them, or was simply ignoring them. Her conception of Verona, it became more and more obvious, was more suited to the French Riviera of today than to a brutal Renaissance city of the early sixteenth century. (It was, for that matter, no different from the attitude displayed by George Cukor in his lush 1936 Hollywood version of this same play, which starred Leslie Howard and Norma Shearer.) The people populating her play were, for the most part, good upstanding, clean-living, middle-class mannequins; at the very most, they were only actors in pretty costumes. In her findings there was not the slightest hint of a real world—no intrigue, no desire, only love of the purest kind, no dirty streets, and nobody, apparently, who ever sweated. It was all good clean fun—a little sad at the end, however. Finally, it was asked how she *saw* this play; through what lens did she view all those events of so long ago. Her actual reply: "Through the eyes of love"; that was her answer and only reason. Questioned more closely as to where she got this particular way of thinking about the play, what caused her to take this approach, she said, "From the garden scene—you know, the balcony scene. This is about the most important scene in the play, and so I just wanted to do the play through the eyes of Romeo and Juliet, since they are also the most important people in the play and we have to see the way they do." It was pointed out that the scene *was* important, but that it was (1) a scene totally *different* from practically every other scene, and (2) in order for it to retain its individuality, it must be shown to be different by *contrasting* it to the others, not by making it exactly alike. Her attention was then called to a few other scenes unlike this one in order to point out some of the more brutal moments she had apparently missed in her reading. She was requested, in addition, to read to the rest of the class—slowly—Juliet's monologue describing the horrors of being locked up alive in the tomb and was then asked to give a visualization of what the tomb might look like according to the information Juliet imparts. She was also asked to describe a street brawl and what might happen to those involved in such an event. (It was apparent that nobody ever bled in her Verona. Her reply to all these questions was, "You are always talking about horrible things and blood in these plays." We had been working on *Macbeth* too.) It became more and more clear that the play was still nothing more to her than words on a page, that her conception of the play was every bit as clean and sterile as that printed page from which she read. It was then pointed out that Shakespeare himself could not get more than four lines into the play without mentioning blood and that was just what he meant.

We have reached another juncture in our designing process. Having assembled a certain amount of information and having approached this information from a certain point of view (mostly exterior in nature), we are now able to explore some practical possibilities that might lead eventually to the design of this scene.

Yet while it is possible for the scenographer, at this stage, to create a design that will include all the foregoing considerations and give to the director a workable plan, rarely does this final step happen so quickly or effortlessly. On the contrary, usually another period of experimental work precedes the scenographic concept and the finished working plans and sketches. It is during this second period that the scenographer will find it necessary to make a number of drawings, none complete in statement or complicated in execution. These pictures are actually less than

pictures and more a form of visual shorthand the scenographer employs to make his ideas easier to understand for both himself and the director. So, before we continue our design of a scene from *Romeo and Juliet*, let us look at the way this visual shorthand is accomplished. These drawings will be called action drawings, because that is precisely what they show—action.

Many scenographers foster germinal ideas for a design, especially in relation to the basic shape of the playing area, by "directing" scenes in their own imaginations—seeing the action of the characters in relation to each other and to their surroundings—and then setting down these observations and ideas in a series of quick sketches. These sketches are, unlike those of painters or draftsmen, meant to show *action possibilities* rather than *pictorial composition* or likenesses. Action drawings do not show complete settings in a frame but, rather, fragments of a scene not necessarily viewed from a single fixed point or an audience position. They are diagrams that chart movements of characters as they relate to each other and to the surrounding environment and especially to those objects or pieces of scenery necessary for motivation or for completion of actions. (These drawings differ from a director's blocking diagrams in one major way: while in the director's plan the exact shape of the playing area has been previously confirmed, along with everything contained within that area, in the scenographer's preliminary drawings, nothing is set for certain. She is, in fact, attempting to determine what the director will eventually use.) To the scenographer, these drawings visually clarify space relationship possibilities and help her determine the physical needs of the actors as they perform a scene. Quite often the scenographer will make a number of these action drawings before she is able to determine a definite shape or pattern to a playing area. And she must consider not only the flat floor but levels as well, since often actors must be given the possibility of moving up and down from the stage floor as well as around its surface. The concept behind this activity is not, as some scenographers apparently believe, to decide arbitrarily on a shape or form for the playing areas and then force patterns of movement into it; rather, the concept is to define the boundaries of this area progressively as the needs of the actors become evident through the investigation of successive actions.

These sketches should be done quickly, though not thoughtlessly. Only essentials should be included; in other words, only that space or those items directly needed or concerned with the actor in a limited sequence of actions should be put down and studied. It is a mistake to try to make one action drawing show too many movements. It is also more helpful for the scenographer to concentrate on high points of the scene first and then work backward to less important happenings. She will find that by considering the actions of the performers as part of her own work—not only climactic moments but those of less importance as well—she is more able to assist the director in clarification of a scene that, in turn, might also help the actor to reinforce his work.

In *The Theatre of Bertolt Brecht*, John Willett relates just how important the scenographer can be to the director (and also to the playwright) in planning and influencing action, as well as in creating a place where it will take place.

Brecht was extremely sensitive to grouping and gestures, which in all the early rehearsals were designed simply to tell the story, in an almost silent-film way, and only later became refined and polished up. In this he depended often on his old friend and associate Caspar Neher, who would not only design the setting and the costumes but in dozen of sketches would suggest the action too: Puntila having his bath for example, or Matti haranguing a broom as he sweeps out the yard. . . .

. . . In Brecht's theatre he (Neher) played a decisive part from school days on, providing him with drawings and projections and teaching him to use the elements of scenery as if they were simply properties on a bigger scale. In his kind of setting every item that matters to the play is as authentic and tangible as it can be made, and all else is merely indicated: a real door, a real fence, a real streetlamp, standing solid and fit for use on an otherwise almost empty stage.

As Brecht himself tells us, "our friend [Neher] always starts with the people themselves and what is happening to or through them. . . . He constructs the space for people to experience something in. . . . above all he is an ingenious story-teller. *He knows better than anyone that whatever does not further the narrative harms it*"

(italics mine). Neher did not think of these small drawings as finished pictures with intrinsic artistic value. They were, rather, only a means by which actions are recorded for use on the stage. Like Neher's drawings, ours are meant to show the actors in relation to each other and to their most basic environmental needs. For instance, if walls are needed, as they are in the following example, their decoration and style are not as important as it is to determine their functional purposes. Although decorative matters must be considered at some point, they are not important to the task at hand.

Earlier, the street brawls which occur periodically in the play were discussed in visual terms—but words were used to describe the street and the events taking place on them, not actual diagrams or pictures. Now we are going to show how the scenographer might develop these ideas into diagrams. Only three will be shown to illustrate the process, although it would be more likely that three dozen would actually need to be made. But, before any diagrams are made, let us look at an existing street similar to those in Verona at the time of the play (fig. 199). In studying this image it is easy to see that it contains many

Fig. 199. Italian city street

features we might expect to show up in the final design. But just how usable is this information at this time? Can we simply copy this street with all its details and put it directly on the stage? Perhaps we could; the Hollywood approach to film design during the twenties and thirties of this century was essentially not much more than this. What the actors were required to do was really not a consideration of any importance to the scenographer; he was more concerned with the looks of the setting than its potential service to the actor or to the drama. And, when presented any latitude of selection, the pretty picture always won the day; the 1936 cinema version of *Romeo and Juliet*, when compared with the more recent Zeffirelli production, shows this very clearly.

But, while we must make use of such pictures as the street illustration at some time during our research, only certain features of it are of any great value to us at the present time. This street might very well be diagramed in this manner; we are not as interested in pictorial aspects of the locale as we are in its spatial qualities (fig. 200). All we are interested in are the essential

features of such a street, not its outward details and surfaces. This is also true for the people who inhabit these diagrams; we are concerned less with their costumes or external features than with their actions. These actions can be adequately expressed by the use of simple stick figures rather than elaborately drawn costumed ones (fig. 201). For our purposes, A is no more helpful than B. Now, let us return to the construction of the diagrams.

Situation 1. Two retainers of the house of Capulet are walking along one of the narrow streets of Verona. They are boasting about what they would do should they encounter members of the rival house of Montague. Suddenly, at the other end of the street, two servants of that house do appear. There is no escape for either pair (both pairs probably less brave than they would like to appear and would, if they could, avoid open conflict), the walls more or less channeling their possibilities of movement—either backward (retreat) or forward, almost certain conflict of some sort (verbal or physical). Figure 202 is a diagram of this moment when they first see each other.

Situation 2. Both parties have had to advance to save face. The men from the one house begin to bait the men of the other. The conflict is only one on the verbal level at this point. Their actions quite possibly are those similar to the combatants in a boxing ring or cockfight—basically circular—while each takes the measure of the other, waiting for the best time to strike. If possible, a fight is to be avoided. But this is contingent on the assumption that one side will give way to the superiority of the other (fig. 203).

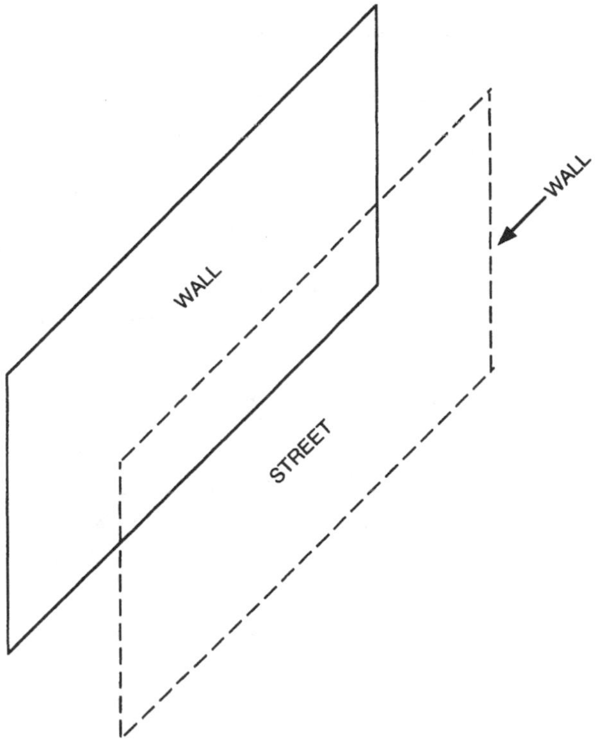

Fig. 200. Diagram of street

Fig. 201. Figure in action

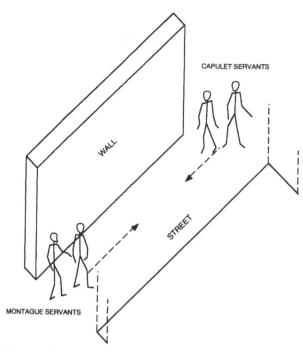

Fig. 202. Encounter of characters in street

Situation 3. The two groups taunt each other until one person begins a physical attack. Very soon all four are fighting, and in a few moments others have come onto the street to join the fray. The fight becomes larger and involves more people until finally the two heads of the rival households appear. Our drawing at this point is not adequate—we need to have some idea of where these other people are coming from. The draw-

ing must be extended to help us visualize the paths these other combatants might take to get to the area where the fight is taking place. In other words, we are extending our image to satisfy the need of the actors for an access to the place of action. So, our drawing must grow to include these areas as well as those first drawn. The acting space increases, therefore, as the need for it becomes evident. This is the organic way that stage space and the shape of the immediate acting area are determined (fig. 204).

The scenographer must make dozens of these drawings for each and every separate scene. At this stage, however, we are not too concerned with the possible relationship of these individual spaces to each other. (Although they will, at a later stage in the design, have to be correlated, combined, and given a priority; some scenes demand less space or definition, some more. The needs of some of these lesser scenes can be combined and then absorbed in the requirements of a more important scene.) The final design, while not evident now, will eventually be determined by just such ideas and drawings. At a later stage of work, specific plans must be made about the exact shape and size of the playing area, whether or not it has levels, and the appearance of the setting as a whole. For now, these decisions are still waiting to be resolved from future drawings. Making these action drawings is only a first step; but it is a most important and necessary one, especially for the student scenographer. Action drawings build bridges between the macrocosm of the playwright's world and the microcosm of the scenographer's design.

These, then, are the types of drawings the scenographer might make and show to the direc-

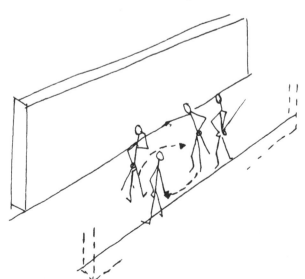

Fig. 203. Encounter of characters in street

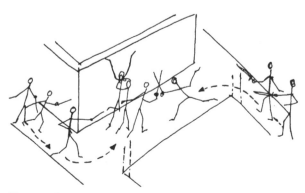

Fig. 204. Encounter of characters in street

tor or work out with him in conference. It is quite possible that the director will undertake some of these sketches himself, since the skill required for such work is negligible in terms of formal art training. It is, in fact, a good practice to urge the director to make such drawings; if nothing else, it saves a great deal of time, especially if the director does have firm convictions concerning space utilization. It is much easier, most scenographers will agree, to work with a director who is able to think in graphic terms, who has firm (not inflexible) ideas, and who is able to contribute his own ideas—as well as accept those of a scenographer—in visual form, rudimentary though they be.

At first glance this whole mode of thinking may seem to encroach on the director's territory and function; but, as it has been noted before, designing a set is to a large extent directing; the scenographer causes the actor to move in certain ways and in predetermined directions even if they never exchange so much as one word. The wise director always takes advantage of this situation. It greatly accounts, in fact, for the desire of many to use scenographers with whom they are familiar or have worked successfully before; in such a collaboration, each not only knows the way the other thinks and works but knows how to make the objectives of the other more meaningful and productive.

Most directors will admit that working with scenographers who evolve designs from the standpoint of action is easier than working with those who are only concerned with visual aspects of the setting; some will even admit that the scenographer actively concerned with space and the actor's needs many times suggests ideas that they had not considered. Yet by putting ourselves in the role of director or actor, we do not necessarily lose our own identities as scenographers; it merely gives us a different and, quite possibly, more inclusive perspective. It also helps us to comprehend better the playwright's hidden reasons for selecting the particular place he has to set his play. While it is only possible for a scenographer to accomplish this understanding in a limited way, even the attempt to do so is a healthy attitude that will make him much more ready and willing to think first of the production as a whole and not just as an opportunity to exhibit his designs. Furthermore,

if a sincere attempt is made by the scenographer to put himself in the place of the director and the actor, he will begin to develop that all-important inner eye without which no scenographer can hope to become an artist.

The most important thing for the scenographer to learn, although it may take years to attain, is *how to design scenes that promote action, not pictures that promote scenery.*

The greatest danger in the balcony scene, as we have noted before, lies in the possibility that the scenographer may see the entire production in terms of this one scene. It is quite appropriate that the scenographer evokes a garden that is unlike the city outside it—romantic and beautiful. This scene, however, virtually stands alone in the play in regard to the kind of romantic vision it represents. To insist on, however, and to maintain this vision throughout the whole play, as sometimes is the case, are wrong on at least two counts. First, the scene is denied its uniqueness, and second, it does not allow the hard cruel background—which is much more the natural condition of the time and this play— to assume its proper role. Romeo and Juliet become much more important to us, their plight all the more pathetic, if we see them pitted *against* a physical situation that has little beauty or romance about it. Too many scenographers have forgotten the important fundamental principle of any art form: that contrast in background gives importance to that which is placed before it.

Just how was this garden scene done on Shakespeare's own stage? To date, no scholar has given a completely satisfying explanation of the means by which the action in the street just before the main portion of the scene is transferred into the garden itself; with the little actual knowledge we have of the workings of this stage, it is not clear whether this was done with some accepted convention (and there must have been many used in this form of theater) or by using an actual scenic device—not part of the permanent stage structure—that an actor could climb over and hide behind. Nothing in the various works that purport to explain the workings of Shakespearian stagecraft illuminates this particular scene; no one, although there have been many conjectural inquiries into this question, has been able to agree or to give a satisfactory explanation of what does really happen. (In the theater that uses scenery, such as the proscenium stage, it is not too difficult to find ways of solving this problem; on the open stage, however, a workable solution would not be as easily found.) It is interesting to compare the quarto of 1597 with more recent texts:

Quarto 1597

NURSE: Come your mother staies for you, Ille goe a long with you.
Exeunt

Enter Romeo *alone.*

ROM: Shall I goe forward and my heart is here? Turne backe dull earth and finde thy Center out.

Enter Benvolio Mercutio

BEN: Romeo, my cofen Romeo.

MER: Doeft thou heare he is wise, Vpon my life he hath stolne him home to bed.

BEN: He came this way, and leapt this Orchard wall.
Call good Mercutio.

MER: Call, nay lle coniure too. . . .

MER: . . . Come lets away, for tis but vaine, To seek him heare that meanes not to be found

ROM: He iefts at fcars that neuer felt a wound: But soft, what light from yonder window breakes?

And we then begin the garden scene proper. Here, now, is the same scene from an accepted modern-day version of this play.

Modern Version

NURSE: Anon, anon!
Come, let's away; the strangers all are gone.

Enter Chorus.

Now old Desire doth in his death-bed lie,
And young Affection gapes to be his heir: . . .
But passion lends them power, times means, to meet,
Temp'ring extremities with extreme sweet.

Exit Chorus.

ACT II

Scene I. *A lane by the wall of Capulet's orchard.*

Enter Romeo, *alone.*

ROM: Can I go forward when my heart is here?
Turn back, dull earth, and find thy centre out.

[*He climbs the wall, and leaps down within it.*]

BEN: Romeo! my cousin Romeo! Romeo!

MER: He is wise; And, on my life, hath stol'n him home to bed.

BEN: He ran this way, and leap'd this orchard wall.
Call good Mercutio.

MER: Nay, I'll conjure too. . . .

BEN: Go, then; for 'tis in vain To seek him here that means not to be found.

Exeunt

Scene II. *Capulet's orchard*

Enter Romeo.

ROM: He jests at scars that never felt a wound.

Juliet appears above, at a window.

But, soft! what light through yonder window breaks?

There are, as one can easily see, distinct differences between the earlier and later texts. Let us consider just what can be deduced from a study of these variations. First, a few of the more obvious differences should be noted:

1. In the quarto the action is continuous; there is no Chorus (which many feel was not even written by Shakespeare because of its lack of purpose and its generally inferior writing).

2. In the modern version editors have written in stage directions based on what they thought was occurring, and they have broken the one scene into two (street-garden).

3. There is an interior reference to Romeo climbing over a wall. (And it had to be done on stage, there is no opportunity for him to leave the stage.)

4. Romeo has to be where he can hear what is said. The noted Shakespearian critic E. K. Chambers has surmised that Romeo is in the garden at the beginning of the scene and Mercutio and Benvolio are on the outside in the street: "As there is no indication in the Qq and Fi of Romeo's entrance here, it is not impossible that in the old arrangement of the scene the wall was represented as dividing the stage, so that the audience could see Romeo on one side and Mercutio on the other." R. G. White, another nineteenth-century scholar, has a more detailed explanation.

From the beginning of this Act to the entrance of the Friar, there is not the slightest implication of a supposed change of scene, but rather the contrary; and the arrangement in question [Rowe's] seems to have been the consequence of an assumption that Benvolio's remark (II, i, 5) is made on the outside of the wall; whereas the text rather implies that the whole of this Act, from the entrance of Romeo to his exit after his interview with Juliet, passes within Capulet's garden; for after the stage direction, "Enter Romeo alone" (which has a like particularly in all the old copies), Romeo says, "Can I go forward while my heart is here?"—not in the street or outside the wall, but here, in the dwelling-place of his love, which is before he eyes. After he speaks the next lines, the old copies (from the absence of scenery) could not direct him to "climb the wall and leap down within it"; but, had he been supposed to do this, some intimation would have been given that he was to go out of eye-shot of Mer. and Benv.; as, for instance, in Love's Lab. . . . Again Benvolio's remark that Romeo "*hath hid* himself among *these trees*" must surely be made within the enclosure where Romeo is, unless we suppose Benv. able to see farther into a stone wall than most folk can.

Here we have the complete scene beginning with Romeo's entrance ("Can I go forward when my heart is here?") with Romeo already *within* the orchard along with Mercutio and Benvolio. If we accept this situation we cannot honor the stage directions that have come to be accepted in the later texts.

In any case, however, while it is difficult to have complete faith in Chamber's speculation, White's explanation also lacks absolute credibility. So, what should we do? Perhaps the best plan would be to reconstruct, using as much in formation as we can get from all commentaries and our own thoughts, the scene just before the entrance of Romeo. (And we must, as best we can, approach this scene from the actor's viewpoint.)

After the end of the Capulet ball scene, the garden scene begins (discounting the spurious Chorus that separates the two). Our question is, *Just where is Romeo entering from, where is he, and what is the motivation for his entrance?* Let us accept the proposition that he is in the street when he first comes into view. His remark, "Can I go forward [i.e., on down the street and away from where Juliet lives] while my heart is here?" does not have to mean that he is actually inside the garden wall; the proximity of the actor to the house is certainly enough to give sense and meaning to the remark. He is probably trying to

give his friends the slip, even though he may not be completely aware of what he intends to do. Their calls are motive enough for him to hide and the hiding places are fairly limited. Going over the wall and into the garden seems a logical solution to his problem. Once Romeo is in the garden our attention must go with him; that is, we as scenographers must put ourselves in his place to see—our first time and probably Romeo's too—just how this garden appears.

But what do we see? And just how did we really find our way here? The answer, quite obviously, is by following the progress of Romeo in our imaginations as he acts out the scene. With the aid of the action-drawing process we begin to comprehend the action requirements of the scene, as well as its visual needs. First, however, let us think back over what we already know about these two places—the garden and the street outside it. We know much more of the second than we do of the first; we know, for instance, a number of facts concerning the streets of Verona in general: narrow, dirty, the scene of brutal and cruel brawls, probably not well lit at night and subject to a number of roving bands of Renaissance "juvenile delinquents" who would, simply for the thrill of it, attack the single traveler unlucky enough to be walking these streets alone after dark. We can also surmise a number of things about the garden (although we know, at this point, considerably less about it than we do the streets). Being private property, it is probably not only secluded and protected but more peaceful, more carefully attended, and, in short, all the things that the streets outside are not. These are, literally, two different worlds separate and kept apart by a wall. Diagrammatically these places could be presented as shown in figure 205.

We are now ready to trace the action of this scene through the use of action drawings. Often young scenographers ask if this process is more or less practiced by all scenographers when they are evolving a design for the stage out of printed text. The answer is quite obviously no. At least few do it to the extent and in the detail presented here. Many of them can and do accomplish everything that is shown here without setting a pencil to paper; that is, they can *see* these actions in their imaginations. And some who have worked in this manner at one point in their artis-

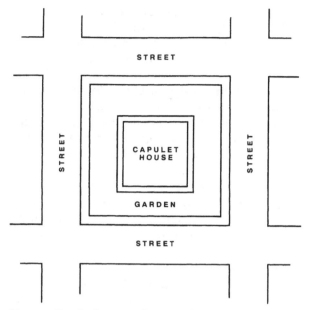

Fig. 205. Capulet house and surrounding area

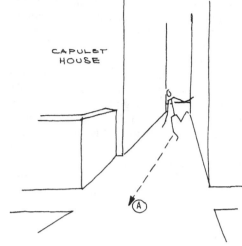

Fig. 207. Street scene before garden scene

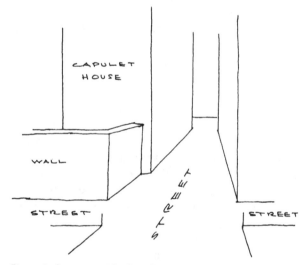

Fig. 206. Street outside Capulet house

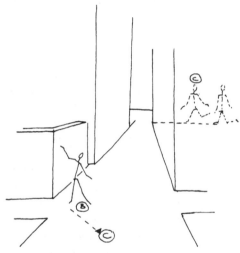

Fig. 208. Street scene before garden scene

tic careers no longer do it as much at a later phase. The real value in this activity is, though, that the more you do this sort of analyzing in your formative stage of development, the stronger your spatial imagination becomes and the less you need detailed analysis as you become a more experienced scenographer. In other words, it is a technique of working that frankly is geared to the learning process, but one that greatly aids the building of the imaginative skills peculiar to scenography. And while some scenographers continue to use these action sketches

throughout their careers, the student learning his art should not underestimate the value of this activity even if, at a later time, he no longer feels it necessary to work in this manner. A simple sketch of the foregoing diagram might look something like figure 206. Remember, though, at this point we are not trying so much to work out a stage setting as we are trying to get a clear view of what elements must go into it.

A (fig. 207). Romeo enters street. He is running away, we will discover, from his friends.

B (fig. 208). "Can I go forward when my heart is here?" (In the Capulet house with Juliet.)

C (fig. 208). He hears Benvolio and Mercutio calling for him and not too far behind. He does not want to leave nor does he want to be discovered. He must hide somewhere.

D (fig. 209). He climbs over the wall (How high is it?). But Benvolio must *see* him just as he goes over. (Benvolio remarks directly as to this action shortly after this.)

E (fig. 210). Benvolio and Mercutio come near the wall. Romeo is now hidden on the other side but can hear what is being said about him. Benvolio also remarks a little later that "he hath hid himself among these trees" (which are probably in the garden). *Problem*: We need to see both Romeo and the two other men. How?

F (fig. 211). Mercutio calls to Romeo (know-

ing where he is but pretending that he does not.

G (fig. 211). Benvolio starts to go down the street. He tells Mercutio it is a vain quest to seek Romeo out any longer, he doesn't mean to be found.

H (fig. 212). Benvolio and Mercutio leave. *Problem*: Our angle of vision must now shift to the inside of the garden where the rest of the scene is to take place. (Perhaps this should happen as Romeo goes over the wall so that

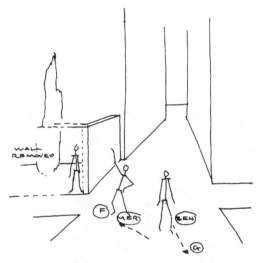

Fig. 211. Street scene before garden scene

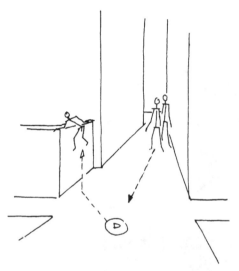

Fig. 209. Street scene before garden scene

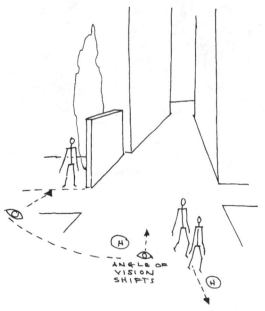

Fig. 212. Focus of scene shifting to garden

Fig. 210. Street scene before garden scene

Fig. 213. Focus of scene shifted to garden

Fig. 214. Garden scene

Fig. 215. Setting for street scene

he is seen during the short scene with Benvolio and Mercutio.) How can this be done?

I (fig. 213). Now the second part of the scene begins. ("He jests at scars . . .") *Problem*: Romeo mentions a window. Where is it? We know it is a second-story one, even though the stage direction, "Juliet appears above at a window," does not appear in the 1597 quarto. No entrance is provided at all in that version. But, even if the play were completely unfamiliar to the scenographer (an unlikely possibility), he would shortly learn, from internal evidence, that it was a room not at ground level. We can also suppose from further study of the scene that she stands on a balcony structure. (What size?)

J (fig. 214). At this point, we still have a lot to determine before a design can be made. (How big is the area we need in the garden? What kind of trees? How big is the balcony, what architectural style is it and the window, and how far from the ground are they? These are but a few of the questions that must be eventually answered.

Even though this discussion of *Romeo and Juliet* has consumed a great deal of time, the scenographer would soon discover, were he given the task of working out all the problems for an actual production, that only the surface has been scratched; a complete investigation, along the lines pursued here, would be worth a deliberation at least a dozen times as long as it has been given. For our purposes, however, there is a point of diminishing returns; therefore, we will stop now, even though nothing conclusive has been decided or shown concerning the production as a whole. Perhaps this will be incentive to the student scenographer to carry on from here to complete a design or, preferably, return again to the beginning in order that individual ideas of what the script "tells" can be discerned.

Let it be repeated once more that the conclusions to these investigations are not half so important as is the fact they were reached by a process that includes both rational and intuitional aspects of the scenographer's mind. Most important of all, it should be understood that there is a process of scenography that does not depend merely on an emotional (or unthinking) response to a play by an artist peculiarly talented in scenography. This process, however, has been sufficiently exposed so that further explanation could serve no purpose. Furthermore, the

Fig. 216. Wall mechanism for scene change

actual problems of putting these findings into designs and onto the stage cannot be solved once and for all; although many of these findings may remain conceptually valid for the play in general, every new production will demand that the problems be confronted and resolved anew.

Little can be added at this point other than to demonstrate how one particular problem—the shift in scene from the street into the garden—was accomplished in an actual production. Although not the definitive solution to this scene, its evolution was based directly on research materials and the techniques of employing those materials into a design that we have just been studying. The setting for this particular production was, for the most part, nothing more than a series of walls some of which were stationary and some moveable. This plan allowed different areas on the stage to be given variable size and form for different scenes, with a minimum of physical change.

For instance, figures 215 and 217 are scene sketches where both inner walls were designed to open toward the center of the stage: in figure 215 these walls are in position for a street scene; but jump ahead to figure 216 and you see that the inner wall to your right (marked A in the working diagram [fig. 216]) is opened toward the center to expose better the garden of the Capulet house. Wall A is opened at the same time Romeo climbs onto the wall—thus it is possible to see him climb over it and down into the garden without losing sight of his action. The garden is exposed by the time Mercutio and Benvolio have entered.

Fig. 217. Setting for the garden scene

The Nature of the Scenographic Concept

An image is symbolic when it implies something more than its obvious and immediate meaning. It has a wider "unconscious" aspect that is never precisely defined or fully explained. Nor can one hope to define or explain it. As the mind explores the symbol, it is led to ideas that lie beyond the grasp of reason. . . . Because there are innumerable things beyond the range of human understanding, we constantly use symbolic terms to represent concepts that we cannot define or fully comprehend.
—Carl Jung, *Man and His Symbols*

All that is profound needs a mask.
—Frederich Nietzche

"O, what a world of unseen visions and heard silences, this insubstantial country of the mind! What ineffable essences, these touchless rememberings and unshowable reveries! . . . A whole kingdom where each of us reigns reclusively alone, questioning what we will, commanding what we can. A hidden hermitage where we may study out the troubled book of what we have done and yet may do." Thus Julian Jaynes, the noted psychologist, describes that unique possession we all have, the human mind; "An introcosm that is more myself," he goes on to say, "than anything I can find in a mirror."

And so we come to the most difficult of all questions we must consider in the education of the scenographer: the role that the individual imagination plays in the creation of theatrical art. For without the presence of this element, the theater is a dead world.

The senses perceive, the mind interprets. During all of man's waking life this process is taking place; this is no less true in the theater than it is in the street outside. But there are some differences between what is experienced in the theater and what takes place in that world outside it. Although we can never catalogue all those differences, we can make one general observation that is likely to remain true in most instances: the viewer of an event in the theater (no matter how practical or prosaic a person he might be outside) is much more likely to accept that what he is seeing on the stage has a significance for him over and above the actual act he is witnessing. He is, it could be said, primed from the moment he steps from the street outside into the theater to be receptive to images and actions that have meanings (often, as Jung speculates, *beyond the grasp of reason*) that lie far beyond surface perceptions. Moreover, the spectator unconsciously bridges that gap that exists between "real life" and the stage without ever once consciously thinking, "What I am witnessing is a synthesis of life in symbolic form, not life as I left it outside this theater." This realization has little to do with theatrical conventions (although, of course, they must be consciously understood). This is equally true for a production that closely imitates life today (naturalism) or a production that presents a form of ritual thousands of years old with little or no naturalistic semblance. It has nothing at all to do so with the twentieth century's most debated question: *Is what we see in the theater an integral part of life as it is lived outside the theater, or is the theater a phantasy world that remains strictly apart from the cares and limitations of everyday life?* Regardless of philosophy or political bent, the person who goes to the theater—it is reasonable to contend—never is so swept away with the illusion of the stage that he thinks that what he is seeing is really happening for the first time and happening "for real."

The scenographer, along with all other theater workers, may always safely assume that his work, while it may be admired for its fanciful invention or for its illusory verisimilitude is part of the world of the theater; a world where locations dictated by the text have, to a large degree, been selected to enhance or, more to the point, further the action of the work at hand. (One of the most telling aspects of Shakespeare's genius is that his scenes all take place in the one and only possible location he sets it; not only does

the scene allow the particular actions required, it almost always promotes those actions that transpire. For instance, *Hamlet* could not possibly begin in any other location except the parapet on the periphery of the castle; not one line would make sense otherwise. One of the most devastating effects of nineteenth-century production practice of his plays was that in order to facilitate massive settings for some scenes others were relocated, chopped, rewritten, or cut entirely simply because it was not possible to move the scenery; thus forced into locales for which they were not written, many of these scenes were incomprehensible.)

The scenographer's work will always be a part of that intricate relationship between what the senses perceive through direct experience of life outside the theater and what the mind interprets from the work of others inside. It is for this reason that all scenographers must be trained (and, more importantly, must train themselves) to think as interpretive artists and not merely as commissionable artisans with unique and original visions looking for a large frame in which to exhibit their work.

The scenographic concept must not be a superficial eye-catching surprise; instead, it must speak to us of levels in our experience that are worth the while to show to others. Unlike the glossy imagery of Madison Avenue, which seeks to sell that which we do not need, the scenographic image must sell us something we do have use for and can make a part of our own expanding experience and understanding. To do this the images we attempt to bring to the stage must have a firm basis in communal experience but they must go beyond the commonplace perceptions which usually surround them. Let me draw your attention to the kind of image making and image perception I believe the scenographer must be able to comprehend and use in his work on the stage. In Loren Eiseley's *Unexpected Universe*, he describes a moment in his life when he happened onto a startling image that helped him to understand a concept that still has a certain currency in speech and thought; *the web of life*.

Some time ago I had occasion one summer morning to visit a friend's grave in a country cemetery. The event made a profound impression on me. By some trick of midnight circumstance a multitude of graves in the untended grass were covered and interwoven together in a shimmering sheet of gossamer, whose threads ran indiscriminately over sunken grave mounds and head-stones.

It was as if the dead were still linked as in life, as if that frail network, touched by the morning sun, had momentarily succeeded in bringing the inhabitants of the grave into some kind of persisting relationship with the living. The night-working spiders had produced a visual facsimile of the intricate web in which past life is intertwined with all that lives and in which the living constitute a subtle, though not totally inescapable, barrier to any newly emergent creature that might attempt to break out of the enveloping strands of the existing world.

As I watched, a gold-winged glittering fly, which had been resting below the net, essayed to rise into the sun. Its wings were promptly entrapped. The analogy was complete. Life did bear a relationship to the past and was held in the grasp of the present. The dead in the grass were, figuratively, the sustaining base that controlled the direction of the forces exerted throughout the living web.

Here we have a striking image that although accidentally encountered immediately "speaks" to the viewer in a moving and profound way. It is the scenographer's function to bring to the stage just such images for just such purposes; to create, in Eiseley's words, "visual facsimiles" that illuminate insubstantial but nonetheless important feelings or concepts. There is one thing more to be noted about the image Eiseley saw; it is this: as striking and provocative as the static image of the network of strands between the graves was, the image did not reveal its full meaning until the fly attempted to move out of it. The very same can be said of the scenographic concept: it is not complete in and of itself, no matter how visually striking its static form is; action by something that is not an actual part of it is required for its meaning to be made manifest.

The scenographic concept, then, is that which links the world of imagination to the world of practical craft; it must never be a cosmetic feature of a production simply to dazzle an audience with its own unique presence. A scenographic concept must, in point of fact, not ever attempt to do the work of the playwright or the performer or to come between them and the audience. Any scenographic concept that is consciously evident to an audience has failed its purpose; it must remain a skeleton of thought,

a structure that supports the underlying meaning of the rest, not something that we as scenographers wish to present as evidence of our own particular skill and art. And while the twentieth century has come to find as much beauty in the underlying structure of things as in their surface features, it must never be the scenographer's presumption that it is his task to reveal this structure to an audience for its own sake. More than anything else, a scenographic concept is the way that all artists working in a single production find to achieve a common focus and path of intention. To the extent that the scenographic concept is or becomes anything else—no matter who has had a hand in fashioning it—it is worse than no concept at all, at best a useless self-serving exercise.

The scenographic concept must have a deep and continuing connection with the production at all levels; the reason for using a compelling image or series of images should never be just for the sake of keeping up with the latest scenographic trend. Mordecai Gorelik was one of the very first theater artists in this century to see the importance of methodically examining the ways in which conceptual imagery arising from the written text can be correlated to the physical needs of the setting. He is justifiably famous for his long promotion of a better understanding of the role that metaphor can play in the theater. At the same time, he is pragmatic in his approach to the subject.

I don't think anyone will quarrel with the statement that the setting must be related to the play *poetically*. But the formulation is too vague. The poetic relationship must be *pin-pointed*. It is the *metaphor* of the setting which makes the relationship specific.

What is a metaphor? It is an analogy between two things, otherwise unrelated, in order to show a certain resemblance between them. You may say that a man is like a lion if he is powerful and courageous. You may say that a woman is like a flower if she is delicate, appealing. These comparisons, which make use of the word "like," are called *similes*. If you leave out the word "like" and say, instead, "This man is a lion," "This woman is a flower," you are using metaphors. Perhaps the only practical difference between a simile and a metaphor is that you leave out the word "like." I prefer the metaphor simply because it is more dramatic. . . . It may be that very few designers use the word "metaphor" in their imaginative work. They may talk of the "quality" of the setting, its "essence" or its "atmosphere." It seems to me of little moment whether you use the word "metaphor," "simile," "quality," or no word at all—provided you make the setting thoroughly fit the play. The fact is that there is no way to discuss the thematic significance of a setting except in terms of a poetic analogy. Except, perhaps, in mathematics, language offers no other way to make a comparison.

The scenographic concept, when it is too obvious, tends to lose much of its power to affect an audience deeply. When its intent is clearly perceived, the attention of the spectator is diverted from the main subject the concept is employed to support; any object or action that blatantly exposes its meaning too easily becomes the object of attention and not a means of focusing that attention. Even the business of advertising commercial products has learned much about the increased power of subliminal selling as opposed to obvious linkages of symbol and product. Figure 218 is a 1900 advertisement for Ivory Soap; it is a clever image that makes an extremely obvious statement: *Cleanliness is next to godliness.* Perhaps this was effective in its time; the same kind of thinking is often used by present-day scenographers who wish to assure that their visual points are made. But to adopt the use of symbols and concepts at this level can only be at the expense of the deeper meanings of the production these concepts are created to serve.

This is not to say, however, that the more obscure or hidden the concept is the more affective it will be; there does need to be a strong tie between a scenographic concept and the dramatic message it attempts to convey. But the scenographer should always ask himself this: *Am I supporting that dramatic message in a truly cooperative way, or am I seeking to tell it all by myself?*

The scenographic concept must provide a focus without becoming the focus itself. For example, in a production of *Hamlet* some few years ago, the director made these decisions: (1) that Hamlet could be interpreted primarily as a psychological casebook study and, in particular, in Freudian terms; (2) that the terminology of Freud could be used directly in the staging of the play. To this end he had not one Hamlet on stage, but *four*: Hamlet—the perceivable character written

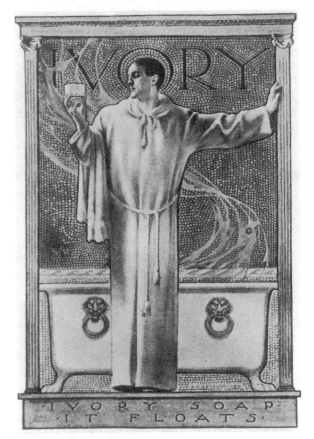

Fig. 218. Ivory Soap advertisement, 1900. Courtesy of Dover Publications, Inc.

by Shakespeare—Hamlet's alter ego, Hamlet's id, and Hamlet's subconscious. Accordingly, the lines usually spoken by the single performer were parceled out to those other Hamlets as the director deemed appropriate. The concept was perfectly clear to even the most unsophisticated of audience members: here is a *Hamlet* in which we can follow the progress of Hamlet's thought as it arises from the various levels of Hamlet's tormented mind (even when he himself cannot or may not be aware that such thoughts are in process or in evidence). We in the audience, the director believed, will never be confused as to which aspect of Hamlet's mind is speaking, since the appropriate aspect-character speaks words arising from the appropriate level. This, he thought, will clarify Shakespeare's original intentions to a modern-day audience.

Unfortunately, this concept, in dividing the mind of Hamlet, also divided the corporeal reality of Hamlet. We saw four Hamlets, not one;

the play became more a study of multiple personality, each with a claim to totality, not, as I believe Shakespeare intended, the portrait of a man certainly divided in mind and purpose but just as certainly caught in a single form. The conflict arises from the very fact that he is caught in a single form, which makes his plight all the more dramatically interesting.

The concept of this production certainly had its carefully thought-out aspects; those associated with it worked diligently and with conviction. But it did not work. The main reason was that the concept could not be employed without calling direct attention to the *modus operandi* of the concept; it did not fail because it was innovative, it failed because the concept *stood between* the playwright and the audience. More important still, the concept *fractured* the attention of the audience rather than focusing it. Most important of all, the performer playing Hamlet was denied the opportunity to reveal those aspects of Hamlet's mind through performance. There are two very sound principles that every theater artist should seriously entertain if not adopt outright. These are:

1. A clever idea can be of great use in the production of a theatrical work; a really clever idea can be disastrous.

2. The scenographic concept is part of the apparatus for transmitting the meaning or message of a production; *it is not the message itself.*

While there is only one basic scenographic concept in a production (more than one could result in conflicting messages being sent to a confused audience), it should be expected that the usefulness of this form of thinking would manifest itself in smaller ways in the working out of a production. Metaphorical thought is not, however, restricted to the proposition that there is only one major image in a production to which all other lesser images must directly correspond. In *Romeo and Juliet*, for instance, the dominant literary image in the play is, according to Caroline Spurgeon, "light, every form and manifestation of it; the sun, moon, stars, fire, lightning, the flash of gunpowder, the reflected light of beauty and love." There is, in addition to this predominance of light imagery, another level that corresponds to a more physical aspect of the city: walls.

In music drama, for over a hundred years

now, there has been a device that greatly assists the composer to focus an audience's attention in very precise ways. This device is called a leitmotiv; its basic purpose is to identify a person, situation or idea that recurs in the progress of the drama. It provides a key to the development of action and helps to keep the relationships of the characters more understandable. Even when an audience does not consciously identify the recurring motif at the time heard, the use of this device helps to build an underlying structure of meaning that helps to clarify the lines of the unfolding story; an audience is "moved" in the direction the composer wishes to take them, even when they are unaware they are being so manipulated. Conductors, especially, study a score for such recurring motifs and seek to understand, at any one point in the total work, just how the motif works, why it is quoted at that point, and the precise way the motif should be treated at that time. Correctly understood, these leitmotivs help both to give an overall unity to the work and, at the same time, to provide inner nodes of energy by which the work may develop from point to point.

Scenographers—no less than directors—are counterparts of the orchestral conductor in their function to identify the visual leitmotivs in a theatrical work and to render them on the stage in their proper relationship to the production. More than anything else, this means that the scenographer's work can never be viewed as finished when one has merely provided a workable environment for performers. Let us take a single recent example of how a visual motif—the mirror in *A Chorus Line*—can be employed in the manner just discussed.

Until only fairly recently, large mirrored surfaces were not technically or economically feasible on the stage. However, with the advent of Mylar and similar plastic materials, an entire stage can now be enclosed with mirrored surfaces at nominal cost. The dramatic possibilities of the mirror are unlimited; space can be vastly extended; images can be multiplied or distorted to suit dramatic purposes; the audience itself can be made part of the scenographic environment. The question that scenographers must now address is to what purposes will these new possibilities be put? For if he uses the mirror merely because it is now available, he runs the risk of distorting the underlying concept of a production, transferring the attention of an audience from the performer to the scenic environment, and ultimately, fracturing the unity of the whole. The mirror, then, can only be beneficial if it in some fundamental way furthers the inherent imagery of the production.

Chorus Line began in 1974 as a simple set of ideas, feelings, and observations concerning the lives of professional chorus-line dancers. It grew over a period of time, changing form and even physical place of performance, before it finally became a finished production capable of repetition and duplication. The scenographic environment started as simply as the concept which engendered the project: a bare stage on which dancers could work. As the project developed and became more complex, the question of "scenery" began to emerge. The locale was, and always remained, a stage in a theater; in some ways it was an abstract space, in another sense, it was a particular place with specific properties. And, setting aside the metaphorical dictum of Shakespeare that "all the world's a stage," the necessity of making this locale something more than what it was simply did not fit the intention of those involved in fashioning the production. Yet, as *Chorus Line* evolved, two very definite needs arose: first, was the need for variety of imagery associated with Broadway musical production and, second (and in many ways much more important to the integral needs of the "story"), some way to externalize the conceptual basis of the performer's existence. Robin Wagner, the designer of *Chorus Line*, quite probably did not introduce the mirrors into the production single-handedly; it is much more probable that it was a group decision or, at the very least, the designer's very astute response to an underlying group need. The introduction of the mirror into the production scheme was, however, a solution that eminently satisfied both those needs listed. Most important of all, the use of mirrors is as much a psychological statement as it is a clever solution to sustain the visual interest of an audience. Let us be more precise as to some of the possibilities that emerge when the mirror is introduced into the production scheme:

1. *The mirror as a basic tool of the dancer.* Most dance training involves the use of large mirrors.

Positioning, body line, posture—these are all a matter of exact visual importance to the dancer. On the one hand, a dancer can *feel* what he is doing in his own body and can be *told* by a teacher what is being done correctly or incorrectly; but the mirror is the objective critic that *shows* if what is being felt is being projected. Dancers come to rely on "that other person in the mirror" to instruct them. There is no doubt that a duality exists in the dancer's psyche and that the constant proximity of the mirror helps to bring this duality into existence.

2. *The mirror as a verification of the dancer's art.* Spending so much time in front of mirrors, both in training and as an adjunct in preparing for a performance (applying makeup to its best advantage, adjusting costume to the best effect), a dancer comes to regard the mirror sometimes as a helpful friend, sometimes as a recalcitrant enemy. As the years pass, this relationship becomes more intimate and more complex. The mirror to a performer becomes something more than just a flat reflective surface; it also reflects that passing of time that makes the other person in the mirror a stranger. In *Chorus Line*, the question of time and the limited time left are integral to the "plot." In what is possibly the climax of the production—a dance by the "lead," and appropriately named "The Music and the Mirror"—the performer is at once confronted and confirmed in multiple images by a semicircle of mirrors that both reflect her accomplishment and goad her to excel her past performances. There is a demonic quality to this scene as well as an exhilarating one. The mirrors turn her into a chorus line comprising only herself. The structure of this scene, indeed the meaning of it in relation to the total meaning of the production, would not have been possible without the use of the circle of mirrors. The medium very much becomes the message.

3. *The mirror as a device for changing the point of view of the audience.* In *Chorus Line*, the use of mirrors provides many moments that are truly breathtaking, but there is one that cannot be described in any other terms than magical. It is the moment when the back wall of the stage, which is composed of a number of vertical revolving units, turns to present the mirrored side for the first time. The audience is suddenly transported from the front of the stagehouse, looking

toward the stage, *to the back of the stage, looking out at itself*. For many—for most, quite probably—it is the first time ever they have been thrust into the position of the performer. The effect is both exhilarating and somewhat disturbing; anyone who has ever been on the stage, even the most seasoned professional, never quite overcomes those conflicting feelings when performing in front of a live audience. And it is only through the use of the mirror that this magic is possible, that an audience can begin to share this experience with the performer. Although the individual member of the audience does not suddenly say, "Ah, yes! Now I understand what it feels like to be a performer as she confronts that vast sea of faces," her viewpoint has altered even if she does not consciously acknowledge the change.

The use of mirrors, as with numerous other technical advances in the theater, can serve a great deal more than just being up-to-date scenographically. It can, as in *Chorus Line*, be the most effective means of presenting the basic meanings of a production. The scenographer is not the purveyor of the latest technical achievement possible in the theater but, rather, the artist who selects the technology most appropriate to the individual problem at hand. The real point to keep in mind is that the scenographic concept and the visual motif must serve the production at a very deep level; the integration of these most basic images is essential, or else the results will always be patently cosmetic.

The Scenographic Concept on the Stage: *The Glass Menagerie*

It has been many years since the first performance of *The Glass Menagerie*, Tennessee Williams's initial success in the theater. It would be almost impossible to recount just how many times it has been put on the stage since then and how many ways it has been done. Jo Mielziner first designed it, and there probably have been many more individual and original interpretations by actors and directors than there have been by scenographers, not that his design has been merely duplicated down through the years. Still, the basic concepts behind this particular design have all but gone unquestioned in a great

many of those productions seen on the stage. And the fact that Williams himself agreed with the design offered by Mielziner, at least tacitly, has further reinforced the feeling that this is the "right" way, the correct solution. Before we go further, let us look at a simplified version of the plan of the setting used in the original production. Basically it consisted of certain specific areas arranged as shown in figure 219. In this design, the setting is oriented to a proscenium theater arrangement and in no way violates the limitations of such a theater, which, usually, keeps audience (fig. 220A) and actors (fig. 220B) in separate and isolated units. Movement in depth and at oblique angles is limited; action of the play is essentially horizontal rather than multidimensional. In short, the design approach is basically pictorial.

Let us, for a moment, examine this question of approach and, at the same time, examine the question of originality. Scenographers should always ask themselves for what reasons would they want to redesign a basic plan thought out by a talented and successful professional just to "show you can do it too"? This is, in many instances, part of the motive, but it's not the whole truth, the complete rationale. No, the creative urge in most scenographers lies in a somewhat different direction or at least has a deeper impetus and motivation.

Quite often a student scenographer will say that what he wants to do with a project, a design, is to "think it out for myself and do something different." And while it is difficult to disagree with this desire totally, some objection could be made to the last words of that statement, to the implication of the "do something different" part. Originality is certainly not a bad thing to strive for; but one should always carefully examine the motives inherent in the desire for it. Perhaps this statement should be amended to read, "When I approach a play with the intent of designing it, I would like to think it out." Period. Dylan Thomas once said that the business of posterity was to look after itself; maybe it is the business of originality to do likewise and not be pursued as the most important element of the design. This is especially true in an age that has put such an emphasis and premium (too much possibly) on originality for its own sake. To be new and different just to be new and different is a reason,

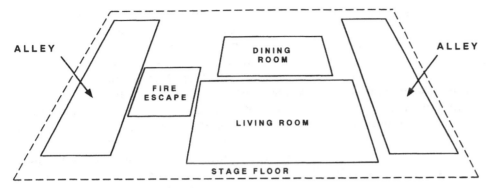

Fig. 219. Mielziner's setting with acting areas

it must be admitted; it is not necessarily a good reason, however, at least not good enough for the serious mature scenographer to make it his complete *raison d'être*. This, then, often becomes the truly creative scenographer's problem when faced with designing the "war horses" of theater: to be able to see the play in a new light and with fresh eyes, not in terms of doing it differently just to be original; to be able to create a right environment (very few will deny there is more than one acceptable variation), not just an impressively new or cleverly different setting. All too often, when we attempt to evolve a style for a production, we add on a veneer, when our real problem should be to clear away and start from scratch. A scenographer must not be afraid to begin at the beginning.

The designing of *The Glass Menagerie* was begun with the basic assumption that the world of the play is a macrocosm, a complete and specific world, even though it is merely conceptual, and one that is unlimited by artificial restrictions (such as the proscenium arch). Someday, all too soon as it usually happens, this larger world must be presented as a microcosm and will be bound by the limitations of the stage, that is, accomplished with its devices and subject to its principles. But, it is valuable, as long as possible, to keep the freedom of the first from being unduly hampered by the shortcomings of the second. This is the best reason one can find for not blindly accepting the design solution of another artist, no matter how successful that design might have been.

The design for the present production of *The Glass Menagerie* began, then, by attempting to clear away what was already known, by going

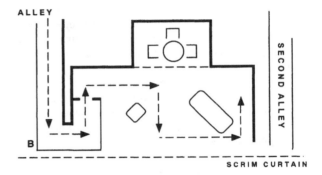

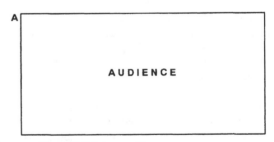

Fig. 220. Plan of Mielziner setting

back to the script itself. In doing this, however, certain considerations could not be avoided entirely. First, was knowledge of the various ways it had been done before: this backlog of observation included such diverse items as cinema version, a telecast, and a recording, as well as having seen a number of stage presentations ranging from proscenium arch productions to thrust stage to full arena. All helped in some way; there are always those little revelations—sometimes planned, most often accidental—even in the worst productions that made it worth seeing. Still, this accumulated information is of little use to the scenographer confronted with the job of realizing Williams's particular world of memory for a new production.

A second consideration, and a more useful one, was Williams's own words in a short essay accompanying the recorded version of the play. While this material is primarily "literary"—not directly related to stage production of the play— certain thoughts in it give valuable hints to the scenographer.

When my family first moved to St. Louis from the South, we were forced to live in a congested apartment neighborhood. . . . The apartment we lived in was about as cheerful as an Arctic winter. There were outside windows only in the front room and kitchen. The rooms between had windows that opened upon a narrow areaway that was virtually sunless and which we named "Death Valley" for a reason which is amusing only in retrospect.

There were a great many alley cats in the neighborhood which were constantly fighting the dogs. Every now and then some unwary young cat would allow itself to be pursued into this areaway which had only one opening. The end of the cul-de-sac was directly beneath my sister's bedroom window and it was here that the cats would have to turn around to face their pursuers in mortal combat. . . . For this reason . . . she kept the shade constantly drawn so that the interior of her bedroom had a perpetual twilight atmosphere. . . . My sister and I painted all her furniture white; she put white curtains at the window and on the shelves around the room she collected a large assortment of little glass articles. . . .

When I left home a number of years later, it was this room that I recalled most vividly and poignantly when looking back on our home life in St. Louis. . . . The areaway where the cats were torn to pieces was one thing—my sister's white curtains and tiny menagerie of glass were another. Somewhere between them was the world that we lived in.

This passage, written in Williams's characteristically visual style, gives the scenographer valuable clues as to the kind of the world necessary on the stage. And It would be possible to find actual visual research material to support the images conjures up by the playwright's words. But any interpreter of Williams's plays should not believe that there exists a direct relationship between the playwright's and the actual world in which he lived; the world seen on the stage, no matter how seemingly accurate in historical detail, is a composite construction fashioned

from the imagination of the playwright, who has reworked the raw materials of factual materials into something that lies beyond mere reportage. Scenographers—as well as all other theater artists—must take these transformations of historical fact into theatrical images as a necessary part of the interpretation process. Williams himself was quite aware that *The Glass Menagerie* was not a historical document of his own past life. Those who knew him have left their own recollections and records that shed some light as to how this process happens. Here is a brief selection from Donald Windham's memoir, *Lost Friendships*:

He helped create legends and created them himself—as he had since the days when he made up the name Tennessee. It was publicity fodder from the start that he based the characters of Laura and Amanda on his sister and mother—although he himself later pointed out that there was very little of his sister in Laura. (There was more of himself, I would say.) In truth, when he was writing the play, he neither intended nor considered it a transformed-but-essentially-truthful portrait of his early home life in St. Louis. But this is what he implied he had done in the article he wrote for the N.Y. *Herald Tribune* following the opening.

Tennessee called Menagerie a memory play. I would say that it is a dream play. The central fact of Tennessee's home life in St. Louis was the presence of his father. And although the elimination of a father from the Wingfield family can be explained as an act of wish fulfillment, the remaining characters in Menagerie are not in any family situation that, from my knowledge, Tennessee ever experienced. He worked for a period at the shoe company where his father was employed, but he did not contribute to the support of his family. He had heard from me and others of the times in our homes when the gas and electricity were turned off because the bills were not paid; but despite the early years in dreary apartments these were not things he had experienced in the St. Louis houses furnished with Oriental rugs, mahogany diningroom suites, a grand piano in the parlor, where his mother gave teas for the D.A.R., with ices, sandwiches and cakes from a caterer.

He borrowed whatever was useful, from any direction, from his own life and other's lives. And he carried this freehand appropriation over into his presentation of himself. I don't think anyone will ever know, for instance, how much he borrowed for himself—from Philip Horton's biography of Hart Crane—of Crane's love for his grandmother. This appropriation was another of the clues to his character that I didn't recognize until later. He assumed surrogate personalities, surrogate biographies, trying them on like suits of other people's clothes and substituting them for his own when they fitted the part he was playing sometimes briefly, sometimes more or less permanently. (Italics mine)

The physical world the scenographer creates in the theater is not unlike that which the playwright creates on the page: it is a composite world whose selective elements have been gleaned from fact and transformed into something beyond historical documentation. While Windham seems to find Williams's manipulation of fact into myth something less than admirable, one must point out that such manipulations lie at the heart of the process; such borrowings and "appropriations"—to use Windham's words— is standard procedure for both playwright and scenographer. Knowing what to "borrow" and what to excise, moreover, is an important part of any artist's craft. (See "Furniture and Set Properties," under "The Scenographer's Areas of Influence" part 2, for Tennessee Williams's reflections on the furniture in his St. Louis home.) For instance, in the play, Laura's bedroom is not shown, but what is revealed in Williams's description of it (and especially Laura's relationship to its nature and contents) clearly must, in some way, be incorporated into any stage presentation. The grim, cruel aspect of the outside "real" world and the quietly luminous twilight quality of the inside of the bedroom are constructive information, pertinent to the play and useful to a scenographer. In any case, this double world, simultaneously represented, is probably the most important element of the play's environment. In the successful productions of this play (and this was true of the Mielziner design), this fundamental relationship was observed, regardless of the differences in the way it was accomplished; in the unsuccessful ones, it has been lacking or was mishandled and the play suffered accordingly.

Yet the most valuable clue to a workable solution to the design was obtained—as it often is— by accident. It was revealed by a young student actor quite unaware that he summed up in one short phrase the whole key to the riddle. The play was being discussed in a context totally unrelated to any design problem. Questioning him about how he would feel and react were he Tom and faced with the economic and family ties Tom had, he said, "I would do what was necessary as quickly· as possible. I guess that you have to do that. But then I'd split." Almost immediately his word "split" seemed to have meaning, although it was not until sometime later that the full realization of just how valuable this word was became apparent. He had simply referred, of course, to the present-day vernacular for the act of leaving; the train of thought he provoked, however, had more to do with the situation of the three people who composed the family than it did with his meaning or casual use of the term.

About this time there was another disturbing and intriguing question that was occasioned by a statement of Tom's made during the final moments of the play: "time is the longest distance between two places . . . [and so I] followed, from then on, in my father's footsteps, attempting to find in motion what was lost in space." With these thoughts in mind, an image began to evolve of this family as they existed in time rather than in their allotted space, their apartment. The problem, then, was to construct a diagram that would resolve these two insistent thoughts, *time and a split*, into a meaningful visual image, an image that would clarify and describe the basic action of the play. After many tries, the image shown in figure 221 evolved. This diagram provided several important visual ideas. Some of those were:

1. They were a single unit at one time. In the past, when they first moved to St. Louis, Tom was younger and, although not happy with his lot, was not in the stagnant position, both in his work and family life, he occupies during the course of the play.

2. At the time of the play's action, they have reached the point when the splits are, although ignored actively by the mother and Laura, just beginning to become serious.

3. Tom does eventually go his own way, but Laura is left, as is Amanda. For both Laura and Amanda, this is the end of the road, as it were. However, one other split is suggested here (although not actively examined in the course of the play), and that is the split between Laura and Amanda after the last attempt (the plot of the play) to get a husband for Laura. Amanda, when

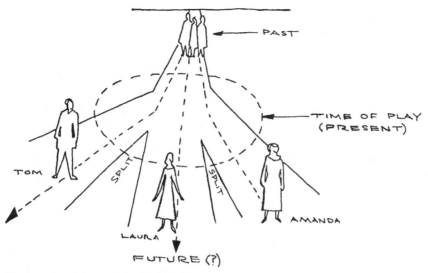

Fig. 221. Scenic concept in diagram form

this attempt fails, does move away from Laura and allows her to be alone, which, of course, is what she has come to accept already.

4. While we cannot be absolutely certain of the future of these three, we can be relatively sure that the end of the play should somehow imply they will never be "together" as a unit again. Each is left in a separate world.

From these speculations there occurred a better understanding of those final moments of the play, the time when all three find themselves isolated and alone (fig. 222). This brought to mind, incidentally, that the first scene of the play, directly following the prologuelike speech of Tom, was one that showed them together at the table; although there is an uneasy peace among them, they are as close as they ever are in the play. From that moment the splits begin to widen.

This image also suggested several practical ideas; for one thing, it clarified a desire to violate the proscenium arch (which was the type of theater where the design would be done) so that the separateness of the individual characters could be intensified. Second, if Tom chooses the outside—that is, the world—and Laura is left in the room where she was happiest—with her menagerie—then Amanda also needed a place of her own—a practical world where she can keep busy and useful. In the Mielziner design, this world of Amanda had been stuck off in the back and was subordinate to the other two worlds. Quite possibly it needed to be out where it could be visually and practically more important. A kitchen also seemed a natural and necessary adjunct to Amanda's particular place and so that, too, should somehow be included in the total design. By now the areas needed had increased from the two basic ones described in the play to three. This meant, in all probability, that space on the stage would be more limited than if the original Broadway (Mielziner's) plan was followed.

Environment is not always or entirely a matter of *how* a place looks. It takes into consideration its spatial qualities as well. In *The Glass Menagerie*, environment is concerned primarily with the juxtaposition of spaces along with their

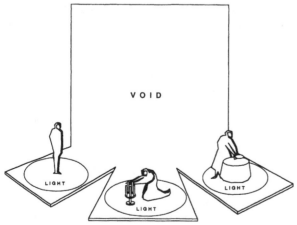

Fig. 222. Last moments of *The Glass Menagerie*

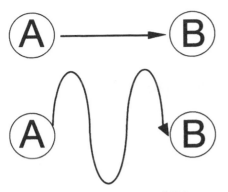

Fig. 223. Actor movement possibilities

individual and opposing qualities, not alone with a historically accurate pictorial representation, that is, showing how a St. Louis alley looked in 1939. There is no doubt this period of time and its peculiar look and feel should be evoked; but this is not simply a matter of copying factual visual details.

In other words, the space through which the characters of this play move, the shape of it, and the objects and barriers it contains are more important than the background against which they are seen, no matter how visually right it is. We cannot avoid the diagrammatic implication of Williams's last sentence: "The areaway . . . was one thing—my sister's white curtains and tiny menagerie of glass were another. Somewhere between them was the world that we lived in."

Whenever more than one place is put on the single stage space, the scenographer is faced

with a basic problem; he must compress the individual spaces to fit the total space and, at the same time, expand the possibility for movement of the actors in those spaces. Practically no major play Williams has ever written deals with a single limited area. In almost all his plays, he writes into the fabric of the play situations that cannot be acted out in a single unit of space, such as a room. The scenographer cannot avoid these demands for settings more fluid than single locales, nor is he given time to substitute one place for another in a sequence (changing one set for another by mechanical means). But the sense of space can be created without an actual, large amount of space if certain things are done with it; for instance, substituting time and distance for space. This simply means that the scenographer causes a character to walk a much longer distance to get to a place that is actually and physically quite close if approached the nearest possible way. The actor's path and progress (fig. 223) are carefully controlled by various means so that he cannot go from A to B in a direct manner but must make his approach in this longer way.

In the Mielziner design, the main part of the action was confined to the boxlike structure set in the middle of the stage (fig. 224). The proscenium arch theater, with its relatively poor sight lines, undoubtedly dictated the placement of crucial areas in his design. (The second alley, quite possibly, was created because of the sightline problem, even though in the directions of

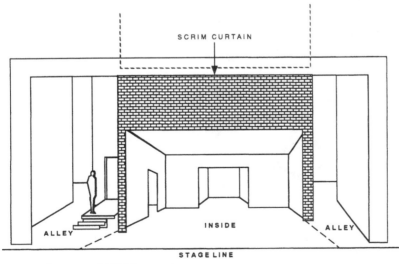

Fig. 224. Diagram of Mielziner setting

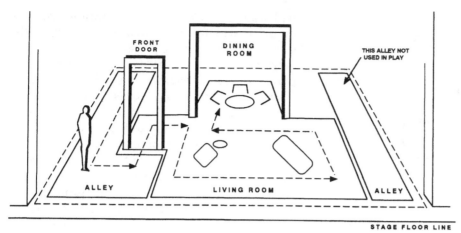

Fig. 225. Movement possibilities of Mielziner setting

the playwright—and in the description of his original model, the actual locale itself—there was no second possibility of access or escape.)

Now, since there was a desire to show more of the dining room and also add a kitchen area (not used in the original design), this added space must be paid for at the expense of the other two areas (the alley and the living room). It also became clear that an expanded hall area was necessary in order to go from room to room, and a bedroom door was needed primarily for escape purposes during the short blackouts. The need for a *sense* of space becomes, therefore, even more critical than before. In the Mielziner solution, the space is resolved basically as shown in figure 225.

By using this dining room-kitchen area in a more prominent way, it would be necessary to make the paths of movement more circuitous than he did, and, at the same time, work in depth rather than horizontally as he had done. The traffic followed roughly the pattern in figure 226.

In the present design, the proscenium arch line was violated and no curtain was used to bring the action of the play, which is extremely intimate in scope and nature, in closer proximity to the audience. This made it necessary for most of the actual physical boundaries of the rooms, the walls, to be removed. The feeling of being "boxed in," which Tom constantly alludes to and reacts against, so well conceived in the Mielziner

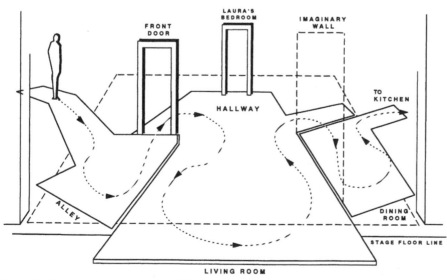

Fig. 226. Alternate movement possibilities

design had, therefore, to be resolved in a different manner altogether. This was accomplished primarily through the use of a brick wall placed at the rear of the apartment, which rose up behind and over the rather low ceiling line of the exterior. The wall, blank and unpenetrated by any opening, was carried out of sight and lost in the darkness of the upper portion of the stage house. There was, literally, no way out of Williams's "cul-de-sac" except the narrow passage of the alley into the street.

This wall (along with all the other details of the setting), while as literal environment was token in nature, was realistic in execution and did, although not entirely surrounding the apartment and alley, give the desired feeling of claustrophobic enclosure. It should also be noted here, perhaps, that even though the details of the setting were almost naturalistic when examined separately, the composition of these elements was not, at least not to the extent of the Mielziner design. If any prevalent influence is discernible, it would probably be Brechtian in nature.

The greatest advantage of the open stage form featured in this design (fig. 227), however, was that in extending the acting areas out and beyond the walls and into the auditorium, the actors could, by light, be more effectively iso-lated and separated from the setting. This ability to isolate a character from his environment is essential to the structure and nature of this particular play since it purports to be memory, and memory tends to disassociate and separate the significant act and detail from its original, all-inclusive, comprehensive background. This need to define and isolate characters, and at the same time obliterate all else, is especially necessary in the Laura-Jim section during the final scene of the play. Williams, himself, motivates this need by causing the action to be confined to a small circle of light from a few candles.

In the final stages of the design, what had evolved was this: a mood, a feeling of period and place, was accomplished (this is something that the Mielziner design did superbly). At the same time, it was necessary to depart from his basic plan in order (1) to open up the apartment and expose more effectively some areas that he and his director decided not to show or use and (2) to make use of the image of the three major characters split one from the other and each alone on his own solitary path. What has been done in this design (fig. 228) is certainly not a matter of being newer (except chronologically) or more original (that was never an intent or even a serious question) or better but a matter of how well the design served the actors and

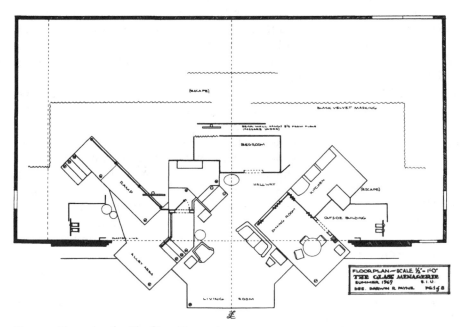

Fig. 227. Floor plan for *The Glass Menagerie*

Fig. 228. Design for *The Glass Menagerie*

director; in fact, that is the only criterion really acceptable in judging the merit of any scenographic design. What was attempted, and to some extent accomplished, was a resolution of the original thesis, which was to think the problem through from the ground up (finding in that process a workable and satisfying solution) rather than to rely on or react against an earlier one by another scenographer. Finally, let it be said, if there is a sense of competition in the scenographer's makeup, and it is hard to believe that any creative artist is totally without it in some respect, it should be directed more inwardly, striving with one's own limitations, and not outward, that is, attempting to "do it better" than someone else.

Scenography during the Past Forty Years

Until now our attention has been directed primarily toward scenographic designs created from a traditional and fairly literal point of view; in these designs an audience would have little difficulty relating what they saw on the stage to their own conceptions of what reality

was or should be. It is hoped that this procedure has had some value, partly for its own sake but also as a preparation for studying scenographic concepts that are not as literally based.

It is time to take a step beyond this approach—or at least to affirm there are others—and to make a brief examination of how scenographers create designs that have as their premise that the stage setting need not always be representational images of reality as perceived outside the theater. While discussion of this view has been purposely avoided until now, even the most cursory glance at the output of today's scenographers will quickly reveal to the student scenographer a wide spectrum of possibilities of which he should be aware. At the same time, it must be remembered that the most advanced design theory owes much more to past concepts than it might appear at first glance.

Theater tends to be a closed system, a conservative activity where change comes slowly; the world of "show business" presents to many an escape from the "real" world. During the last one hundred fifty years the most popular style of production has been varying degrees of naturalism. The desire to reproduce reality on the stage still remains strong not only for audiences but for professional theater artists as well. And yet during this century change has accelerated as each decade passed. By the early 1960s change for its own sake had all but supplanted traditional approaches to almost every aspect of life. Theater certainly did not escape these new anticonservative attitudes. As a result, scenographers working during the past forty years find they must look at the world both inside and outside the theater with different eyes than their predecessors did. Naturalism and the reproduction of literal images on the stage have all but given way to a hybrid form of production that borrows from every age, from every style, from every production philosophy that has been tried heretofore. Along with this trend there is a parallel attempt on the part of those who produce works for the stage to uncover and to display that which lies beneath the surface of physical things and events. There seems to be an intense desire to fracture, reorganize, and synthesize raw visual impressions into hybrid forms and structures that do not mirror life so much as present its dominate feature more directly: *change as it occurs in time and motion.*

It is easier to note, however, that profound alterations are being made in the way the scenographer thinks and performs than it is to chart the directions and import of those alterations. Moreover, by the time new concepts and practices filter into the classroom, often they have lost their initial vitality and usually much of their original "meaning"; for this reason, the young scenographer sometimes adopts only the outer forms of these newer approaches (and all too often only the most obvious and spectacular elements of them) without really understanding the underlying reasons for their initial creation. (There is more truth than we care to admit in Faulkner's observation that "immature artists copy, great artists steal." Knowing what and when to steal is very much a part of the scenographer's self-education.)

Although the theater of the past four decades has been the target of numerous forces, undoubtedly the most significant change has been the emergence of a more ritualistic form of theater that has put an emphasis on the emotional, nonverbal (sensory) engagement of an audience. Along with this trend there has been a marked lack of emphasis on elaborate production as well as an intense effort to break down the traditional barriers that have grown up during the past three hundred years between performer and audience. A corresponding trend has been the virtual dethronement of the playwright as the single most important person in theater. As a direct result of this development, the play, once considered as the sacrosanct corner block of the production, has become less important. The hierarchy of the theater—playwright down to director down to actor, scenographer, and technician—in a great many instances has all but given way to a loosely bonded confederation of artists each who, by mutual agreement, "does his own thing." Some playwrights writing today, however, are more "idea" men who supply scenarios and situations to actors who then improvise from those germinal ideas. Television and cinema often are collaborative ventures where the group makes decisions as to what audiences see or hear. This does not imply that everyone in theater has suddenly jettisoned traditional methods and standards of theater production; tradition in theater is much too strong; productions are being mounted in most companies as they have been for centuries. Nevertheless, there are few professional artists, especially directors and scenographers, who have not been influenced by the experiments of the more avant-garde theater groups that have gained attention during the last forty years. In addition, directors are encouraging scenographers to take more liberties, to be more adventuresome in their designs than producers have in the past. In many cases, scenographers simply seems to be taking these liberties for granted. This does not necessarily imply that they are becoming self-serving, ego-oriented exhibitionists; most scenographers still design settings—although these settings are now more generally referred to as scenic environments—that they sincerely believe are in the best interests of the total production. But they are in many instances accepting less outside advice as to what those best interests are; this, I believe, accounts for the significant number of scenographers who have turned to stage directing in addition to scenography. At the very least, there is a distinct understanding among most scenographers that the situation in which they work has become a more coequal one than it was in the

Fig. 229. *Der Mond* design

past. In some ways, this thinking is less an innovation of today than it is a return to theater practices prior to the middle of the nineteenth century when Richard Wagner and the Duke of Saxe-Meiningen began their crusade to make all aspects of a production merge into a unified whole (and if this production was to be reflective of any single personality, it was to be theirs). The difference between then and now, however, is that the scenographer, then often only an artisan who supplied scenic backgrounds according to strict specifications, is now very much an individual with strong artistic views and a philosophy to support those opinions.

What is essentially new to the present-day theater (and something for which the modern scenographer is greatly responsible) is the conception of the stage setting not as a static or fixed unit—a "set"—confined to a limited, predetermined area of space but, rather, as an image or series of images which, like the human universe it reflects, is in a constant state of flux. This concept gives rise to a number of principles, some of which have been conventions of past ages of theater, although others are strictly twen-

tieth century in origin. A few of these conventions—although not all—are:

1. The action of the production can take place anywhere within viewing range of the spectator (and may even require the spectator to move from place to place to view the action—rather than having the performer come to him), and the spectator's vision may be amplified, channeled, or distorted by mechanical means (closed-circuit television—cinema—projections or light effects).

2. The setting need not be a single unified image but can be a number of unrelated ones shown in series or simultaneously.

3. The duration of any single image or group of images is not directly related to the duration of the script's stated or intended divisions (acts, scenes, episodes, etc.). In fact, the images may move and change in arbitrary rhythms contrary to the progression of the script's intentions or to the actions of the performers. The scenic environment, in short, may be every bit as kinetic as any of the other elements in the production.

4. The scenic environment may visually (as well as physically) support the nature of the pro-

duction without literal or historical references may consist solely of forms and images the scenographer feels best displays the abstract qualities of the production (fig. 229).

Vladimir Jindra, the noted Czechoslovakian scenographer, has given an extremely succinct appraisal of just how all these trends add up: "The artificial rules and artificial relationships in the world of a drama derive from the principle that a human being can't die, can't live, can't represent all his life in two hours as a dramatic person, as an actor does: nor can human beings be transported from one place to another with the ease of dramatic characters. There is a very simple conclusion we can make from these facts: *each dramatic piece has its own unique rules, determined by the space, by the time, by the movements, and by the dramatic personalities involved"* italics mine).

In the next example, we will concentrate only on one area of these various possibilities: making the setting an embodiment of abstract qualities instead of a literal representation of a historical or geographical locale. Multimedia productions certainly figure importantly in current production practices. To discuss them adequately is, however, far beyond the scope of this text and presupposes a level of investigation which we have not intended. Little has been written on this subject to date; the material that has found its way into print usually deals with past productions (accounts of how a certain production was accomplished) or observations in the most general terms. The young scenographer should expect these newer trends in scenography to accelerate in the future; but much of what he learns about how to produce such a design must be gained from experience, not books, since one of the prime features of a multimedia production—the mobility of images—is incapable of being shown.

Scenography as a Physical Embodiment of Abstract Qualities: *The Caretaker*

Although the scenographer may use actual, realistic source materials in the preparation of a design, he may sometimes be more interested in refining from those materials what he considers to be the visual and tactile essences. His purpose is to create a design that while not recognizably "real" will in some way increase the involvement, understanding, and pleasure of the spectator viewing it and the actor performing within it. In creating such a design, the scenographer is still doing research much in the manner that we have already observed, but he allows his imagination to take greater liberties with his findings than has been the case in previous examples. He may, for instance, strip away surfaces from their substructures, juxtapose incongruent images and objects in various scales, fracture natural elements or architectural forms, and then recombine them into new structures and arrangements. Let us take a closer look at how and why a scenographer might choose to work in this manner.

Harold Pinter's play *The Caretaker* takes place in a single location, a room in a derelict building in an old section of London; the time of the action originally was 1959 (the date of the play's composition), but it could very well be the present time with little harm done to the text or intention of the play. While there is no reason to believe that the actual room in which Pinter sets the action of the play exists, it is quite probable that hundreds of such rooms not only do exist in London but could be found and duplicated on the stage. But would this really satisfy the underlying requirements of the script? Would a naturalistic setting necessarily make the play more correctly produced—or better in the eyes of the spectator? Would it possibly hinder the production in any way? While these questions could never be completely answered without thinking in terms of an actual, proposed production, any close inspection of the play will quickly reveal that Pinter relies heavily on physical things to create an atmosphere that while it is never less than real is always something more than factual reportage; nor does the dialogue, no matter how disjoined or abstract it becomes, ever proceed very far without direct reference to, or use of, something physical and close at hand. (In many ways, the locales of his plays are almost always totally closed systems; that is, the rooms in which the actions of his plays take place are not only complete worlds in themselves, but are isolated from any others.)

Any scenographer would agree that it is impossible to design this particular play without a very careful analysis of the physical features of the room where the action transpires—the exact placement of doors, windows—with an equally intense study of the objects in it (and since it is a kind of storehouse, the problems of placement and relationships of objects become critical). But what about the intent of the play itself; what about its verbal structure? Who could deny that the dialogue is naturalistic to the point of being pointless? Or is it? Is it possible that Pinter is operating on more than one level and with more than one purpose? Quite obviously he is. It is equally obvious that his locale is closely tied to what he is trying to show. Should, then, the scenographer create a scenic environment that mirrors exactly only one level, the naturalistic one? Can you, in fact, have naturalistic acting (and that is obviously the technique demanded of the performers if not the underlying intent) in a "theatrical" setting, that is, a setting that is not "real"? Of course, only an accepted philosophy of presentation can give the answer to such a general question, but the answer it gives in today's practice is *yes*.

This is not so contradictory as it might seem to be at first glance. Perhaps one of the solutions to understanding this situation lies in the fact that an actor's performance can and should lie on several levels simultaneously; whereas the scenographer's work, while also striving to possess levels of meaning other than the purely literal one, is more restricted to harder-lined images and symbols that are not as illusion-creating (and therefore not as mysterious) as those created by the actor.

What if the scenographer decides to create a design *that exhibits a level of meaning other than the naturalistic one*; a level in which he presents to an audience the qualities he perceives in this room in abstract form, not hidden behind the details of naturalistic reproduction? In essence, this is what has happened in much of today's production; the scenographer has been given just such a liberty. And whether or not one agrees with this philosophy (there are, in fact, many who do not), it should be recognized that is does exist; the scenographer training today would be well advised not only to expect this freedom of ex-

pression but, more and more, to expect that many directors will not only allow but also thrust it upon him. Let us take a closer look at how the design for this play, *The Caretaker*, was approached in the production discussed here. In this production questions similar to those we have just raised were part of the scenographer's task. These were not the only problems; others had to be addressed such as:

1. How, in the open stage version planned, could the atmosphere of a closed-up, cutoff place be obtained; how to get the effect of a tight, cramped space on a stage with a wall possible on one side only, the other three removed to facilitate an audience's vision?

2. How to make the characters seem to be held down and contained or, as the director desired, "wedged into a situation." While the actors were to perform their roles as naturalistically as possible, the place where they were to perform should be "less an actual room than a structure which is open and closed at the same time; a particular room and a timeless place; a construction that catches smells, is permanent but capable of disintegrating momentarily—a world solid and full of holes."

3. A floor pattern that allows for the maximum mobility of action (there is much more of this inherent in the script than seems at first reading) while seeming to prevent it.

Preliminary research turned up enough materials to allow a drawing to be made that would satisfy many of the integral necessities of the play's action: a room on the second floor of a fairly large house with a number of rooms, hallways, and so on, all in a state of disrepair (fig. 230). Literal features of the room thus reconstructed: walls—wallpaper dirty with age, peeling, stained; plaster beneath cracked, patches falling off to reveal substructure (lath and rough plaster); moldings and trims scarred, dirty, rough from repeated coats of paint and varnish; floors—worn, warped, scarred, edges of planks chipped and splintered. The whole building shows the effect of heat, cold, moisture, and hard use with little upkeep. While these are all facts (strong possibilities at least), research cannot end here; a greater refinement of these findings is necessary before they can be directly incorporated into a final design. But where to from

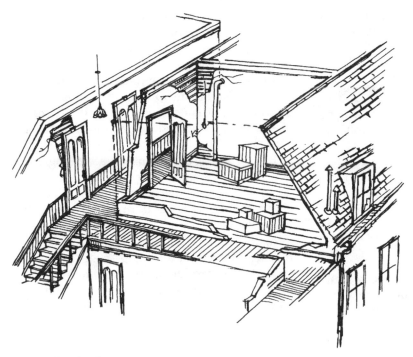

Fig. 230. London house

here; what direction will turn up anything more useful than this information or determine its possible use?

Research, as it has been pointed out before, is not always just a matter of finding appropriate visual details. Literary sources can be tremendously helpful to the scenographer when he is seeking to pinpoint illusive qualities of a playscript; they might very well assist the scenographer in knowing what out of his raw research materials to keep and use and what to discard. Granted, these sources are much harder to find than visual materials; you almost have to know where this written material is before searching for it. This is all the more reason for the scenographer to maintain a wide undirected reading program. Paradoxically, being able to verbalize images is more important to the scenographer of abstract settings than it might be for the scenographer creating more literal ones; words become clues to visual ideas. For instance, when I first read *The Caretaker* and began to consider what the room where it takes place should look and—more important—feel like, I recalled a passage I had once read in a book by Rainer Maria Rilke, *The Notebooks of Malte Laurids Brigge*. The passage

was a description of an old tenement building that was being torn down, and this is what the protagonist, Brigge, saw and recorded in his notebook:

Will anyone believe that there are such houses? . . . But, to be precise, they were houses that were no longer there. Houses that had been pulled down from top to bottom. What *was* there was the other houses, those that stood alongside of them, tall neighboring houses. Apparently these were in danger of falling down, since everything alongside had been taken away; for a whole scaffolding of long, tarred timbers had been rammed slantwise between the rubbish-strewn ground and the bared wall. I don't know whether I have already said that it is this wall I mean. But it was, so to speak, not the first wall of the existing houses (as one would have supposed), but the last of those that had been there. One saw its inner side. One saw at the different storeys the walls of rooms to which the paper still clung, and here and there the join of floor or ceiling. Beside these room-walls there still remained, along the whole length of the wall, a dirty-white area, and through this crept in unspeakably disgusting motions, worm-soft as if digesting, the open, rust-spotted channel of the water-closet pipe. Grey, dusty traces of the paths the lighting-gas had taken remained at the ceiling edges, and here and there, quite unexpectedly, they bent sharp around and came running into the colored wall and into a hole that had been torn out black and ruthless. But most unforgettable of all were the walls themselves. The stubborn life of these rooms had not let itself be trampled out. It was still there; it clung to the nails that had been left, it stood on the remaining hands-breadth of flooring, it crouched under the corner joints where there was still a little bit of interior. One could see that it was in the paint, which, year by year, it had slowly altered: blue into moldy green, green into grey, and yellow into an old, stale rotting white. But it was also in the spots that had kept fresher, behind mirrors, pictures, and wardrobes; for it had drawn and re-drawn their contours, and had been with spiders and dust even in these hiding places that now lay bared. It was in every flayed strip, it was in the damp blisters at the lower edges of the wallpapers; it wavered in the torn-off shreds, and sweated out of the foul patches that had come into being long ago. And from these walls once blue and green and yellow, which were framed by the fracture-tracts of the demolished parti-tions, the breath of these lives stood out—the clammy, sluggish, musty breath, which no wind had yet scat-tered. There stood the middays and the sicknesses and the exhaled breath and the smoke of years, and the sweat that breaks out under armpits and makes clothes heavy, and the stale breath of mouths, and the fusel odor of sweltering feet. There stood the tang of urine and the burn of soot and the grey reek of pota-toes, and the heavy, smooth stench of ageing grease. The sweet, lingering smell of neglected infants was there, and the fear-smell of children who go to school, and the sultriness out of the beds of nubile youths. To these was added much that had come from below, from the abyss of the street, which reeked, and more that had oozed down from above with the rain, which over cities is not clean.

The observations that Rilke has Brigge make are essentially those I found in my own research; but there is a vast difference, it can easily be seen, between my casual catalogue of isolated "facts" and this intensely depicted total vision. Of the two, Rilke's words are more helpful to me than my own visual findings; his description is not a substitute, it merely clarifies my own think-ing by helping me to recognize the "right" solu-tion when I hit upon it. Moreover, there is a direct relationship between the subterranean levels on which Pinter's play moves and the thoughts and feelings experienced by Brigge when he viewed those walls to rooms no longer

in existence. It is precisely this mode of thought that the scenographer must apply to his work, especially when creating settings that directly present to an audience essences and abstract qualities of recognizable details in a literal con-text. It is also significant that Brigge is most af-fected by what is *not* there rather than what is; one could say exactly the same thing about Pint-er's plays.

Both the director and the scenographer agreed that the setting for *The Caretaker* should have a similar feeling, should evoke something of the same response from an audience that Brigge felt when he viewed the remaining walls of the torn-down building. But now it was time to begin the task of applying these thoughts to the particular production at hand; to begin solv-ing the unique problems it presented. Since the nature of the open stage made it impossible to close in the sides of the room with solid walls, it was decided to make the best use of the re-maining elements—the ceiling, the floor, the back wall (fig. 231). It was also decided to inten-sify, in some way, the overhanging force of the ceiling (and, incidentally, facilitate the hanging of lighting instruments); this was accomplished in two major ways: (1) by slanting it; this idea presented itself in several photographs showing rooms with outer walls merging into roof lines (the earlier drawing [fig. 230] includes this fea-ture in it); and (2) by forcing the perspective in an obvious manner (fig. 232). As a result of these two decisions, a strong downward thrust was given to the whole ceiling (fig. 233). This helped obtain the director's desire for a space into which the action could be "wedged." (In the final de-sign, as it was realized on the stage, there was an ominous quality imparted by this ceiling that

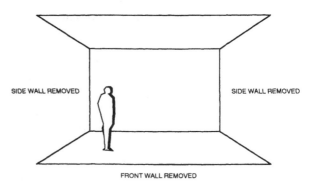

Fig. 231. Room with three walls removed

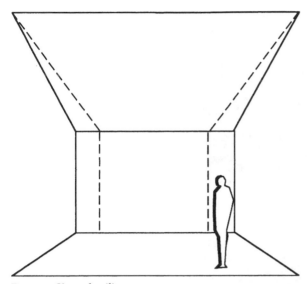

Fig. 232. Slanted ceiling

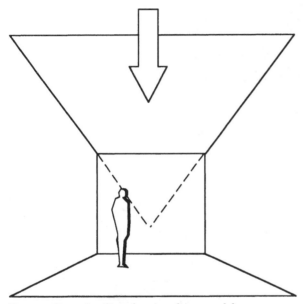

Fig. 233. Slanted ceiling showing downward force

can be explained in terms of design principles; that is, strong downward forces when coupled with diagonals equals dynamic instability.)

There was only one access to the room (and there should be only one); this was placed in the back wall. This door led to a hallway that led to downstairs and other parts of the house. Architecturally, a ceiling such as we had now did not make much sense; aesthetically, we felt, it did: feasibility lost out to artistic license. Figure 234 is a photographic image that seemed to sum up

a number of desirable features (a stark simplicity but, at the same time, a certain mysterious quality: perhaps the resulting combination of the aged wooden structures with the extreme angle of perspective).

Thus far, a basic form had been evolved, although at this stage of development it is certainly not a complete or usable one. Various possibilities for treating this shell now came under consideration; one possibility was to make the ceiling and wall a simulation of what might be found in the actual building. (And this was considered at one point in the planning stages of this production.) This did not, however, seem to take full advantage of the images summoned up by Rilke: a room whose physical existence was all but destroyed but whose "stubborn life . . . had not let itself be trampled out." Perhaps there was something in the actual construction of the building that would provide the feeling of enclosure and at the same time seem to be in the process of disappearing. ("A world solid and full of holes.") And so the walls and ceiling had its various layers of building materials—wallpapers, coats of paint, plaster—removed until only the bare lath and framework remained (fig. 235).

Unlike the framework of a house being constructed, which plainly exhibits its new wood, this structure must show the effects of its age and disintegration; moreover, these effects should be presented on their own terms, not merely as naturalistic details. They are, in fact, the physical correlatives of Rilke's verbal images, "the tang of urine . . . the burn of soot . . . the grey reek of potatoes . . . the heavy, smooth stench of ageing grease." Verbal images suggest physical ones; but how they are put into physical is not always an easy or predictable task. To assure the required result, not only must the scenographer create the appropriate forms and structures, he must also provide instruction to the shops for the application of textured materials to these forms (special plastic sands mixed into paints, crumbled cork, appliques of metal foils, fiber-glass forms and finishes, vacuum-formed plastic, etc.). The day when scenery was only wood, canvas, and scene paint is probably gone forever. A scenographer must also ensure that these forms and textures are finished with a careful selection of color (and, again, Rilke provides valuable clues to a proper palette for *The Care-*

Fig. 234. Wooden house by Charles Lichtenstein. Courtesy of Katharine Kuh

taker: "blue into moldy green, green into grey, and yellow into an old stale rotting white"). Even though the scenographer may have had many careful color sketches and paint specifications, they are rarely sufficient. It is not uncommon in actual production for him to go to the shops and seek the proper effect by working directly on the actual scenery—handling three-dimensional materials much as a sculptor would and painting and repainting the scenery a number of times. Only the amateur gets what he wants on the first try.

As it has been noted before, this room is filled with a great number of items; ostensibly, there is no apparent order to their placement. In reality, a random order to these things would immobilize the actor (and the relationship of each item to the others is implicitly—and carefully—worked out in the text of the play, fig. 236).

What must be done, therefore, is determine (with the director) just what these space relation-

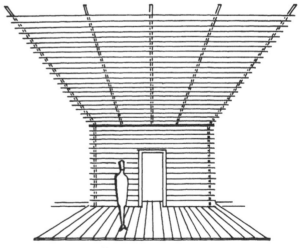

Fig. 235. Slanted ceiling with lath construction exposed

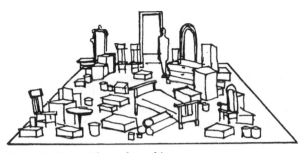

Fig. 236. Floor with random objects

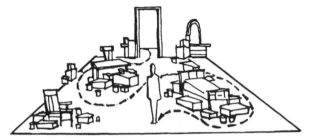

Fig. 237. Floor with objects in islands

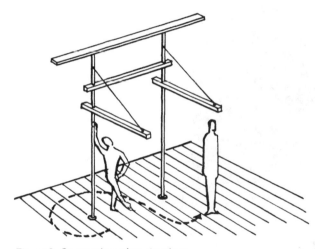

Fig. 238. Supporting pipe structure

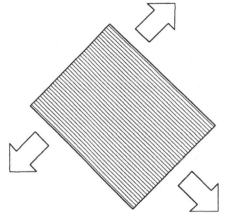

Fig. 239. Floor extension possibilities

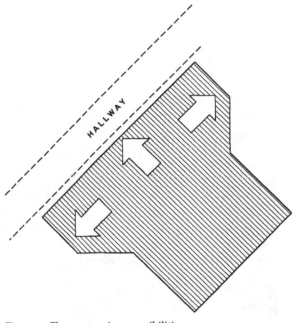

Fig. 240. Floor extension possibilities

ships are and then mass all the items that are necessary to the progress of the play (along with those that are simply needed for visual effect) into islands around and through which the action patterns of the performers can move (fig. 237). Sight lines, naturally, limit the height of the objects that could be placed around the outer edge of the stage; this made it necessary to "store" furniture and objects above the heads of the performers. It also intensifies the claustrophobic feeling that they are hemmed in by these things without really being so.

While a structure was designed specifically for this purpose, it also functioned in other ways as well; the pipe frame with its outrigger beams not only provided hanging room for overhead storage but also helped to cut off and define the total area of the room into smaller more individual areas. Not only did it seem a logical supporting device for the ceiling—as well as a structure around which the actors can gravitate, lean against, and otherwise use in numerous ways—it also helped to integrate the physical setting into the total stage space without hindering the spectator's vision (fig. 238). Once the basic form of the setting was settled, a floor plan had to be determined that would incorporate all the needs of the play (and the actors) and then be resolved in terms of actual space available, which, on the open stage is always at a premium. The basic form of the stage could not be extended in any of these directions (fig. 239). This made it necessary to expand the playing area in the only directions possible while still preserving the basic thrust of the stage (fig. 240).

While the preceding pages should give a fairly clear picture of how a design for *The Caretaker* evolved, it would be impossible to draw attention to all the many steps and decisions that are made for any one project; some of these will be reasoned out along the lines presented here; not a few will be compromises. Finally, what resulted in this case was, more than anything else, a large sculpture form in which the action

of play, it was felt, transpired appropriately (figs. 241, 242).

There is little question that scenographers today must be more knowledgeable in all fields of art, history, and social studies than their predecessors were or needed to be. While we cannot know for certain what the future of scenography will be—or what path theater production in the future will take—it is safe to assume that the old world of canvas flats and illusory painting is fast waning, taking with it the box-set mentality that has plagued the theater for so long.

"Epic Scene Design"
By Mordecai Gorelik

The controversial nature of the Epic stage form, as developed in the 1920's in Berlin, is

Fig. 241. Design for *The Caretaker*

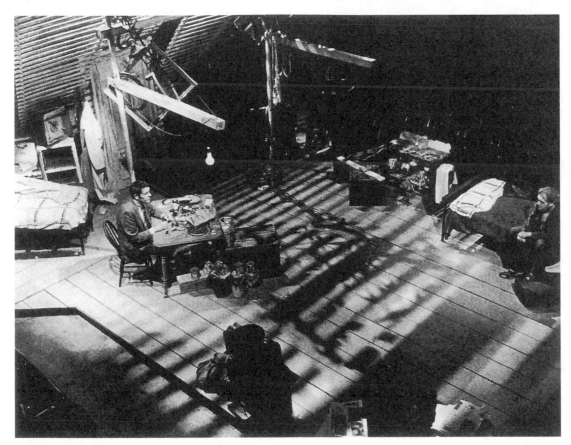

Fig. 242. Scene from *The Caretaker*

nowhere more evident than in its scene design. By 1924 the director Erwin Piscator, with his staging of Alfons Paquet's *Flags*, had inaugurated the use of film sequences on stage, a method that was to characterize many of his productions. An example was his staging of Ernst Toller's *Hoppla, We Live!* (1927). The play is about a man who comes out of a lunatic asylum for the first time in nine years, gets a look at the world, then decided to hurry back to the asylum; before he can get there, however, he is caught up in the violence of contemporary history, and escapes from an insane world only by hanging himself. The director provided, as a prologue, a newsreel review of the past nine years of world events. During the rest of the action, scenes on stage alternated with film episodes. Two movie screens were used, one behind the other, the front one being, on occasion, transparent.

For *Rasputin*, in the same year, Piscator used three film projectors and two thousand meters of film. The stage setting resembled a segment of a globe that opened in sections and turned on a revolving platform. The globe itself formed above it, while at one side of the stage a narrow filmic "calendar" kept marginal notes on the multitude of events of World War I. At times captions were superimposed on the film as it ran along. Thus there appeared, over a shot of the battle of the Somme, the words "Loss—a half-million dead; gain—three hundred square kilometers."

Also, in 1927, came *The Good Soldier Schweik*, which recounts the adventures of a sly peasant soldier, a Czech conscript who endures all the horrors of the World War, including its hopelessly snarled red tape. Under Piscator's direction, two treadmills, parallel with the footlights, formed the depth of the stage and brought scraps of settings on and off. Behind the treadmills a translucent projection screen was provided for the antimilitarist animated cartoons of George Grosz and for movie sequences showing the road that Schweik traveled on his famous march to Budweis. In addition, full-size cutout cartoons of freight cars and soldiers passed by on the treadmills.

Leo Lania's *Competition* (1928), also staged by Piscator, tells what happens when an oil well is discovered and two international oil concerns begin a ruthless competition. The play opens on a bare stage. Three travelers lie down to sleep. They discover the oil, then hammer a crude stake into the stage floor. Now begins the sale of parts of the stage. Large signs go up as the rival companies fence off portions with barbed wire. The drillers arrive, followed by loads of lumber for the derricks, which are erected then and there. Finally, the stage is crowded with oil derricks.

Piscator's experiments were matched, in the same era, by those of the dramatist-director Bertolt Brecht. Brecht's *The Threepenny Opera* (1928) had, as a permanent background, a pipe organ outlined in electric lights. A small orchestra occupied the middle of the stage. The production employed freestanding pieces of scenery, including iron-barred prison cages and a long stairway on casters. Unlike Piscator, Brecht never resorted to films on stage, but he, too, made use of projection screens, usually on either side of the stage, or above the actor's heads. On those screens explanatory titles and illustrations were shown. Thus the wedding scene of *The Threepenny Opera*, a stable in Soho, London, had the projected title: "Deep in the heart of Soho the bandit Macheath celebrates his marriage to Polly Peachum, daughter of the King of Beggars."

In the New York production of Brecht's *Mother* (1935), a small revolving stage stood just left of stage center and was partitioned through the middle with wooden panels a little more than head-high. A projection screen hung above it. At stage right were two grand pianos. The stage was illuminated by visible spotlights hanging in the proscenium opening. Illustrations and information were flashed on the screen: a photo of the factory where the workers were employed, a portrait of the owner of the factory, a list of food prices in Mother's untutored hand. The Hollywood, California, production of Brecht's *Galileo* (1947) also contained projections; these consisted of illustrations taken from Galileo's book, the *Dialogo*. Introductory titles for each of the scenes of *Galileo* were thrown on a half curtain that was used to mask scene shifts.

The half curtains strung on wires across the stage became a feature of Brecht's staging, much as the film sequences typified Piscator. They served again for Brecht's *Mother Courage and Her Children*, a play that may well be remembered as Brecht's finest work and very likely as one of the great dramas of this century. *Mother Courage* was produced in Zurich (1941) and East Berlin (1949). It is still in the repertory of the Berliner Ensemble, a company devoted to the production of Brecht's plays and of plays in Epic style. Its story is that of the marketwoman, Anna Fierling, who follows the armies of King Charles X of Sweden during the Thirty Years' War, losing her three children in the course of many adventures. The production, as directed by Brecht and Erich Engel, contains no settings in the ordinary sense, only stage properties. Of these the most important is Mother Courage's market wagon, which rolls on from year to year and country to country, maintaining its place against the movement of a huge revolving stage. There is no background except a bare plaster cyclorama, but when a more enclosed quality is needed, curtains of rough cloth are hung from visible battens upstage. The many locales of the action are indicated by means of names woven out of tree branches and let down from the flies. The lighting is entirely uncolored. For the song numbers the actors take a "singing position" downstage, and at the same time there is lowered from the flies a special property made up of battle flags, drums, trumpets, and three or four illuminated glass globes. As the war drags on, this prop becomes dusty and battle-stained and the glass globes are broken and left unlit.

New York recently saw an example of Epic design in the setting for Friedrich Dürrenmatt's *The Visit* (1958). These consisted in part of a backdrop painted with deliberate crudity to indicated a small town, before which appeared mere scraps of scenery—the facade of a small railway station, the counter of a grocery store, the balcony of a hotel. Cutout lettering, let down from above, names each locale specifically.

The Visit's designer, Teo Otto, a Swiss, also did the settings for *Mother Courage* in collaboration with Heinrich Kilger. Other European artists who have worked in Epic style include, most notably, Caspar Neher, designer of the original *Threepenny Opera* and of a number of other

Brechtian dramas, including *The Rise and Fall of the City of Mahagonny* (1930), the Brechtian *Antigone* (Chur, Switzerland, 1948), *Herr Puntila and His Handy Man Matti* (Berlin, 1949), *The Tutor* (Berlin, 1950), *Mother* (Berlin, 1951) and *Galileo* (Berlin, 1957). Since the founding of the Berliner Ensemble, several new designers have been initiated into the Epic method, principally Karl von Appen, who contributed the settings of Brecht's *The Good Woman of Setzuan* (1957) and *The Caucasian Chalk Circle* (1954), Farquhar's *Drums and Trumpets* (*The Recruiting Officer*) (1955), Vishnevski's *The Optimistic Tragedy* (1958), and Synge's *The Playboy of the Western World* (1956).

To my knowledge the first original Epic settings by an American designer were my own, for the New York production of Brecht's *Mother*, already described. (The settings were dismissed as "braggart paucity" in a contemporary *Theatre Arts* review by Edith J. R. Isaacs.) I have been given little further opportunity to work in Epic style. However, my designs for the off-Broadway *Volpone* (1957) were in the Epic tradition, and so was the setting for Michael V. Gazzo's *A Hatful of Rain* (1955). In the latter production a tenement flat in Manhattan was indicated by means of screenlike walls and a kitchen on a raked platform; an iron ladder and a fire escape led up from each side of the stage, and a skylight hung independently over a hallway area. My designs for John Wexley's *They Shall Not Die*, were an Epic project (1934) never realized on stage.

During the era of Federal Theatre, the Living Newspaper unit, in dramatizing topical events and statistics, made use of fragmentary settings, projections and film sequences, borrowing freely from the pioneer work of Piscator. Especially noteworthy was the work of Hjalmar Hermansen for *Triple A Plowed Under* (1936) and of Howard Bay for *One Third of a Nation* (1938) [fig. 243].

During his American period at the Dramatic Workshop, the school he founded in New York, Piscator carried out a number of productions of unusual interest scenically. The settings for Pogodin's *Aristocrats* (1945) consisted mainly of changing projections on a group of screens. Klabond's *The Circle of Chalk* (1941) had an arrangement of Venetian blinds. Robert Penn Warren's *All the King's Men* (1948) made use of spiral stair-

case, flanked by projection screens and supplemented by mobile platforms. Piscator has since put on a new series of experimental productions in western Germany and elsewhere in Europe. His staging of Arthur Miller's *The Crucible* (1954), and Faulkner's *Requiem for a Nun* (1955) and Tolstoy's *War and Peace* (1955) featured translucent platforms, jutting into the center of the auditorium and lighted from below. In the case of *War and Peace* the stage floor had sectional maps of Europe projected on it from underneath [fig. 244].

Present-day scene design in the professional theatre of the United States is mainly in the tradition of selective naturalism, varied by Theatricalism in its more imaginative work. But some tendencies toward Epic may be noted. These recent trends may be related to the work of Brecht and Piscator only by coincidence, but whether coincidental or not, they are noteworthy. Thus it is now common practice for American musical comedies to use fragments of settings that work arbitrarily in space in front of more permanent backdrops. A parallel to the method of Piscator's *Competition* may be seen in the design by Peter Larkin for the construction of a teahouse on a stage in *The Teahouse of the August Moon* (1953). Boris Aronson's setting for *J.B.* (1958), though Theatricalist in conception, utilized furniture and properties with Epic precision.

Even more epic in quality were Jo Mielziner's settings for *Cat on a Hot Tin Roof* (1955) and *Sweet Bird of Youth* (1959). Working with the boldly imaginative director Elia Kazan, Mielziner began in those plays to push beyond Theatricalism. His designs remained romantic and had a confusing residue of Theatricalist make-believe (as in the use of invisible doors or the invisible pull-cords of Venetian blinds); but he proceeded nevertheless to the free use of properties and furniture in space, and to the reduction of environment to a "report" (projections of porch columns and fireworks in *Cat*, projections of Venetian blinds and of palm trees and seascapes in *Bird*). Specifically and tellingly Epic was Kazan's use of a television sequence in *Bird*, in which a demagogue and his henchmen were shown in action. This scenic element was no mere novelty but a legitimate device for an Epic widening of Tennessee Williams's story. A projected sequence of this sort occurred in a now-forgotten play by

Fig. 243. Setting for *One Third of a Nation*. Courtesy of Howard Bay

George S. Brooks and Walter B. Lister, *Spread Eagle* (1927). As directed by Jed Harris, with settings by Norman Bel Geddes, this unusual Broadway drama, epic in scope, had a scene of a film-showing in a movie theatre in order to illustrate the use of high-powered propaganda in drumming a nation into war.

The scenic innovations of Epic theatre have attracted attention and are undoubtedly influencing world theatre. But they are more than novelties or bright ideas. On the contrary, they are the product of a whole new philosophy of production, part of a theatre larger in scope than the theatre of today. Piscator used projected comment and film shorts in order to make up for the deficiency of his scripts, which were written in the prevailing naturalistic or romantic style. In an attempt to add historic perspective to the scripts, he wove in movie sequences that gave some of the background of the stage events, and used projected captions that started trains of thought not suggested by the dialogue. Seeking this wider view, Piscator rebelled against the concentration of the single setting; instead he tended to break up the action into a flowing movement of a great many scenes. His adaptation of Tolstoy's *War and Peace*, with its forty-five scenes, could almost serve as a film shooting script. In view of the demands he has made upon the shifting mechanism of the stage, it is not surprising that Piscator finds today's stage machinery out of date. There is no reason he thinks, why the modern stage should not be as beautifully equipped as the modern factory.

Brecht was less interested than Piscator in the use of stage machinery, but he, too, objected to the "well-made" play and its naturalistic setting. These he considered not only old fashioned but part of a "magical" technique for tricking an audience into a cheap emotional jag. The principle of alienation underlies not only Brecht's writings but the kind of scenic production his plays re-

Fig. 244. Setting for *War and Peace*. Courtesy of Mordecai Gorelik

quire. He wished to "alienate," to "cool off" the dramatic story, to "hold it at arm's length," so to speak. In that way he hoped to make audiences more reflective and critical, to keep them from being "entranced" by a spuriously exciting, over-emotional empathy. His use of lettered comment, or of projected titles summarizing the action of each scene in advance, was intended mainly to put a brake on such excitement. Any director in quest of excitement and emotion would tear his hair at such recommendations. But Brecht was not interested in "schmaltz." He called his own dramas "learningplays," and did not hesitate to declare that pedagogy is the true purpose of drama.

Scenically Brecht rejected not only naturalism but the picturesque, atmospheric stage picture as well. Instead of surrounding his actors with an atmospheric reproduction of a locale, he asked his scene designers to proceed by what he called "the inductive instead of the deductive" method. In practice, that meant beginning by giving the actors the furniture and properties necessary for the action, and following up with a "report on the environment." The "reports" are painted or projected tokens of locale: a photo-graph or framed picture of a house, town or countryside; a drop, painted so obviously that it cannot create any illusion; the name of a town in cutout lettering hung over the stage. All in all, the Epic setting becomes so utterly functional that it cannot be distinguished from an organized group of stage properties. Even a whole house on stage retains the quality of a stage prop.

Such an approach runs head on into the doctrine of theatrical *synthesis* as formulated by Richard Wagner and endorsed by artists like Gordon Craig, Adolphe Appia and Robert Edmond Jones. Brecht was not disposed to soften the impact of that collision. Instead he demanded that *autonomy* be restored to all the production elements, including the setting. The setting must not be allowed, he said, to blend "magically" with the costumes, lighting, properties, music and acting in order to create an overwhelming emotional experience. Rather, the setting, and each of the other elements of staging, ought to function, autonomously, in the same manner as the elements of a scientific lecture-demonstration, in which retorts and Bunsen burners are brought into play as their use becomes necessary.

The cyclorama, or sky drop, with its suggestion of infinite space, is banished from the Epic setting, which is *sachlich*, finite. Furniture, pieces of rooms, sections of walls, doors or windows— sometimes without surrounding walls—may be used to serve the action. The stage lighting, employing, usually, only naked white light, does not pretend to be sunlight, moonlight, or the glow of a fireplace or a lamp. Stage light may be colored in primitive fashion, however: a simple blue tone, perhaps, to indicate night, or a color to distinguish an event, as amber when a song is sung, or pink to illuminate the visiting Chinese gods to *The Good Woman of Setzuan*.

Though Epic design may be new in some of its aspects, it lays no claim to being unprecedented. In common with Theatricalism it accepts the platform stage as against the picture stage, and it shares with Theatricalism the opinion that the setting must be a frank scenic construction or apparatus, not an imitation—however selective—of "life itself." But Epic design accords much more with Chinese and Japanese Theatricalism than with the European Theatricalist tradition. The Oriental influence upon Epic is evident in its clean-cut functionalism and in its appreciation of the unadorned textures of wood, stone, metal, plaster, and fiber. Epic designs differ from both Eastern and Western Theatricalism in insisting that everything scenic that appears on stage must be "the object itself," not an allusion of the object. A backdrop must never pretend to be anything but painted cloth; an electric bulb may be used to represent a star, but must not give the illusion of a star. Nor must anything be theatrically stylized; a baroque door, an Empire chair, a Victorian wardrobe must all have historic and geographic documentation, even if the door stands on the open stage without a wall around it.

Epic goes beyond all previous styles in its emphasis on function. But it should be remembered that good scene design in any style knows that it must justify its presence on stage, and that the designer who does not help the actors is nothing but an interloper. In *My Life in Art* Stanislavsky declared that he would rather have one good armchair on stage than all the backdrops painted for his theatre by the best artists

in Russia. He was exaggerating, of course, but the remark is to the point. It should be added that Epic design is by no means casual, disorderly or poverty-stricken. It requires at least as much organization and care as any previous method, and can be equally rich and colorful. Almost always it is more dynamic than its predecessors.

For those who become intrigued by the scenic novelties of Epic theatre, a word of warning may be necessary. Epic is an honest attempt to bring some of the principles of science into the theatre. It is not intended to be a snobbish exercise for "brilliant" designers or directors, nor a new plaything for technicians who are keen on "experiment." A designer does not automatically become gifted and modern if he makes use of projections or half curtains on a wire; indeed, there is always the possibility that a designer with a genuine feeling for naturalism or Theatricalism may be out of his element with Epic. The half curtains, the movie sequences, the projected titles happen to be the personal trademarks of Brecht and Piscator. They are no guarantee that we are witnessing an Epic production. They are what Brecht himself called primitive Epic design—first steps toward a technique that may someday embody, in scenic form, the principles of a classic, scientifically minded theatre of the future.

No one can foresee what Epic design will look like eventually. Since it departs radically from current practice, and since it has a genuine philosophic basis, it opens a whole field of scenic invention. Most striking is its scientific bent. I once indicated, for a town square in Brecht's *Round Heads and Peaked Heads*, a collection of shopkeepers' signs hung over the center of the stage. "The Gorelik effect," Brecht called it, after he had used it and found it effective. He proposed very seriously to begin cataloguing scenic effects of proven worth as contributions to a classic future form of stage setting. The very notion of such a catalogue will, no doubt, horrify many talented designers; but there may be others, equally talented, who will not feel that there is an impassable barrier between art and science. Indeed, they may find that the reverse is true: The spirit of science may yet enable scenic art to reach new levels of imagination.

Bibliography

Index

Bibliography

While it is not expected that the scenographic student would find it necessary to own all the works listed below, a number of them should be considered prudent investments; these texts are indicated by asterisks. The continual building of a permanent working library of research resources is a highly recommended practice that will aid the working scenographer amply repaying the time and cost incurred. Although the latest printing has been included here, it should be expected that many of the works cited will continue to be updated in subsequent editions.

Aesthetics and Theories

*Appia, Adolphe. *Music and the Art of the Theatre*. Coral Gables, Fla.: University of Miami Press, 1962.

Artaud, Antonin. *The Theater and Its Double*. New York: Grove Press, 1958.

Bentley, Eric. *The Life of the Drama*. New York: Atheneum, 1964.

*Brecht, Bertolt. *Brecht on Theatre*. Translated by John Willett. New York: Hill and Wang, 1964.

Brockett, Oscar G., and Robert R. Findlay. *Century of Innovation: A History of European and American Theatre and Drama since 1870*. Englewood Cliffs N.J.: Prentice Hall, 1973.

*Brook, Peter. *The Empty Space*. New York: Avon Books, 1969.

Brustein, Robert. *The Theatre of Revolt: An Approach to Modern Drama*. Boston: Little, Brown, 1964.

Clark, Barrett H. *European Theories of the Drama*. 3d ed. Revised by Henry Popkin. New York: Crown, 1965.

Clay, James H., and Daniel Crempel. *The Theatrical Image*. New York: McGraw-Hill, 1967.

Clurman, Harold. *Lies Like Truth*. New York: Macmillan, 1958.

Craig, Gordon. *The Theatre Advancing*. Boston: Little, Brown, 1919.

———. *Scene*. London: Milford, 1923.

*———. *On the Art of the Theatre*. Boston: Small, Maynard, 1974.

Ehrensweig, Anton. *The Hidden Order of Art*. Berkeley: University of California Press, 1971.

*Grotowski, Jerzy. *Towards a Poor Theatre*. New York: Simon and Schuster, 1970.

*Jones, Robert Edmond. *The Dramatic Imagination*. New York: Theatre Arts Books, 1941.

*Kott, Jan. *Shakespeare Our Contemporary*. New York: Doubleday, 1964.

Langer, Suzanne. *Philosophy in a New Key*. Cambridge, Mass.: Harvard University Press, 1951.

———. *Feeling and Form: A Theory of Art*. New York: Archon Books, 1964.

Meyerhold, Vsevolod. *Meyerhold on Theatre*. Edited by Edward Braun. New York: Hill and Wang, 1969.

*Miller, Jonathan. *Subsequent Performances*. New York: Viking, 1986.

Miller, William J. *Modern Playwrights at Work*. New York: Samuel French, 1968.

Rybczynski, Witold. *Home*. New York: Viking, 1987

Simonson, Lee. *Part of a Lifetime*. New York: Duell, Sloan and Pearce, 1943.

Southern, Richard. *Seven Ages of the Theatre*. New York: Hill and Wang, 1961.

Styan, J. L. *The Dramatic Experience*. London: Cambridge University Press, 1965.

Taylor, Gary. *Reinventing Shakespeare*. New York and London: Oxford University Press, 1989.

Taylor, Gordon Rattray. *The Natural History of the Mind*. New York: E. P. Dutton, 1979.

Willett, John. *Brecht in Context*. London and New York: Methuen, 1984.

Young, Stark. *The Theatre*. New York: Hill and Wang, 1963.

Historical Theater Practice

Arnott, Peter D. *Greek Scenic Conventions in the Fifth Century B.C.* Oxford: Clarendon Press, 1962.

*Basoli, Antonio. *Collezione di Varie Scene Teatrali*. New York: Benjamin Blom, 1969.

Bauer-Heinbold, Margarete. *The Baroque Theatre*. New York: McGraw-Hill, 1967.

*Brockett, Oscar G. *History of the Theatre*. 3d ed. Boston: Allyn and Bacon, 1977.

Eckardt, Wolf Von, and Sander L. Gilman. *Bertolt Brecht's Berlin*. New York: Doubleday, 1975.

Ernst, Earle. *The Kabuki Theatre*. New York: Oxford University Press, 1956.

Ewen, David. *American Musical Theatre*. New York: Holt, Rinehart and Winston, 1959.

Fox, Levi. *The Shakespeare Handbook*. Boston: G. K. Hall, 1987.

*Gorelik, Mordecai. *New Theatres for Old*. New York: Octagon Books, 1975.

Hewitt, Barnard, ed. *The Renaissance Stage: Documents of Serlio, Sabbatini and Furttenbach*. Coral Gables, Fla., 1958.

*Hodges, C. Walter. *The Globe Restored*. New York: Coward-McCann, 1954.

———. *Shakespeare's Second Globe*. London: Oxford University Press, 1973.

Hollywood. Michael Webb, ed. Boston: Little, Brown, 1986.

Jacobson, Robert. *Magnificence Onstage at the Met*. New York: Simon and Schuster, 1985.

Jones, Richard David. *Great Directors at Work*. Berkeley: University of California Press, 1986.

Leacroft, Richard, and Helen Leacroft. *Theatre and Playhouse*. London: Methuen, 1985.

*Macgowan, Kenneth, and Robert E. Jones. *Continental Stagecraft*. New York: Harcourt, Brace and World, 1922.

———, and William Melnitz. *The Living Stage*. Englewood Cliffs, N.J.: Prentice Hall, 1964.

Mello, Bruno. *Trattato di Scenotechnica*. Milano: Gorlich Editors, 1962.

The Metropolitan Opera Encyclopedia. Edited by David Hamilton. New York: Simon and Schuster, 1987.

*Moynet, J. J. *French Theatrical Production in the Nineteenth Century*. Translated and augmented by Allan S. Jackson with M. Glen Wilson. Edited by Marvin A. Carlson. Binghamton, N.Y.: Max Reinhardt Foundation with the Center for Modern Theater Research, 1976.

*Nagler, A. M. *A Source Book in Theatrical History*. New York: Dover Publications, 1959.

The New York Stage: Famous Productions in Photographs. Edited by Stanley Appelbaum. New York: Dover Publications, 1976.

Nicoll, Allardyce. *Stuart Masques and the Renaissance Stage*. New York: Benjamin Blom, 1963.

———. *The Development of the Theatre*. 5th ed. London: Harrap, 1966.

———. *The Garrick Stage*. Manchester: Manchester University Press, 1981.

Osborne, Charles. *The World Theatre of Wagner*. New York: Macmillan, 1982.

*Rosenfeld, Sybil. *A Short History of Scene Design in Great Britain*. Oxford: Basil Blackwell, 1973.

Sayler, Oliver M., ed. *Max Reinhardt and His Theatre*. New York: Benjamin Blom, 1968.

*Scholz, Janos. *Baroque and Romantic Stage Design*. New York: Beechurst Press, 1955.

The Simon and Schuster Book of the Ballet. New York: Simon and Schuster, 1979.

The Simon and Schuster Book of the Opera. New York: Simon and Schuster, 1977.

Simonson, Lee. *The Stage Is Set*. New York: Atheneum, 1965.

Southern, Richard. *Changeable Scenery: Its Origins and Development*. London: Faber and Faber, 1952.

The Twin City Scenic Collection. Minneapolis: University of Minnesota, 1987.

*Willett, John. *The Theatre of Bertolt Brecht*. New York: New Directions, 1959.

Theater Design and Architecture

Boyle, Walden P. *Central and Flexible Staging*. Berkeley: University of California Press, 1956.

*Burris-Meyer, Harold, and Edward C. Cole. *Theatres and Auditoriums*. 2d ed. New York: Van Nostrand Reinhold, 1964.

*Cogswell, Margaret, ed. *The Ideal Theater: Eight Concepts*. New York: American Federation of Arts.

*Glasstone, Victor. *Victorian and Edwardian Theatres*. London: Thames and Hudson, 1975.

*Izenour, George. *Theater Design*. New York: McGraw-Hill, 1977.

Joseph, Stephen. *New Theatre Forms*. London: Sir Isaac Pitman and Sons, 1968.

*Mielziner, Jo. *The Shapes of Our Theatre*. New York: Atheneum, 1965.

Orrell, John. *The Quest for Shakespeare's Globe*. Cambridge: Cambridge University Press, 1983.

Roose-Evans, James. *Experimental Theatre*. New York: Universe Books, 1970.

Southern, Richard. *The Georgian Playhouse*. London: Pleiades Books, 1948.

Theatre Check List: A Guide to the Planing and Construction of Proscenium and Open Stage Theatres. Edited by the American Theatre Planning Board. Middletown, Conn.: Wesleyan University Press, n.d.

General Design Theory

Van Nostrand Reinhold Co., 450 West Thirty-third Street, New York, N.Y. 10001, publishes a wide variety and great number of design-related books. A careful study of their entire listings is recommended.

*Ching, Francis D. K. *Architecture: Form, Space and Order*. New York: Van Nostrand Reinhold., 1979.

Kuh, Katharine. *Break-Up*. Greenwich, Conn.: New York Graphic Society, 1965.

Middleton, Michael. *Group Practice in Design*. New York: George Braziller, 1969.

*Munari, Bruno. *Design as Art*. Baltimore, Md.: Penguin Books, 1971.

*Potter, Norman. *What Is a Designer: Education and Practice*. New York: Van Nostrand Reinhold, 1969.

*Pye, David. *The Nature and Aesthetics of Design*. New York: Van Nostrand Reinhold Co., 1978.

Rubin, William S. *Dada and Surrealist Art*. New York: Harry N. Abrams, 1969.

Sausmarez, Maurice de. *Basic Design: The Dynamics of Visual Form*. New York: Van Nostrand Reinhold, 1971.

*Seitz, William C. *The Art of Assemblage*. Museum of Modern Art. Garden City, N.Y.: Doubleday, 1961.

Wescher, Herta. *Collage*. Translated by Robert E. Wolf. New York: Harry N. Abrams, 1968.

Scenographic Art and Artists

Aronson, Arnold. *American Set Design*. New York: Theatre Communications Group, 1985.

Art and the Stage in the Twentieth Century. Edited by Henning Rischbieter. Documented by Wolfgang Storch. Greenwich, Conn.: New York Graphic Society, 1970.

Bablet, Denis. *Edward Gordon Craig*. London: Heinemann, 1966.

———. *The Revolutions of Stage Design in the 20th Century*. Paris and New York: Leon Amiel-Publisher, 1977.

Barsacq, Leon. *Caligari's Cabinet and Other Grand Illu-sions*. Boston: New York Graphic Society; Little, Brown, 1976.

*Bay, Howard. *Stage Design*. New York: Drama Book Specialists, 1974.

Beaumont, Cyril W. *Ballet Design: Past and Present*. London: The Studio, 1940.

British Theatre Design: 1979–1983. Oxford: Holywell Press Ltd., n.d.

British Theatre Design: 1983–1987. Oxford: Twynam Publishing Ltd., n.d.

*Burian, Jarka. *The Scenography of Josef Svoboda*. Middletown, Conn.: Wesleyan University Press, 1971.

Contemporary Stage Design U.S.A. Edited by Elizabeth Burdick, Peggy C. Hansen, and Brenda Zanger. Middletown, Conn.: Wesleyan University Press, 1974.

Film Design. Compiled and edited by Terence St. John Marner. New York: A. S. Barnes, 1974.

Friedman, Martin. *Hockney Paints the Stage*. New York: Abbeville Press, 1983.

*Fuerst, W. R., and S. J. Hume. *Twentieth Century Stage Decoration*. 2 Vols. New York: Dover Publishing, 1967.

*Hainaux, Rene. *Stage Design throughout the World since 1935*. New York: Theatre Arts Books, 1957.

———. *Stage Design throughout the World since 1950*. New York: Theatre Arts Books, 1964.

———. *Stage Design throughout the World since 1960*. New York: Theatre Arts Books, 1973.

———. *Stage Design throughout the World since 1970–75*. New York: Theatre Arts Books. 1976.

*Hartmann, Rudolpf, ed. *Opera*. New York: William Morrow, 1977.

Larson, Orville, ed. *Scene Design for Stage and Screen*. East Lansing: Michigan State University Press, 1961.

Laver, James. *Drama, Its Costume and Decor*. London: Studio Publications, 1951.

Mayor, A. Hyatt. *The Bibiena Family*. New York: Bittner, 1945.

Manvell, Roger. *Shakespeare and the Film*. New York: Praeger, 1971.

Maximowna, Ita. *Bühnenbilderbuch*. Würzburg: Verlag Ernst Wasmuth Tübingen, 1982.

Mielziner, Jo. *Designing for the Theatre: A Memoir and Portfolio*. New York: Atheneum, 1965.

Oenslager, Donald. *Scenery Then and Now*. New York: W. W. Norton, 1936.

———. *Stage Design*. New York: Viking Press, 1975.

———. *The Theatre of Donald Oenslager*. Middletown, Conn.: Wesleyan University Press, 1978.

*Pendleton, Ralph, ed. *The Theatre of Robert Edmond Jones*. Middletown, Conn.: Wesleyan University Press, 1958.

*Rich, Frank, with Lisa Aronson. *The Theatre Art of Boris Aronson*. New York: Alfred A. Knopf, 1987.

Rowell, Kenneth. *Stage Design*. New York: Van Nostrand Reinhold, 1968.

*Simonson, Lee. *The Art of Scenic Design*. New York: Harper and Brothers, 1950.

Spencer, Charles. *Leon Bakst*. London: Academy Editions, 1973.

———. *The World of Serge Diaghilev*. Chicago, Henry Regnery, 1974.

———. *Cecil Beaton Stage and Film Designs*. New York: St. Martin's Press, 1977.

Theatrical Designs from the Baroque through Neo-Classicism. 3 vols. New York: H. Bittner, 1940.

Warre, Michael. *Designing and Making Stage Scenery*. New York: Van Nostrand Reinhold, 1966.

Willett, John. *Caspar Neher: Brecht's Designer*. London and New York: Methuen, 1986.

Leyda, Jay, and Zina Voynow. *Eisenstein at Work*. New York: Pantheon Books, 1982.

General Research Source Materials:
Architecture, Crafts, Furniture, Costume

Ayres, James. *The Artist's Craft*. Oxford: Phaidon, 1985.

Abbott, Berenice. *The World of Atget*. New York: Horizon Press, 1964.

*Annan, Thomas. *Photographs of the Old Closes and Streets of Glasgow, 1868—1877*. New York: Dover Publications, 1977.

*Aronson, Joseph. *The Encyclopedia of Furniture*. New York: Crown Publishers, 1959.

*Barton, Lucy. *Historic Costume for the Stage*. Boston: Baker's Plays, 1961.

*Chippendale, Thomas. *The Gentleman and Cabinet-Maker's Director*. New York: Dover Publications, 1966.

*Cooper, Nicholas. *The Opulent Eye*. London: Architectural Press, 1976.

*Cornforth, John. *English Interiors, 1790–1848*. London: Barrie and Jenkins, 1978.

Decoration. Vols. 1 and 2. Edited by Souren Melikian. New York: French and European Publications, 1963.

Dictionary of Design and Decoration. Edited by Robert Harling. New York: Viking Press, 1973.

*Doré, Gustave, and Blanchard Jerrod. *London: A Pilgrimage*. New York: Benjamin Blom, 1968.

*Duncan, Alastair. *Art Noveau and Art Deco Lighting*. New York: Simon and Schuster, 1978.

*Feininger, Andreas. *Roots of Art*. New York: Viking Press, 1975.

Garrett, Elizabeth Donaghy. *At Home: The American Family, 1750–1870*. New York: Harry N. Abrams, 1990.

Gere, Charlotte. *Nineteenth-Century Decoration: The Art of the Interior*. New York: Harry N. Abrams, 1989.

The Golden Age of Shop Design: European Shop Interiors 1880—1939. Edited by Alexandra Artley. London: Architectural Press, 1975.

Great Architecture of the World. Edited by John Julius Norwich. New York: Random House, in association with American Heritage Publishing, 1975.

The History of Furniture. New York: William Morrow, 1976.

Jellicoe, Geoffrey, and Susan Jellicoe. *The Landscape of Man*. New York: Viking Press, 1975.

*Kettell, Russell Hawes. *Early American Rooms, 1650–1858*. New York: Dover Publications, 1967.

*Lancaster, Clay. *New York Interiors at the Turn of the Century*. New York: Dover Publications, 1976.

*Meyer, Franz Sales. *Handbook of Ornament*. New York: Dover Publications, 1957.

*Motley. *Designing and Making Stage Costumes*. New York: Watson-Guptill Publications, 1964.

*Nutting, Wallace, *Furniture Treasury*. New York: Macmillan, 1961.

Palmes, J. C. *Sir Banister Fletcher's A History of Architecture*. New York: Charles Scribner's Sons, 1975.

*Payne, Blanche. *History of Costume from the Ancient Egyptians to the Twentieth Century*. New York: Harper and Row, 1965.

*Praz, Mario. *An Illustrated History of Furnishings*. New York: Braziller, 1964.

*Racinet, A. C. *Handbook of Ornaments in Color*. Vols. 1–4. Translated by J. A. Underwood. New York: Van Nostrand Reinhold, 1978.

*Rust, Graham. *The Painted House*. New York: Alfred A. Knopf, 1988.

*Sitwell, Sacheverell. *Great Houses of Europe*. New York: G. P. Putman's Sons, 1961.

*Smith, Whitney. *Flags through the Ages and across the World*. New York: McGraw-Hill Book, 1975.

*Speltz, Alexander. *The Styles of Ornament*. New York: Dover Publications, 1957.

Thornton, Peter. *Authentic Decor: The Domestic Interior, 1620–1920*. New York: Viking, 1984.

200 Years of American Sculpture. New York: David R. Godine, 1956.

*Vituvius. *The Ten Books of Architecture*. New York: Dover Publications, 1960.

Wolberg, Lewis R. *Micro-Art, Art Images in a Hidden World*. New York: Abrams, n.d.

*Yarwood, Doreen. *The English Home*. London: B. T. Batsford, 1956.

*———. *The Architecture of Britain*: London: B. T. Batsford, 1978.

Scenographic Construction, Lighting, and Related Crafts

*Bellman, Willard F. *Lighting the Stage: Art and Practice.* 2d ed. New York: Thomas Y. Crowell, 1974.

———. *Scenography and Stage Technology.* New York: Thomas Y. Cromwell, 1974.

Bentham, Frederick. *The Art of Stage Lighting.* 2d ed. London: Sir Isaac Pitman and Sons, 1968.

*Burris-Meyer, Harold, and Edward C. Cole. *Scenery for the Theatre.* Rev. ed. Boston: Little, Brown, 1971.

*Ching, Frank. *Architectural Graphics.* New York: Van Nostrand Reinhold, 1975.

Corey, Irene. *The Mask of Reality: An Approach to Design in the Theater.* Anchorage, 1968.

*Dubery, Fred, and John Willats. *Drawing Systems.* New York: Van Nostrand Reinhold, 1972.

Gillette, Arnold. *Stage Scenery.* Rev. ed. New York: Harper and Row, 1960.

*Kook, Edward F. *Images of Light for the Living Theatre.* New York: Privately Published, 1963.

*McCandless, Stanley. *A Method of Lighting the Stage.* 3d rev. ed. New: York: Theatre Arts Books, 1947.

*Payne, Darwin R. *Theory and Craft of the Scenographic Model.* Rev. ed. Carbondale and Edwardsville: Southern Illinois University Press, 1985.

*Pecktal, Lynn. *Designing and Painting for the Theatre.* New York: Holt, Rinehart and Winston, 1975.

*Pilbrow, Richard. *Stage Lighting.* New York: Van Nostrand Reinhold, 1971.

*Rosenthal, Jean, and Lael Wertenbacker. *The Magic of Light.* Boston: Little, Brown, 1972.

*Rubin, Joel E., and Leland Watson. *Theatrical Lighting Practice.* New York: Theatre Arts Books, 1954.

Vero, Radu. *Understanding Perspective.* New York: Van Nostrand Reinhold, 1980.

General Reading Both inside and outside the Theater

Addenbrooke, David. *The Royal Shakespeare Company.* London: William Kimber, 1974.

*Asimov, Isaac. *Asimov's Guide to Shakespeare.* Garden City, N.Y.: Doubleday, 1970.

*Austin, James H. *Chase, Chance, and Creativity.* New York: Columbia University Press, 1978.

*Bronowski, J. *The Ascent of Man.* New York: Little, Brown, 1973.

*Clark, Kenneth. *Civilization.* New York: Harper and Row, 1969.

*Clurman, Harold. *On Directing.* New York: Macmillan, 1972.

Cole, Toby, ed. *Playwrights on Playwriting.* New York: Hill and Wang, 1961.

———, and Helen Krich Chinoy, eds. *Directors on Directing.* Rev. ed. Indianapolis: Bobbs-Merrill, 1963.

Davydoff, Mariamna. *Memoirs of a Russian Lady.* New York: Harry N. Abrams, 1986.

Engle, Lehmann. *Planning and Producing the Musical Show.* New York: Crown Publishers, 1957.

Erlande-Brandenburg, Alain. *Gothic Art.* New York: Harry N. Abrams, 1989.

Esslin, Martin. *The Theatre of the Absurd.* Rev. ed. New York: Overlook Press, 1973.

Ewen, David. *American Musical Theatre.* New York: Holt, Rinehart and Winston, 1959.

*Feldman, Edmond Burke. *Varieties of Visual Experience.* New York: Harry N. Abrams, n.d.

Grun, Bernard. *The Timetables of History.* New York: Simon and Schuster, 1975.

*Hall, Edward T. *The Hidden Dimension.* Garden City, N.Y.: Doubleday, 1966.

———. *Beyond Culture.* Garden City, N.Y.: Anchor Press/Doubleday, 1977.

*Hamilton, Edith. *The Greek Way.* New York: W. W. Norton, 1952.

The Harper Atlas of World History. New York: Harper and Row, 1986.

Hunt, Hugh. *The Director in the Theatre.* London: Routledge and Kegan Paul, 1954.

Marshall, Norman. *The Producer and the Play.* London: McDonald, 1962.

*Matlaw, Myron. *Modern World Drama.* New York: E. P. Dutton, 1972.

The Oxford Companion to the Theatre. 3d ed. Edited by Phyllis Hartnoll. London: Oxford University Press, 1967.

The Oxford History of the Classical World. Edited by John Boardman, Jasper Griffin, and Oxwyn Murry. Oxford: Oxford University Press, 1986.

Private Life in the Fifteenth Century. Edited by Roger Virgo. New York: Weidenfeld and Nicolson, 1989.

Roberts, Vera Mowry. *The Nature of the Theatre.* New York: Harper and Row, 1971.

*Spurgeon, Caroline. *Shakespeare's Imagery.* Cambridge: Cambridge University Press, 1968.

Stanislavsky, Konstantin. *Building a Character.* Translated by R. E. Hapgood. New York: Theater Arts Books, 1948.

———. *My Life in Art.* Translated by J. J. Robbins. Boston: Meridan Books, 1956.

Index

Darwin Reid Payne is an adjunct professor in theater at Wake Forest University at Winston-Salem, North Carolina. He was formerly chairman of the theater department of Southern Illinois University at Carbondale. In addition to designing and directing at regional theaters throughout the United States and Canada, he is also writing a book on the use of computers in scenography.